JavaScript™
For Programmers
Deitel® Developer Series

Deitel® Ser

How to Program Series

Java How to Program, 7/E

C++ How to Program, 6/E

Visual C++® 2008 How to Program, 2/E

C How to Program, 5/E

Internet & World Wide Web How to Program, 4/E

Visual Basic® 2008 How to Program

Visual C#® 2008 How to Program, 3/E

Small Java™ How to Program, 6/E

Small C++ How to Program, 5/E

Simply Series

Simply C++: An Application-Driven Tutorial Approach

Simply Java™ Programming: An Application-Driven Tutorial Approach

Simply C#: An Application-Driven Tutorial Approach

Simply Visual Basic® 2008, 3/E: An Application-Driven Tutorial Approach

SafariX Web Books

www.deitel.com/books/SafariX.html

C++ How to Program, 5/E & 6/E

Java How to Program, 6/E & 7/E

Simply C++: An Application-Driven Tutorial Approach

Simply Visual Basic 2008: An Application-Driven Tutorial Approach, 3/E

Small C++ How to Program, 5/E

Small Java How to Program, 6/E

Visual Basic 2008 How to Program

Visual C# 2008 How to Program, 3/E

ies Page

To follow the Deitel publishing program, please register for the free *Deitel® Buzz Online* e-mail newsletter at:

   www.deitel.com/newsletter/subscribe.html

To communicate with the authors, send e-mail to:

   deitel@deitel.com

For information on government and corporate *Dive-Into®* Series on-site seminars offered by Deitel & Associates, Inc. worldwide, visit:

   www.deitel.com/training/

or write to

   deitel@deitel.com

For continuing updates on Prentice Hall/Deitel publications visit:

   www.deitel.com
   www.prenhall.com/deitel

Check out our Resource Centers for valuable web resources that will help you master Visual C#, other important programming languages, software and Internet- and web-related topics:

   www.deitel.com/ResourceCenters.html

The publisher offers excellent discounts on this book when ordered in quantity for bulk purchases or special sales, which may include electronic versions and/or custom covers and content particular to your business, training goals, marketing focus, and branding interests. For more information, please contact:

    U. S. Corporate and Government Sales
    (800) 382-3419
    corpsales@pearsontechgroup.com

For sales outside the U. S., please contact:

    International Sales
    international@pearsoned.com

Visit us on the Web: www.phptr.com

Library of Congress Cataloging-in-Publication Data

`On file`

© 2010 Pearson Education, Inc.

Text printed in the United States on recycled paper at R.R . Donnelley in Crawfordsville, Indiana.
First printing, February 2009

JavaScript™ FOR PROGRAMMERS

DEITEL® DEVELOPER SERIES

Paul J. Deitel
Deitel & Associates, Inc.

Harvey M. Deitel
Deitel & Associates, Inc.

PRENTICE HALL

Upper Saddle River, NJ • Boston • Indianapolis • San Francisco
New York • Toronto • Montreal • London • Munich • Paris • Madrid
Capetown • Sydney • Tokyo • Singapore • Mexico City

Trademarks

DEITEL, the double-thumbs-up bug and DIVE INTO are registered trademarks of Deitel & Associates, Inc.

Apache is a trademark of The Apache Software Foundation.

CSS, DOM, XHTML and XML are registered trademarks of the World Wide Web Consortium.

Firefox is a registered trademark of the Mozilla Foundation.

Google is a trademark of Google, Inc.

JavaScript, Java and all Java-based marks are trademarks or registered trademarks of Sun Microsystems, Inc. in the United States and other countries.

Microsoft, Internet Explorer and the Windows logo are either registered trademarks or trademarks of Microsoft Corporation in the United States and/or other countries.

MySpace is a registered trademark of MySpace.com.

UNIX is a registered trademark of The Open Group.

Web 2.0 is a service mark of CMP Media.

Wikipedia is a registered trademark of WikiMedia.

Throughout this book, trademarks are used. Rather than put a trademark symbol in every occurrence of a trademarked name, we state that we are using the names in an editorial fashion only and to the benefit of the trademark owner, with no intention of infringement of the trademark.

To Brendan Eich:

For creating the JavaScript language while at Netscape Communications Corporation.

Paul and Harvey Deitel

Deitel Resource Centers

Our Resource Centers focus on the vast amounts of free content available online. Find resources, downloads, tutorials, documentation, books, e-books, journals, articles, blogs, RSS feeds and more on many of today's hottest programming and technology topics. For the most up-to-date list of our Resource Centers, visit:

www.deitel.com/ResourceCenters.html

Let us know what other Resource Centers you'd like to see! Also, please register for the free *Deitel®* *Buzz Online* e-mail newsletter at:

www.deitel.com/newsletter/subscribe.html

Computer Science
Functional Programming
Regular Expressions

Programming
ASP.NET 3.5
Adobe Flex
Ajax
Apex
ASP.NET Ajax
ASP.NET
C
C++
C++ Boost Libraries
C++ Game Programming
C#
Code Search Engines and
   Code Sites
Computer Game
   Programming
CSS 2.1
Dojo
Facebook Developer Plat-
   form
Flash 9
Functional Programming
Java
Java Certification and
   Assessment Testing
Java Design Patterns
Java EE 5
Java SE 6
Java SE 7 (Dolphin)
   Resource Center
JavaFX
JavaScript
JSON
Microsoft LINQ
Microsoft Popfly
.NET
.NET 3.0
.NET 3.5
OpenGL
Perl
PHP
Programming Projects
Python
Regular Expressions
Ruby
Ruby on Rails

Silverlight
Visual Basic
Visual C++
Visual Studio Team Sys-
   tem
Web 3D Technologies
Web Services
Windows Presentation
   Foundation
XHTML
XML

**Games and Game
   Programming**
Computer Game Pro-
   gramming
Computer Games
Mobile Gaming
Sudoku

Internet Business
Affiliate Programs
Competitive Analysis
Facebook Social Ads
Google AdSense
Google Analytics
Google Services
Internet Advertising
Internet Business
   Initiative
Internet Public Relations
Link Building
Location-Based Services
Online Lead Generation
Podcasting
Search Engine Optimiza-
   tion
Selling Digital Content
Sitemaps
Web Analytics
Website Monetization
YouTube and AdSense

Java
Java
Java Certification and
   Assessment Testing
Java Design Patterns
Java EE 5
Java SE 6

Java SE 7 (Dolphin)
   Resource Center
JavaFX

Microsoft
ASP.NET
ASP.NET 3.5
ASP.NET Ajax
C#
DotNetNuke (DNN)
Internet Explorer 7 (IE7)
Microsoft LINQ
.NET
.NET 3.0
.NET 3.5
SharePoint
Silverlight
Visual Basic
Visual C++
Visual Studio Team
   System
Windows Presentation
   Foundation
Windows Vista
Microsoft Popfly

**Open Source &
   LAMP Stack**
Apache
DotNetNuke (DNN)
Eclipse
Firefox
Linux
MySQL
Open Source
Perl
PHP
Python
Ruby

Software
Apache
DotNetNuke (DNN)
Eclipse
Firefox
Internet Explorer 7 (IE7)
Linux
MySQL
Open Source
Search Engines

SharePoint
Skype
Web Servers
Wikis
Windows Vista

Web 2.0
Alert Services
Attention Economy
Blogging
Building Web
   Communities
Community Generated
   Content
Facebook Developer
   Platform
Facebook Social Ads
Google Base
Google Video
Google Web Toolkit
   (GWT)
Internet Video
Joost
Location-Based Services
Mashups
Microformats
Recommender Systems
RSS
Social Graph
Social Media
Social Networking
Software as a Service
   (SaaS)
Virtual Worlds
Web 2.0
Web 3.0
Widgets

**Dive Into® Web 2.0
   eBook**
Web 2 eBook

Other Topics
Computer Games
Computing Jobs
Gadgets and Gizmos
Ring Tones
Sudoku

Contents

4   JavaScript: Introduction to Scripting   74

5   JavaScript: Control Statements I   96

6   JavaScript: Control Statements II   117

Preface

... the challenges are for the designers of these applications: to forget what we think we know about the limitations of the Web, and begin to imagine a wider, richer range of possibilities. It's going to be fun.

> —Jesse James Garrett, Adaptive Path
> "Ajax: A New Approach to Web Applications"
> (adaptivepath.com/ideas/essays/archives/000385.php)

Introduction

Welcome to *JavaScript for Programmers*! We've worked hard to create what we hope you'll find to be an informative, entertaining and challenging learning experience. At Deitel & Associates, we write programming language professional books and textbooks for Prentice Hall, deliver corporate training at organizations worldwide and develop Internet businesses.

This book reflects the *client side* of today's Web 2.0, Ajax-based, Rich Internet Application-development methodologies. The technologies you'll learn here are appropriate for experienced professionals who build substantial web-based applications. You'll find "industrial-strength" code examples that are clear, straightforward and promote best practices.

Today's users are accustomed to desktop applications with rich graphical user interfaces (GUIs), such as those used on Apple's Mac OS X systems, Microsoft Windows systems, various Linux systems and others. Users want applications that can run on the Internet and the web and communicate with other applications. Users want to apply database technologies for storing and manipulating their business and personal data. They want applications that are not limited to the desktop or even to some local computer network, but that can integrate Internet and web components, and remote databases. Programmers want to use all these capabilities in a truly portable manner so that applications will run without modification on a variety of platforms.

We focus on the client side of web-based applications (i.e., the portions that typically run in web browsers such as Mozilla's Firefox, Microsoft's Internet Explorer, Apple's Safari, Opera, Google's Chrome and other web browsers), using technologies such as XHTML, JavaScript, CSS, Extensible Markup Language (XML) the DOM (Document Object Model) and Ajax (Asynchronous JavaScript and XML).

This book was extracted from the front half our Prentice Hall textbook *Internet & World Wide Web How to Program, 4/e*. That book also provides substantial treatments of key Rich Internet Applications development *server-side* technologies, including web servers, database, PHP, Ruby on Rails, ASP.NET/ASP.NET Ajax, JavaServer Faces and web services.

Perhaps most important, this book presents over 100 working code examples and shows the outputs produced when these examples are rendered in browsers. We present all concepts in the context of complete working programs. We call this the "live-code approach." All of the source code is available for download from

> www.deitel.com/books/jsfp/

Please see the Before You Begin section following the Preface for details on downloading these examples.

If you have questions as you read this book, send an e-mail to deitel@deitel.com—we'll respond promptly. For updates on the book and the status of all supporting software, and for the latest news on Deitel publications and services, visit www.deitel.com. Sign up at www.deitel.com/newsletter/subscribe.html for the free *Deitel® Buzz Online* e-mail newsletter and check out www.deitel.com/ResourceCenters.html for our growing list of Internet and web programming, Internet business, Web 2.0 and related Resource Centers. Each week we announce our latest Resource Centers in the newsletter.

Key Features

Here's some of the key features of *JavaScript for Programmers*:

- Reflects the client side of today's Web 2.0, Ajax-based, Rich Internet Application-development methodologies in which you create web applications with the interactivity of desktop applications.

- Covers the two leading web browsers—Internet Explorer and Firefox. All client-side applications in the book run correctly on both browsers.

- Focuses on Web 2.0 technologies and concepts.

- Chapter on building Ajax-enabled web applications with "raw" Ajax and with the Dojo JavaScript libraries. Applications in this chapter demonstrate core Web 2.0 capabilities—partial-page updates and type-ahead.

- Significant treatment of client-side scripting with JavaScript.

- Significant treatments of XHTML DOM manipulation and JavaScript events.

- Significant treatment of XML DOM manipulation with JavaScript.

- Client-side case studies that enable you to interact with preimplemented server-side applications and web services that we host at test.deitel.com.

- Case studies including Deitel Cover Viewer (JavaScript/DOM), Address Book (Ajax) and Calendar (Ajax with the Dojo Toolkit).

All of this has been carefully reviewed distinguished industry developers and academics.

JavaScript for Programmers Achitecture

Figure 1 shows the architecture of *JavaScript for Programmers*. The book is divided into five parts. The first part, Chapter 1, introduces the Internet, the web and Web 2.0.

The second part, Chapters 2–3, focuses on the markup (XHTML) and presentation (CSS) technologies that enable you to build web pages. You'll want to test your web applications across many browsers and platforms. The examples for the book execute correctly on both Microsoft's Internet Explorer 7 and Mozilla's Firefox 3 browsers. Most of the examples will also work in other browsers such as Opera, Apple's Safari and Google's

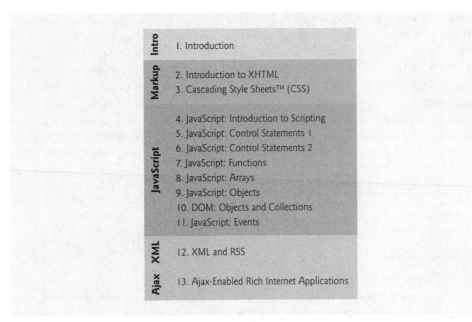

Fig. 1 | Architecture of *JavaScript for Programmers*

Chrome, but may not work on earlier browsers. Microsoft Windows users of this book should use Internet Explorer 7 or Firefox 3; readers who have other operating systems should install Firefox 3. Firefox 2 will also work with this book.

The third part of the book, Chapters 4–11, presents an eight-chapter treatment of JavaScript, including an introduction followed by control statements, functions, arrays and objects. Chapter 10 focuses on the objects and collections that enable you to manipulate web page elements from JavaScript. Chapter 11 demonstrates event handling in JavaScript, which enables you to respond to user interaction with web page elements. Chapters 4–11 depend on the XHTML and CSS concepts presented in Chapters 2–3.

The fourth part of the book, Chapter 12, presents XML and RSS—two technologies used frequently in Web 2.0 applications to transmit data between servers and clients. Finally, our presentation concludes with Chapter 13's treatment of Ajax development. Ajax is not a new technology—we've been writing about all but one of its component technologies since the first edition of our book *Internet & World Wide Web How to Program* in 1999, and many of the technologies existed before that. However, Ajax is one of the key technologies of Web 2.0 and RIAs. The chapter starts with "raw" Ajax development then discusses "encapsulated" Ajax development with the Dojo libraries. Chapters 12–13 depend on the concepts presented in Chapters 2–11.

Teaching Approach

JavaScript for Programmers contains a rich collection of examples. The book concentrates on the principles of good software engineering and stresses program clarity. We are educators who teach leading-edge topics in industry classrooms worldwide. The Deitels have taught courses at all levels to government, industry, military and academic clients of Deitel & Associates, Inc.

Live-Code Approach. *JavaScript for Programmers* is loaded with "live-code" examples—each new concept is presented in the context of a complete working web application that is immediately followed by one or more screen captures showing the application's functionality. This style exemplifies the way we teach and write about programming; we call this the "live-code approach."

Syntax Shading. We syntax shade all the code, similar to the way most integrated-development environments and code editors syntax color code. This improves code readability—an important goal, given that this book contains about 6,000 lines of code in complete, working programs. Our syntax-shading conventions are as follows:

```
comments appear in italic
keywords appear in bold italic
errors appear in bold black
constants and literal values appear in bold gray
all other code appears in black
```

Code Highlighting. We place white rectangles around each program's key code segments.

Using Fonts for Emphasis. We place the key terms and the index's page reference for each defining occurrence in ***bold italic*** text for easier reference. We emphasize on-screen components in the **bold Helvetica** font (e.g., the **File** menu) and emphasize program text in the Lucida font (e.g., int x = 5).

Web Access. All of the source-code examples for *JavaScript for Programmers* are available for download from:

www.deitel.com/books/jsfp/

Site registration is quick, easy and free. Download all the examples, then run each program in a browser as you read the corresponding text discussions. Making changes to the examples and seeing the effects of those changes is a great way to enhance your Internet and web programming learning experience.

Objectives. Each chapter begins with a statement of objectives. This lets you know what to expect and gives you an opportunity to determine if you have met these goals after reading the chapter.

Quotations. The objectives are followed by quotations. Some are humorous, some are philosophical, others offer interesting insights. We hope that you enjoy relating the quotations to the chapter material.

Outline. The chapter outline helps you approach the material in a top-down fashion, so you can anticipate what is to come and set a comfortable learning pace.

Illustrations/Figures. Abundant charts, tables, line drawings, programs and program output are included.

Programming Tips. We include programming tips to help you focus on important aspects of program development. These tips and practices represent the best we have gleaned from a combined seven decades of programming and teaching experience. One of our readers told us that she feels this approach is like the highlighting of axioms, theorems and corollaries in mathematics books—it provides a basis on which to build good software.

Good Programming Practices

Good Programming Practices *call attention to techniques that will help you produce programs that are clearer, more understandable and more maintainable.*

Common Programming Errors

Pointing out these Common Programming Errors *reduces the likelihood that you'll make the same mistakes.*

Error-Prevention Tips

These tips contain suggestions for exposing bugs and removing them from your programs; many describe techniques for preventing bugs in the first place.

Performance Tips

These tips highlight opportunities for making your programs run faster or minimizing the amount of memory that they occupy.

Portability Tips

We include Portability Tips *to help you write code that will run on a variety of platforms, and to explain how to achieve a high degree of portability.*

Software Engineering Observations

The Software Engineering Observations *highlight architectural and design issues that affect the construction of software systems, especially large-scale systems.*

Thousands of Index Entries. We've included an extensive index which is especially useful when you use the book as a reference.

Deitel® Buzz Online Free E-mail Newsletter

Each week, the free *Deitel® Buzz Online* newsletter announces our latest Resource Center(s) and includes commentary on industry trends and developments, links to free articles and resources from our published books and upcoming publications, product-release schedules, errata, challenges, anecdotes, information on our corporate instructor-led training courses and more. It's also a good way for you to keep posted about issues related to *JavaScript for Programmers*. To subscribe, visit:

    www.deitel.com/newsletter/subscribe.html

Deitel Online Resource Centers

Our website, www.deitel.com, provides scores of Resource Centers on various topics including programming languages, software, Web 2.0, Internet business and open source projects. You can view the complete list of Resource Centers in the first few pages of this book or at www.deitel.com/ResourceCenters.html. These Resource Centers evolve out of the research we do to support our books and business endeavors. We list many exceptional (mostly free) resources including tutorials, documentation, software downloads, articles, blogs, podcasts, videos, code samples, books, e-books and more. We announce our latest Resource Centers in the *Deitel® Buzz Online.*Acknowledgments
It is a great pleasure to acknowledge the efforts of many people whose names may not appear on the cover, but whose hard work, cooperation, friendship and understanding were

crucial to the production of the book. Many people at Deitel & Associates, Inc. devoted long hours to this project—thanks especially to Abbey Deitel and Barbara Deitel.

We'd also like to thank the participants in our Honors Internship program who contributed to this publication—Ilana Segall, a mathematical and computational science major at Stanford University; Scott Wehrwein, a computer science major at Middlebury College; and Mark Kagan, a computer science, economics and math major at Brandeis University.

We are fortunate to have worked on this project with the talented and dedicated team of publishing professionals at Prentice Hall. We appreciate the extraordinary efforts of Mark Taub, Editor-in-Chief of Prentice Hall Professional; John Fuller, Managing Editor of Prentice Hall Professional and Marcia Horton, Editorial Director of Prentice Hall's Engineering and Computer Science Division. Carole Snyder and Dolores Mars did a remarkable job recruiting the book's review team and managing the review process. Sandra Schroeder and Chuti Prasertsith did a wonderful job designing the book's cover. Bob Engelhardt and Scott Disanno did a marvelous job managing the book's production.

This book was adapted from our book *Internet & World Wide Web How to Program, 4/e*. We wish to acknowledge the efforts of our reviewers on that book who worked on the corresponding chapters. Adhering to a tight time schedule, they scrutinized the text and the programs, providing countless suggestions for improving the accuracy and completeness of the presentation.

Reviewers

Umachitra Damodaran (Sun Microsystems), Vadiraj Deshpande (Sun Microsystems), Molly E. Holtzschlag (W3C), Ralph Hooper (University of Alabama, Tuscaloosa), Johnvey Hwang (Splunk, Inc.), Eric Lawrence (Microsoft), Billy B. L. Lim (Illinois State University), Shobana Mahadevan (Sun Microsystems), Anand Narayanaswamy (Microsoft), John Peterson (Insync and V.I.O., Inc.), Jennifer Powers (University of Albany), José Antonio González Seco (Parlamento de Andalucia), Dr. George Semeczko (Royal & SunAlliance Insurance Canada), Steven Shaffer (Penn State University), Karen Tegtmeyer (Model Technologies, Inc.), Eric M. Wendelin (Auto-trol Technology Corporation), Raymond F. Wisman (Indiana University) and Daniel Zappala (Brigham Young University).

We hope you enjoy this look at the exciting world of JavaScript-based, client-side web applications development. As you read the book, we'd sincerely appreciate your comments, criticisms, corrections and suggestions for improving the text. Please address all correspondence to deitel@deitel.com. We'll respond promptly, and post corrections and clarifications at www.deitel.com/books/jsfp/. We hope you enjoy reading *JavaScript for Programmers* as much as we enjoyed writing it!

Paul J. Deitel
Dr. Harvey M. Deitel
Maynard, Massachusetts

About the Authors

Paul J. Deitel, CEO and Chief Technical Officer of Deitel & Associates, Inc., has almost three decades of experience in the computer field. Paul is a graduate of MIT's Sloan School of Management, where he studied Information Technology. Through Deitel & Associates, Inc., he has delivered web programming, Java, C#, Visual Basic, C++ and C courses to industry clients, including Cisco, IBM, Sun Microsystems, Dell, Lucent Technologies, Fidelity, NASA at the Kennedy Space Center, White Sands Missile Range, the National Severe Storm Laboratory, Rogue Wave Software, Boeing, Stratus, Hyperion Software, Adra Systems, Entergy, CableData Systems, Nortel Networks, Puma, iRobot, Invensys and many more. He holds the Sun Certified Java Programmer and Java Developer certifications and has been designated by Sun Microsystems as a Java Champion. He has lectured on Java and C++ for the Boston Chapter of the Association for Computing Machinery. He and his father, Dr. Harvey M. Deitel, are the world's best-selling programming-language textbook authors.

Dr. Harvey M. Deitel, Chairman and Chief Strategy Officer of Deitel & Associates, Inc., earned B.S. and M.S. degrees from MIT and a Ph.D. from Boston University. He earned tenure and served as the Chairman of the Computer Science Department at Boston College before founding Deitel & Associates, Inc., with his son, Paul J. Deitel. Harvey and Paul are the co-authors of dozens of books and multimedia packages and they are writing many more. The Deitels' texts have earned international recognition with translations published in Japanese, German, Russian, Spanish, Traditional Chinese, Simplified Chinese, Korean, French, Polish, Italian, Portuguese, Greek, Urdu and Turkish. Dr. Deitel has delivered hundreds of professional seminars to major corporations, academic institutions, government organizations and the military.

About Deitel & Associates, Inc.

Deitel & Associates, Inc., is an internationally recognized corporate training and authoring organization specializing in computer programming languages, Internet and web software technology, object technology education and Internet business development through its Web 2.0 Internet Business Initiative. The company provides instructor-led courses on major programming languages and platforms, such as C++, Java, C, C#, Visual C++, Visual Basic, XML, object technology and Internet and web programming. The founders of Deitel & Associates, Inc. are Paul J. Deitel and Dr. Harvey M. Deitel. The company's clients include many of the world's largest companies, government agencies, branches of the military, and academic institutions. Through its 32-year publishing partnership with Prentice Hall, Deitel & Associates, Inc. publishes leading-edge programming professional books, textbooks, interactive multimedia *Cyber Classrooms* and online and offline *LiveLessons* video courses. Deitel & Associates, Inc., and the authors can be reached via e-mail at:

deitel@deitel.com

To learn more about Deitel & Associates, Inc., its publications and its worldwide *Dive Into*® Series Corporate Training curriculum, visit:

www.deitel.com/training/

and subscribe to the free *Deitel*® *Buzz Online* e-mail newsletter at:

www.deitel.com/newsletter/subscribe.html

Check out the growing list of online Resource Centers at:

www.deitel.com/ResourceCenters.html

Individuals wishing to purchase Deitel publications can do so through:

www.deitel.com/books/index.html

The publisher offers discounts on this book when ordered in quantity for bulk purchases or special sales, which may include electronic versions and/or custom covers and content particular to your business, training goals, marketing focus, and branding interests. For more information, please contact:

U. S. Corporate and Government Sales
(800) 382-3419
corpsales@pearsontechgroup.com

For sales outside the U. S., please contact:

International Sales
international@pearsoned.com

Visit the publisher at www.phptr.com.

Before You Begin

Please follow these instructions to download the book's examples and ensure you have a current web browser before you begin using this book.

Downloading the *JavaScript for Programmers* Source Code

The source code in *JavaScript for Programmers* can be downloaded as a ZIP archive file from www.deitel.com/books/jsfp/. After you register and log in, click the link for the examples under **Download Code Examples and Other Premium Content for Registered Users**. Extract the example files to your hard disk using a ZIP file extractor program, such as WinZip (www.winzip.com). On Windows, we suggest that you extract the files to a folder such as C:\jsfp_examples. On Mac OS X and Linux, we suggest that you extract the files to a folder named jsfp_examples in your home folder.

Web Browsers Used in This Book

We've tested every example in this book using Mozilla's Firefox 2 and 3, and Microsoft's Internet Explorer 7 web browsers. Before you begin, ensure that you have one or both of these browsers installed on your computer. Internet Explorer 7 is available only for Microsoft Windows operating systems. If you are a Windows user and do not have Internet Explorer 7, you can download it from www.update.microsoft.com using Microsoft's Windows Update service. Firefox is available for most platforms. You can download Firefox 3 from www.firefox.com.

Many of the book's examples *will not work* in Internet Explorer 6. Though most or all of the examples in this book might run on other recent web browsers, such as Opera (www.opera.com), Apple's Safari (www.apple.com/safari/) and Google's Chrome (www.google.com/chrome/), we haven't tested the examples on these or any other browsers.

You are now ready to begin reading *JavaScript for Programmers*. We hope you enjoy the book! If you have any questions, please e-mail us at deitel@deitel.com. We'll respond promptly.

1

Introduction

The renaissance of interest in the web that we call Web 2.0 has reached the mainstream.
—Tim O'Reilly

Billions of queries stream across the servers of these Internet services—the aggregate thoughtstream of humankind, online.
—John Battelle, *The Search*

People are using the web to build things they have not built or written or drawn or communicated anywhere else.
—Tim Berners-Lee

Some people take what we contribute and extend it and contribute it back. That's really the basic open source success story.
—David Heinemeier Hansson, interviewed by Chris Karr at www.Chicagoist.com

OBJECTIVES

In this chapter you'll learn:

- The evolution of the Internet and the World Wide Web.
- What Web 2.0 is and why it's having such an impact among Internet-based and traditional businesses.
- What Rich Internet Applications (RIAs) are and the key software technologies used to build RIAs.
- How object technology is improving the software development process.
- The importance of JavaScript as the universal client scripting language.

1.1 Introduction

Welcome to Internet and World Wide Web programming and Web 2.0! We've worked hard to create what we hope you'll find to be an informative, entertaining and challenging learning experience. As you read this book, you may want to refer to

www.deitel.com/books/jsfp/

for updates and additional information.

The technologies you'll learn in this book are appropriate for experienced professionals who build substantial information systems. You'll find "industrial-strength" code examples. We have attempted to write in a clear and straightforward manner using best programming and documentation practices.

Perhaps most important, the book includes over 100 working code examples and shows the outputs produced when these examples are rendered in browsers or run on computers. We present all concepts in the context of complete working programs. We call this the "live-code approach." All of the source code is available for download from www.deitel.com/books/jsfp/.

We present a carefully paced introduction to "client-side" web programming, using the popular JavaScript language and the closely related technologies of XHTML (Extensible HyperText Markup Language), CSS (Cascading Style Sheets) and the DOM (Document Object Model). We often refer to "programming" as scripting—for reasons that will soon become clear.

JavaScript is among today's most popular software development languages for web-based applications. In this book, we present a number of powerful software technologies that will enable you to build such applications. We concentrate on using technologies such as the Extensible HyperText Markup Language (XHTML), JavaScript, CSS, and Extensible Markup Language (XML) to build the portions of web-based applications that reside on the *client side* (i.e., the portions of applications that typically run in your web browsers such as Mozilla's Firefox, Microsoft's Internet Explorer, Opera, Google's Chrome or Apple's Safari). The *server side* of web-based applications typically runs on "heavy-duty" computer systems on which organizations' business-critical websites reside. By mastering the technologies in this book, you'll be able to build the client side of substantial web-based, client/server, database-intensive, "multitier" applications. Our sister book, *Internet & World Wide Web How to Program, 4/e*, contains both the client-side programming material from *JavaScript for Programmers*, and also presents a variety of server-side programming technologies.

To keep up to date with Internet and web programming developments, and the latest information on *JavaScript for Programmers* at Deitel & Associates, please register for our free e-mail newsletter, the *Deitel® Buzz Online,* at

```
www.deitel.com/newsletter/subscribe.html
```

Please check out our growing list of Internet and web programming, and Internet business Resource Centers at

```
www.deitel.com/resourcecenters.html
```

Each week, we announce our latest Resource Centers in the newsletter. A list of Deitel Resource Centers at the time of this writing is located in the first few pages of the book. The Resource Centers include links to, and descriptions of, key tutorials, demos, free software tools, articles, e-books, white papers, videos, podcasts, blogs, RSS feeds and more that will help you deepen your knowledge of most of the subjects we discuss in this book.

Errata and updates for the book are posted at

```
www.deitel.com/books/jsfp/
```

You're embarking on a challenging and rewarding path. We hope that you'll enjoy *JavaScript for Programmers.* As you proceed, if you have any questions, send e-mail to

```
deitel@deitel.com
```

and we'll respond promptly.

1.2 History of the Internet and World Wide Web

In the late 1960s, one of the authors (HMD) was a graduate student at MIT. His research at MIT's Project MAC (now the Laboratory for Computer Science—the home of the World Wide Web Consortium) was funded by ARPA—the Advanced Research Projects Agency of the Department of Defense. ARPA sponsored a conference at which several dozen ARPA-funded graduate students were brought together at the University of Illinois at Urbana-Champaign to meet and share ideas. During this conference, ARPA rolled out the blueprints for networking the main computer systems of about a dozen ARPA-funded universities and research institutions. They were to be connected with communications lines operating at a then-stunning 56 Kbps (i.e., 56,000 bits per second)—this at a time when most people (of the few who could) were connecting over telephone lines to computers at a rate of 110 bits per second. There was great excitement at the conference. Researchers at Harvard talked about communicating with the Univac 1108 "supercomputer" at the University of Utah to handle calculations related to their computer graphics research. Many other intriguing possibilities were raised. Academic research was about to take a giant leap forward. Shortly after this conference, ARPA proceeded to implement the *ARPANET,* which eventually evolved into today's *Internet.*

Communicating Quickly and Easily
Things worked out differently from what was originally planned. Rather than enabling researchers to share each other's computers, it rapidly became clear that enabling researchers to communicate quickly and easily via what became known as *electronic mail* (*e-mail,* for

short) was the key early benefit of the ARPANET. This is true even today on the Internet, as e-mail and instant messaging facilitates communications of all kinds among more than a billion people worldwide.

Mutiple Users Sending and Receiving Information Simultaneously

One of the primary goals for ARPANET was to allow multiple users to send and receive information simultaneously over the same communications paths (e.g., phone lines). The network operated with a technique called *packet switching*, in which digital data was sent in small bundles called *packets*. The packets contained address, error-control and sequencing information. The address information allowed packets to be routed to their destinations. The sequencing information helped in reassembling the packets—which, because of complex routing mechanisms, could actually arrive out of order—into their original order for presentation to the recipient. Packets from different senders were intermixed on the same lines. This packet-switching technique greatly reduced transmission costs, as compared with the cost of dedicated communications lines.

The network was designed to operate without centralized control. If a portion of the network failed, the remaining working portions would still route packets from senders to receivers over alternative paths for reliability.

Protocols for Communication

The protocol for communicating over the ARPANET became known as *TCP*—the *Transmission Control Protocol*. TCP ensured that messages were properly routed from sender to receiver and that they arrived intact.

As the Internet evolved, organizations worldwide implemented their own networks for both intraorganization (i.e., within the organization) and interorganization (i.e., between organizations) communications. A wide variety of networking hardware and software appeared. One challenge was to get these different networks to communicate. ARPA accomplished this with the development of *IP*—the *Internet Protocol*—truly creating a *"network of networks,"* the current architecture of the Internet. The combined set of protocols is now commonly called *TCP/IP*.

Commercial Internet Use

Initially, Internet use was limited to universities and research institutions; then the military began using the Internet. Eventually, the government decided to allow access to the Internet for commercial purposes. Initially, there was resentment in the research and military communities—these groups were concerned that response times would become poor as "the Net" became saturated with users.

In fact, the exact opposite has occurred. Businesses rapidly realized that they could tune their operations and offer new and better services to their clients, so they started spending vast amounts of money to develop and enhance the Internet. This generated fierce competition among communications carriers and hardware and software suppliers to meet this demand. The result is that *bandwidth* (i.e., the information-carrying capacity) of the Internet has increased tremendously and costs have plummeted.

World Wide Web

The *World Wide Web* allows computer users to locate and view multimedia-based documents on almost any subject over the Internet. Though the Internet was developed decades ago, the web is a relatively recent creation. In 1989, *Tim Berners-Lee* of CERN (the European Organization for Nuclear Research) began to develop a technology for sharing information via hyperlinked text documents. Berners-Lee called his invention the *Hyper-Text Markup Language* (*HTML*). He also wrote communication protocols to form the backbone of his new information system, which he called the World Wide Web. In particular, he wrote the *Hypertext Transfer Protocol* (*HTTP*)—a communications protocol for sending information over the web. Web use exploded with the availability in 1993 of the Mosaic browser, which featured a user-friendly graphical interface. Marc Andreessen, whose team at NCSA (the University of Illinois' National Center for Supercomputing Applications) developed Mosaic, went on to found Netscape®, the company that many people credit with initiating the explosive Internet economy of the late 1990s. Netscape's version of the Mosaic browser has been evolved by the Mozilla Corporation into the enormously popular open source Mozilla Firefox browser.

Making Our Work and Lives Easier

In the past, most computer applications ran on computers that were not connected to one another, whereas today's applications can be written to communicate among the world's computers. The Internet mixes computing and communications technologies. It makes our work easier. It makes information instantly and conveniently accessible worldwide. It enables individuals and small businesses to get worldwide exposure. It is changing the way business is done. People can search for the best prices on virtually any product or service. Special-interest communities can stay in touch with one another. Researchers can be made instantly aware of the latest breakthroughs. The Internet and the web are surely among humankind's most profound creations.

1.3 World Wide Web Consortium (W3C)

In October 1994, Tim Berners-Lee founded an organization—called the *World Wide Web Consortium* (*W3C*)—devoted to developing nonproprietary, interoperable technologies for the World Wide Web. One of the W3C's primary goals is to make the web universally accessible—regardless of ability, language or culture. The W3C (www.w3.org) provides extensive resources on Internet and web technologies.

The W3C is also a standardization organization. Web technologies standardized by the W3C are called *Recommendations*. W3C Recommendations include the Extensible HyperText Markup Language (XHTML), Cascading Style Sheets (CSS), HyperText Markup Language (HTML—now considered a "legacy" technology) and the Extensible Markup Language (XML). A recommendation is not an actual software product, but a document that specifies a technology's role, syntax rules and so forth.

1.4 Web 2.0

In 2003 there was a noticeable shift in how people and businesses were using the web and developing web-based applications. The term *Web 2.0* was coined by *Dale Dougherty* of *O'Reilly® Media*[1] in 2003 to describe this trend. Although it became a major media buzz-

---

1. O'Reilly, T. "What is Web 2.0: Design Patterns and Business Models for the Next Generation of Software." September 2005 <http://www.oreillynet.com/pub/a/oreilly/tim/news/2005/09/30/what-is-web-20.html?page=1>.

word, few people really know what Web 2.0 means. Generally, Web 2.0 companies use the web as a platform to create collaborative, community-based sites (e.g., social networking sites, blogs, wikis, etc.).

Web 1.0

Web 1.0 (the state of the web through the 1990s and early 2000s) was focused on a relatively small number of companies and advertisers producing content for users to access (some people called it the "brochure web"). Web 2.0 *involves* the user—not only is the content often created by the users, but users help organize it, share it, remix it, critique it, update it, etc. One way to look at Web 1.0 is as a *lecture*, a small number of professors informing a large audience of students. In comparison, Web 2.0 is a *conversation*, with everyone having the opportunity to speak and share views.

Architecture of Participation

Web 2.0 is providing new opportunities and connecting people and content in unique ways. Web 2.0 embraces an *architecture of participation*—a design that encourages user interaction and community contributions. You, the user, are the most important aspect of Web 2.0—so important, in fact, that in 2006, *TIME Magazine*'s "Person of the Year" was "you."[2] The article recognized the social phenomenon of Web 2.0—the shift away from a powerful few to an empowered many. Several popular blogs now compete with traditional media powerhouses, and many Web 2.0 companies are built almost entirely on user-generated content. For websites like MySpace®, Facebook®, Flickr™, YouTube, eBay® and Wikipedia®, users create the content, while the companies provide the platforms. These companies *trust their users*—without such trust, users cannot make significant contributions to the sites.

Collective Intelligence

The architecture of participation has influenced software development as well. Open source software is available for anyone to use and modify with few or no restrictions. Using *collective intelligence*—the concept that a large diverse group of people will create smart ideas—communities collaborate to develop software that many people believe is better and more robust than proprietary software. Rich Internet Applications (RIAs) are being developed using technologies (such as Ajax) that have the look and feel of desktop software, enhancing a user's overall experience. Software as a Service (SaaS)—software that runs on a server instead of a local computer—has also gained prominence because of sophisticated new technologies and increased broadband Internet access.

Search engines, including Google™, Yahoo!®, MSN®, Ask™, and many more, have become essential to sorting through the massive amount of content on the web. Social bookmarking sites such as del.icio.us and Ma.gnolia allow users to share their favorite sites with others. Social media sites such as Digg™, Spotplex™ and Netscape enable the community to decide which news articles are the most significant. The way we find the information on these sites is also changing—people are *tagging* (i.e., labeling) web content by subject or keyword in a way that helps anyone locate information more effectively.

---

2. Grossman, L. "TIME's Person of the Year: You." *TIME*, December 2006 <http://www.time.com/time/magazine/article/0,9171,1569514,00.html>.

Web Services

Web services have emerged and, in the process, have inspired the creation of many Web 2.0 businesses. Web services allow you to incorporate functionality from existing applications and websites into your own web applications quickly and easily. For example, using Amazon Web Services™, you can create a specialty bookstore to run your website and earn revenues through the Amazon Associates Program; or, using Google™ Maps web services with eBay web services, you can build location-based "mashup" applications to find auction items in certain geographical areas. Web services, inexpensive computers, abundant high-speed Internet access, open source software and many other elements have inspired new, exciting, *lightweight business models* that people can launch with only a small investment. Some types of websites with rich and robust functionality that might have required hundreds of thousands or even millions of dollars to build in the 1990s can now be built for nominal amounts of money.

Semantic Web

In the future, we'll see computers learn to understand the meaning of the data on the web—the beginnings of the Semantic Web are already appearing. Continual improvements in hardware, software and communications technologies will enable exciting new types of applications.

See our Web 2.0 Resource Center at www.deitel.com/web2.0/ for more information on the major characteristics and technologies of Web 2.0, key Web 2.0 companies and Web 2.0 Internet business and monetization models. The Resource Center also includes information on user-generated content, blogging, content networks, social networking, location-based services and more. We have separate Resource Centers on many Web 2.0 concepts and technologies. You can view a list of our Resource Centers in the first few pages of this book and at www.deitel.com/ResourceCenters.html.

1.5 Key Software Trend: Object Technology

One of the authors, HMD, remembers the great frustration felt in the 1960s by software development organizations, especially those working on large-scale projects. During his undergraduate years, he had the privilege of working summers at a leading computer vendor on the teams developing timesharing, virtual-memory operating systems. This was a great experience for a college student. But, in the summer of 1967, reality set in when the company "decommitted" from producing as a commercial product the particular system on which hundreds of people had been working for many years. It was difficult to get this thing called software right—software is "complex stuff."

Improvements to software technology did emerge, with the benefits of structured programming and the related disciplines of structured systems analysis and design being realized in the 1970s. Not until the technology of object-oriented programming became widely used in the 1990s, though, did software developers feel they had the necessary tools for making major strides in the software development process.

What are objects and why are they special? Actually, object technology is a packaging scheme that helps us create meaningful software units. These can be large and are highly focused on particular applications areas. There are date objects, time objects, paycheck objects, invoice objects, audio objects, video objects, file objects, record objects and so on. In fact, almost any noun can be reasonably represented as an object.

We live in a world of objects. Just look around you. There are cars, planes, people, animals, buildings, traffic lights, elevators and the like. Before object-oriented languages appeared, procedural programming languages (such as Fortran, COBOL, Pascal, BASIC and C) were focused on actions (verbs) rather than on things or objects (nouns). Programmers living in a world of objects programmed primarily using verbs. This made it awkward to write programs. Now, with the availability of popular object-oriented languages, such as C++, Java, Visual Basic and C#, programmers continue to live in an object-oriented world *and* can program in an object-oriented manner. This is a more natural process than procedural programming and has resulted in significant productivity gains.

A key problem with procedural programming is that the program units do not effectively mirror real-world entities, so these units are not particularly reusable. It's not unusual for programmers to "start fresh" on each new project and have to write similar software "from scratch." This wastes time and money, as people repeatedly "reinvent the wheel." With object technology, the software entities created (called classes), if properly designed, tend to be reusable on future projects. Using libraries of reusable componentry can greatly reduce effort required to implement certain kinds of systems (compared to the effort that would be required to reinvent these capabilities on new projects).

Software Engineering Observation 1.1

Extensive class libraries of reusable software components are available on the Internet. Many of these libraries are free.

Software Engineering Observation 1.2

Some organizations report that the key benefit object-oriented programming gives them is not software that is reusable but, rather, software that is more understandable, better organized and easier to maintain, modify and debug. This can be significant, because perhaps as much as 80 percent of software cost is associated not with the original efforts to develop the software, but with the continued evolution and maintenance of that software throughout its lifetime.

1.6 JavaScript: Object-Based Scripting for the Web

JavaScript is a powerful object-based scripting language with strong support for proper software engineering techniques. You'll create and manipulate objects from the start in JavaScript. JavaScript is available free in today's popular web browsers.

You'll see that JavaScript is a portable scripting language and that programs written in JavaScript can run in many web browsers. Actually, portability is an elusive goal.

Portability Tip 1.1

Although it is easier to write portable programs in JavaScript than in many other programming languages, differences among interpreters and browsers make portability difficult to achieve. Simply writing programs in JavaScript does not guarantee portability. You'll occasionally need to research platform variations and write your code accordingly.

Portability Tip 1.2

When writing JavaScript programs, you need to deal directly with cross-browser portability issues. Such issues are hidden by JavaScript libraries, such as Dojo (discussed in Chapter 13), Prototype, Script.aculo.us and ASP.NET Ajax, which provide powerful, ready-to-use capabilities that simplify JavaScript coding by making it cross-browser compatible.

Error-Prevention Tip 1.1

Always test your JavaScript programs on all systems and in all web browsers for which they are intended.

JavaScript was created by Netscape, which created the first widely successful web browser. Both Netscape and Microsoft have been instrumental in standardizing JavaScript through ECMA International (formerly the European Computer Manufacturers Association) as ECMAScript. Adobe Flash uses another scripting language named ActionScript. ActionScript and JavaScript are converging in the JavaScript standard's next version (JavaScript 2/ECMA Script version 4) currently under development. This will result in a universal client scripting language, greatly simplifying web application development.

1.7 Browser Portability

Ensuring a consistent look and feel on client-side browsers is one of the great challenges of developing web-based applications. Currently, a standard does not exist to which software developers must adhere when creating web browsers. Although browsers share a common set of features, each browser might render pages differently. Browsers are available in many versions and on many different platforms (Microsoft Windows, Apple Macintosh, Linux, UNIX, etc.). Vendors add features to each new version that sometimes cause cross-platform incompatibility issues. Clearly it is difficult to develop web pages that render correctly on all versions of all browsers. In this book we develop web applications that execute on the Internet Explorer 7 and Firefox 2 (and higher) browsers. Most examples will operate correctly in other recent browsers such as Opera, Apple's Safari and Google's Chrome, but we have not explicitly tested the applications on these other browsers.

Portability Tip 1.3

The web is populated with many different browsers, which makes it difficult for authors and web application developers to create universal solutions. The W3C is working toward the goal of a universal client-side platform.

1.8 Web Resources

www.deitel.com/
Check this site frequently for updates, corrections and additional resources for all Deitel & Associates, Inc., publications.

www.deitel.com/ResourceCenters.html
Check out the complete list of Deitel Resource Centers, including numerous programming, open source, Web 2.0 and Internet business topics.

www.w3.org
The World Wide Web Consortium (W3C) website offers a comprehensive description of web technologies. For each Internet technology with which the W3C is involved, the site provides a description of the technology, its benefits to web designers, the history of the technology and the future goals of the W3C in developing the technology.

www.deitel.com/Ajax/
www.deitel.com/XML/
www.deitel.com/XHTML/
www.deitel.com/CSS21/
www.deitel.com/Dojo/

2

Introduction to XHTML

OBJECTIVES

In this chapter you'll learn:

- Important components of XHTML documents.
- To use XHTML to create web pages.
- To add images to web pages.
- To create and use hyperlinks to navigate web pages.
- To mark up lists of information.
- To create tables with rows and columns of data and control table formatting.
- To create and use forms to get user input.
- To make web pages accessible to search engines using <meta> tags.

To read between the lines
was easier than to follow the
text.
—Henry James

High thoughts must have
high language.
—Aristophanes

Yea, from the table of my
memory
I'll wipe away all trivial
fond records.
—William Shakespeare

He had a wonderful talent
for packing thought close,
and rendering it portable.
—Thomas Babington
Macaulay

Outline

2.1 Introduction

Welcome to the world of opportunity created by the World Wide Web. The Internet is almost four decades old, but it wasn't until the web's growth in popularity in the 1990s and the recent start of the Web 2.0 era that the explosion of opportunity we are experiencing began. Exciting new developments occur almost daily—the pace of innovation is unprecedented. In this chapter, you'll develop your own web pages. As the book proceeds, you'll create increasingly appealing and powerful web pages.

This chapter begins unlocking the power of web-based application development with *XHTML*—the *Extensible HyperText Markup Language*. Later in the chapter, we introduce more sophisticated XHTML techniques such as *internal linking* for easier page navigation, *forms* for collecting information from a web-page visitor and *tables*, which are particularly useful for structuring information from *databases* (i.e., software that stores structured sets of data). In the next chapter, we discuss a technology called *Cascading Style Sheets™* (*CSS*), a technology that makes web pages more visually appealing.

Unlike procedural programming languages such as C, C++, or Java, XHTML is a *markup language* that specifies the format of the text that is displayed in a web browser such as Microsoft's Internet Explorer or Mozilla Firefox.

One key issue when using XHTML is the separation of the *presentation* of a document (i.e., the document's appearance when rendered by a browser) from the *structure* of the document's information. XHTML is based on HTML (HyperText Markup Language)—a legacy technology of the World Wide Web Consortium (W3C). In HTML, it was common to specify both the document's structure and its formatting. Formatting might specify where the browser placed an element in a web page or the fonts and colors used to display an element. The *XHTML 1.0 Strict* recommendation (the version of XHTML that we use in this book) allows only a document's structure to appear in a valid XHTML document, and *not* its formatting. Normally, such formatting is specified with Cascading Style Sheets (Chapter 3). All our examples in this chapter are based on the XHTML 1.0 Strict Recommendation.

2.2 Editing XHTML

In this chapter, we write XHTML in its *source-code form*. We create *XHTML documents* by typing them in a text editor (e.g., Notepad, TextEdit, vi, emacs) and saving them with either an .html or an .htm filename extension.

Good Programming Practice 2.1

Assign filenames to documents that describe their functionality. This practice can help you identify documents faster. It also helps people who want to link to a page, by giving them an easy-to-remember name. For example, if you are writing an XHTML document that contains product information, you might want to call it products.html.

Computers called *web servers* running specialized software store XHTML documents. Clients (e.g., web browsers) request specific *resources* such as the XHTML documents from web servers. For example, typing www.deitel.com/books/downloads.html into a web browser's address field requests downloads.html from the books directory on the web server running at www.deitel.com. For now, we simply place the XHTML documents on our computer and render them by opening them locally with a web browser such as Internet Explorer or Firefox.

2.3 First XHTML Example

This chapter presents XHTML markup and provides screen captures that show how a browser renders (i.e., displays) the XHTML. You can download the examples from www.deitel.com/books/jsfp/. Every XHTML document we show has line numbers for your convenience—these line numbers are not part of the XHTML documents. As you read this book, open each XHTML document in your web browser so you can view and interact with it as it was originally intended.

Figure 2.1 is an XHTML document named main.html. This first example displays the message "Welcome to XHTML!" in the browser. The key line in the program is line 13, which tells the browser to display "Welcome to XHTML!" Now let us consider each line of the program.

```
1   <?xml version = "1.0" encoding = "utf-8"?>
2   <!DOCTYPE html PUBLIC "-//W3C//DTD XHTML 1.0 Strict//EN"
3      "http://www.w3.org/TR/xhtml1/DTD/xhtml1-strict.dtd">
4
5   <!-- Fig. 2.1: main.html -->
6   <!-- First XHTML example. -->
7   <html xmlns = "http://www.w3.org/1999/xhtml">
8      <head>
9         <title>Welcome</title>
10     </head>
11
12     <body>
13        <p>Welcome to XHTML!</p>
14     </body>
15  </html>
```

Fig. 2.1 | First XHTML example. (Part 1 of 2.)

Title bar shows
contents of `title`
element

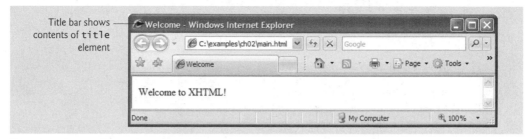

Fig. 2.1 | First XHTML example. (Part 2 of 2.)

Lines 1–3 are required in XHTML documents to conform with proper XHTML syntax. For now, copy and paste these lines into each XHTML document you create. The meaning of these lines is discussed in detail in Chapter 12.

Lines 5–6 are *XHTML comments*. XHTML document creators insert comments to improve markup readability and describe the content of a document. Comments also help other people read and understand an XHTML document's markup and content. Comments do not cause the browser to perform any action when the user loads the XHTML document into the web browser to view it. XHTML comments always start with `<!--` and end with `-->`. Each of our XHTML examples includes comments that specify the figure number and filename and provide a brief description of the example's purpose. Subsequent examples include comments in the markup, especially to highlight new features.

Good Programming Practice 2.2

Place comments throughout your markup. Comments help other programmers understand the markup, assist in debugging and list useful information that you do not want the browser to render. Comments also help you understand your own markup when you revisit a document to modify or update it in the future.

XHTML markup contains text that represents the content of a document and *elements* that specify a document's structure. Some important elements of an XHTML document are the *html* element, the *head* element and the *body* element. The html element encloses the *head section* (represented by the head element) and the *body section* (represented by the body element). The head section contains information about the XHTML document, such as its *title*. The head section also can contain special document formatting instructions called *style sheets* and client-side programs called *scripts* for creating dynamic web pages. (We introduce style sheets in Chapter 3 and scripting with JavaScript in Chapter 4.) The body section contains the page's content that the browser displays when the user visits the web page.

XHTML documents delimit an element with *start* and *end* tags. A start tag consists of the element name in angle brackets (e.g., `<html>`). An end tag consists of the element name preceded by a forward slash (/) in angle brackets (e.g., `</html>`). In this example, lines 7 and 15 define the start and end of the html element. Note that the end tag in line 15 has the same name as the start tag, but is preceded by a / inside the angle brackets. Many start tags have *attributes* that provide additional information about an element. Browsers can use this additional information to determine how to process the element. Each attribute has a *name* and a *value* separated by an equals sign (=). Line 7 specifies a required attribute (`xmlns`) and value (`http://www.w3.org/1999/xhtml`) for the html element in an XHTML document. For now, simply copy and paste the html element start tag in line 7 into your XHTML documents. We discuss the details of the xmlns attribute in Chapter 12.

Common Programming Error 2.1

Not enclosing attribute values in either single or double quotes is a syntax error. However, some web browsers may still render the element correctly.

Common Programming Error 2.2

Using uppercase letters in an XHTML element or attribute name is a syntax error. However, some web browsers may still render the element correctly.

An XHTML document divides the html element into two sections—head and body. Lines 8–10 define the page's head section with a head element. Line 9 specifies a title element. This is called a ***nested element*** because it is enclosed in the head element's start and end tags. The head element is also a nested element because it is enclosed in the html element's start and end tags. The title element describes the web page. Titles usually appear in the ***title bar*** at the top of the browser window, in the browser tab that the page is displayed on, and also as the text identifying a page when users add the page to their list of **Favorites** or **Bookmarks** that enables them to return to their favorite sites. Search engines (i.e., sites that allow users to search the web) also use the title for indexing purposes.

Good Programming Practice 2.3

Indenting nested elements emphasizes a document's structure and promotes readability.

Common Programming Error 2.3

XHTML does not permit tags to overlap—a nested element's end tag must appear in the document before the enclosing element's end tag. For example, the nested XHTML tags <head><title>hello</head></title> cause a syntax error, because the enclosing head element's ending </head> tag appears before the nested title element's ending </title> tag.

Good Programming Practice 2.4

Use a consistent title-naming convention for all pages on a site. For example, if a site is named "Bailey's Website," then the title of the contact page might be "Bailey's Website—Contact." This practice can help users better understand the website's structure.

Line 12 begins the document's body element. The body section of an XHTML document specifies the document's content, which may include text and elements.

Some elements, such as the ***paragraph element*** (denoted with <p> and </p>) in line 13, mark up text for display in a browser. All the text placed between the <p> and </p> tags forms one paragraph. When the browser renders a paragraph, a blank line usually precedes and follows paragraph text.

This document ends with two end tags (lines 14–15). These tags close the body and html elements, respectively. The </html> tag in an XHTML document informs the browser that the XHTML markup is complete.

To open an XHTML example from this chapter, open the folder where you saved the book's examples, browse to the ch04 folder and double click the file to open it in your default web browser. At this point your browser window should appear similar to the sample screen capture shown in Fig. 2.1. (Note that we resized the browser window to save space in the book.)

2.4 W3C XHTML Validation Service

Programming web-based applications can be complex, and XHTML documents must be written correctly to ensure that browsers process them properly. To promote correctly written documents, the World Wide Web Consortium (W3C) provides a *validation service* (`validator.w3.org`) for checking a document's syntax. Documents can be validated by providing a URL that specifies the file's location, by uploading a file to `validator.w3.org/file-upload.html` or by pasting code directly into a text area. Uploading a file copies the file from the user's computer to another computer on the Internet. The W3C's web page indicates that the service name is **MarkUp Validation Service** and that the validation service is able to validate the syntax of XHTML documents. All the XHTML examples in this book have been validated successfully using `validator.w3.org`.

By clicking **Choose...**, users can select files on their own computers for upload. After selecting a file, clicking the **Check** button uploads and validates the file. If a document contains syntax errors, the validation service displays error messages describing the errors.

Error-Prevention Tip 2.1

Most current browsers attempt to render XHTML documents even if they are invalid. This often leads to unexpected and possibly undesirable results. Use a validation service, such as the W3C **MarkUp Validation Service***, to confirm that an XHTML document is syntactically correct.*

2.5 Headings

Some text in an XHTML document may be more important than other text. For example, the text in this section is considered more important than a footnote. XHTML provides six *headings*, called *heading elements*, for specifying the relative importance of information. Figure 2.2 demonstrates these elements (h1 through h6). Heading element h1 (line 13) is considered the most significant heading and is typically rendered in a larger font than the other five headings (lines 14–18). Each successive heading element (i.e., h2, h3, etc.) is typically rendered in a progressively smaller font.

Portability Tip 2.1

The text size used to display each heading element can vary significantly between browsers. In Chapter 3, we discuss how to control the text size and other text properties.

Look-and-Feel Observation 2.1

Placing a heading at the top of every XHTML page helps viewers understand the purpose of each page.

Look-and-Feel Observation 2.2

Use larger headings to emphasize more important sections of a web page.

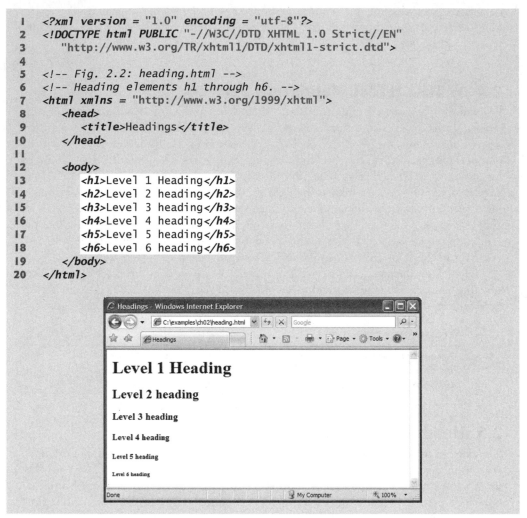

```
 1    <?xml version = "1.0" encoding = "utf-8"?>
 2    <!DOCTYPE html PUBLIC "-//W3C//DTD XHTML 1.0 Strict//EN"
 3       "http://www.w3.org/TR/xhtml1/DTD/xhtml1-strict.dtd">
 4
 5    <!-- Fig. 2.2: heading.html -->
 6    <!-- Heading elements h1 through h6. -->
 7    <html xmlns = "http://www.w3.org/1999/xhtml">
 8       <head>
 9          <title>Headings</title>
10       </head>
11
12       <body>
13          <h1>Level 1 Heading</h1>
14          <h2>Level 2 heading</h2>
15          <h3>Level 3 heading</h3>
16          <h4>Level 4 heading</h4>
17          <h5>Level 5 heading</h5>
18          <h6>Level 6 heading</h6>
19       </body>
20    </html>
```

Fig. 2.2 | Heading elements h1 through h6.

2.6 Linking

One of the most important XHTML features is the *hyperlink*, which references (or *links* to) other resources, such as XHTML documents and images. When a user clicks a hyperlink, the browser tries to execute an action associated with it (e.g., navigate to a URL, open an e-mail client, etc.). In XHTML, both text and images can act as hyperlinks. Web browsers typically underline text hyperlinks and color their text blue by default, so that users can distinguish hyperlinks from plain text. In Fig. 2.3, we create text hyperlinks to four different websites.

Line 14 introduces the *strong element*, which indicates that its contents has high importance. Browsers typically display such text in a bold font.

Links are created using the *a* (*anchor*) element. Line 17 defines a hyperlink to the URL assigned to attribute *href*, which specifies the location of a linked resource, such as

```
 1    <?xml version = "1.0" encoding = "utf-8"?>
 2    <!DOCTYPE html PUBLIC "-//W3C//DTD XHTML 1.0 Strict//EN"
 3       "http://www.w3.org/TR/xhtml1/DTD/xhtml1-strict.dtd">
 4
 5    <!-- Fig. 2.3: links.html -->
 6    <!-- Linking to other web pages. -->
 7    <html xmlns = "http://www.w3.org/1999/xhtml">
 8       <head>
 9          <title>Links</title>
10       </head>
11
12       <body>
13          <h1>Here are my favorite sites</h1>
14          <p><strong>Click a name to go to that page.</strong></p>
15
16          <!-- Create four text hyperlinks -->
17          <p><a href = "http://www.deitel.com">Deitel</a></p>
18          <p><a href = "http://www.prenhall.com">Prentice Hall</a></p>
19          <p><a href = "http://www.yahoo.com">Yahoo!</a></p>
20          <p><a href = "http://www.usatoday.com">USA Today</a></p>
21       </body>
22    </html>
```

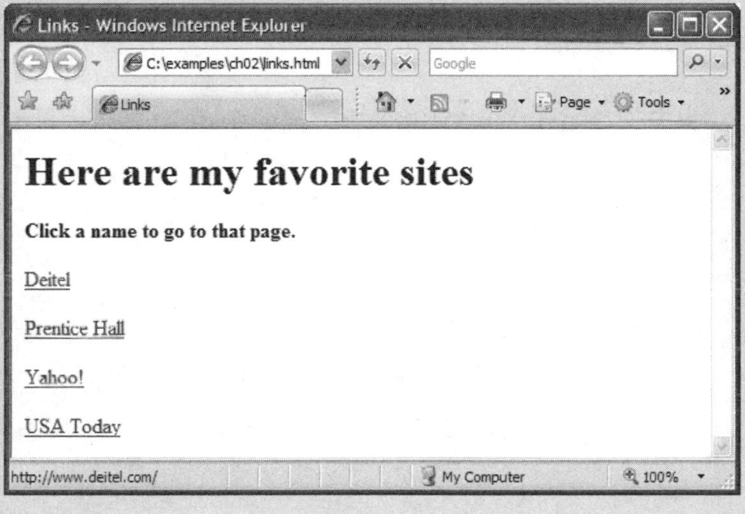

Fig. 2.3 | Linking to other web pages.

a web page, a file or an e-mail address. This particular anchor element links the text `Deitel` to a web page located at `http://www.deitel.com`. When a URL does not indicate a specific document on the website, the web server returns a default web page. This page is often called `index.html`; however, most web servers can be configured to use any file as the default web page for the site. If the web server cannot locate a requested document, it returns an error indication to the web browser, and the browser displays a web page containing an error message to the user.

Hyperlinking to an E-Mail Address
Anchors can link to e-mail addresses using a *mailto:* URL. When someone clicks this type of anchored link, most browsers launch the default e-mail program (e.g., Microsoft Outlook or Mozilla Thunderbird) to enable the user to write an e-mail message to the linked address. Figure 2.4 demonstrates this type of anchor. Lines 15–17 contain an e-mail link. The form of an e-mail anchor is `<a href = "mailto:emailAddress">...</a>`. In this case, we link to the e-mail address `deitel@deitel.com`.

```
 1   <?xml version = "1.0" encoding = "utf-8"?>
 2   <!DOCTYPE html PUBLIC "-//W3C//DTD XHTML 1.0 Strict//EN"
 3      "http://www.w3.org/TR/xhtml1/DTD/xhtml1-strict.dtd">
 4
 5   <!-- Fig. 2.4: contact.html -->
 6   <!-- Linking to an e-mail address. -->
 7   <html xmlns = "http://www.w3.org/1999/xhtml">
 8      <head>
 9         <title>Contact Page</title>
10      </head>
11
12      <body>
13         <p>
14            My email address is
15            <a href = "mailto:deitel@deitel.com">
16               deitel@deitel.com
17            </a>
18            . Click the address and your default email client
19             will open an e-mail message and address it to me.
20         </p>
21      </body>
22   </html>
```

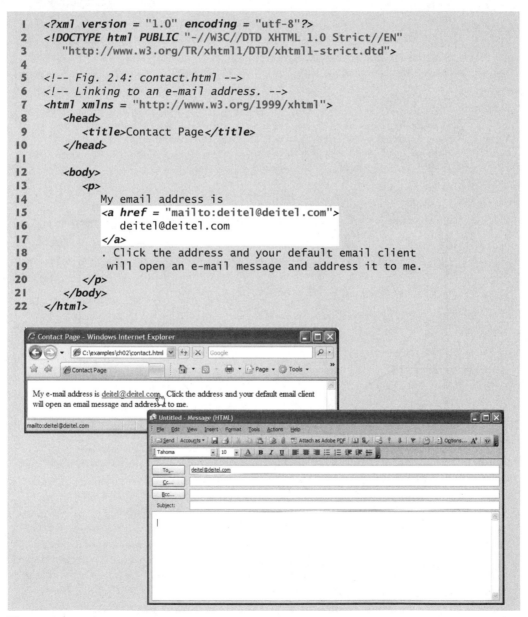

Fig. 2.4 | Linking to an e-mail address.

2.7 Images

The examples discussed so far demonstrate how to mark up documents that contain only text. However, most web pages contain both text and images. In fact, images are an equally important, if not essential, part of web-page design. The three most popular image formats used by web developers are Graphics Interchange Format (GIF), Joint Photographic Experts Group (JPEG) and Portable Network Graphics (PNG) images. Users can create images using specialized software, such as Adobe Photoshop Elements (www.adobe.com), G.I.M.P. (http://www.gimp.org) and Inkscape (http://www.inkscape.org). Images may also be acquired from various websites. Figure 2.5 demonstrates how to incorporate images into web pages.

Lines 14–15 use an *img element* to insert an image in the document. The image file's location is specified with the img element's *src attribute*. This image is located in the same directory as the XHTML document, so only the image's filename is required. Optional attributes *width* and *height* specify the image's width and height, respectively. You can

```
1   <?xml version = "1.0" encoding = "utf-8"?>
2   <!DOCTYPE html PUBLIC "-//W3C//DTD XHTML 1.0 Strict//EN"
3      "http://www.w3.org/TR/xhtml1/DTD/xhtml1-strict.dtd">
4
5   <!-- Fig. 2.5: picture.html -->
6   <!-- Images in XHTML files. -->
7   <html xmlns = "http://www.w3.org/1999/xhtml">
8      <head>
9         <title>Images</title>
10     </head>
11
12     <body>
13        <p>
14           <img src = "cpphtp6.jpg" width = "92" height = "120"
15              alt = "C++ How to Program book cover" />
16           <img src = "jhtp.jpg" width = "92" height = "120"
17              alt = "Java How to Program book cover" />
18        </p>
19     </body>
20  </html>
```

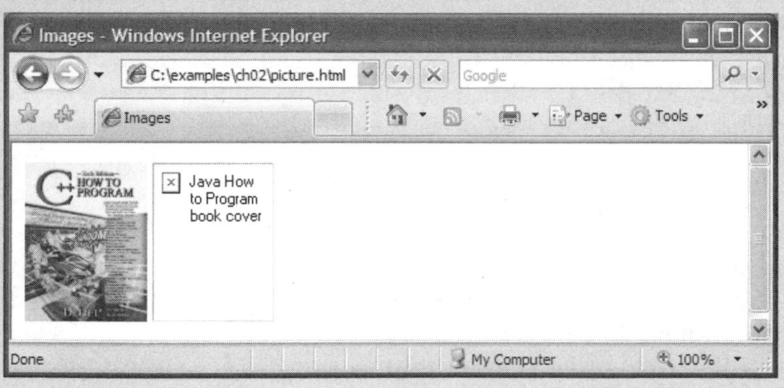

Fig. 2.5 | Images in XHTML files.

scale an image by increasing or decreasing the values of the image `width` and `height` attributes. If these attributes are omitted, the browser uses the image's actual width and height. Images are measured in *pixels* ("picture elements"), which represent dots of color on the screen. Any image-editing program will have a feature that displays the dimensions, in pixels, of an image. The image in Fig. 2.5 is 92 pixels wide and 120 pixels high.

Good Programming Practice 2.5

Always include the `width` and the `height` of an image inside the `<img>` tag. When the browser loads the XHTML file, it will know immediately from these attributes how much screen space to provide for the image and will lay out the page properly, even before it downloads the image.

Performance Tip 2.1

Including the `width` and `height` attributes in an `<img>` tag can help the browser load and render pages faster.

Common Programming Error 2.4

Entering new dimensions for an image that change its inherent width-to-height ratio distorts the appearance of the image. For example, if your image is 200 pixels wide and 100 pixels high, you should ensure that any new dimensions have a 2:1 width-to-height ratio.

Every `img` element in an XHTML document must have an *alt attribute*. If a browser cannot render an image, the browser displays the `alt` attribute's value. A browser may not be able to render an image for several reasons. It may not support images—as is the case with a *text-based browser* (i.e., a browser that can display only text)—or the client may have disabled image viewing to reduce download time. Figure 2.5 shows Internet Explorer 7 rendering an X symbol and displaying the `alt` attribute's value, signifying that the image (`jhtp.jpg`) cannot be found.

The `alt` attribute helps you create *accessible* web pages for users with disabilities, especially those with vision impairments who use text-based browsers. Specialized software called a *speech synthesizer* can "speak" the `alt` attribute's value so that a user with a visual impairment knows what the browser is displaying.

Some XHTML elements (called *empty elements*) contain only attributes and do not mark up text (i.e., text is not placed between the start and end tags). Empty elements (e.g., `img`) must be terminated, either by using the *forward slash character* (`/`) inside the closing right angle bracket (`>`) of the start tag or by explicitly including the end tag. When using the forward slash character, we add a space before it to improve readability (as shown at the ends of lines 15 and 17). Rather than using the forward slash character, lines 16–17 could be written with a closing `</img>` tag as follows:

```
<img src = "jhtp.jpg" width = "92" height = "120"
    alt = "Java How to Program book cover"></img>
```

Using Images as Hyperlinks

By using images as hyperlinks, web developers can create graphical web pages that link to other resources. In Fig. 2.6, we create six different image hyperlinks.

Lines 14–17 create an *image hyperlink* by nesting an `img` element in an anchor (a) element. The value of the `img` element's `src` attribute value specifies that this image (`links.jpg`) resides in a directory named `buttons`. The `buttons` directory and the

```
 1    <?xml version = "1.0" encoding = "utf-8"?>
 2    <!DOCTYPE html PUBLIC "-//W3C//DTD XHTML 1.0 Strict//EN"
 3       "http://www.w3.org/TR/xhtml1/DTD/xhtml1-strict.dtd">
 4
 5    <!-- Fig. 2.6: nav.html -->
 6    <!-- Images as link anchors. -->
 7    <html xmlns = "http://www.w3.org/1999/xhtml">
 8       <head>
 9          <title>Navigation Bar</title>
10       </head>
11
12       <body>
13          <p>
14             <a href = "links.html">
15                <img src = "buttons/links.jpg" width = "65"
16                   height = "50" alt = "Links Page" />
17             </a>
18
19             <a href = "list.html">
20                <img src = "buttons/list.jpg" width = "65"
21                   height = "50" alt = "List Example Page" />
22             </a>
23
24             <a href = "contact.html">
25                <img src = "buttons/contact.jpg" width = "65"
26                   height = "50" alt = "Contact Page" />
27             </a>
28
29             <a href = "table1.html">
30                <img src = "buttons/table.jpg" width = "65"
31                   height = "50" alt = "Table Page" />
32             </a>
33
34             <a href = "form.html">
35                <img src = "buttons/form.jpg" width = "65"
36                   height = "50" alt = "Feedback Form" />
37             </a>
38          </p>
39       </body>
40    </html>
```

Fig. 2.6 | Images as link anchors. (Part 1 of 2.)

Fig. 2.6 | Images as link anchors. (Part 2 of 2.)

XHTML document are in the same directory. Images from other web documents also can be referenced by setting the src attribute to the name and location of the image. Note that if you're hosting a publicly available web page that uses an image from another site, you should get permission to use the image and host a copy of image on your own website. If you refer to an image on another website, the browser has to request the image resource from the other site's server. Clicking an image hyperlink takes a user to the web page specified by the surrounding anchor element's href attribute. Notice that when the mouse hovers over a link of any kind, the URL that the link points to is displayed in the status bar at the bottom of the browser window.

2.8 Special Characters and Horizontal Rules

When marking up text, certain characters or symbols (e.g., <) may be difficult to embed directly into an XHTML document. Some keyboards do not provide these symbols, or the presence of these symbols may cause syntax errors. For example, the markup

```
<p>if x < 10 then increment x by 1</p>
```

results in a syntax error because it uses the less-than character (<), which is reserved for start tags and end tags such as <p> and </p>. XHTML provides *character entity references* (in the form &*code*;) for representing special characters. We could correct the previous line by writing

```
<p>if x &lt; 10 then increment x by 1</p>
```

which uses the character entity reference *<* for the less-than symbol (<).

Figure 2.7 demonstrates how to use special characters in an XHTML document. Lines 24–25 contain other special characters, which can be expressed as either character entity references (coded using word abbreviations such as & for ampersand and

```
 1   <?xml version = "1.0" encoding = "utf-8"?>
 2   <!DOCTYPE html PUBLIC "-//W3C//DTD XHTML 1.0 Strict//EN"
 3      "http://www.w3.org/TR/xhtml1/DTD/xhtml1-strict.dtd">
 4
 5   <!-- Fig. 2.7: contact2.html -->
 6   <!-- Inserting special characters. -->
 7   <html xmlns = "http://www.w3.org/1999/xhtml">
 8      <head>
 9         <title>Contact Page</title>
10      </head>
11
12      <body>
13         <p>
14            Click
15            <a href = "mailto:deitel@deitel.com">here</a>
16            to open an email message addressed to
17            deitel@deitel.com.
18         </p>
19
20         <hr /> <!-- inserts a horizontal rule -->
21
22         <!-- special characters are entered -->
23         <!-- using the form &code; -->
24         <p>All information on this site is <strong>&copy;
25            Deitel &amp; Associates, Inc. 2007.</strong></p>
26
27         <!-- to strike through text use <del> tags -->
28         <!-- to subscript text use <sub> tags -->
29         <!-- to superscript text use <sup> tags -->
30         <!-- these tags are nested inside other tags -->
31         <p><del>You may download 3.14 x 10<sup>2</sup>
32            characters worth of information from this site.</del>
33            Only <sub>one</sub> download per hour is permitted.</p>
34         <p><em>Note: &lt; &frac14; of the information
35            presented here is updated daily.</em></p>
36      </body>
37   </html>
```

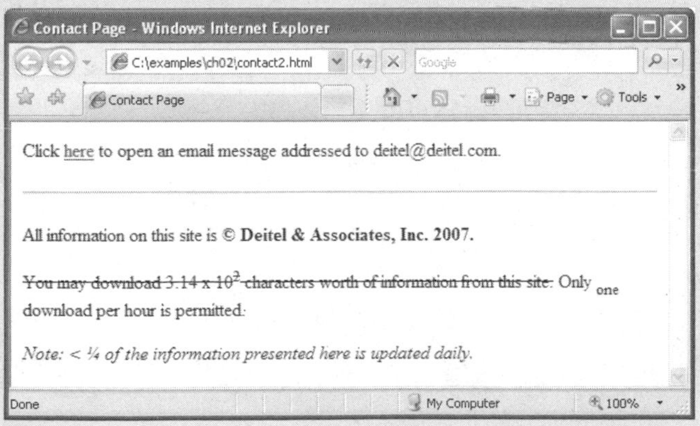

Fig. 2.7 | Inserting special characters.

© for copyright) or *numeric character references*—decimal or *hexadecimal* (*hex*) values representing special characters. For example, the & character is represented in decimal and hexadecimal notation as & and &, respectively. Hexadecimal numbers are base 16 numbers—digits in a hexadecimal number have values from 0 to 15 (a total of 16 different values). The letters A–F represent the hexadecimal digits corresponding to decimal values 10–15. Thus in hexadecimal notation we can have numbers like 876 consisting solely of decimal-like digits, numbers like DA19F consisting of digits and letters, and numbers like DCB consisting solely of letters.

In lines 31–33, we introduce four new elements. Most browsers render the *del* element as strike-through text. With this format users can easily indicate document revisions. To *superscript* text (i.e., raise text above the baseline and decreased font size) or *subscript* text (i.e., lower text below the baseline and decreased font size), use the *sup* or *sub* element, respectively. The paragraph in lines 34–35 contains an *em element*, which indicates that its contents should be emphasized. Browsers usually render em elements in an italic font. We also use character entity reference < for a less-than sign and ¼ for the fraction 1/4 (line 34).

In addition to special characters, this document introduces a *horizontal rule*, indicated by the *<hr />* tag in line 22. Most browsers render a horizontal rule as a horizontal line with a blank line above and below it.

2.9 Lists

Up to this point, we have presented basic XHTML elements and attributes for linking to resources, creating headings, using special characters and incorporating images. In this section, we discuss how to organize information on a web page using lists. In the next section, we introduce another feature for organizing information, called a table. Figure 2.8 displays text in an *unordered list* (i.e., a list that does not order its items by letter or number). The unordered list element *ul* creates a list in which each item begins with a bullet symbol (called a disc). Each entry in an unordered list (element ul in line 17) is an *li* (*list item*) element (lines 19–22). Most web browsers render each li element on a new line with a bullet symbol indented from the beginning of the line.

```
 1   <?xml version = "1.0" encoding = "utf-8"?>
 2   <!DOCTYPE html PUBLIC "-//W3C//DTD XHTML 1.0 Strict//EN"
 3      "http://www.w3.org/TR/xhtml1/DTD/xhtml1-strict.dtd">
 4
 5   <!-- Fig. 2.8: links2.html -->
 6   <!-- Unordered list containing hyperlinks. -->
 7   <html xmlns = "http://www.w3.org/1999/xhtml">
 8      <head>
 9         <title>Links</title>
10      </head>
11
12      <body>
13         <h1>Here are my favorite sites</h1>
14         <p><strong>Click on a name to go to that page.</strong></p>
15
```

Fig. 2.8 | Unordered list containing hyperlinks. (Part 1 of 2.)

```
16          <!-- create an unordered list -->
17          <ul>
18              <!-- add four list items -->
19              <li><a href = "http://www.deitel.com">Deitel</a></li>
20              <li><a href = "http://www.w3.org">W3C</a></li>
21              <li><a href = "http://www.yahoo.com">Yahoo!</a></li>
22              <li><a href = "http://www.cnn.com">CNN</a></li>
23          </ul>
24      </body>
25  </html>
```

Fig. 2.8 | Unordered list containing hyperlinks. (Part 2 of 2.)

Nested Lists

Lists may be nested to represent hierarchical relationships, as in an outline format. Figure 2.9 demonstrates nested lists and *ordered lists*. The ordered list element *ol* creates a list in which each item begins with a number.

A web browser indents each nested list to indicate a hierarchical relationship. The first ordered list begins at line 30. Items in an ordered list are enumerated one, two, three and so on. Nested ordered lists are enumerated in the same manner. The items in the outermost unordered list (line 16) are preceded by discs. List items nested inside the unordered list of line 16 are preceded by circular bullets. Although not demonstrated in this example, subsequent nested list items are preceded by square bullets.

```
1   <?xml version = "1.0" encoding = "utf-8"?>
2   <!DOCTYPE html PUBLIC "-//W3C//DTD XHTML 1.0 Strict//EN"
3       "http://www.w3.org/TR/xhtml1/DTD/xhtml1-strict.dtd">
4
5   <!-- Fig. 2.9: list.html -->
6   <!-- Nested and ordered lists. -->
7   <html xmlns = "http://www.w3.org/1999/xhtml">
```

Fig. 2.9 | Nested and ordered lists. (Part 1 of 3.)

```
 8      <head>
 9         <title>Lists</title>
10      </head>
11
12      <body>
13         <h1>The Best Features of the Internet</h1>
14
15         <!-- create an unordered list -->
16         <ul>
17            <li>You can meet new people from countries around
18               the world.</li>
19            <li>
20               You have access to new media as it becomes public:
21
22               <!-- this starts a nested list, which uses a -->
23               <!-- modified bullet. The list ends when you -->
24               <!-- close the <ul> tag. -->
25               <ul>
26                  <li>New games</li>
27                  <li>New applications
28
29                     <!-- nested ordered list -->
30                     <ol>
31                        <li>For business</li>
32                        <li>For pleasure</li>
33                     </ol>
34                  </li> <!-- ends line 27 new applications li -->
35
36                  <li>Around the clock news</li>
37                  <li>Search engines</li>
38                  <li>Shopping</li>
39                  <li>Programming
40
41                     <!-- another nested ordered list -->
42                     <ol>
43                        <li>XML</li>
44                        <li>Java</li>
45                        <li>XHTML</li>
46                        <li>Scripts</li>
47                        <li>New languages</li>
48                     </ol>
49                  </li> <!-- ends programming li of line 39 -->
50               </ul> <!-- ends the nested list of line 25 -->
51            </li>
52
53            <li>Links</li>
54            <li>Keeping in touch with old friends</li>
55            <li>It is the technology of the future!</li>
56         </ul> <!-- ends the unordered list of line 16 -->
57      </body>
58   </html>
```

Fig. 2.9 | Nested and ordered lists. (Part 2 of 3.)

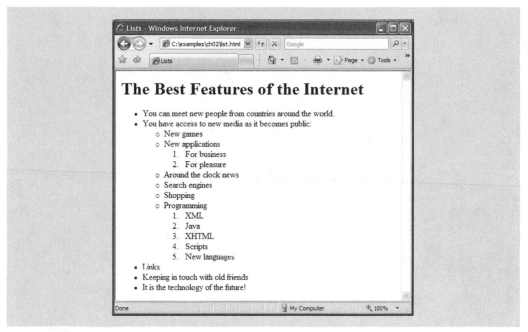

Fig. 2.9 | Nested and ordered lists. (Part 3 of 3.)

2.10 Tables

Tables are frequently used to organize data into rows and columns. Our first example (Fig. 2.10) creates a table with six rows and two columns to display price information for fruit.

Tables are defined with the **table** element (lines 15–62). Lines 15–17 specify the start tag for a table element that has several attributes. The **border** attribute specifies the table's border width in pixels. To create a table without a border, set border to "0". This example assigns attribute **width** the value "40%" to set the table's width to 40 percent of the browser's width. A developer can also set attribute width to a specified number of pixels. Try resizing the browser window to see how the width of the window affects the width of the table.

```
 1    <?xml version = "1.0" encoding = "utf-8"?>
 2    <!DOCTYPE html PUBLIC "-//W3C//DTD XHTML 1.0 Strict//EN"
 3       "http://www.w3.org/TR/xhtml1/DTD/xhtml1-strict.dtd">
 4
 5    <!-- Fig. 2.10: table1.html -->
 6    <!-- Creating a basic table. -->
 7    <html xmlns = "http://www.w3.org/1999/xhtml">
 8       <head>
 9          <title>A simple XHTML table</title>
10       </head>
11
```

Fig. 2.10 | Creating a basic table. (Part 1 of 3.)

```
12    <body>
13
14       <!-- the <table> tag opens a table -->
15       <table border = "1" width = "40%"
16          summary = "This table provides information about
17             the price of fruit">
18
19          <!-- the <caption> tag summarizes the table's -->
20          <!-- contents (this helps the visually impaired) -->
21          <caption><strong>Price of Fruit</strong></caption>
22
23          <!-- the <thead> section appears first in the table -->
24          <!-- it formats the table header area -->
25          <thead>
26             <tr> <!-- <tr> inserts a table row -->
27                <th>Fruit</th> <!-- insert a heading cell -->
28                <th>Price</th>
29             </tr>
30          </thead>
31
32          <!-- the <tfoot> section appears last in the table -->
33          <!-- it formats the table footer -->
34          <tfoot>
35             <tr>
36                <th>Total</th>
37                <th>$3.75</th>
38             </tr>
39          </tfoot>
40
41          <!-- all table content is enclosed -->
42          <!-- within the <tbody> -->
43          <tbody>
44             <tr>
45                <td>Apple</td> <!-- insert a data cell -->
46                <td>$0.25</td>
47             </tr>
48             <tr>
49                <td>Orange</td>
50                <td>$0.50</td>
51             </tr>
52             <tr>
53                <td>Banana</td>
54                <td>$1.00</td>
55             </tr>
56             <tr>
57                <td>Pineapple</td>
58                <td>$2.00</td>
59             </tr>
60          </tbody>
61       </table>
62
63    </body>
64 </html>
```

Fig. 2.10 | Creating a basic table. (Part 2 of 3.)

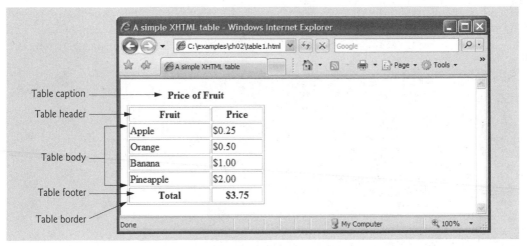

Fig. 2.10 | Creating a basic table. (Part 3 of 3.)

As its name implies, attribute *summary* (lines 16–17) describes the table's contents. Speech devices use this attribute to make the table more accessible to users with visual impairments. The *caption* element (line 21) describes the table's content and helps text-based browsers interpret the table data. Text inside the <caption> tag is rendered above the table by most browsers. Attribute summary and element caption are two of the many XHTML features that make web pages more accessible to users with disabilities.

A table has three distinct sections—*head*, *body* and *foot*. The head section (or header cell) is defined with a *thead* element (lines 25–30), which contains header information such as column names. Each *tr* element (lines 26–29) defines an individual *table row*. The columns in the head section are defined with *th* elements. Most browsers center text formatted by th (table header column) elements and display them in bold. Table header elements are nested inside table row elements (lines 27–28).

The body section, or *table body*, contains the table's primary data. The table body (lines 43–60) is defined in a *tbody* element. In the body, each tr element specifies one row. *Data cells* contain individual pieces of data and are defined with *td* (*table data*) elements in each row.

The foot section (lines 34–39) is defined with a *tfoot* (table foot) element. The text placed in the footer commonly includes calculation results and footnotes. Like other sections, the foot section can contain table rows, and each row can contain cells. As in the head section, cells in the foot section are created using th elements, instead of the td elements used in the table body. Note that the table foot section must be above the body section in the code, but the table foot displays at the bottom of the table.

Using rowspan and colspan

Figure 2.10 explored a basic table's structure. Figure 2.11 presents another table example and introduces two new attributes that allow you to build more complex tables.

The table begins in line 15. Table cells are sized to fit the data they contain. Document authors can create larger data cells using the attributes *rowspan* and *colspan*. The values assigned to these attributes specify the number of rows or columns occupied by a cell. The th element at lines 23–26 uses the attribute rowspan = "2" to allow the cell containing the picture of the camel to use two vertically adjacent cells (thus the cell *spans* two rows). The th element in lines 29–32 uses the attribute colspan = "4" to widen the header cell (containing Camelid comparison and Approximate as of 6/2007) to span four cells.

```
 1   <?xml version = "1.0" encoding = "utf-8"?>
 2   <!DOCTYPE html PUBLIC "-//W3C//DTD XHTML 1.0 Strict//EN"
 3      "http://www.w3.org/TR/xhtml1/DTD/xhtml1-strict.dtd">
 4
 5   <!-- Fig. 2.11: table2.html -->
 6   <!-- Complex XHTML table. -->
 7   <html xmlns = "http://www.w3.org/1999/xhtml">
 8      <head>
 9         <title>Tables</title>
10      </head>
11
12      <body>
13         <h1>Table Example Page</h1>
14
15         <table border = "1">
16            <caption>Here is a more complex sample table.</caption>
17
18            <thead>
19               <!-- rowspans and colspans merge the specified -->
20               <!-- number of cells vertically or horizontally -->
21               <tr>
22                  <!-- merge two rows -->
23                  <th rowspan = "2">
24                     <img src = "camel.gif" width = "205"
25                        height = "167" alt = "Picture of a camel" />
26                  </th>
27
28                  <!-- merge four columns -->
29                  <th colspan = "4">
30                     <h1>Camelid comparison</h1>
31                     <p>Approximate as of 6/2007</p>
32                  </th>
33               </tr>
34               <tr>
35                  <th># of Humps</th>
36                  <th>Indigenous region</th>
37                  <th>Spits?</th>
38                  <th>Produces Wool?</th>
39               </tr>
40            </thead>
41            <tbody>
42               <tr>
43                  <th>Camels (bactrian)</th>
44                  <td>2</td>
45                  <td>Africa/Asia</td>
46                  <td>Yes</td>
47                  <td>Yes</td>
48               </tr>
```

Fig. 2.11 | Complex XHTML table. (Part 1 of 2.)

```
49                        <tr>
50                            <th>Llamas</th>
51                            <td>1</td>
52                            <td>Andes Mountains</td>
53                            <td>Yes</td>
54                            <td>Yes</td>
55                        </tr>
56                    </tbody>
57                </table>
58            </body>
59    </html>
```

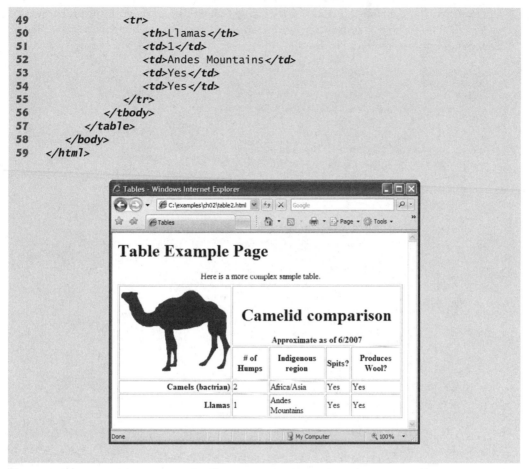

Fig. 2.11 | Complex XHTML table. (Part 2 of 2.)

2.11 Forms

When browsing websites, users often need to provide such information as search keywords, e-mail addresses and zip codes. XHTML provides a mechanism, called a form, for collecting data from a user.

Data that users enter on a web page is normally sent to a web server that provides access to a site's resources (e.g., XHTML documents, images). These resources are located either on the same machine as the web server or on a machine that the web server can access through the network. When a browser requests a web page or file that is located on a server, the server processes the request and returns the requested resource. A request contains the name and path of the desired resource and the method of communication (called a *protocol*). XHTML documents use the Hypertext Transfer Protocol (HTTP).

Figure 2.12 is a simple form that sends data to the web server, which passes the form data to a program. The program processes the data received from the web server and typically returns information to the web server. The web server then sends the information as an XHTML document to the web browser. [*Note:* This example demonstrates client-side functionality. If the form is submitted (by clicking **Submit**), nothing will happen, because we don't yet know how to process the form data. In Chapter 13, we'll invoke a server-side form handler to process data in a form.]

```
1    <?xml version = "1.0" encoding = "utf-8"?>
2    <!DOCTYPE html PUBLIC "-//W3C//DTD XHTML 1.0 Strict//EN"
3       "http://www.w3.org/TR/xhtml1/DTD/xhtml1-strict.dtd">
4
5    <!-- Fig. 2.12: form.html -->
6    <!-- Form with hidden fields and a text box. -->
7    <html xmlns = "http://www.w3.org/1999/xhtml">
8       <head>
9          <title>Forms</title>
10      </head>
11
12      <body>
13         <h1>Feedback Form</h1>
14
15         <p>Please fill out this form to help
16            us improve our site.</p>
17
18         <!-- this tag starts the form, gives the -->
19         <!-- method of sending information and the -->
20         <!-- location of form script -->
21         <form method = "post" action = "">
22            <p>
23               <!-- hidden inputs contain non-visual -->
24               <!-- information -->
25               <input type = "hidden" name = "recipient"
26                  value = "deitel@deitel.com" />
27               <input type = "hidden" name = "subject"
28                  value = "Feedback Form" />
29               <input type = "hidden" name = "redirect"
30                  value = "main.html" />
31            </p>
32
33            <!-- <input type = "text"> inserts a text box -->
34            <p><label>Name:
35               <input name = "name" type = "text" size = "25"
36                  maxlength = "30" />
37            </label></p>
38
39            <p>
40               <!-- input types "submit" and "reset" insert -->
41               <!-- buttons for submitting and clearing the -->
42               <!-- form's contents -->
43               <input type = "submit" value = "Submit" />
44               <input type = "reset" value = "Clear" />
45            </p>
46         </form>
47      </body>
48   </html>
```

Fig. 2.12 | Form with hidden fields and a text box. (Part 1 of 2.)

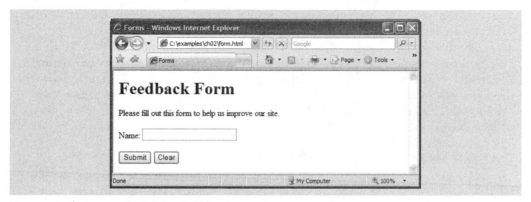

Fig. 2.12 | Form with hidden fields and a text box. (Part 2 of 2.)

Forms can contain visual and nonvisual components. Visual components include clickable buttons and other graphical user interface components with which users interact. Nonvisual components, called *hidden inputs*, store any data that you specify, such as e-mail addresses and XHTML document filenames that act as links. The form is defined in lines 21–46 by a *form* element.

Attribute *method* (line 21) specifies how the form's data is sent to the web server. Using method = "*post*" appends form data to the browser request, which contains the protocol (HTTP) and the requested resource's URL. This method of passing data to the server is transparent—the user doesn't see the data after the form is submitted. The other possible value, method = "*get*", appends the form data directly to the end of the URL of the script, where it is visible in the browser's **Address** field.

The *action* attribute in the <form> tag in line 21 specifies the URL of a script on the web server that will be invoked to process the form's data. Since we haven't introduced server-side programming yet, we leave this attribute empty for now.

Lines 25–44 define six *input* elements that specify data to provide to the script that processes the form (also called the *form handler*). There are several types of input elements. An input's type is determined by its *type attribute*. This form uses a text input, a submit input, a reset input and three hidden inputs.

The *text* input in lines 35–36 inserts a *text box* in the form. Users can type data in text boxes. The label element (lines 34–37) provides users with information about the input element's purpose. The input element's *size* attribute specifies the number of characters visible in the text box. Optional attribute *maxlength* limits the number of characters input into the text box—in this case, the user is not permitted to type more than 30 characters.

 Look-and-Feel Observation 2.3

Include a label element for each form element to help users determine the purpose of each form element.

Two input elements in lines 43–44 create two buttons. The *submit* input element is a button. When the submit button is pressed, the user is sent to the location specified in the form's action attribute. The *value* attribute sets the text displayed on the button. The *reset* input element allows a user to reset all form elements to their default values. The value attribute of the `reset` input element sets the text displayed on the button (the default value is **Reset** if you omit the `value` attribute).

The three `input` elements in lines 25–30 have the `type` attribute `hidden`, which allows you to send form data that is not input by a user. The three hidden inputs are an e-mail address to which the data will be sent, the e-mail's subject line and a URL for the browser to open after submission of the form. Two other `input` attributes are ***name***, which identifies the `input` element, and ***value***, which provides the value that will be sent (or posted) to the web server.

Good Programming Practice 2.6

Place hidden `input` elements at the beginning of a form, immediately after the opening `<form>` tag. This placement allows document authors to locate hidden `input` elements quickly.

Additional Form Elements

In the previous example, you saw basic elements of XHTML forms. Now that you know the general structure of a form, we introduce elements and attributes for creating more complex forms. Figure 2.13 contains a form that solicits user feedback about a website.

In line 32, we introduce the ***br*** element, which most browsers render as a =*line break*. Any markup or text following a `br` element is rendered on the next line. Like the `img` element, `br` is an example of an empty element terminated with a forward slash. We add a space before the forward slash to enhance readability.

The ***textarea*** element (lines 33–34) inserts a multiline text box, called a ***text area***, into the form. The number of rows is specified with the ***rows*** attribute, and the number of columns (i.e., characters per line) is specified with the ***cols*** attribute. In this example, the `textarea` is four rows high and 36 characters wide. To display default text in the text area, place the text between the `<textarea>` and `</textarea>` tags. Default text can be specified in other `input` types, such as text boxes, by using the `value` attribute.

The ***password*** input in line 41 inserts a password box with the specified `size` (maximum number of characters allowed). A password box allows users to enter sensitive information, such as credit card numbers and passwords, by "masking" the information input with asterisks (*). The actual value input is sent to the web server, not the characters that mask the input.

```
1   <?xml version = "1.0" encoding = "utf-8"?>
2   <!DOCTYPE html PUBLIC "-//W3C//DTD XHTML 1.0 Strict//EN"
3      "http://www.w3.org/TR/xhtml1/DTD/xhtml1-strict.dtd">
4
5   <!-- Fig. 2.13: form2.html -->
6   <!-- Form using a variety of components. -->
7   <html xmlns = "http://www.w3.org/1999/xhtml">
8      <head>
9         <title>More Forms</title>
10     </head>
11
12     <body>
13        <h1>Feedback Form</h1>
```

Fig. 2.13 | Form using a variety of components. (Part 1 of 4.)

```
14      <p>Please fill out this form to help
15          us improve our site.</p>
16
17      <form method = "post" action = "">
18          <p>
19              <input type = "hidden" name = "recipient"
20                  value = "deitel@deitel.com" />
21              <input type = "hidden" name = "subject"
22                  value = "Feedback Form" />
23              <input type = "hidden" name = "redirect"
24                  value = "main.html" />
25          </p>
26
27          <p><label>Name:
28              <input name = "name" type = "text" size = "25" />
29          </label></p>
30
31          <!-- <textarea> creates a multiline textbox -->
32          <p><label>Comments:<br />
33              <textarea name = "comments"
34                  rows = "4" cols = "36">Enter comments here.</textarea>
35          </label></p>
36
37          <!-- <input type = "password"> inserts a -->
38          <!-- textbox whose display is masked with -->
39          <!-- asterisk characters -->
40          <p><label>E-mail Address:
41              <input name = "email" type = "password" size = "25" />
42          </label></p>
43
44          <p>
45              <strong>Things you liked:</strong><br />
46
47              <label>Site design
48                  <input name = "thingsliked" type = "checkbox"
49                      value = "Design" /></label>
50              <label>Links
51                  <input name = "thingsliked" type = "checkbox"
52                      value = "Links" /></label>
53              <label>Ease of use
54                  <input name = "thingsliked" type = "checkbox"
55                      value = "Ease" /></label>
56              <label>Images
57                  <input name = "thingsliked" type = "checkbox"
58                      value = "Images" /></label>
59              <label>Source code
60                  <input name = "thingsliked" type = "checkbox"
61                      value = "Code" /></label>
62          </p>
63
64          <!-- <input type = "radio" /> creates a radio -->
65          <!-- button. The difference between radio buttons -->
```

Fig. 2.13 | Form using a variety of components. (Part 2 of 4.)

```
66              <!-- and checkboxes is that only one radio button -->
67              <!-- in a group can be selected. -->
68          <p>
69              <strong>How did you get to our site?:</strong><br />
70
71              <label>Search engine
72                  <input name = "howtosite" type = "radio"
73                      value = "search engine" checked = "checked" /></label>
74              <label>Links from another site
75                  <input name = "howtosite" type = "radio"
76                      value = "link" /></label>
77              <label>Deitel.com Website
78                  <input name = "howtosite" type = "radio"
79                      value = "deitel.com" /></label>
80              <label>Reference in a book
81                  <input name = "howtosite" type = "radio"
82                      value = "book" /></label>
83              <label>Other
84                  <input name = "howtosite" type = "radio"
85                      value = "other" /></label>
86          </p>
87
88          <p>
89              <label>Rate our site:
90
91                  <!-- the <select> tag presents a drop-down -->
92                  <!-- list with choices indicated by the -->
93                  <!-- <option> tags -->
94              <select name = "rating">
95                  <option selected = "selected">Amazing</option>
96                  <option>10</option>
97                  <option>9</option>
98                  <option>8</option>
99                  <option>7</option>
100                 <option>6</option>
101                 <option>5</option>
102                 <option>4</option>
103                 <option>3</option>
104                 <option>2</option>
105                 <option>1</option>
106                 <option>Awful</option>
107             </select>
108             </label>
109         </p>
110
111         <p>
112             <input type = "submit" value = "Submit" />
113             <input type = "reset" value = "Clear" />
114         </p>
115     </form>
116     </body>
117 </html>
```

Fig. 2.13 | Form using a variety of components. (Part 3 of 4.)

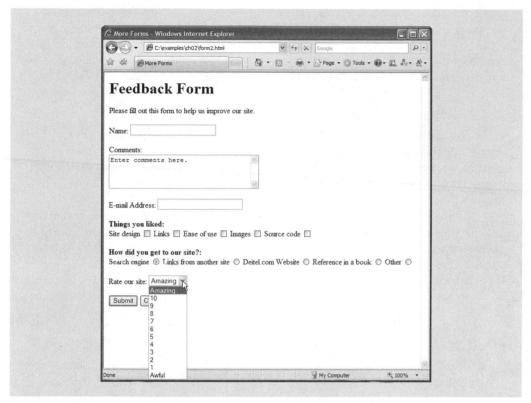

Fig. 2.13 | Form using a variety of components. (Part 4 of 4.)

Lines 47–61 introduce the **checkbox** form element. Checkboxes enable users to select from a set of options. When a user selects a checkbox, a check mark appears in the checkbox. Otherwise, the checkbox remains empty. Each **"checkbox"** input creates a new checkbox. Checkboxes can be used individually or in groups. Checkboxes that belong to a group are assigned the same name (in this case, "thingsliked").

Common Programming Error 2.5

When your form has several checkboxes with the same name, you must make sure that they have different values, or the scripts running on the web server will not be able to distinguish them.

After the checkboxes, we present two more ways to allow the user to make choices. In this example, we introduce two new input types. The first type is the **radio button** (lines 71–85) specified with type **"radio"**. Radio buttons are similar to checkboxes, except that only one radio button in a group of radio buttons may be selected at any time. The radio buttons in a group all have the same name attributes and are distinguished by their different value attributes. The attribute–value pair checked = "checked" (line 73) indicates which radio button, if any, is selected initially. The checked attribute also applies to checkboxes.

Common Programming Error 2.6

Not setting the name attributes of the radio buttons in a form to the same name is a logic error because it lets the user select all of them at the same time.

The *select* element (lines 94–107) provides a drop-down list from which the user can select an item. The name attribute identifies the drop-down list. The *option* elements (lines 95–106) add items to the drop-down list. The option element's *selected* attribute specifies which item initially is displayed as the selected item in the select element. If no option element is marked as selected, the browser selects the first option by default.

2.12 Internal Linking

Earlier in the chapter, we discussed how to hyperlink one web page to another. Figure 2.14 introduces *internal linking*—a mechanism that enables the user to jump between locations in the same document. Internal linking is useful for long documents that contain many sections. Clicking an internal link enables users to find a section without scrolling through the entire document.

Line 14 contains a tag with the id attribute (set to "features") for an internal hyperlink. To link to a tag with this attribute inside the same web page, the href attribute of an anchor element includes the id attribute value preceded by a pound sign (as in #features). Line 56 contains a hyperlink with the id features as its target. Selecting this hyperlink in a web browser scrolls the browser window to the h1 tag in line 14. Note that you may have to resize your browser to a small window and scroll down before clicking the link to see the browser scroll to the h1 element.

```
1   <?xml version = "1.0" encoding = "utf-8"?>
2   <!DOCTYPE html PUBLIC "-//W3C//DTD XHTML 1.0 Strict//EN"
3      "http://www.w3.org/TR/xhtml1/DTD/xhtml1-strict.dtd">
4
5   <!-- Fig. 2.14: internal.html -->
6   <!-- Internal hyperlinks to make pages more navigable. -->
7   <html xmlns = "http://www.w3.org/1999/xhtml">
8      <head>
9         <title>Internal Links</title>
10     </head>
11
12     <body>
13        <!-- id attribute creates an internal hyperlink destination -->
14        <h1 id = "features">The Best Features of the Internet</h1>
15
16        <!-- an internal link's address is "#id" -->
17        <p><a href = "#bugs">Go to <em>Favorite Bugs</em></a></p>
18
19        <ul>
20           <li>You can meet people from countries
21              around the world.</li>
22           <li>You have access to new media as it becomes public:
23              <ul>
24                 <li>New games</li>
25                 <li>New applications
26                    <ul>
27                       <li>For Business</li>
28                       <li>For Pleasure</li>
```

Fig. 2.14 | Internal hyperlinks to make pages more navigable. (Part 1 of 3.)

```
29                          </ul>
30                      </li>
31
32                  <li>Around the clock news</li>
33                  <li>Search Engines</li>
34                  <li>Shopping</li>
35                  <li>Programming
36                      <ul>
37                          <li>XHTML</li>
38                          <li>Java</li>
39                          <li>Dynamic HTML</li>
40                          <li>Scripts</li>
41                          <li>New languages</li>
42                      </ul>
43                  </li>
44              </ul>
45          </li>
46
47          <li>Links</li>
48          <li>Keeping in touch with old friends</li>
49          <li>It is the technology of the future!</li>
50      </ul>
51
52      <!-- id attribute creates an internal hyperlink destination -->
53      <h1 id = "bugs">My 3 Favorite Bugs</h1>
54      <p>
55          <!-- internal hyperlink to features -->
56          <a href = "#features">Go to <em>Favorite Features</em></a>
57      </p>
58      <ol>
59          <li>Fire Fly</li>
60          <li>Gal Ant</li>
61          <li>Roman Tic</li>
62      </ol>
63  </body>
64 </html>
```

Fig. 2.14 | Internal hyperlinks to make pages more navigable. (Part 2 of 3.)

Fig. 2.14 | Internal hyperlinks to make pages more navigable. (Part 3 of 3.)

Look-and-Feel Observation 2.4

Internal hyperlinks are useful in XHTML documents that contain large amounts of information. Internal links to different parts of the page make it easier for users to navigate the page— they do not have to scroll to find the section they want.

Although not demonstrated in this example, a hyperlink can specify an internal link in another document by specifying the document name followed by a pound sign and the id value, as in:

> href = "*filename*.html#*id*"

For example, to link to a tag with the id attribute called booklist in books.html, href is assigned "books.html#booklist". You can also send the browser to an internal link on another site by appending the pound sign and id value of an element to any URL, as in:

> href = "*URL*/filename.html#*id*"

2.13 meta Elements

Search engines usually catalog sites by following links from page to page (often known as spidering or crawling) and saving identification and classification information for each page. One way that search engines catalog pages is by reading the content in each page's **meta** elements, which specify information about a document.

Two important attributes of the meta element are **name**, which identifies the type of meta element, and **content**, which provides the information search engines use to catalog pages. Figure 2.15 introduces the meta element.

```
1   <?xml version = "1.0" encoding = "utf-8"?>
2   <!DOCTYPE html PUBLIC "-//W3C//DTD XHTML 1.0 Strict//EN"
3      "http://www.w3.org/TR/xhtml1/DTD/xhtml1-strict.dtd">
4
```

Fig. 2.15 | meta elements provide keywords and a description of a page. (Part 1 of 2.)

```
5   <!-- Fig. 2.15: meta.html -->
6   <!-- meta elements provide keywords and a description of a page. -->
7   <html xmlns = "http://www.w3.org/1999/xhtml">
8      <head>
9         <title>Welcome</title>
10
11         <!-- <meta> tags provide search engines with -->
12         <!-- information used to catalog a site -->
13         <meta name = "keywords" content = "web page, design,
14            XHTML, tutorial, personal, help, index, form,
15            contact, feedback, list, links, deitel" />
16         <meta name = "description" content = "This website will
17            help you learn the basics of XHTML and web page design
18            through the use of interactive examples and
19            instruction." />
20      </head>
21      <body>
22         <h1>Welcome to Our Website!</h1>
23
24         <p>We have designed this site to teach about the wonders
25         of <strong><em>XHTML</em></strong>. <em>XHTML</em> is
26         better equipped than <em>HTML</em> to represent complex
27         data on the Internet. <em>XHTML</em> takes advantage of
28         XML's strict syntax to ensure well-formedness. Soon you
29         will know about many of the great features of
30         <em>XHTML.</em></p>
31
32         <p>Have Fun With the Site!</p>
33      </body>
34   </html>
```

Fig. 2.15 | meta elements provide keywords and a description of a page. (Part 2 of 2.)

Lines 13–15 demonstrate a "keywords" meta element. The content attribute of such a meta element provides search engines with a list of words that describe a page. These words are compared with words in search requests. Thus, including meta elements and their content information can draw more viewers to your site.

Lines 16–19 demonstrate a "description" meta element. The content attribute of such a meta element provides a three- to four-line description of a site, written in sentence form. Search engines also use this description to catalog your site and sometimes display this information as part of the search results. Note that this use of the meta element is one of many methods of search engine optimization (SEO). For more information on SEO, visit Deitel's SEO Resource Center at www.deitel.com/searchengineoptimization.

Software Engineering Observation 2.1

meta elements are not visible to users and must be placed inside the head section of your XHTML document. If meta elements are not placed in this section, they will not be read by search engines.

2.14 Web Resources

www.deitel.com/xhtml

Visit our online XHTML Resource Center for links to some of the best XHTML information on the web. There you'll find categorized links to introductions, tutorials, books, blogs, forums, sample chapters, and more. Also check out links about XHTML 2, the upcoming version of the XHTML standard.

Cascading Style Sheets™ (CSS)

Fashions fade, style is eternal.
—Yves Saint Laurent

A style does not go out of style as long as it adapts itself to its period. When there is an incompatibility between the style and a certain state of mind, it is never the style that triumphs.
—Coco Chanel

How liberating to work in the margins, outside a central perception.
—Don DeLillo

I've gradually risen from lower-class background to lower-class foreground.
—Marvin Cohen

OBJECTIVES

In this chapter you'll learn:

- To control the appearance of a website by creating style sheets.
- To use a style sheet to give all the pages of a website the same look and feel.
- To use the `class` attribute to apply styles.
- To specify the precise font, size, color and other properties of displayed text.
- To specify element backgrounds and colors.
- To understand the box model and how to control margins, borders and padding.
- To use style sheets to separate presentation from content.

3.1 Introduction

In Chapter 2, we introduced the Extensible HyperText Markup Language (XHTML) for marking up information to be rendered in a browser. In this chapter, we shift our focus to formatting and presenting information. To do this, we use a W3C technology called *Cascading Style Sheets™* (*CSS*) that allows document authors to specify the presentation of elements on a web page (e.g., fonts, spacing, colors) separately from the structure of the document (section headers, body text, links, etc.). This *separation of structure from presentation* simplifies maintaining and modifying a web page.

XHTML was designed to specify the content and structure of a document. Though it has some attributes that control presentation, it is better not to mix presentation with content. If a website's presentation is determined entirely by a style sheet, a web designer can simply swap in a new style sheet to completely change the appearance of the site. CSS provides a way to apply style outside of XHTML, allowing the XHTML to dictate the content while the CSS dictates how it's presented.

As with XHTML, the W3C provides a CSS code validator located at `jigsaw.w3.org/css-validator/`. It is a good idea to validate all CSS code with this tool to make sure that your code is correct and works on as many browsers as possible.

CSS is a large topic. As such, we can introduce only the basic knowledge of CSS that you'll need to understand the examples in the rest of the book. For more CSS references and resources, check out our CSS Resource Center at `www.deitel.com/css21`.

The W3C's CSS specification is currently in its second major version, with a third in development. The current versions of most major browsers support much of the functionality in CSS 2. This allows programmers to make full use of its features. In this chapter, we introduce CSS, demonstrate some of the features introduced in CSS 2 and discuss some of the upcoming CSS 3 features. As you read this book, open each XHTML document in your web browser so you can view and interact with it in a web browser, as it was originally intended.

Remember that the examples in this book have been tested in Internet Explorer 7 and Firefox 2 (and higher). The latest versions of many other browsers (e.g., Safari, Opera,

Konqueror, Chrome) should render this chapter's examples properly, but we have not tested them. Some examples in this chapter *will not work* in older browsers, such as Internet Explorer 6 and earlier. Make sure you have either Internet Explorer 7 (Windows only) or Firefox (available for all major platforms) installed before running the examples in this chapter.

3.2 Inline Styles

You can declare document styles in several ways. This section presents *inline styles* that declare an individual element's format using the XHTML attribute **style**. Inline styles override any other styles applied using the techniques we discuss later in the chapter. Figure 3.1 applies inline styles to p elements to alter their font size and color.

Good Programming Practice 3.1

Inline styles do not truly separate presentation from content. To apply similar styles to multiple elements, use embedded stylesheets or external style sheets, introduced later in this chapter.

The first inline style declaration appears in line 17. Attribute style specifies an element's style. Each *CSS property* (**font-size** in this case) is followed by a colon and a value. In line 17, we declare this particular p element to use 20-point font size.

Line 21 specifies the two properties, font-size and **color**, separated by a semicolon. In this line, we set the given paragraph's color to light blue, using the hexadecimal code #6666ff. Color names may be used in place of hexadecimal codes.

```
 1   <?xml version = "1.0" encoding = "utf-8"?>
 2   <!DOCTYPE html PUBLIC "-//W3C//DTD XHTML 1.0 Strict//EN"
 3      "http://www.w3.org/TR/xhtml1/DTD/xhtml1-strict.dtd">
 4
 5   <!-- Fig. 3.1: inline.html -->
 6   <!-- Using inline styles -->
 7   <html xmlns = "http://www.w3.org/1999/xhtml">
 8      <head>
 9         <title>Inline Styles</title>
10      </head>
11      <body>
12         <p>This text does not have any style applied to it.</p>
13
14         <!-- The style attribute allows you to declare -->
15         <!-- inline styles. Separate multiple style properties -->
16         <!-- with a semicolon. -->
17         <p style = "font-size: 20pt">This text has the
18            <em>font-size</em> style applied to it, making it 20pt.
19         </p>
20
21         <p style = "font-size: 20pt; color: #6666ff">
22         This text has the <em>font-size</em> and
23         <em>color</em> styles applied to it, making it
24         20pt. and light blue.</p>
25      </body>
26   </html>
```

Fig. 3.1 | Using inline styles. (Part 1 of 2.)

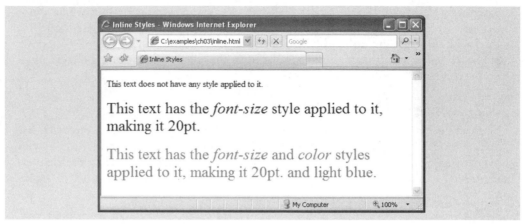

Fig. 3.1 | Using inline styles. (Part 2 of 2.)

3.3 Embedded Style Sheets

A second technique for using style sheets is *embedded style sheets*. Embedded style sheets enable a you to embed an entire CSS document in an XHTML document's head section. To achieve this separation between the CSS code and the XHTML that it styles, we'll use *CSS selectors*. Figure 3.2 creates an embedded style sheet containing four styles.

```
 1   <?xml version = "1.0" encoding = "utf-8"?>
 2   <!DOCTYPE html PUBLIC "-//W3C//DTD XHTML 1.0 Strict//EN"
 3      "http://www.w3.org/TR/xhtml1/DTD/xhtml1-strict.dtd">
 4
 5   <!-- Fig. 3.2: embedded.html -->
 6   <!-- Embedded style sheets. -->
 7   <html xmlns = "http://www.w3.org/1999/xhtml">
 8      <head>
 9         <title>Style Sheets</title>
10
11         <!-- this begins the style sheet section -->
12         <style type = "text/css">
13            em       { font-weight: bold;
14                       color: black }
15            h1       { font-family: tahoma, helvetica, sans-serif }
16            p        { font-size: 12pt;
17                       font-family: arial, sans-serif }
18            .special { color: #6666ff }
19         </style>
20      </head>
21      <body>
22         <!-- this class attribute applies the .special style -->
23         <h1 class = "special">Deitel &amp; Associates, Inc.</h1>
24
25         <p>Deitel &amp; Associates, Inc. is an internationally
26         recognized corporate training and publishing organization
```

Fig. 3.2 | Embedded style sheets. (Part 1 of 2.)

```
27        specializing in programming languages, Internet/World
28        Wide Web technology and object technology education.
29        The company provides courses on Java, C++, Visual Basic,
30        C#, C, Internet and World Wide Web programming, Object
31        Technology, and more.</p>
32
33        <h1>Clients</h1>
34        <p class = "special"> The company's clients include many
35        <em>Fortune 1000 companies</em>, government agencies,
36        branches of the military and business organizations.
37        Through its publishing partnership with Prentice Hall,
38        Deitel &amp; Associates, Inc. publishes leading-edge
39        programming textbooks, professional books, interactive
40        web-based multimedia Cyber Classrooms, satellite
41        courses and World Wide Web courses.</p>
42     </body>
43  </html>
```

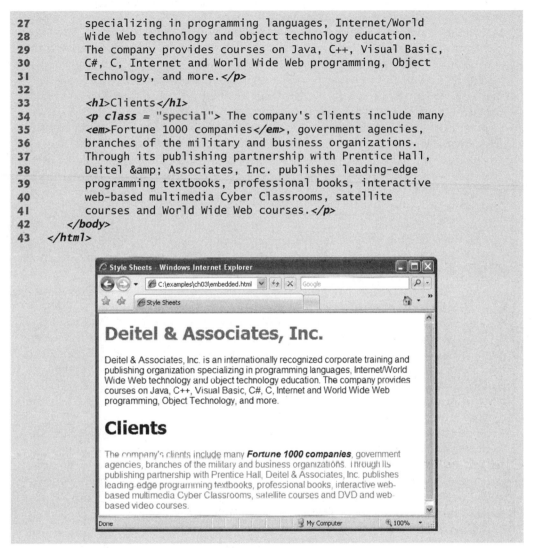

Fig. 3.2 | Embedded style sheets. (Part 2 of 2.)

The style element (lines 12–19) defines the embedded style sheet. Styles placed in the head apply to matching elements wherever they appear in the entire document. The style element's type attribute specifies the *Multipurpose Internet Mail Extensions (MIME) type* that describes a file's content. CSS documents use the MIME type text/css. Other MIME types include image/gif (for GIF images), text/javascript (for the JavaScript scripting language, which we discuss in Chapters 4–9), and more.

The body of the style sheet (lines 13–18) declares the *CSS rules* for the style sheet. A CSS selector determines which elements will be styled according to a rule. Our first rule begins with the selector em (line 13) to select all em elements in the document. The *font-weight* property in line 13 specifies the "boldness" of text. Possible values are bold, normal (the default), bolder (bolder than bold text) and lighter (lighter than normal text). Boldness also can be specified with multiples of 100, from 100 to 900 (e.g., 100, 200, ..., 900). Text specified as normal is equivalent to 400, and bold text is equivalent to 700. However, many systems do not have fonts that can scale with this level of precision, so using the values from 100 to 900 might not display the desired effect.

In this example, all em elements will be displayed in a bold font. We also apply styles to all h1 (line 15) and p (lines 16–17) elements. The body of each rule is enclosed in curly braces ({ and }).

Line 18 uses a new kind of selector to declare a *style class* named special. Style classes define styles that can be applied to any element. In this example, we declare class special, which sets color to blue. We can apply this style to any element type, whereas the other rules in this style sheet apply only to specific element types defined in the style sheet (i.e., em, h1 or p). Style-class declarations are preceded by a period. We'll discuss how to apply a style class momentarily.

CSS rules in embedded style sheets use the same syntax as inline styles; the property name is followed by a colon (:) and the value of the property. Multiple properties are separated by semicolons (;). In the rule for em elements, the color property specifies the color of the text, and property font-weight makes the font bold.

The *font-family* property (line 15) specifies the name of the font to use. Not all users have the same fonts installed on their computers, so CSS allows you to specify a comma-separated list of fonts to use for a particular style. The browser attempts to use the fonts in the order they appear in the list. It's advisable to end a font list with a *generic font family name* in case the other fonts are not installed on the user's computer. In this example, if the tahoma font is not found on the system, the browser will look for the helvetica font. If neither is found, the browser will display its default sans-serif font. Other generic font families include serif (e.g., times new roman, Georgia), cursive (e.g., script), fantasy (e.g., critter) and monospace (e.g., courier, fixedsys).

The *font-size* property (line 16) specifies a 12-point font. Other possible measurements in addition to pt (point) are introduced later in the chapter. Relative values— xx-small, x-small, small, smaller, medium, large, larger, x-large and xx-large—also can be used. Generally, relative values for font-size are preferred over point sizes because an author does not know the specific measurements of the display for each client. Relative font-size values permit more flexible viewing of web pages.

For example, a user may wish to view a web page on a handheld device with a small screen. Specifying an 18-point font size in a style sheet will prevent such a user from seeing more than one or two characters at a time. However, if a relative font size is specified, such as large or larger, the actual size is determined by the browser that displays the font. Using relative sizes also makes pages more accessible to users with disabilities. Users with impaired vision, for example, may configure their browser to use a larger default font, upon which all relative sizes are based. Text that the author specifies to be smaller than the main text still displays in a smaller size font, yet it is clearly visible to each user. Accessibility is an important consideration—in 1998, Congress passed the Section 508 Amendment to the Rehabilitation Act of 1973, mandating that websites of government agencies are required to be accessible to disabled users.

Line 23 uses the XHTML attribute *class* in an h1 element to apply a style class—in this case class special (declared with the .special selector in the style sheet in line 18). When the browser renders the h1 element, note that the text appears on screen with the properties of both an h1 element (arial or sans-serif font defined in line 17) and the .special style class applied (the color #6666ff defined in line 18). Also notice that the browser still applies its own default style to the h1 element—the header is still displayed in a large font size. Similarly, all em elements will still be italicized by the browser, but they will also be bold as a result of our style rule.

The formatting for the p element and the .special class is applied to the text in lines 34–41. In many cases, the styles applied to an element (the *parent* or *ancestor element*) also apply to the element's nested elements (*child* or *descendant elements*). The em element nested in the p element in line 35 *inherits* the style from the p element (namely, the 12-point font size in line 16) but retains its italic style. In other words, styles defined for the paragraph and not defined for the em element is applied to the em element. Because multiple values of one property can be set or inherited on the same element, they must be reduced to one style per element before being rendered. We discuss the rules for resolving these conflicts in the next section.

3.4 **Conflicting Styles**

Styles may be defined by a *user*, an *author* or a *user agent* (e.g., a web browser). A user is a person viewing your web page, you are the author—the person who writes the document—and the user agent is the program used to render and display the document. Styles "cascade," or flow together, such that the ultimate appearance of elements on a page results from combining styles defined in several ways. Styles defined by the user take precedence over styles defined by the user agent, and styles defined by authors take precedence over styles defined by the user.

Most styles defined for parent elements are also inherited by child (nested) elements. While it makes sense to inherit most styles, such as font properties, there are certain properties that we don't want to be inherited. Consider for example the background-image property, which allows the programmer to set an image as the background of an element. If the body element is assigned a background image, we don't want the same image to be in the background of every element in the body of our page. Instead, the background-image property of all child elements retains its default value of none. In this section, we discuss the rules for resolving conflicts between styles defined for elements and styles inherited from parent and ancestor elements.

Figure 3.2 presented an example of *inheritance* in which a child em element inherited the font-size property from its parent p element. However, in Fig. 3.2, the child em element had a color property that conflicted with (i.e., had a different value than) the color property of its parent p element. Properties defined for child and descendant elements have a greater *specificity* than properties defined for parent and ancestor elements. Conflicts are resolved in favor of properties with a higher specificity. In other words, the styles explicitly defined for a child element are more specific than the styles defined for the child's parent element; therefore, the child's styles take precedence. Figure 3.3 illustrates examples of inheritance and specificity.

Line 12 applies property text-decoration to all a elements whose class attribute is set to nodec. The text-decoration property applies *decorations* to text in an element. By default, browsers underline the text of an a (anchor) element. Here, we set the text-decoration property to none to indicate that the browser should not underline hyperlinks.

Other possible values for text-decoration include overline, line-through, underline and blink. [*Note:* blink is not supported by Internet Explorer.] The .nodec appended to a is a more specific class selector; this style will apply only to a (anchor) elements that specify nodec in their class attribute.

 Portability Tip 3.1

To ensure that your style sheets work in various web browsers, test them on all the client web browsers that will render documents using your styles, as well as using the W3C CSS Validator.

```
1   <?xml version = "1.0" encoding = "utf-8"?>
2   <!DOCTYPE html PUBLIC "-//W3C//DTD XHTML 1.0 Strict//EN"
3       "http://www.w3.org/TR/xhtml1/DTD/xhtml1-strict.dtd">
4
5   <!-- Fig. 3.3: advanced.html -->
6   <!-- Inheritance in style sheets. -->
7   <html xmlns = "http://www.w3.org/1999/xhtml">
8      <head>
9         <title>More Styles</title>
10        <style type = "text/css">
11           body      { font-family: arial, helvetica, sans-serif }
12           a.nodec   { text-decoration: none }
13           a:hover   { text-decoration: underline }
14           li em     { font-weight: bold }
15           h1, em    { text-decoration: underline }
16           ul        { margin-left: 20px }
17           ul ul     { font-size: .8em }
18        </style>
19     </head>
20     <body>
21        <h1>Shopping list for Monday:</h1>
22
23        <ul>
24           <li>Milk</li>
25           <li>Bread
26              <ul>
27                 <li>White bread</li>
28                 <li>Rye bread</li>
29                 <li>Whole wheat bread</li>
30              </ul>
31           </li>
32           <li>Rice</li>
33           <li>Potatoes</li>
34           <li>Pizza <em>with mushrooms</em></li>
35        </ul>
36
37        <p><em>Go to the</em>
38           <a class = "nodec" href = "http://www.deitel.com">
39              Grocery store</a>
40        </p>
41     </body>
42   </html>
```

Fig. 3.3 | Inheritance in style sheets. (Part 1 of 2.)

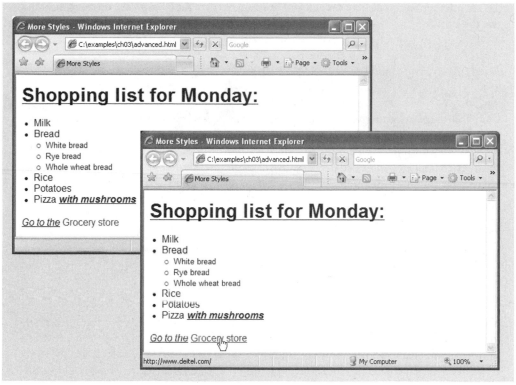

Fig. 3.3 | Inheritance in style sheets. (Part 2 of 2.)

Line 13 specifies a style for hover, which is a ***pseudoclass***. Pseudoclasses give the author access to content not specifically declared in the document. The ***hover pseudoclass*** is activated dynamically when the user moves the mouse cursor over an element. Note that pseudoclasses are separated by a colon (with no surrounding spaces) from the name of the element to which they are applied.

Common Programming Error 3.1

Including a space before or after the colon separating a pseudoclass from the name of the element to which it is applied is an error that prevents the pseudoclass from being applied properly.

Line 14 causes all em elements that are children of li elements to be bold. In the screen output of Fig. 3.3, note that **Go to the** (contained in an em element in line 37) does not appear bold, because the em element is not in an li element. However, the em element containing **with mushrooms** (line 34) is nested in an li element; therefore, it is formatted in bold. The syntax for applying rules to multiple elements is similar. In line 15, we separate the selectors with a comma to apply an underline style rule to all h1 and all em elements.

Line 16 assigns a left margin of 20 pixels to all ul elements. We'll discuss the margin properties in detail in Section 3.9. A pixel is a *relative-length measurement*—it varies in size, based on screen resolution. Other relative lengths include **em** (the *M*-height of the font, which is usually set to the height of an uppercase *M*), **ex** (the *x*-height of the font, which is usually set to the height of a lowercase *x*) and percentages (e.g., font-size: 50%).

To set an element to display text at 150 percent of its default text size, the author could use the syntax

> **font-size:** 1.5em

Alternatively, you could use

> **font-size:** 150%

Other units of measurement available in CSS are *absolute-length measurements*—i.e., units that do not vary in size based on the system. These units are *in* (inches), *cm* (centimeters), *mm* (millimeters), *pt* (points; 1 pt = 1/72 in) and *pc* (picas; 1 pc = 12 pt). Line 17 specifies that all nested unordered lists (ul elements that are descendants of ul elements) are to have font size .8em. [*Note:* When setting a style property that takes a measurement (e.g. font-size, margin-left), no units are necessary if the value is zero.]

Good Programming Practice 3.2

Whenever possible, use relative-length measurements. If you use absolute-length measurements, your document may not be readable on some client browsers (e.g., wireless phones).

3.5 Linking External Style Sheets

Style sheets are a convenient way to create a document with a uniform theme. With *external style sheets* (i.e., separate documents that contain only CSS rules), you can provide a uniform look and feel to an entire website. Different pages on a site can all use the same style sheet. When changes to the styles are required, the author needs to modify only a single CSS file to make style changes across the entire website. Note that while embedded style sheets separate content from presentation, both are still contained in a single file, preventing a web designer and a content author from working in parallel. External style sheets solve this problem by separating the content and style into separate files.

Software Engineering Observation 3.1

Always use an external style sheet when developing a website with multiple pages. External style sheets separate content from presentation, allowing for more consistent look-and-feel, more efficient development, and better performance.

Figure 3.4 presents an external style sheet. Lines 1–2 are *CSS comments*. Like XHTML comments, CSS comments describe the content of a CSS document. Comments may be placed in any type of CSS code (i.e., inline styles, embedded style sheets and external style sheets) and always start with /* and end with */. Text between these delimiters is ignored by the browser.

```
1   /* Fig. 3.4: styles.css */
2   /* External stylesheet */
3
4   body    { font-family: arial, helvetica, sans-serif }
5
6   a.nodec { text-decoration: none }
```

Fig. 3.4 | External style sheet. (Part 1 of 2.)

```
7
8    a:hover   { text-decoration: underline }
9
10   li em     { font-weight: bold }
11
12   h1, em    { text-decoration: underline }
13
14   ul        { margin-left: 20px }
15
16   ul ul     { font-size: .8em; }
```

Fig. 3.4 | External style sheet. (Part 2 of 2.)

Figure 3.5 contains an XHTML document that references the external style sheet in Fig. 3.4. Lines 10–11 (Fig. 3.5) show a *link* element that uses the *rel* attribute to specify a *relationship* between the current document and another document. In this case, we declare the linked document to be a *stylesheet* for this document. The type attribute specifies the MIME type of the related document as text/css. The href attribute provides the URL for the document containing the style sheet. In this case, styles.css is in the same directory as external.html.

```
1    <?xml version = "1.0" encoding = "utf-8"?>
2    <!DOCTYPE html PUBLIC "-//W3C//DTD XHTML 1.0 Strict//EN"
3       "http://www.w3.org/TR/xhtml1/DTD/xhtml1-strict.dtd">
4
5    <!-- Fig. 3.5: external.html -->
6    <!-- Linking an external style sheet. -->
7    <html xmlns = "http://www.w3.org/1999/xhtml">
8       <head>
9          <title>Linking External Style Sheets</title>
10         <link rel = "stylesheet" type = "text/css"
11            href = "styles.css" />
12      </head>
13      <body>
14         <h1>Shopping list for <em>Monday</em>:</h1>
15
16         <ul>
17            <li>Milk</li>
18            <li>Bread
19               <ul>
20                  <li>White bread</li>
21                  <li>Rye bread</li>
22                  <li>Whole wheat bread</li>
23               </ul>
24            </li>
25            <li>Rice</li>
26            <li>Potatoes</li>
27            <li>Pizza <em>with mushrooms</em></li>
28         </ul>
29
```

Fig. 3.5 | Linking an external style sheet. (Part 1 of 2.)

```
30        <p><em>Go to the</em>
31            <a class = "nodec" href = "http://www.deitel.com">
32                Grocery store</a>
33        </p>
34    </body>
35 </html>
```

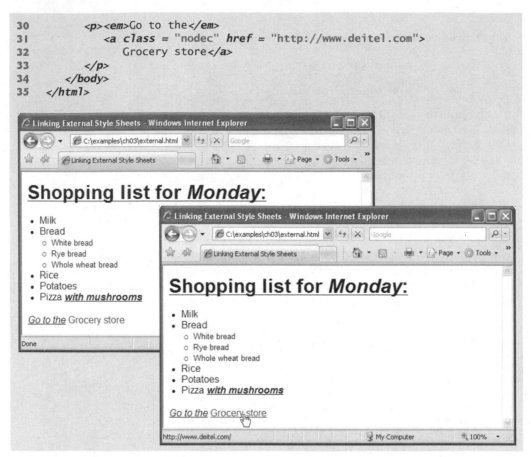

Fig. 3.5 | Linking an external style sheet. (Part 2 of 2.)

Software Engineering Observation 3.2

External style sheets are reusable. Creating them once and reusing them reduces programming effort.

Performance Tip 3.1

Reusing external style sheets reduces load time and bandwidth usage on a server, since the style sheet can be downloaded once, stored by the web browser, and applied to all pages on a website.

3.6 Positioning Elements

Before CSS, controlling the positioning of elements in an XHTML document was difficult—the browser determined positioning. CSS introduced the *position* property and a capability called ***absolute positioning***, which gives authors greater control over how document elements are displayed. Figure 3.6 demonstrates absolute positioning.

Normally, elements are positioned on the page in the order that they appear in the XHTML document. Lines 11–14 define a style called bgimg for the first img element (i.gif) on the page. Specifying an element's position as absolute removes the element from the normal flow of elements on the page, instead positioning it according to the distance from the top, left, right or bottom margins of its ***containing block-level element*** (i.e., an element such as body or p). Here, we position the element to be 0 pixels away from both the top and left margins of its containing element. In line 28, this style is applied to the image, which is contained in a p element.

The ***z-index*** property allows you to layer overlapping elements properly. Elements that have higher z-index values are displayed in front of elements with lower z-index values. In this example, i.gif has the lowest z-index (1), so it displays in the background. The .fgimg CSS rule in lines 15–18 gives the circle image (circle.gif, in lines 31–32) a z-index of 2, so it displays in front of i.gif. The p element in line 34 (Positioned Text) is given a z-index of 3 in line 22, so it displays in front of the other two. If you do not specify a z-index or if elements have the same z-index value, the elements are placed from background to foreground in the order they are encountered in the document.

```
 1   <?xml version = "1.0" encoding = "utf-8"?>
 2   <!DOCTYPE html PUBLIC "-//W3C//DTD XHTML 1.0 Strict//EN"
 3      "http://www.w3.org/TR/xhtml1/DTD/xhtml1-strict.dtd">
 4
 5   <!-- Fig. 3.6: positioning.html -->
 6   <!-- Absolute positioning of elements. -->
 7   <html xmlns = "http://www.w3.org/1999/xhtml">
 8      <head>
 9         <title>Absolute Positioning</title>
10         <style type = "text/css">
11            .bgimg     { position: absolute;
12                         top: 0px;
13                         left: 0px;
14                         z-index: 1 }
15            .fgimg     { position: absolute;
16                         top: 25px;
17                         left: 100px;
18                         z-index: 2 }
19            .text      { position: absolute;
20                         top: 25px;
21                         left: 100px;
22                         z-index: 3;
23                         font-size: 20pt;
24                         font-family: tahoma, geneva, sans-serif }
25         </style>
26      </head>
27      <body>
28         <p><img src = "bgimg.gif" class = "bgimg"
29            alt = "First positioned image" /></p>
30
31         <p><img src = "fgimg.gif" class = "fgimg"
32            alt = "Second positioned image" /></p>
33
34         <p class = "text">Positioned Text</p>
35      </body>
36   </html>
```

Fig. 3.6 | Absolute positioning of elements. (Part 1 of 2.)

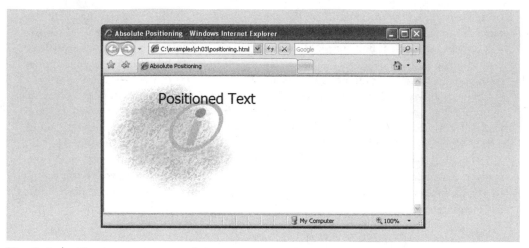

Fig. 3.6 | Absolute positioning of elements. (Part 2 of 2.)

Absolute positioning is not the only way to specify page layout. Figure 3.7 demonstrates *relative positioning*, in which elements are positioned relative to other elements.

```
1   <?xml version = "1.0" encoding = "utf-8"?>
2   <!DOCTYPE html PUBLIC "-//W3C//DTD XHTML 1.0 Strict//EN"
3      "http://www.w3.org/TR/xhtml1/DTD/xhtml1-strict.dtd">
4
5   <!-- Fig. 3.7: positioning2.html -->
6   <!-- Relative positioning of elements. -->
7   <html xmlns = "http://www.w3.org/1999/xhtml">
8      <head>
9         <title>Relative Positioning</title>
10        <style type = "text/css">
11           p              { font-size: 1.3em;
12                            font-family: verdana, arial, sans-serif }
13           span           { color: red;
14                            font-size: .6em;
15                            height: 1em }
16           .super         { position: relative;
17                            top: -1ex }
18           .sub           { position: relative;
19                            bottom: -1ex }
20           .shiftleft     { position: relative;
21                            left: -1ex }
22           .shiftright    { position: relative;
23                            right: -1ex }
24        </style>
25     </head>
26     <body>
27        <p>The text at the end of this sentence
28        <span class = "super">is in superscript</span>.</p>
29
```

Fig. 3.7 | Relative positioning of elements. (Part 1 of 2.)

```
30          <p>The text at the end of this sentence
31          <span class = "sub">is in subscript</span>.</p>
32
33          <p>The text at the end of this sentence
34          <span class = "shiftleft">is shifted left</span>.</p>
35
36          <p>The text at the end of this sentence
37          <span class = "shiftright">is shifted right</span>.</p>
38      </body>
39  </html>
```

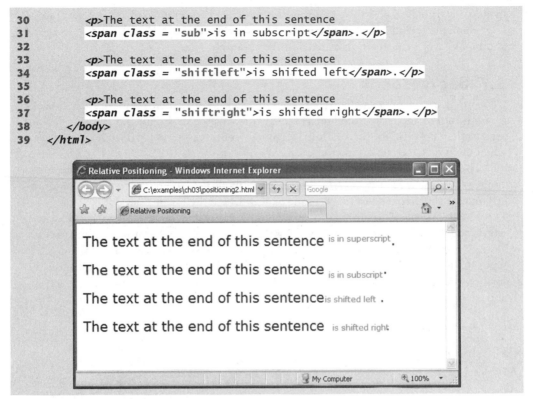

Fig. 3.7 | Relative positioning of elements. (Part 2 of 2.)

Setting the position property to relative, as in class super (lines 16–17), lays out the element on the page and offsets it by the specified top, bottom, left or right value. Unlike absolute positioning, relative positioning keeps elements in the general flow of elements on the page, so positioning is relative to other elements in the flow. Recall that ex (line 17) is the *x*-height of a font, a relative-length measurement typically equal to the height of a lowercase *x*.

 Common Programming Error 3.2

Because relative positioning keeps elements in the flow of text in your documents, be careful to avoid unintentionally overlapping text.

Inline and Block-Level Elements

We introduce the *span* element in line 28. Lines 13–15 define the CSS rule for all span elements. The height of the span determines how much vertical space the span will occupy. The font-size determines the size of the text inside the span.

Element span is a *grouping element*—it does not apply any inherent formatting to its contents. Its primary purpose is to apply CSS rules or id attributes to a section of text. Element span is an *inline-level element*—it applies formatting to text without changing the flow of the document. Examples of inline elements include span, img, a, em and strong. The *div* element is also a grouping element, but it is a *block-level element*. This means it is displayed on its own line and has a virtual box around it. Examples of block-level elements include div, p and heading elements (h1 through h6). We'll discuss inline and block-level elements in more detail in Section 3.9.

3.7 Backgrounds

CSS provides control over the background of block-level elements. CSS can set a background color or add background images to XHTML elements. Figure 3.8 adds a corporate logo to the bottom-right corner of the document. This logo stays fixed in the corner even when the user scrolls up or down the screen.

The **background-image** property (line 11) specifies the image URL for the image logo.gif in the format url(*fileLocation*). You can also set the **background-color** property in case the image is not found (and to fill in where the image does not cover).

The **background-position** property (line 12) places the image on the page. The keywords top, bottom, center, left and right are used individually or in combination for vertical and horizontal positioning. An image can be positioned using lengths by specifying the horizontal length followed by the vertical length. For example, to position the image as horizontally centered (positioned at 50 percent of the distance across the screen) and 30 pixels from the top, use

   background-position: 50% 30px;

```
1   <?xml version = "1.0" encoding = "utf-8"?>
2   <!DOCTYPE html PUBLIC "-//W3C//DTD XHTML 1.0 Strict//EN"
3      "http://www.w3.org/TR/xhtml1/DTD/xhtml1-strict.dtd">
4
5   <!-- Fig. 3.8: background.html -->
6   <!-- Adding background images and indentation. -->
7   <html xmlns = "http://www.w3.org/1999/xhtml">
8      <head>
9         <title>Background Images</title>
10        <style type = "text/css">
11           body   { background-image: url(logo.gif);
12                    background-position: bottom right;
13                    background-repeat: no-repeat;
14                    background-attachment: fixed;
15                    background-color: #eeeeee }
16           p      { font-size: 18pt;
17                    color: #1144AA;
18                    text-indent: 1em;
19                    font-family: arial, sans-serif; }
20           .dark  { font-weight: bold }
21        </style>
22     </head>
23     <body>
24        <p>
25        This example uses the background-image,
26        background-position and background-attachment
27        styles to place the <span class = "dark">Deitel
```

Fig. 3.8 | Adding background images and indentation. (Part 1 of 2.)

```
28        &amp; Associates, Inc.</span> logo in the bottom,
29        right corner of the page. Notice how the logo
30        stays in the proper position when you resize the
31        browser window. The background-color fills in where
32        there is no image.
33      </p>
34    </body>
35  </html>
```

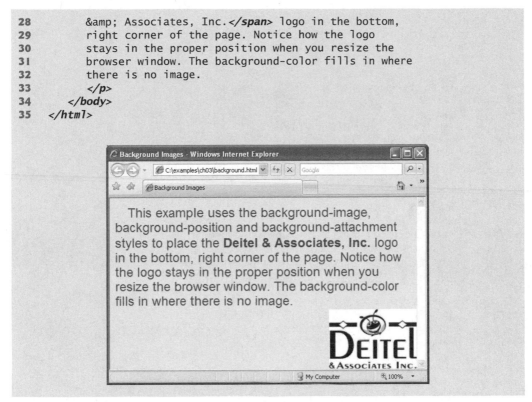

Fig. 3.8 | Adding background images and indentation. (Part 2 of 2.)

The ***background-repeat*** property (line 13) controls background image *tiling*, which places multiple copies of the image next to each other to fill the background. Here, we set the tiling to no-repeat to display only one copy of the background image. Other values include repeat (the default) to tile the image vertically and horizontally, repeat-x to tile the image only horizontally or repeat-y to tile the image only vertically.

The final property setting, ***background-attachment: fixed*** (line 14), fixes the image in the position specified by ***background-position***. Scrolling the browser window will not move the image from its position. The default value, scroll, moves the image as the user scrolls through the document.

Line 18 uses the ***text-indent*** property to indent the first line of text in the element by a specified amount, in this case 1em. An author might use this property to create a web page that reads more like a novel, in which the first line of every paragraph is indented.

The CSS property ***font-style*** property allows you to set the text style to none, italic or oblique (oblique is simply more slanted than italic—the browser will default to italic if the system or font does not support oblique text).

3.8 Element Dimensions

In addition to positioning elements, CSS rules can specify the actual dimensions of each page element. Figure 3.9 demonstrates how to set the dimensions of elements.

```
 1   <?xml version = "1.0" encoding = "utf-8"?>
 2   <!DOCTYPE html PUBLIC "-//W3C//DTD XHTML 1.0 Strict//EN"
 3      "http://www.w3.org/TR/xhtml1/DTD/xhtml1-strict.dtd">
 4
 5   <!-- Fig. 3.9: width.html -->
 6   <!-- Element dimensions and text alignment. -->
 7   <html xmlns = "http://www.w3.org/1999/xhtml">
 8      <head>
 9         <title>Box Dimensions</title>
10         <style type = "text/css">
11            div { background-color: #aaccff;
12                  margin-bottom: .5em;
13                  font-family: arial, helvetica, sans-serif }
14         </style>
15      </head>
16      <body>
17         <div style = "width: 20%">Here is some
18         text that goes in a box which is
19         set to stretch across twenty percent
20         of the width of the screen.</div>
21
22         <div style = "width: 80%; text-align: center">
23         Here is some CENTERED text that goes in a box
24         which is set to stretch across eighty percent of
25         the width of the screen.</div>
26
27         <div style = "width: 20%; height: 150px; overflow: scroll">
28         This box is only twenty percent of
29         the width and has a fixed height.
30         What do we do if it overflows? Set the
31         overflow property to scroll!</div>
32      </body>
33   </html>
```

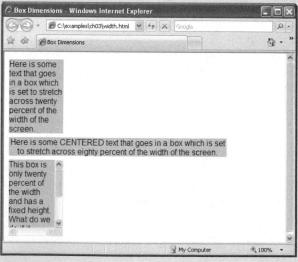

Fig. 3.9 | Element dimensions and text alignment.

The inline style in line 17 illustrates how to set the *width* of an element on screen; here, we indicate that the div element should occupy 20 percent of the screen width. The height of an element can be set similarly, using the *height* property. The height and width values also can be specified as relative or absolute lengths. For example,

> *width:* 10em

sets the element's width to 10 times the font size. Most elements are left aligned by default; however, this alignment can be altered to position the element elsewhere. Line 22 sets text in the element to be center aligned; other values for the *text-align* property include left and right.

In the third div, we specify a percentage height and a pixel width. One problem with setting both dimensions of an element is that the content inside the element can exceed the set boundaries, in which case the element is simply made large enough for all the content to fit. However, in line 27, we set the *overflow* property to scroll, a setting that adds scroll bars if the text overflows the boundaries.

3.9 Box Model and Text Flow

All block-level XHTML elements have a virtual box drawn around them based on what is known as the *box model*. When the browser renders elements using the box model, the content of each element is surrounded by *padding*, a *border* and a *margin* (Fig. 3.10).

CSS controls the border using three properties: *border-width*, *border-color* and *border-style*. We illustrate these three properties in Fig. 3.11.

Property border-width may be set to any valid CSS length (e.g., em, ex, px, etc.) or to the predefined value of thin, medium or thick. The *border-color property* sets the color. [*Note:* This property has different meanings for different style borders.] The border-style options are none, hidden, dotted, dashed, solid, double, groove, ridge, inset and outset. Borders groove and ridge have opposite effects, as do inset and outset. When border-style is set to none, no border is rendered.

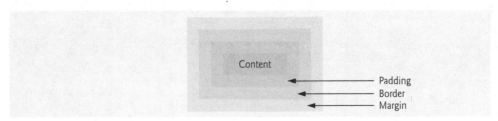

Fig. 3.10 | Box model for block-level elements.

```
1   <?xml version = "1.0" encoding = "utf-8"?>
2   <!DOCTYPE html PUBLIC "-//W3C//DTD XHTML 1.0 Strict//EN"
3      "http://www.w3.org/TR/xhtml11/DTD/xhtml11-strict.dtd">
4
5   <!-- Fig. 3.11: borders.html -->
6   <!-- Borders of block-level elements. -->
```

Fig. 3.11 | Borders of block-level elements. (Part 1 of 2.)

```
 7   <html xmlns = "http://www.w3.org/1999/xhtml">
 8      <head>
 9         <title>Borders</title>
10         <style type = "text/css">
11            div      { text-align: center;
12                       width: 50%;
13                       position: relative;
14                       left: 25%;
15                       border-width: 4px }
16            .medium { border-width: medium }
17            .thin    { border-width: thin }
18            .solid   { border-style: solid }
19            .double { border-style: double }
20            .groove { border-style: groove }
21            .inset   { border-style: inset }
22            .outset { border-style: outset }
23            .dashed { border-style: dashed }
24            .red     { border-color: red }
25            .blue    { border-color: blue }
26         </style>
27      </head>
28      <body>
29         <div class = "solid">Solid border</div><hr />
30         <div class = "double">Double border</div><hr />
31         <div class = "groove">Groove border</div><hr />
32         <div class = "inset">Inset border</div><hr />
33         <div class = "dashed">Dashed border</div><hr />
34         <div class = "thin red solid">Thin Red Solid border</div><hr />
35         <div class = "medium blue outset">Medium Blue Outset border</div
36      </body>
37   </html>
```

Fig. 3.11 | Borders of block-level elements. (Part 2 of 2.)

Each border property may be set for an individual side of the box (e.g., border-top-style or border-left-color). Note that we assign more than one class to an XHTML element by separating multiple class names with spaces, as shown in lines 36–37.

As we have seen with absolute positioning, it is possible to remove elements from the normal flow of text. *Floating* allows you to move an element to one side of the screen; other content in the document then flows around the floated element. Figure 3.12 demonstrates how floats and the box model can be used to control the layout of an entire page.

```
 1   <?xml version = "1.0" encoding = "utf-8"?>
 2   <!DOCTYPE html PUBLIC "-//W3C//DTD XHTML 1.0 Strict//EN"
 3      "http://www.w3.org/TR/xhtml1/DTD/xhtml1-strict.dtd">
 4
 5   <!-- Fig. 3.12: floating.html -->
 6   <!-- Floating elements. -->
 7   <html xmlns = "http://www.w3.org/1999/xhtml">
 8      <head>
 9         <title>Flowing Text Around Floating Elements</title>
10         <style type = "text/css">
11            div.heading { background-color: #bbddff;
12                          text-align: center;
13                          font-family: arial, helvetica, sans-serif;
14                          padding: .2em }
15            p           { text-align: justify;
16                          font-family: verdana, geneva, sans-serif;
17                          margin: .5em }
18            div.floated { background-color: #eeeeee;
19                          font-size: 1.5em;
20                          font-family: arial, helvetica, sans-serif;
21                          padding: .2em;
22                          margin-left: .5em;
23                          margin-bottom: .5em;
24                          float: right;
25                          text-align: right;
26                          width: 50% }
27            div.section { border: 1px solid #bbddff }
28         </style>
29      </head>
30      <body>
31         <div class = "heading"><img src = "deitel.png" alt = "Deitel" />
32         </div>
33         <div class = "section">
34            <div class = "floated">Corporate Training and Publishing</div>
35            <p>Deitel &amp; Associates, Inc. is an internationally
36            recognized corporate training and publishing organization
37            specializing in programming languages, Internet/World
38            Wide Web technology and object technology education.
39            The company provides courses on Java, C++, Visual Basic, C#,
40            C, Internet and web programming, Object
41            Technology, and more.</p>
42         </div>
43         <div class = "section">
44            <div class = "floated">Leading-Edge Programming Textbooks</div>
45            <p>Through its publishing
46            partnership with Prentice Hall, Deitel &amp; Associates,
47            Inc. publishes leading-edge programming textbooks,
```

Fig. 3.12 | Floating elements. (Part 1 of 2.)

```
48            professional books, interactive CD-ROM-based multimedia
49            Cyber Classrooms, satellite courses and DVD and web-based
50            video courses.</p>
51        </div>
52      </body>
53    </html>
```

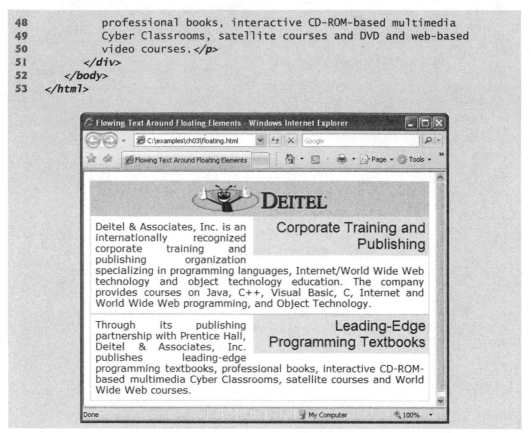

Fig. 3.12 | Floating elements. (Part 2 of 2.)

Looking at the XHTML code, we can see that the general structure of this document consists of a header and two main sections. Each section contains a subheading and a paragraph of text.

Block-level elements (such as divs) render with a line break before and after their content, so the header and two sections will render vertically one on top of another. In the absence of our styles, the subheading divs would also stack vertically on top of the text in the p tags. However, in line 24 we set the float property to right in the class floated, which is applied to the subheadings. This causes each subheading div to float to the right edge of its containing element, while the paragraph of text will flow around it.

Line 17 assigns a margin of .5em to all paragraph tags. The **margin property** sets the space between the outside of the border and all other content on the page. In line 21, we assign .2em of padding to the floated divs. The **padding property** determines the distance between the content inside an element and the inside of the element's border. Margins for individual sides of an element can be specified (lines 22–23) by using the properties **margin-top**, **margin-right**, **margin-left** and **margin-bottom**. Padding can be specified in the same way, using **padding-top**, **padding-right**, **padding-left** and **padding-bottom**. To see the effects of margins and padding, try putting the margin and padding properties inside comments and observing the difference.

In line 27, we assign a border to the section boxes using a shorthand declaration of the border properties. CSS allows shorthand assignments of borders to allow you to define all three border properties in one line. The syntax for this shorthand is border: <width> <style> <color>. Our border is one pixel thick, solid, and the same color as the background-color property of the heading div (line 11). This allows the border to blend with the header and makes the page appear as one box with a line dividing its sections.

3.10 Media Types

CSS *media types* allow a programmer to decide what a page should look like depending on the kind of media being used to display the page. The most common media type for a web page is the ***screen media type***, which is a standard computer screen. Other media types in CSS 2 include ***handheld***, ***braille***, ***aural*** and ***print***. The handheld medium is designed for mobile Internet devices, while braille is for machines that can read or print web pages in braille. aural styles allow the programmer to give a speech-synthesizing web browser more information about the content of the web page. This allows the browser to present a web page in a sensible manner to a visually impaired person. The print media type affects a web page's appearance when it is printed. For a complete list of CSS media types, see http://www.w3.org/TR/REC-CSS2/media.html#media-types.

Media types allow a programmer to decide how a page should be presented on any one of these media without affecting the others. Figure 3.13 gives a simple example that applies one set of styles when the document is viewed on the screen, and another when the document is printed. To see the difference, look at the screen captures below the paragraph or use the **Print Preview** feature in Internet Explorer or Firefox.

```
1   <?xml version = "1.0" encoding = "utf-8"?>
2   <!DOCTYPE html PUBLIC "-//W3C//DTD XHTML 1.0 Strict//EN"
3      "http://www.w3.org/TR/xhtml/DTD/xhtml1-strict.dtd">
4
5   <!-- Fig. 3.13: mediatypes.html -->
6   <!-- CSS media types. -->
7   <html xmlns = "http://www.w3.org/1999/xhtml">
8      <head>
9         <title>Media Types</title>
10        <style type = "text/css">
11           @media all
12           {
13              body   { background-color: #4488aa }
14              h1     { font-family: verdana, helvetica, sans-serif;
15                       color: #aaffcc }
16              p      { font-size: 12pt;
17                       color: white;
18                       font-family: arial, sans-serif }
19           } /* end @media all declaration. */
20           @media print
21           {
22              body   { background-color: white }
23              h1     { color: #008844}
```

Fig. 3.13 | CSS media types. (Part 1 of 2.)

```
24                 p       { font-size: 14pt;
25                         color: #4488aa;
26                         font-family: "times new roman", times, serif }
27            } /* end @media print declaration. */
28        </style>
29     </head>
30     <body>
31        <h1>CSS Media Types Example</h1>
32
33        <p>
34        This example uses CSS media types to vary how the page
35        appears in print and how it appears on any other media.
36        This text will appear one font on the screen and a
37        different font on paper or in a print preview. To see
38        the difference in Internet Explorer, go to the Print
39        menu and select Print Preview. In Firefox, select Print
40        Preview from the File menu.
41        </p>
42     </body>
43  </html>
```

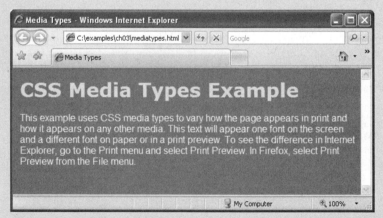

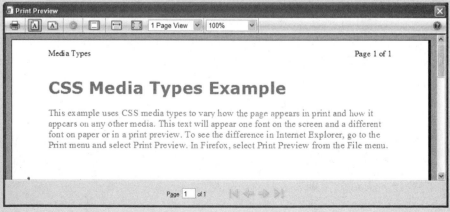

Fig. 3.13 | CSS media types. (Part 2 of 2.)

In line 11, we begin a block of styles that applies to all media types, declared by `@media all` and enclosed in curly braces (`{` and `}`). In lines 13–18, we define some styles for all media types. Lines 20–27 set styles to be applied only when the page is printed, beginning with the declaration `@media print` and enclosed in curly braces.

The styles we applied for all media types look nice on a screen but would not look good on a printed page. A colored background would use a lot of ink, and a black-and-white printer may print a page that's hard to read because there isn't enough contrast between the colors. Also, `sans-serif` fonts like `arial`, `helvetica`, and `geneva` are easier to read on a screen, while `serif` fonts like `times new roman` are easier to read on paper.

Look-and-Feel Observation 3.1

Pages with dark background colors and light text use a lot of ink and may be difficult to read when printed, especially on a black-and white-printer. Use the print media type to avoid this.

Look-and-Feel Observation 3.2

In general, sans-serif fonts look better on a screen, while serif fonts look better on paper. The print media type allows your web page to display sans-serif font on a screen and change to a serif font when it is printed.

To solve these problems, we apply specific styles for the `print` media type. We change the `background-color` of the body, the `color` of the h1 tag, and the `font-size`, `color`, and `font-family` of the p tag to be more suited for printing and viewing on paper. Notice that most of these styles conflict with the declarations in the section for all media types. Since the `print` media type has higher specificity than `all` media types, the `print` styles override the styles for all media types when the page is printed. Since the `font-family` property of the h1 tag is not overridden in the `print` section, it retains its old value even when the page is printed.

3.11 Building a CSS Drop-Down Menu

Drop-down menus are a good way to provide navigation links on a website without using a lot of screen space. In this section, we take a second look at the `:hover` pseudoclass and introduce the `display` property to create a drop-down menu using CSS and XHTML.

We've already seen the `:hover` pseudoclass used to change a link's style when the mouse hovers over it. We'll use this feature in a more advanced way to cause a menu to appear when the mouse hovers over a menu button. The other important property we need is the **display** property. This allows a programmer to decide whether an element is rendered on the page or not. Possible values include `block`, `inline` and `none`. The `block` and `inline` values display the element as a block element or an inline element, while `none` stops the element from being rendered. The code for the drop-down menu is shown in Fig. 3.14.

```
1    <?xml version = "1.0" encoding = "utf-8"?>
2    <!DOCTYPE html PUBLIC "-//W3C//DTD XHTML 1.0 Strict//EN"
3        "http://www.w3.org/TR/xhtml1/DTD/xhtml1-strict.dtd">
4
```

Fig. 3.14 | CSS drop-down menu. (Part 1 of 3.)

```
5   <!-- Fig. 3.14: dropdown.html -->
6   <!-- CSS drop-down menu. -->
7   <html xmlns = "http://www.w3.org/1999/xhtml">
8      <head>
9         <title>
10           Drop-Down Menu
11        </title>
12        <style type = "text/css">
13           body               { font-family: arial, sans-serif }
14           div.menu           { font-weight: bold;
15                                color: white;
16                                border: 2px solid #225599;
17                                text-align: center;
18                                width: 10em;
19                                background-color: #225599 }
20           div.menu:hover a   { display: block }
21           div.menu a         { display: none;
22                                border-top: 2px solid #225599;
23                                background-color: white;
24                                width: 10em;
25                                text-decoration: none;
26                                color: black }
27           div.menu a:hover   { background-color: #dfeeff }
28        </style>
29     </head>
30     <body>
31        <div class = "menu">Menu
32           <a href = "#">Home</a>
33           <a href = "#">News</a>
34           <a href = "#">Articles</a>
35           <a href = "#">Blog</a>
36           <a href = "#">Contact</a>
37        </div>
38     </body>
39  </html>
```

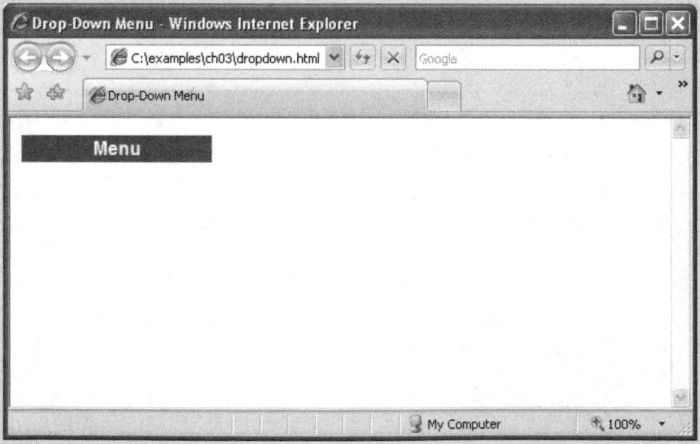

Fig. 3.14 | CSS drop-down menu. (Part 2 of 3.)

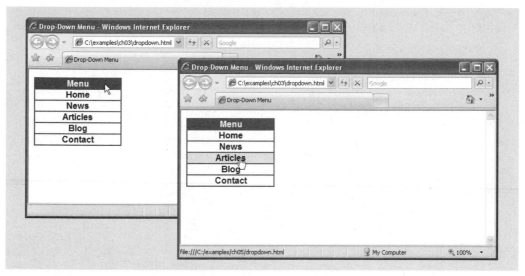

Fig. 3.14 | CSS drop-down menu. (Part 3 of 3.)

First let's look at the XHTML code. In lines 31–37, a div of class menu has the text "Menu" and five links inside it. This is our drop-down menu. The behavior we want is as follows: the text that says "Menu" should be the only thing visible on the page, unless the mouse is over the menu div. When the mouse cursor hovers over the menu div, we want the links to appear below the menu for the user to choose from.

To see how we get this functionality, let's look at the CSS code. There are two lines that give us the drop-down functionality. Line 21 selects all the links inside the menu div and sets their display value to none. This instructs the browser not to render the links. The other important style is in line 20. The selectors in this line are similar to those in line 21, except that this line selects only the a (anchor) elements that are children of a menu div that has the mouse over it. The display: block in this line means that when the mouse is over the menu div, the links inside it will be displayed as block-level elements.

The selectors in line 27 are also similar to lines 20 and 21. This time, however, the style is applied only to any a element that is a child of the menu div when that child has the mouse cursor over it. This style changes the background-color of the currently high-lighted menu option. The rest of the CSS simply adds aesthetic style to the components of our menu. Look at the screen captures or run the code example to see the menu in action.

This drop-down menu is just one example of more advanced CSS formatting. Many additional resources are available online for CSS navigation menus and lists. Specifically, check out List-o-Matic, an automatic CSS list generator located at www.accessify.com/tools-and-wizards/developer-tools/list-o-matic/ and Dynamic Drive's library of vertical and horizontal CSS menus at www.dynamicdrive.com/style/.

3.12 User Style Sheets

Users can define their own *user style sheets* to format pages based on their preferences. For example, people with visual impairments may want to increase the page's text size.

Web page authors need to be careful not to inadvertently override user preferences with defined styles. This section discusses possible conflicts between *author styles* and *user styles*.

Figure 3.15 contains an author style. The font-size is set to 9pt for all <p> tags that have class note applied to them.

User style sheets are external style sheets. Figure 3.16 shows a user style sheet that sets the body's font-size to 20pt, color to yellow and background-color to #000080.

User style sheets are not linked to a document; rather, they are set in the browser's options. To add a user style sheet in IE7, select **Internet Options...**, located in the **Tools** menu. In the **Internet Options** dialog (Fig. 3.17) that appears, click **Accessibility...**, check

```
 1   <?xml version = "1.0" encoding = "utf-8"?>
 2   <!DOCTYPE html PUBLIC "-//W3C//DTD XHTML 1.0 Strict//EN"
 3      "http://www.w3.org/TR/xhtml1/DTD/xhtml1-strict.dtd">
 4
 5   <!-- Fig. 3.15: user_absolute.html -->
 6   <!-- pt measurement for text size. -->
 7   <html xmlns = "http://www.w3.org/1999/xhtml">
 8      <head>
 9         <title>User Styles</title>
10         <style type = "text/css">
11            .note { font-size: 9pt }
12         </style>
13      </head>
14      <body>
15         <p>Thanks for visiting my website. I hope you enjoy it.
16         </p><p class = "note">Please Note: This site will be
17         moving soon. Please check periodically for updates.</p>
18      </body>
19   </html>
```

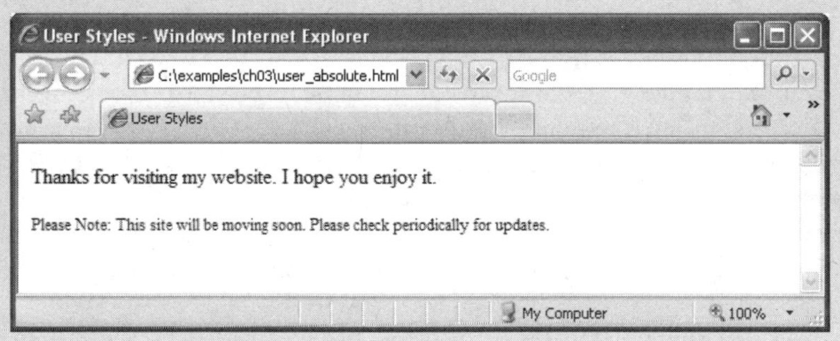

Fig. 3.15 | pt measurement for text size.

```
 1   /* Fig. 3.16: userstyles.css */
 2   /* A user stylesheet */
 3   body     { font-size: 20pt;
 4              color: yellow;
 5              background-color: #000080 }
```

Fig. 3.16 | User style sheet.

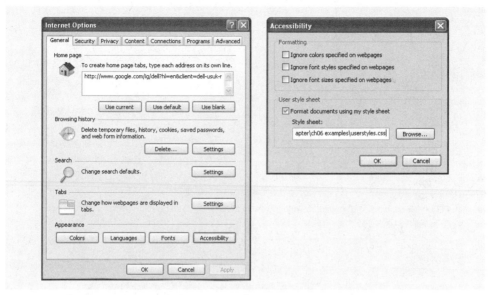

Fig. 3.17 | User style sheet in Internet Explorer 7.

the **Format documents using my style sheet** checkbox, and type the location of the user style sheet. Internet Explorer 7 applies the user style sheet to any document it loads. To add a user style sheet in Firefox, find your Firefox profile using the instructions at `www.mozilla.org/support/firefox/profile#locate` and place a style sheet called `userContent.css` in the chrome subdirectory.

The web page from Fig. 3.15 is displayed in Fig. 3.18, with the user style sheet from Fig. 3.16 applied. In this example, if users define their own `font-size` in a user style sheet, the author style has a higher precedence and overrides the user style. The `9pt` font specified in the author style sheet overrides the `20pt` font specified in the user style sheet. This small font may make pages difficult to read, especially for individuals with visual impairments. You can avoid this problem by using relative measurements (e.g., `em` or `ex`) instead of absolute measurements, such as `pt`. Figure 3.19 changes the `font-size` property to use a relative measurement (line 11) that does not override the user style set in Fig. 3.16. Instead,

Fig. 3.18 | User style sheet applied with `pt` measurement.

```
 1   <?xml version = "1.0" encoding = "utf-8"?>
 2   <!DOCTYPE html PUBLIC "-//W3C//DTD XHTML 1.0 Strict//EN"
 3      "http://www.w3.org/TR/xhtml1/DTD/xhtml1-strict.dtd">
 4
 5   <!-- Fig. 3.19: user_relative.html -->
 6   <!-- em measurement for text size. -->
 7   <html xmlns = "http://www.w3.org/1999/xhtml">
 8      <head>
 9         <title>User Styles</title>
10         <style type = "text/css">
11            .note { font-size: .75em }
12         </style>
13      </head>
14      <body>
15         <p>Thanks for visiting my website. I hope you enjoy it.
16         </p><p class = "note">Please Note: This site will be
17         moving soon. Please check periodically for updates.</p>
18      </body>
19   </html>
```

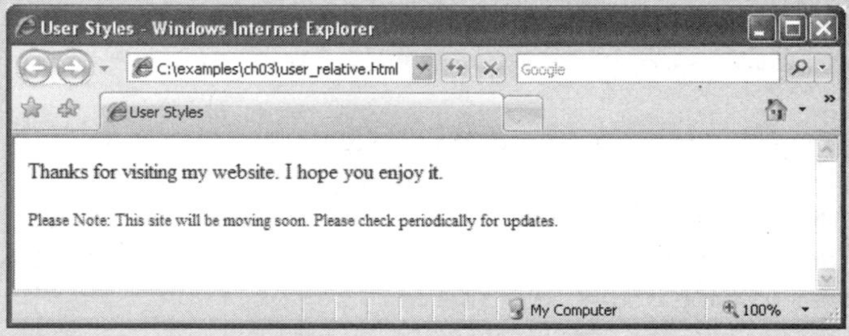

Fig. 3.19 | em measurement for text size.

the font size displayed is relative to the one specified in the user style sheet. In this case, text enclosed in the <p> tag displays as 20pt, and <p> tags that have class note applied to them are displayed in 15pt (.75 times 20pt).

Figure 3.20 displays the web page from Fig. 3.19 with the user style sheet from Fig. 3.16 applied. Note that the second line of text displayed is larger than the same line of text in Fig. 3.18.

Fig. 3.20 | User style sheet applied with em measurement.

3.13 CSS 3

The W3C is currently developing CSS 3 and some browsers are beginning to implement some of the new features that will be in the *CSS 3* specification. We discuss a few of the upcoming features that will most likely be included in CSS 3.

CSS 3 will allow for more advanced control of borders. In addition to the border-style, border-color, and border-width properties, you will be able to set multiple border colors, use images for borders, add shadows to boxes, and create borders with rounded corners.

Background images will be more versatile in CSS 3, allowing you to set the size of a background image, specify an offset to determine where in the element the image should be positioned, and use multiple background images in one element. There will also be properties to set shadow effects on text and more options for text overflow when the text is too long to fit in its containing element.

Additional features will include resizable boxes, enhanced selectors, multicolumn layouts, and more developed speech (aural) styles. The Web Resources section points you to the Deitel CSS Resource Center, where you can find links to the latest information on the development and features of CSS 3.

3.14 Web Resources

http://www.deitel.com/css21
The Deitel CSS Resource Center contains links to some of the best CSS information on the web. There you'll find categorized links to tutorials, references, code examples, demos, videos, and more. Check out the demos section for more advanced examples of layouts, menus, and other web page components.

4

JavaScript: Introduction to Scripting

*Comment is free, but facts
are sacred.*
—C. P. Scott

*The creditor hath a better
memory than the debtor.*
—James Howell

*When faced with a decision,
I always ask, "What would
be the most fun?"*
—Peggy Walker

*Equality, in a social sense,
may be divided into that of
condition and that of rights.*
—James Fenimore Cooper

OBJECTIVES

In this chapter you'll learn:

- To write simple JavaScript programs.
- To use input and output statements.
- Basic memory concepts.
- To use arithmetic operators.
- The precedence of arithmetic operators.
- To write decision-making statements.
- To use relational and equality operators.

4.1 Introduction

In Chapters 2 and 3, we introduced XHTML and Cascading Style Sheets (CSS). In this chapter, we begin our introduction to the *JavaScript*[1] *scripting language*, which facilitates a disciplined approach to designing computer programs that enhance the functionality and appearance of web pages.[2]

Chapters 4–9 present a detailed discussion of JavaScript—the *de facto* standard client-side scripting language for web-based applications, due to its highly portable nature. Our treatment of JavaScript introduces client-side scripting (used in Chapters 4–11), which makes web pages more dynamic and interactive.

We now introduce JavaScript programming and present examples that illustrate several important features of JavaScript. Each example is carefully analyzed one line at a time. In Chapters 5–6, we present a detailed treatment of program development and program control in JavaScript.

Before you can run code examples with JavaScript on your computer, you may need to change your browser's security settings. By default, Internet Explorer 7 prevents scripts on your local computer from running, displaying a yellow warning bar at the top of the window instead. To allow scripts to run in files on your computer, select **Internet Options** from the **Tools** menu. Click the **Advanced** tab and scroll down to the **Security** section of the **Settings** list. Check the box labeled **Allow active content to run in files on My Computer** (Fig. 4.1). Click **OK** and restart Internet Explorer. XHTML documents on your own computer that contain JavaScript code will now run properly. Firefox has JavaScript enabled by default.

---

1. Don't confuse the scripting language JavaScript with the programming language Java (from Sun Microsystems, Inc.). Java is a full-fledged object-oriented programming language. It can be used to develop applications that execute on a range of devices—from the smallest devices (such as cell phones and PDAs) to supercomputers. Java is popular for developing large-scale distributed enterprise applications and web applications. JavaScript is a browser-based scripting language developed by Netscape and implemented in all major browsers.

2. JavaScript was originally created by Netscape. Both Netscape and Microsoft have been instrumental in the standardization of JavaScript by ECMA International as ECMAScript. For more infomation on ECMAScript visit www.ecma-international.org/publications/standards/ECMA-262.htm.

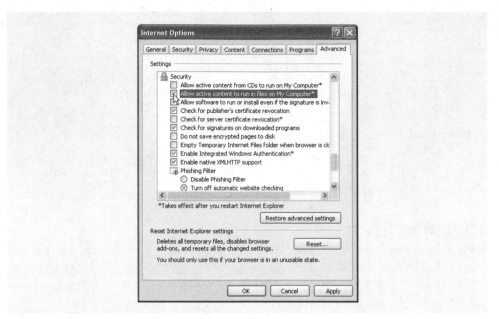

Fig. 4.1 | Enabling JavaScript in Internet Explorer 7

4.2 Simple Program: Displaying a Line of Text in a Web Page

JavaScript uses notations that are familiar to programmers. We begin by considering a simple *script* (or *program*) that displays the text "Welcome to JavaScript Programming!" in the body of an XHTML document. All major web browsers contain *JavaScript interpreters*, which process the commands written in JavaScript. The JavaScript code and its output in Internet Explorer are shown in Fig. 4.2.

```
1   <?xml version = "1.0" encoding = "utf-8"?>
2   <!DOCTYPE html PUBLIC "-//W3C//DTD XHTML 1.0 Strict//EN"
3       "http://www.w3.org/TR/xhtml1/DTD/xhtml1-strict.dtd">
4
5   <!-- Fig. 4.2: welcome.html -->
6   <!-- Displaying a line of text. -->
7   <html xmlns = "http://www.w3.org/1999/xhtml">
8      <head>
9         <title>A First Program in JavaScript</title>
10        <script type = "text/javascript">
11           <!--
12           document.writeln(
13              "<h1>Welcome to JavaScript Programming!</h1>" );
14           // -->
15        </script>
16     </head><body></body>
17  </html>
```

Fig. 4.2 | Displaying a line of text. (Part 1 of 2.)

Fig. 4.2 | Displaying a line of text. (Part 2 of 2.)

This program illustrates several important JavaScript features. We consider each line of the XHTML document and script in detail. As in the preceding chapters, we have given each XHTML document line numbers for your convenience; the line numbers are not part of the XHTML document or of the JavaScript programs. Lines 12–13 do the "real work" of the script, namely, displaying the phrase Welcome to JavaScript Programming! in the web page.

Line 8 indicates the beginning of the <head> section of the XHTML document. For the moment, the JavaScript code we write will appear in the <head> section. The browser interprets the contents of the <head> section first, so the JavaScript programs we write there execute before the <body> of the XHTML document displays. In later chapters on JavaScript and in the chapters on dynamic HTML, we illustrate *inline scripting*, in which JavaScript code is written in the <body> of an XHTML document.

Line 10 uses the *<script>* tag to indicate to the browser that the text which follows is part of a script. The *type* attribute specifies the type of file as well as the *scripting language* used in the script—in this case, a text file written in javascript. Both Internet Explorer and Firefox use JavaScript as the default scripting language.

Line 11 contains the XHTML opening comment tag <!--. Some older web browsers do not support scripting. In such browsers, the actual text of a script often will display in the web page. To prevent this from happening, many script programmers enclose the script code in an XHTML comment, so that browsers that do not support scripts will simply ignore the script. The syntax used is as follows:

```
<script type = "text/javascript">
   <!--
   script code here
   // -->
</script>
```

When a browser that does not support scripts encounters the preceding code, it ignores the <script> and </script> tags and the script code in the XHTML comment. Browsers that do support scripting will interpret the JavaScript code as expected. [*Note:* Some browsers require the *JavaScript single-line comment //* (see Section 4.4 for an explanation) before the ending XHTML comment delimiter (-->) to interpret the script properly. The opening HTML comment tag (<!--) also serves as a single-line comment delimiter in JavaScript, therefore it does not need to be commented.]

Portability Tip 4.1

Some browsers do not support the <script>...</script> tags. If your document is to be rendered with such browsers, enclose the script code between these tags in an XHTML comment, so that the script text does not get displayed as part of the web page. The closing comment tag of the XHTML comment (-->) is preceded by a JavaScript comment (//) to prevent the browser from trying to interpret the XHTML comment as a JavaScript statement.

Lines 12–13 instruct the browser's JavaScript interpreter to perform an *action*, namely, to display in the web page the *string* of characters contained between the *double quotation (") marks*. A string is sometimes called a *character string*, a *message* or a *string literal*. We refer to characters between double quotation marks as strings. Individual white-space characters between words in a string are not ignored by the browser. However, if consecutive spaces appear in a string, browsers condense them to a single space. Also, in most cases, browsers ignore leading white-space characters (i.e., white space at the beginning of a string).

Software Engineering Observation 4.1

Strings in JavaScript can be enclosed in either double quotation marks (") or single quotation marks (').

Lines 12–13 use the browser's *document object*, which represents the XHTML document the browser is currently displaying. The document object allows you to specify text to display in the XHTML document. The browser contains a complete set of objects that allow script programmers to access and manipulate every element of an XHTML document. In later chapters, we overview some of these objects as we discuss the Document Object Model (DOM).

An object resides in the computer's memory and contains information used by the script. The term *object* normally implies that *attributes* (*data*) and *behaviors* (*methods*) are associated with the object. The object's methods use the attributes to perform useful actions for the *client of the object* (i.e., the script that calls the methods). A method may require additional information (*arguments*) to perform its action; this information is enclosed in parentheses after the name of the method in the script. In lines 12–13, we call the document object's *writeln method* to write a line of XHTML markup in the XHTML document. The parentheses following the method name writeln contain the one argument that method writeln requires (in this case, the string of XHTML that the browser is to display). Method writeln instructs the browser to display the argument string. If the string contains XHTML elements, the browser interprets these elements and renders them on the screen. In this example, the browser displays the phrase Welcome to JavaScript Programming! as an h1-level XHTML heading, because the phrase is enclosed in an h1 element.

The code elements in lines 12–13, including document.writeln, its argument in the parentheses (the string) and the *semicolon* (;), together are called a *statement*. Every statement ends with a semicolon (also known as the *statement terminator*), although this practice is not required by JavaScript. Line 15 indicates the end of the script.

Good Programming Practice 4.1

Always include a semicolon at the end of a statement to terminate the statement. This notation clarifies where one statement ends and the next statement begins.

Common Programming Error 4.1

Forgetting the ending `</script>` *tag for a script may prevent the browser from interpreting the script properly and may prevent the XHTML document from loading or rendering properly.*

The `</head>` tag in line 16 indicates the end of the `<head>` section. Also in line 16, the tags `<body>` and `</body>` specify that this XHTML document has an empty body. Line 17 indicates the end of this XHTML document.

We are now ready to view our XHTML document in a web browser—open it in Internet Explorer or Firefox. If the script contains no syntax errors, it should produce the output shown in Fig. 4.2.

Common Programming Error 4.2

JavaScript is case sensitive. Not using the proper uppercase and lowercase letters is a syntax error—a violation of the rules of writing correct statements in the programming language. The JavaScript interpreter in Internet Explorer reports all syntax errors by indicating in a separate popup window that a runtime error has occurred (i.e., a problem occurred while the interpreter was running the script). [Note: To enable this feature in IE7, select **Internet Options...** *from the* **Tools** *menu. In the* **Internet Options** *dialog that appears, select the* **Advanced** *tab and click the checkbox labelled* **Display a notification about every script error** *under the* **Browsing** *category. Firefox has an error console that reports JavaScript errors and warnings. It is accessible by choosing* **Error Console** *from the* **Tools** *menu.]*

4.3 Modifying Our First Program

This section continues our introduction to JavaScript programming with two examples that modify the example in Fig. 4.2.

Displaying a Line of Colored Text

A script can display `Welcome to JavaScript Programming!` several ways. Figure 4.3 uses two JavaScript statements to produce one line of text in the XHTML document. This example also displays the text in a different color, using the CSS `color` property.

```
 1   <?xml version = "1.0" encoding = "utf-8"?>
 2   <!DOCTYPE html PUBLIC "-//W3C//DTD XHTML 1.0 Strict//EN"
 3      "http://www.w3.org/TR/xhtml/DTD/xhtml1-strict.dtd">
 4
 5   <!-- Fig. 4.3: welcome2.html -->
 6   <!-- Printing one line with multiple statements. -->
 7   <html xmlns = "http://www.w3.org/1999/xhtml">
 8      <head>
 9         <title>Printing a Line with Multiple Statements</title>
10         <script type = "text/javascript">
11            <!--
12            document.write( "<h1 style = \"color: magenta\">" );
```

Fig. 4.3 | Printing one line with separate statements. (Part 1 of 2.)

```
13        document.write( "Welcome to JavaScript " +
14           "Programming!</h1>" );
15        // -->
16     </script>
17  </head><body></body>
18 </html>
```

Fig. 4.3 | Printing one line with separate statements. (Part 2 of 2.)

Most of this document is identical to Fig. 4.2, so we concentrate only on lines 12–14 of Fig. 4.3, which display one line of text in the XHTML document. The first statement uses document method **write** to display a string. Unlike writeln, write does not position the output cursor in the XHTML document at the beginning of the next line after writing its argument. [*Note:* The output cursor keeps track of where the next character appears in the XHTML document, not where the next character appears in the web page as rendered by the browser.] The next character written in the XHTML document appears immediately after the last character written with write. Thus, when lines 13–14 execute, the first character written, "W," appears immediately after the last character displayed with write (the > character inside the right double quote in line 12). Each write or writeln statement resumes writing characters where the last write or writeln statement stopped writing characters. So, after a writeln statement, the next output appears on the beginning of the next line. In effect, the two statements in lines 12–14 result in one line of XHTML text. Remember that statements in JavaScript are separated by semicolons (;). Therefore, lines 13–14 represent only one complete statement. JavaScript allows large statements to be split over many lines. However, you cannot split a statement in the middle of a string. The + operator (called the "concatenation operator" when used in this manner) in line 13 joins two strings together and is explained in more detail later in this chapter.

Common Programming Error 4.3

Splitting a statement in the middle of a string is a syntax error.

Note that the characters \" (in line 12) are not displayed in the browser. The *back-slash* (\) in a string is an *escape character*. It indicates that a "special" character is to be used in the string. When a backslash is encountered in a string of characters, the next character is combined with the backslash to form an *escape sequence*. The escape sequence \" is the *double-quote character*, which causes a double-quote character to be inserted into the string. We use this escape sequence to insert double quotes around the attribute value for style without terminating the string. Note that we could also have used single quotes for the attribute value, as in document.write("<h1 style = 'color: magenta'>");, because the single quotes do not terminate a double-quoted string. We discuss escape sequences in greater detail momentarily.

It is important to note that the preceding discussion has nothing to do with the actual rendering of the XHTML text. Remember that the browser does not create a new line of text unless the browser window is too narrow for the text being rendered or the browser encounters an XHTML element that explicitly starts a new line—for example, <br/> to start a new line or <p> to start a new paragraph.

Common Programming Error 4.4

Many people confuse the writing of XHTML text with the rendering of XHTML text. Writing XHTML text creates the XHTML that will be rendered by the browser for presentation to the user.

Displaying Multiple Lines of Text

In the next example, we demonstrate that a single statement can cause the browser to display multiple lines by using line-break XHTML tags (<br/>) throughout the string of XHTML text in a write or writeln method call. Figure 4.4 demonstrates the use of line-break XHTML tags. Lines 12–13 produce three separate lines of text when the browser renders the XHTML document.

```
1   <?xml version = "1.0" encoding = "utf-8"?>
2   <!DOCTYPE html PUBLIC "-//W3C//DTD XHTML 1.0 Strict//EN"
3      "http://www.w3.org/TR/xhtml1/DTD/xhtml1-strict.dtd">
4
5   <!-- Fig. 4.4: welcome3.html -->
6   <!-- Printing on multiple lines with a single statement. -->
7   <html xmlns = "http://www.w3.org/1999/xhtml">
8      <head>
9         <title>Printing Multiple Lines</title>
10        <script type = "text/javascript">
11           <!--
12           document.writeln( "<h1>Welcome to<br />JavaScript" +
13              "<br />Programming!</h1>" );
14           // -->
15        </script>
16     </head><body></body>
17  </html>
```

Fig. 4.4 | Printing on multiple lines with a single statement.

Displaying Text in an Alert Dialog

The first several programs in this chapter display text in the XHTML document. Sometimes it is useful to display information in windows called *dialogs* (or *dialog boxes*) that "pop up" on the screen to grab the user's attention. Dialogs typically display important messages to users browsing the web page. JavaScript allows you easily to display a dialog box containing a message. The program in Fig. 4.5 displays Welcome to JavaScript Programming! as three lines in a predefined dialog called an *alert dialog*.

Line 12 in the script uses the browser's *window* object to display an alert dialog. The argument to the window object's *alert* method is the string to display. Executing the preceding statement displays the dialog shown in the first window of Fig. 4.5. The *title bar*

```
1   <?xml version = "1.0" encoding = "utf-8"?>
2   <!DOCTYPE html PUBLIC "-//W3C//DTD XHTML 1.0 Strict//EN"
3       "http://www.w3.org/TR/xhtml1/DTD/xhtml1-strict.dtd">
4
5   <!-- Fig. 4.5: welcome4.html -->
6   <!-- Alert dialog displaying multiple lines. -->
7   <html xmlns = "http://www.w3.org/1999/xhtml">
8       <head>
9           <title>Printing Multiple Lines in a Dialog Box</title>
10          <script type = "text/javascript">
11              <!--
12                  window.alert( "Welcome to\nJavaScript\nProgramming!" );
13              // -->
14          </script>
15      </head>
16      <body>
17          <p>Click Refresh (or Reload) to run this script again.</p>
18      </body>
19  </html>
```

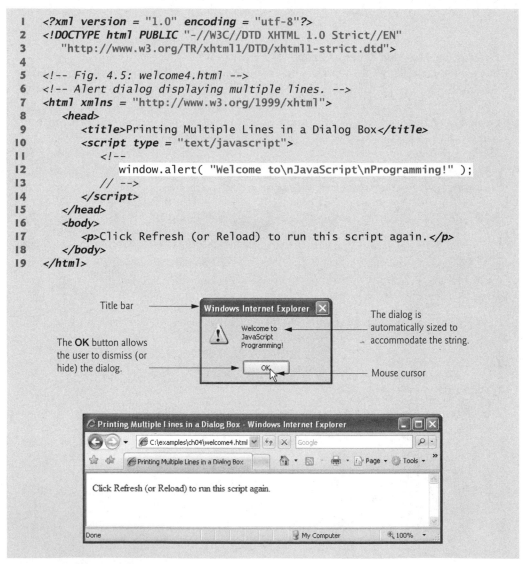

Fig. 4.5 | Alert dialog displaying multiple lines.

of the dialog contains the string **Windows Internet Explorer** to indicate that the browser is presenting a message to the user. The dialog provides an **OK** button that allows the user to *dismiss* (i.e., *close*) the dialog by clicking the button. To dismiss the dialog, position the *mouse cursor* (also called the *mouse pointer*) over the **OK** button and click the mouse. Firefox's alert dialog looks similar, but the title bar contains the text **[JavaScript Application]**.

Common Programming Error 4.5

Dialogs display plain text; they do not render XHTML. Therefore, specifying XHTML elements as part of a string to be displayed in a dialog results in the actual characters of the tags being displayed.

Note that the `alert` dialog contains three lines of plain text. Normally, a dialog displays the characters in a string exactly as they appear between the double quotes. Note, however, that the dialog does not display the characters \n. The escape sequence \n is the *newline character*. In a dialog, the newline character causes the *cursor* (i.e., the current screen position indicator) to move to the beginning of the next line in the dialog. Some other common escape sequences are listed in Fig. 4.6. The \n, \t and \r escape sequences in the table do not affect XHTML rendering unless they are in a *pre element* (this element displays the text between its tags in a fixed-width font exactly as it is formatted between the tags, including leading white-space characters and consecutive white-space characters). The other escape sequences result in characters that will be displayed in plain text dialogs and in XHTML.

Escape sequence	Description
\n	New line. Position the screen cursor at the beginning of the next line.
\t	Horizontal tab. Move the screen cursor to the next tab stop.
\r	Carriage return. Position the screen cursor to the beginning of the current line; do not advance to the next line. Any characters output after the carriage return overwrite the characters previously output on that line.
\\	Backslash. Used to represent a backslash character in a string.
\"	Double quote. Used to represent a double-quote character in a string contained in double quotes. For example, `window.alert( "\"in quotes\"" );` displays `"in quotes"` in an `alert` dialog.
\'	Single quote. Used to represent a single-quote character in a string. For example, `window.alert( '\'in quotes\'' );` displays `'in quotes'` in an `alert` dialog.

Fig. 4.6 | Some common escape sequences.

Common Programming Error 4.6

XHTML elements in an alert dialog's message are not interpreted as XHTML. This means that using <br />, for example, to create a line break in an alert box is an error. The string <br/> will simply be included in your message.

4.4 Obtaining User Input with prompt Dialogs

Scripting gives you the ability to generate part or all of a web page's content at the time it is shown to the user. A script can adapt the content based on input from the user or other variables, such as the time of day or the type of browser used by the client. Such web pages are said to be *dynamic*, as opposed to static, since their content has the ability to change. The next two subsections use scripts to demonstrate dynamic web pages.

4.4.1 Dynamic Welcome Page

Our next script builds on prior scripts to create a dynamic welcome page that obtains the user's name, then displays it on the page. The script uses another predefined dialog box from the window object—a *prompt* dialog—which allows the user to input a value that the script can use. The program asks the user to input a name, then displays the name in the XHTML document. Figure 4.7 presents the script and sample output. [*Note:* In later Java-Script chapters, we obtain input via GUI components in XHTML forms, as introduced in Chapter 2.]

```
 1   <?xml version = "1.0" encoding = "utf-8"?>
 2   <!DOCTYPE html PUBLIC "-//W3C//DTD XHTML 1.0 Strict//EN"
 3      "http://www.w3.org/TR/xhtml1/DTD/xhtml1-strict.dtd">
 4
 5   <!-- Fig. 4.7: welcome5.html -->
 6   <!-- Prompt box used on a welcome screen. -->
 7   <html xmlns = "http://www.w3.org/1999/xhtml">
 8      <head>
 9         <title>Using Prompt and Alert Boxes</title>
10         <script type = "text/javascript">
11            <!--
12            var name; // string entered by the user
13
14            // read the name from the prompt box as a string
15            name = window.prompt( "Please enter your name" );
16
17            document.writeln( "<h1>Hello, " + name +
18               ", welcome to JavaScript programming!</h1>" );
19            // -->
20         </script>
21      </head>
22      <body>
23         <p>Click Refresh (or Reload) to run this script again.</p>
24      </body>
25   </html>
```

Fig. 4.7 | Prompt box used on a welcome screen. (Part 1 of 2.)

Fig. 4.7 | Prompt box used on a welcome screen. (Part 2 of 2.)

Line 12 is a ***declaration*** that contains the JavaScript ***keyword*** var. Keywords are words that have special meaning in JavaScript. The keyword ***var*** at the beginning of the statement indicates that the word name is a ***variable***. A variable is a location in the computer's memory where a value can be stored for use by a program. All variables have a name, type and value, and should be declared with a var statement before they are used in a program. Although using var to declare variables is not required, we'll see in Chapter 7, JavaScript: Functions, that var sometimes ensures proper behavior of a script.

The name of a variable can be any valid ***identifier***. An identifier is a series of characters consisting of letters, digits, underscores (_) and dollar signs ($) that does not begin with a digit and is not a reserved JavaScript keyword. [*Note:* A complete list of keywords can be found in Fig. 5.1.] Identifiers may not contain spaces. Some valid identifiers are Welcome, $value, _value, m_inputField1 and button7. The name 7button is not a valid identifier, because it begins with a digit, and the name input field is not valid, because it contains a space. Remember that JavaScript is ***case sensitive***—uppercase and lowercase letters are considered to be different characters, so name, Name and NAME are different identifiers.

Good Programming Practice 4.2
Choosing meaningful variable names helps a script to be "self-documenting" (i.e., easy to understand by simply reading the script, rather than having to read manuals or extended comments).

Good Programming Practice 4.3
By convention, variable-name identifiers begin with a lowercase first letter. Each subsequent word should begin with a capital first letter. For example, identifier itemPrice has a capital P in its second word, Price.

Common Programming Error 4.7
Splitting a statement in the middle of an identifier is a syntax error.

Declarations end with a semicolon (;) and can be split over several lines with each variable in the declaration separated by a comma—known as a *comma-separated list* of variable names. Several variables may be declared either in one declaration or in multiple declarations.

In line 12, a *single-line comment* that begins with the characters // states the purpose of the variable in the script. This form of comment is called a single-line comment because it terminates at the end of the line in which it appears. A // comment can begin at any position in a line of JavaScript code and continues until the end of the line.

Good Programming Practice 4.4

Declare each variable on a separate line. This format allows for easy insertion of a descriptive comment next to each declaration—a widely followed professional coding standard.

Another comment notation facilitates writing *multiline comments*. For example,

```
/* This is a multiline
   comment. It can be
   split over many lines. */
```

is a multiline comment spread over several lines. Such comments begin with the delimiter /* and end with the delimiter */. All text between the delimiters of the comment is ignored by the interpreter.

Common Programming Error 4.8

Forgetting one of the delimiters of a multiline comment is a syntax error.

Common Programming Error 4.9

Nesting multiline comments (i.e., placing a multiline comment between the delimiters of another multiline comment) is a syntax error.

JavaScript adopted comments delimited with /* and */ from the C programming language and single-line comments delimited with // from the C++ programming language. JavaScript programmers generally prefer C++-style single-line comments over C-style comments. Throughout this book, we use C++-style single-line comments.

Line 14 is a comment indicating the purpose of the statement in the next line. Line 15 calls the window object's prompt method, which displays the dialog in Fig. 4.8. The dialog allows the user to enter a string representing the user's name.

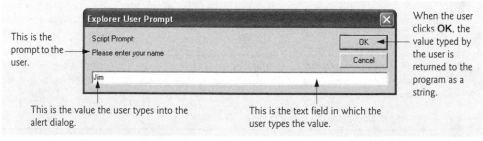

Fig. 4.8 | Prompt dialog displayed by the window object's prompt method.

The argument to `prompt` specifies a message telling the user what to type in the text field. An optional second argument, separated from the first by a comma, may specify the default string displayed in the text field; our code does not supply a second argument. In this case, Internet Explorer displays the default value `undefined`, while Firefox and most other browsers leave the text field empty. The user types characters in the text field, then clicks the **OK** button to submit the string to the program. We normally receive input from a user through a GUI component such as the `prompt` dialog, as in this program, or through an XHTML form GUI component, as we'll see in later chapters.

The user can type anything in the text field of the `prompt` dialog. For this program, whatever the user enters is considered the name. If the user clicks the **Cancel** button, no string value is sent to the program. Instead, the `prompt` dialog submits the value ***null***, a JavaScript keyword signifying that a variable has no value. Note that `null` is not a string literal, but rather a predefined term indicating the absence of value. Writing a `null` value to the document, however, displays the word `null` in the web page.

The statement in line 15 *assigns* the value returned by the `window` object's `prompt` method (a string containing the characters typed by the user—or the default value or `null` if the **Cancel** button is clicked) to variable `name` by using the ***assignment operator***, `=`. The statement is read as, "`name` gets the value returned by `window.prompt( "Please enter your name" )`." The `=` operator is called a ***binary operator*** because it has two ***operands***— `name` and the result of the expression `window.prompt( "Please enter your name" )`. The expression to the right of the assignment operator is always evaluated first.

Good Programming Practice 4.5

Place spaces on either side of a binary operator. This format makes the operator stand out and makes the program more readable.

Lines 17–18 use `document.writeln` to display the new welcome message. The expression inside the parentheses uses the operator `+` to "add" a string (the literal `"<h1>Hello, "`), the variable `name` (the string that the user entered in line 15) and another string (the literal `", welcome to JavaScript programming!</h1>"`). JavaScript has a version of the `+` operator for ***string concatenation*** that enables a string and a value of another data type (including another string) to be combined. The result of this operation is a new (and normally longer) string. If we assume that `name` contains the string literal `"Jim"`, the expression evaluates as follows: JavaScript determines that the two operands of the first `+` operator (the string `"<h1>Hello, "` and the value of variable `name`) are both strings, then concatenates the two into one string. Next, JavaScript determines that the two operands of the second `+` operator (the result of the first concatenation operation, the string `"<h1>Hello, Jim"`, and the string `", welcome to JavaScript programming!</h1>"`) are both strings and concatenates the two. This results in the string `"<h1>Hello, Jim, welcome to JavaScript programming!</h1>"`. The browser renders this string as part of the XHTML document. Note that the space between `Hello,` and `Jim` is part of the string `"<h1>Hello, "`.

As we'll illustrate later, the `+` operator used for string concatenation can convert other variable types to strings if necessary. Because string concatenation occurs between two strings, JavaScript must convert other variable types to strings before it can proceed with the operation. For example, if a variable `age` has the integer value 21, then the expression `"my age is "` + `age` evaluates to the string `"my age is 21"`. JavaScript converts the value of `age` to a string and concatenates it with the existing string literal `"my age is "`.

After the browser interprets the <head> section of the XHTML document (which contains the JavaScript), it then interprets the <body> (lines 22–24) and renders the XHTML. Notice that the XHTML page is not rendered until the prompt is dismissed because the prompt pauses execution in the head, before the body is processed. If you click your browser's **Refresh** (Internet Explorer) or **Reload** (Firefox) button after entering a name, the browser will reload the XHTML document, so that you can execute the script again and change the name. [*Note:* In some cases, it may be necessary to hold down the *Shift* key while clicking the **Refresh** or **Reload** button, to ensure that the XHTML document reloads properly. Browsers often save a recent copy of a page in memory, and holding the *Shift* key forces the browser to download the most recent version of a page.]

4.4.2 Adding Integers

Our next script illustrates another use of prompt dialogs to obtain input from the user. Figure 4.9 inputs two *integers* (whole numbers, such as 7, −11, 0 and 31914) typed by a user at the keyboard, computes the sum of the values and displays the result.

Lines 12–16 declare the variables firstNumber, secondNumber, number1, number2 and sum. Single-line comments state the purpose of each of these variables. Line 19 employs a prompt dialog to allow the user to enter a string representing the first of the two integers that will be added. The script assigns the first value entered by the user to the

```
1   <?xml version = "1.0" encoding = "utf-8"?>
2   <!DOCTYPE html PUBLIC "-//W3C//DTD XHTML 1.0 Strict//EN"
3      "http://www.w3.org/TR/xhtml1/DTD/xhtml1-strict.dtd">
4
5   <!-- Fig. 4.9: addition.html -->
6   <!-- Addition script. -->
7   <html xmlns = "http://www.w3.org/1999/xhtml">
8      <head>
9         <title>An Addition Program</title>
10        <script type = "text/javascript">
11           <!--
12           var firstNumber; // first string entered by user
13           var secondNumber; // second string entered by user
14           var number1; // first number to add
15           var number2; // second number to add
16           var sum; // sum of number1 and number2
17
18           // read in first number from user as a string
19           firstNumber = window.prompt( "Enter first integer" );
20
21           // read in second number from user as a string
22           secondNumber = window.prompt( "Enter second integer" );
23
24           // convert numbers from strings to integers
25           number1 = parseInt( firstNumber );
26           number2 = parseInt( secondNumber );
27
28           sum = number1 + number2; // add the numbers
```

Fig. 4.9 | Addition script. (Part 1 of 2.)

```
29
30              // display the results
31              document.writeln( "<h1>The sum is " + sum + "</h1>" );
32              // -->
33          </script>
34      </head>
35      <body>
36          <p>Click Refresh (or Reload) to run the script again</p>
37      </body>
38  </html>
```

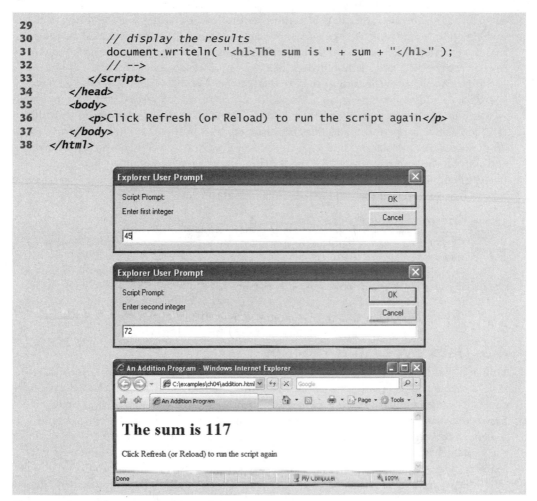

Fig. 4.9 | Addition script. (Part 2 of 2.)

variable firstNumber. Line 22 displays a prompt dialog to obtain the second number to add and assign this value to the variable secondNumber.

As in the preceding example, the user can type anything in the prompt dialog. For this program, if the user either types a noninteger value or clicks the **Cancel** button, a logic error will occur, and the sum of the two values will appear in the XHTML document as *NaN* (meaning *not a number*). A logic error is caused by syntactically correct code that produces an undesired result. In Chapter 9, JavaScript: Objects, we discuss the Number object and its methods that can determine whether a value is not a number.

Recall that a prompt dialog returns to the program as a string the value typed by the user. Lines 25–26 convert the two strings input by the user to integer values that can be used in a calculation. Function *parseInt* converts its string argument to an integer. Line 25 assigns to the variable number1 the integer that function parseInt returns. Line 26 assigns an integer value to variable number2 in a similar manner. Any subsequent references to number1 and number2 in the program use these integer values. [*Note:* We refer to parseInt as a *function* rather than a method because we do not precede the function call with an object name (such as document or window) and a dot (.). The term method means that the function belongs to a particular object. For example, method writeln belongs to the document object and method prompt belongs to the window object.]

Line 28 calculates the sum of the variables number1 and number2 using the *addition operator*, +, and assigns the result to variable sum by using the assignment operator, =. Notice that the + operator can perform both addition and string concatenation. In this case, the + operator performs addition, because both operands contain integers. After line 28 performs this calculation, line 31 uses document.writeln to display the result of the addition on the web page. Lines 33 and 34 close the script and head elements, respectively. Lines 35–37 render the body of XHTML document. Use your browser's **Refresh** or **Reload** button to reload the XHTML document and run the script again.

Common Programming Error 4.10

Confusing the + operator used for string concatenation with the + operator used for addition often leads to undesired results. For example, if integer variable y has the value 5, the expression "y + 2 = " + y + 2 results in "y + 2 = 52", not "y + 2 = 7", because first the value of y (i.e., 5) is concatenated with the string "y + 2 = ", then the value 2 is concatenated with the new, larger string "y + 2 = 5". The expression "y + 2 = " + (y + 2) produces the string "y + 2 = 7" because the parentheses ensure that y + 2 is executed mathematically before it is conveted to a string.

4.5 Data Types in JavaScript

Unlike its predecessor languages C, C++ and Java, JavaScript does not require variables to have a declared type before they can be used in a program. A variable in JavaScript can contain a value of any data type, and in many situations JavaScript automatically converts between values of different types for you. For this reason, JavaScript is referred to as a *loosely typed language*. When a variable is declared in JavaScript, but is not given a value, the variable has an *undefined* value. Attempting to use the value of such a variable is normally a logic error.

When variables are declared, they are not assigned values unless specified by you. Assigning the value null to a variable indicates that it does not contain a value.

4.6 Arithmetic

Many scripts perform arithmetic calculations. The *arithmetic operators* use various special symbols that are not used in algebra. The *asterisk (*)* indicates multiplication; the *percent sign (%)* is the *remainder operator*, which will be discussed shortly. The arithmetic operators are binary operators—each operates on two operands. For example, the expression sum + value contains the binary operator + and the two operands sum and value.

JavaScript provides the remainder operator, %, which yields the remainder after division. [*Note:* The % operator is known as the modulus operator in some programming languages.] The expression x % y yields the remainder after x is divided by y. Thus, 17 % 5 yields 2 (i.e., 17 divided by 5 is 3, with a remainder of 2), and 7.4 % 3.1 yields 1.2. In later chapters, we consider applications of the remainder operator, such as determining whether one number is a multiple of another. There is no arithmetic operator for exponentiation in JavaScript. (Chapter 6, JavaScript: Control Statements II, shows how to perform exponentiation in JavaScript using the Math object's pow method.)

4.7 Decision Making: Equality and Relational Operators

This section introduces a version of JavaScript's *if* statement that allows a program to make a decision based on the truth or falsity of a *condition*. If the condition is met (i.e., the condition is *true*), the statement in the body of the if statement is executed. If the condition is not met (i.e., the condition is *false*), the statement in the body of the if statement is not executed. We'll see an example shortly. [*Note:* Other versions of the if statement are introduced in Chapter 5, JavaScript: Control Statements I.]

Conditions in if statements can be formed by using the *equality operators* and *relational operators* summarized in Fig. 4.10. The relational operators all have the same level of precedence and associate from left to right. The equality operators both have the same level of precedence, which is lower than the precedence of the relational operators. The equality operators also associate from left to right.

Common Programming Error 4.11
It is a syntax error if the operators ==, !=, >= and <= contain spaces between their symbols, as in = =, ! =, > = and < =, respectively.

Common Programming Error 4.12
Reversing the operators !=, >= and <=, as in =!, => and =<, respectively, is a syntax error.

Common Programming Error 4.13
Confusing the equality operator, ==, with the assignment operator, =, is a logic error. The equality operator should be read as "is equal to," and the assignment operator should be read as "gets" or "gets the value of." Some people prefer to read the equality operator as "double equals" or "equals equals."

Standard algebraic equality operator or relational operator	JavaScript equality or relational operator	Sample JavaScript condition	Meaning of JavaScript condition
Equality operators			
=	==	x == y	x is equal to y
≠	!=	x != y	x is not equal to y
Relational operators			
>	>	x > y	x is greater than y
<	<	x < y	x is less than y
≥	>=	x >= y	x is greater than or equal to y
≤	<=	x <= y	x is less than or equal to y

Fig. 4.10 | Equality and relational operators.

The script in Fig. 4.11 uses four if statements to display a time-sensitive greeting on a welcome page. The script obtains the local time from the user's computer and converts it from 24-hour clock format (0–23) to a 12-hour clock format (0–11). Using this value, the script displays an appropriate greeting for the current time of day. The script and sample output are shown in Fig. 4.11.

```
1   <?xml version = "1.0" encoding = "utf-8"?>
2   <!DOCTYPE html PUBLIC "-//W3C//DTD XHTML 1.0 Strict//EN"
3      "http://www.w3.org/TR/xhtml1/DTD/xhtml1-strict.dtd">
4
5   <!-- Fig. 4.11: welcome6.html -->
6   <!-- Using equality and relational operators. -->
7   <html xmlns = "http://www.w3.org/1999/xhtml">
8      <head>
9         <title>Using Relational Operators</title>
10        <script type = "text/javascript">
11           <!--
12           var name; // string entered by the user
13           var now = new Date();      // current date and time
14           var hour = now.getHours(); // current hour (0-23)
15
16           // read the name from the prompt box as a string
17           name = window.prompt( "Please enter your name" );
18
19           // determine whether it is morning
20           if ( hour < 12 )
21              document.write( "<h1>Good Morning, " );
22
23           // determine whether the time is PM
24           if ( hour >= 12 )
25           {
26              // convert to a 12-hour clock
27              hour = hour - 12;
28
29              // determine whether it is before 6 PM
30              if ( hour < 6 )
31                 document.write( "<h1>Good Afternoon, " );
32
33              // determine whether it is after 6 PM
34              if ( hour >= 6 )
35                 document.write( "<h1>Good Evening, " );
36           } // end if
37
38           document.writeln( name +
39              ", welcome to JavaScript programming!</h1>" );
40           // -->
41        </script>
42     </head>
43     <body>
44        <p>Click Refresh (or Reload) to run this script again.</p>
45     </body>
46  </html>
```

Fig. 4.11 | Using equality and relational operators. (Part 1 of 2.)

Fig. 4.11 | Using equality and relational operators. (Part 2 of 2.)

Lines 12–14 declare the variables used in the script. Remember that variables may be declared in one declaration or in multiple declarations. If more than one variable is declared in a single declaration (as in this example), the names are separated by commas (,). This list of names is referred to as a comma-separated list. Once again, note the comment at the end of each line, indicating the purpose of each variable in the program. Also note that some of the variables are assigned a value in the declaration—JavaScript allows you to assign a value to a variable when the variable is declared.

Line 13 sets the variable now to a new ***Date object***, which contains information about the current local time. In Section 4.2, we introduced the document object, an object that encapsulates data pertaining to the current web page. Programmers may choose to use other objects to perform specific tasks or obtain particular pieces of information. Here, we use JavaScript's built-in Date object to acquire the current local time. We create a new instance of an object by using the ***new*** operator followed by the type of the object, Date, and a pair of parentheses. Some objects require that arguments be placed in the parentheses to specify details about the object to be created. In this case, we leave the parentheses empty to create a default Date object containing information about the current date and time. After line 13 executes, the variable now refers to the new Date object. [*Note:* We did not need to use the new operator when we used the document and window objects because these objects always are created by the browser.] Line 14 sets the variable hour to an integer equal to the current hour (in a 24-hour clock format) returned by the Date object's get-Hours method. Chapter 9 presents a more detailed discussion of the Date object's attributes and methods, and of objects in general. As in the preceding example, the script uses window.prompt to allow the user to enter a name to display as part of the greeting (line 17).

To display the correct time-sensitive greeting, the script must determine whether the user is visiting the page during the morning, afternoon or evening. The first if statement (lines 20–21) compares the value of variable hour with 12. If hour is less than 12, then the user is visiting the page during the morning, and the statement at line 21 outputs the string "Good morning". If this condition is not met, line 21 is not executed. Line 24 determines whether hour is greater than or equal to 12. If hour is greater than or equal to 12, then the user is visiting the page in either the afternoon or the evening. Lines 25–36 execute to determine the appropriate greeting. If hour is less than 12, then the JavaScript interpreter does not execute these lines and continues to line 38.

The brace { in line 25 begins a block of statements (lines 27–35) that are executed if hour is greater than or equal to 12—to execute multiple statements inside an if construct, enclose them in curly braces. Line 27 subtracts 12 from hour, converting the current hour from a 24-hour clock format (0–23) to a 12-hour clock format (0–11). The if statement (line 30) determines whether hour is now less than 6. If it is, then the time is between noon and 6 PM, and line 31 outputs the beginning of an XHTML h1 element ("<h1>Good Afternoon, "). If hour is greater than or equal to 6, the time is between 6 PM and midnight, and the script outputs the greeting "Good Evening" (lines 34–35). The brace } in line 36 ends the block of statements associated with the if statement in line 24. Note that if statements can be *nested*, i.e., one if statement can be placed inside another if statement. The if statements that determine whether the user is visiting the page in the afternoon or the evening (lines 30–31 and lines 34–35) execute only if the script has already established that hour is greater than or equal to 12 (line 24). If the script has already determined the current time of day to be morning, these additional comparisons are not performed. (Chapter 5 presents a more in-depth discussion of blocks and nested if statements.) Finally, lines 38–39 output the rest of the XHTML h1 element (the remaining part of the greeting), which does not depend on the time of day.

Good Programming Practice 4.6

Include comments after the closing curly brace of control statements (such as if statements) to indicate where the statements end, as in line 36 of Fig. 4.11.

Note that there is no semicolon (;) at the end of the first line of each if statement. Including such a semicolon would result in a logic error at execution time. For example,

```
if ( hour < 12 ) ;
    document.write( "<h1>Good Morning, " );
```

would actually be interpreted by JavaScript erroneously as

```
if ( hour < 12 )
    ;

document.write( "<h1>Good Morning, " );
```

where the semicolon on the line by itself—called the *empty statement*—is the statement to execute if the condition in the if statement is true. When the empty statement executes, no task is performed in the program. The program then continues with the next statement, which executes regardless of whether the condition is true or false. In this example, "<h1>Good Morning, " would be printed regardless of the time of day.

Common Programming Error 4.14

Placing a semicolon immediately after the right parenthesis of the condition in an if statement is normally a logic error. The semicolon would cause the body of the if statement to be empty, so the if statement itself would perform no action, regardless of whether its condition was true. Worse yet, the intended body statement of the if statement would now become a statement in sequence after the if statement and would always be executed.

Common Programming Error 4.15

Leaving out a condition in a series of if statements is normally a logic error. For instance, check-ing if hour is greater than 12 or less than 12, but not if hour is equal to 12, would mean that the script takes no action when hour is equal to 12. Always be sure to handle every possible con-dition.

Note the use of spacing in lines 38–39 of Fig. 4.11. Remember that white-space char-acters, such as tabs, newlines and spaces, are normally ignored by the browser. So, state-ments may be split over several lines and may be spaced according to your preferences without affecting the meaning of a program. However, it is incorrect to split identifiers and string literals. Ideally, statements should be kept small, but it is not always possible to do so.

The chart in Fig. 4.12 shows the precedence of the operators introduced in this chapter. The operators are shown from top to bottom in decreasing order of precedence. Note that all of these operators, with the exception of the assignment operator, =, associate from left to right. Addition is left associative, so an expression like x + y + z is evaluated as if it had been written as (x + y) + z. The assignment operator, =, associates from right to left, so an expression like x = y = 0 is evaluated as if it had been written as x = (y = 0), which first assigns the value 0 to variable y, then assigns the result of that assignment, 0, to x.

Operators	Associativity	Type
* / %	left to right	multiplicative
+ -	left to right	additive
< <= > >=	left to right	relational
== !=	left to right	equality
=	right to left	assignment

Fig. 4.12 | Precedence and associativity of the operators discussed so far.

4.8 Web Resources

www.deitel.com/javascript

The Deitel JavaScript Resource Center contains links to some of the best JavaScript resources on the web. There you'll find categorized links to JavaScript tutorials, tools, code generators, forums, books, libraries, frameworks and more.

5

JavaScript: Control Statements I

OBJECTIVES

In this chapter you'll learn:

- To use the `if` and `if...else` selection statements to choose among alternative actions.

- To use the `while` repetition statement to execute statements in a script repeatedly.

- Counter-controlled repetition and sentinel-controlled repetition.

- To use the increment, decrement and assignment operators.

5.1 Introduction

When writing a script, it is essential to understand the types of building blocks that are available and to employ proven program-construction principles. In this chapter and in Chapter 6, we discuss JavaScript's control statements, which are similar to those in many other high-level languages. We also introduce JavaScript's assignment operators and explore its increment and decrement operators. These additional operators abbreviate and simplify many program statements.

5.2 Control Statements

JavaScript provides three types of selection statements; we discuss each in this chapter and in Chapter 6. The if selection statement performs (selects) an action if a condition is true or skips the action if the condition is false. The if...else selection statement qperforms an action if a condition is true and performs a different action if the condition is false. The switch selection statement (Chapter 6) performs one of many different actions, depending on the value of an expression.

The *if* statement is called a *single-selection statement* because it selects or ignores a single action (or, as we'll soon see, a single group of actions). The if...else statement is a *double-selection statement* because it selects between two different actions (or groups of actions). The switch statement is a *multiple-selection statement* because it selects among many different actions (or groups of actions).

JavaScript provides four repetition statement types, namely *while*, do...while, for and for...in. (do...while and for are covered in Chapter 6; for...in is covered in Chapter 8.) Each of the words if, else, switch, while, do, for and in is a JavaScript *keyword*. These words are reserved by the language to implement various features, such as JavaScript's control statements. Keywords cannot be used as identifiers (e.g., for variable names). A list of JavaScript keywords is shown in Fig. 5.1.

Common Programming Error 5.1

Using a keyword as an identifier is a syntax error.

JavaScript keywords				
break	case	catch	continue	default
delete	do	else	false	finally
for	function	if	in	instanceof
new	null	return	switch	this
throw	true	try	typeof	var
void	while	with		

Keywords that are reserved but not used by JavaScript

abstract	boolean	byte	char	class
const	debugger	double	enum	export
extends	final	float	goto	implements
import	int	interface	long	native
package	private	protected	public	short
static	super	synchronized	throws	transient
volatile				

Fig. 5.1 | JavaScript keywords.

As we have shown, JavaScript has only eight control structures: sequence, three types of selection and four types of repetition. A program is formed by combining control statements as necessary to implement the program's algorithm.

Single-entry/single-exit control statements make it easy to build programs; the control statements are attached to one another by connecting the exit point of one to the entry point of the next. This process is called *control-statement stacking*. We'll learn that there is only one other way in which control statements may be connected—*control-statement nesting*. Thus JavaScript programs are constructed from only eight different types of control statements combined in only two ways.

5.3 if Selection Statement

A selection statement is used to choose among alternative courses of action in a program. For example, suppose that the passing grade on an examination is 60 (out of 100). Then the JavaScript statement

```
if ( studentGrade >= 60 )
    document.writeln( "Passed" );
```

determines whether the condition "student's grade is greater than or equal to 60" is true or false. If the condition is true, then "Passed" is output in the XHTML document, and the next JavaScript statement in order is performed. If the condition is false, the print statement is ignored, and the next JavaScript statement in order is performed.

Note that the second line of this selection statement is indented. The JavaScript interpreter ignores white-space characters—blanks, tabs and newlines used for indentation and vertical spacing.

The flowchart in Fig. 5.2 illustrates the single-selection if statement. This flowchart contains what is perhaps the most important flowcharting symbol—the diamond symbol

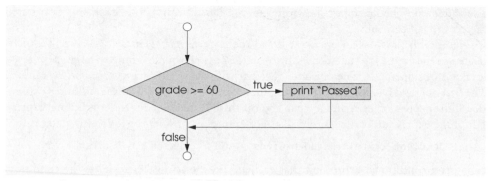

Fig. 5.2 | Flowcharting the single-selection if statement.

(or decision symbol), which indicates that a decision is to be made. The decision symbol contains an expression, such as a condition, that can be either *true* or *false*. The decision symbol has two flowlines emerging from it. One indicates the path to follow in the program when the expression in the symbol is true; the other indicates the path to follow in the program when the expression is false. A decision can be made on any expression that evaluates to a value of JavaScript's boolean type (i.e., any expression that evaluates to true or false—also known as a *boolean expression*).

Software Engineering Observation 5.1

In JavaScript, any nonzero numeric value in a condition evaluates to true, and 0 evaluates to false. For strings, any string containing one or more characters evaluates to true, and the empty string (the string containing no characters, represented as "") evaluates to false. Also, a variable that has been declared with var but has not been assigned a value evaluates to false.

Note that the if statement is a single-entry/single-exit control statement. Flowcharts for the remaining control statements also contain (besides small circle symbols and flowlines) only rectangle symbols, to indicate the actions to be performed, and diamond symbols, to indicate decisions to be made. This type of flowchart represents the *action/decision model of programming*.

5.4 if...else Selection Statement

The if selection statement performs an indicated action only when the condition evaluates to true; otherwise, the action is skipped. The *if...else selection* statement allows you to specify that a different action is to be performed when the condition is true than when the condition is false. For example, the JavaScript statement

```
if ( studentGrade >= 60 )
    document.writeln( "Passed" );
else
    document.writeln( "Failed" );
```

outputs Passed in the XHTML document if the student's grade is greater than or equal to 60 and outputs Failed if the student's grade is less than 60. In either case, after printing occurs, the next JavaScript statement in sequence (i.e., the next statement after the whole if...else statement) is performed. Note that the body of the else part of the structure is also indented. The flowchart shown in Fig. 5.3 illustrates the if...else selection statement's flow of control.

JavaScript provides an operator, called the ***conditional operator*** (***?:***), that is closely related to the if...else statement. The operator ?: is JavaScript's only ***ternary operator***—it takes three operands. The operands together with the ?: form a ***conditional expression***. The first operand is a boolean expression, the second is the value for the conditional expression if the expression evaluates to true and the third is the value for the conditional expression if the expression evaluates to false. For example, consider the following statement

```
document.writeln( studentGrade >= 60 ? "Passed" : "Failed" );
```

contains a conditional expression that evaluates to the string "Passed" if the condition studentGrade >= 60 is true and evaluates to the string "Failed" if the condition is false. Thus, this statement with the conditional operator performs essentially the same operation as the preceding if...else statement. The precedence of the conditional operator is low, so the entire conditional expression is normally placed in parentheses to ensure that it evaluates correctly.

Nested if...else statements test for multiple cases by placing if...else statements inside if...else statements. For example, the following pseudocode statement indicates that the program should print A for exam grades greater than or equal to 90, B for grades in the range 80 to 89, C for grades in the range 70 to 79, D for grades in the range 60 to 69 and F for all other grades:

```
if ( studentGrade >= 90 )
   document.writeln( "A" );
else
   if ( studentGrade >= 80 )
      document.writeln( "B" );
   else
      if ( studentGrade >= 70 )
         document.writeln( "C" );
      else
         if ( studentGrade >= 60 )
            document.writeln( "D" );
         else
            document.writeln( "F" );
```

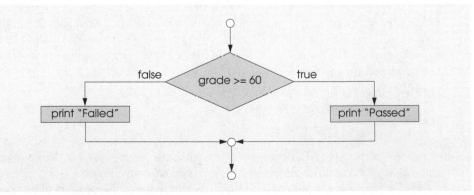

Fig. 5.3 | Flowcharting the double-selection if...else statement.

If studentGrade is greater than or equal to 90, all four conditions will be true, but only the document.writeln statement after the first test will execute. After that particular document.writeln executes, the else part of the outer if...else statements is skipped.

Good Programming Practice 5.1

If there are several levels of indentation, each level should be indented the same additional amount of space.

Most JavaScript programmers prefer to write the preceding if statement as

```
if ( grade >= 90 )
    document.writeln( "A" );
else if ( grade >= 80 )
    document.writeln( "B" );
else if ( grade >= 70 )
    document.writeln( "C" );
else if ( grade >= 60 )
    document.writeln( "D" );
else
    document.writeln( "F" );
```

The two forms are equivalent. The latter form is popular because it avoids the deep indentation of the code to the right. Such deep indentation often leaves little room on a line, forcing lines to be split and decreasing program readability.

It is important to note that the JavaScript interpreter always associates an else with the previous if, unless told to do otherwise by the placement of braces ({}). This situation is referred to as the *dangling-else problem*. For example,

```
if ( x > 5 )
    if ( y > 5 )
        document.writeln( "x and y are > 5" );
else
    document.writeln( "x is <= 5" );
```

appears to indicate with its indentation that if x is greater than 5, the if statement in its body determines whether y is also greater than 5. If so, the body of the nested if statement outputs the string "x and y are > 5". Otherwise, it *appears* that if x is not greater than 5, the else part of the if...else statement outputs the string "x is <= 5".

Beware! The preceding nested if statement does not execute as it appears. The interpreter actually interprets the preceding statement as

```
if ( x > 5 )
    if ( y > 5 )
        document.writeln( "x and y are > 5" );
    else
        document.writeln( "x is <= 5" );
```

in which the body of the first if statement is a nested if...else statement. This statement tests whether x is greater than 5. If so, execution continues by testing whether y is also greater than 5. If the second condition is true, the proper string—"x and y are > 5"—is displayed. However, if the second condition is false, the string "x is <= 5" is displayed, even though we know that x is greater than 5.

To force the preceding nested `if` statement to execute as it was intended originally, it must be written as follows:

```
if ( x > 5 )
{
   if ( y > 5 )
      document.writeln( "x and y are > 5" );
}
else
   document.writeln( "x is <= 5" );
```

The braces (`{}`) indicate to the interpreter that the second `if` statement is in the body of the first `if` statement and that the `else` is matched with the first `if` statement.

The `if` selection statement expects only one statement in its body. To include several statements in an `if` statement's body, enclose the statements in braces (`{` and `}`). This can also be done in the else section of an `if...else` statement. A set of statements contained within a pair of braces is called a ***block***.

Software Engineering Observation 5.2

A block can be placed anywhere in a program that a single statement can be placed.

Software Engineering Observation 5.3

Unlike individual statements, a block does not end with a semicolon. However, each statement within the braces of a block should end with a semicolon.

The following example includes a block in the `else` part of an `if...else` statement:

```
if ( grade >= 60 )
   document.writeln( "Passed" );
else
{
   document.writeln( "Failed<br />" );
   document.writeln( "You must take this course again." );
}
```

In this case, if `grade` is less than 60, the program executes both statements in the body of the `else` and prints

```
Failed.
You must take this course again.
```

Note the braces surrounding the two statements in the `else` clause. These braces are important. Without them, the statement

```
document.writeln( "You must take this course again." );
```

would be outside the body of the `else` part of the `if` and would execute regardless of whether the grade is less than 60.

Common Programming Error 5.2

Forgetting one or both of the braces that delimit a block can lead to syntax errors or logic errors.

Good Programming Practice 5.2

Some programmers prefer to type the beginning and ending braces of blocks before typing the individual statements within the braces. This helps avoid omitting one or both of the braces.

Software Engineering Observation 5.4

Just as a block can be placed anywhere a single statement can be placed, it is also possible to have no statement at all (the empty statement) in such places. The empty statement is represented by placing a semicolon (;) where a statement would normally be.

Common Programming Error 5.3

Placing a semicolon after the condition in an if statement leads to a logic error in single-selection if statement and a syntax error in double-selection if statements (if the if part contains a non-empty body statement).

5.5 while Repetition Statement

A repetition statement allows you to specify that a script is to repeat an action while some condition remains true.

Common Programming Error 5.4

*If the body of a while statement never causes the while statement's condition to become true, a logic error occurs. Normally, such a repetition structure will never terminate—an error called an **infinite loop**. Both Internet Explorer and Firefox show a dialog allowing the user to terminate a script that contains an infinite loop.*

Common Programming Error 5.5

Remember that JavaScript is a case-sensitive language. In code, spelling the keyword while with an uppercase W, as in While, is a syntax error. All of JavaScript's reserved keywords, such as while, if and else, contain only lowercase letters.

As an example of a while statement, consider a program segment designed to find the first power of 2 larger than 1000. Variable product begins with the value 2:

```
var product = 2;

while ( product <= 1000 )
   product = 2 * product;
```

When the while statement finishes executing, product contains the result 1024. The flowchart in Fig. 5.4 illustrates the flow of control of the preceding while statement.

When the script enters the while statement, product is 2. The script repeatedly multiplies variable product by 2, so product takes on the values 4, 8, 16, 32, 64, 128, 256, 512 and 1024 successively. When product becomes 1024, the condition product <= 1000 in the while statement becomes false. This terminates the repetition, with 1024 as product's final value. Execution continues with the next statement after the while statement. [*Note:* If a while statement's condition is initially false, the body statement(s) will never execute.]

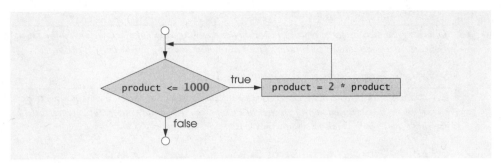

Fig. 5.4 | Flowcharting the `while` repetition statement.

5.6 Counter-Controlled Repetition

Consider the following problem statement:

> *A class of ten students took a quiz. The grades (integers in the range 0 to 100) for this quiz are available to you. Determine the class average on the quiz.*

The class average is equal to the sum of the grades divided by the number of students (10 in this case). The program for this problem (Fig. 5.5) must input each of the grades, perform the averaging calculation and display the result. We use *counter-controlled repetition* to input the grades one at a time. In this example, repetition terminates when the counter exceeds 10.

```
 1  <?xml version = "1.0" encoding = "utf-8"?>
 2  <!DOCTYPE html PUBLIC "-//W3C//DTD XHTML 1.0 Strict//EN"
 3     "http://www.w3.org/TR/xhtml1/DTD/xhtml1-strict.dtd">
 4
 5  <!-- Fig. 5.5: average.html -->
 6  <!-- Counter-controlled repetition to calculate a class average. -->
 7  <html xmlns = "http://www.w3.org/1999/xhtml">
 8     <head>
 9        <title>Class Average Program</title>
10        <script type = "text/javascript">
11           <!--
12           var total; // sum of grades
13           var gradeCounter; // number of grades entered
14           var grade; // grade typed by user (as a string)
15           var gradeValue; // grade value (converted to integer)
16           var average; // average of all grades
17
18           // Initialization Phase
19           total = 0; // clear total
20           gradeCounter = 1; // prepare to loop
21
22           // Processing Phase
23           while ( gradeCounter <= 10 ) // loop 10 times
24           {
25
```

Fig. 5.5 | Counter-controlled repetition to calculate a class average. (Part 1 of 2.)

```
26              // prompt for input and read grade from user
27              grade = window.prompt( "Enter integer grade:", "0" );
28
29              // convert grade from a string to an integer
30              gradeValue = parseInt( grade );
31
32              // add gradeValue to total
33              total = total + gradeValue;
34
35              // add 1 to gradeCounter
36              gradeCounter = gradeCounter + 1;
37          } // end while
38
39          // Termination Phase
40          average = total / 10; // calculate the average
41
42          // display average of exam grades
43          document.writeln(
44              "<h1>Class average is " + average + "</h1>" );
45          // -->
46      </script>
47   </head>
48   <body>
49      <p>Click Refresh (or Reload) to run the script again<p>
50   </body>
51 </html>
```

This dialog is displayed 10 times. User input is 100, 88, 93, 55, 68, 77, 83, 95, 73 and 62.

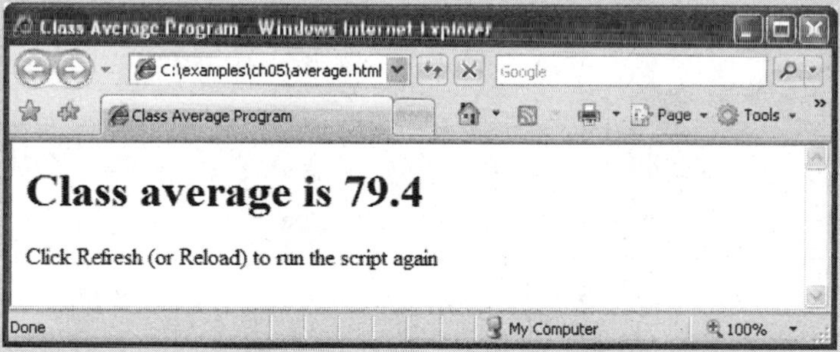

Fig. 5.5 | Counter-controlled repetition to calculate a class average. (Part 2 of 2.)

Lines 12–16 declare variables total, gradeCounter, grade, gradeValue, average. The variable grade will store the string the user types into the prompt dialog. The variable gradeValue will store the integer value of the grade the user enters into the prompt dialog.

Lines 19–20 are assignment statements that initialize total to 0 and gradeCounter to 1. Note that variables total and gradeCounter are initialized before they are used in a calculation.

Common Programming Error 5.6

Not initializing a variable that will be used in a calculation results in a logic error that produces the value NaN–Not a Number. You must initialize the variable before it is used in a calculation.

Line 23 indicates that the `while` statement continues iterating while the value of `gradeCounter` is less than or equal to 10. Line 27 corresponds to the pseudocode statement *"Input the next grade."* The statement displays a prompt dialog with the prompt `"Enter integer grade:"` on the screen.

After the user enters the grade, line 30 converts it from a string to an integer. We must convert the string to an integer in this example; otherwise, the addition statement in line 33 will be a string-concatenation statement rather than a numeric sum.

The program now is ready to increment the variable `gradeCounter` to indicate that a grade has been processed and to read the next grade from the user. Line 36 adds 1 to `gradeCounter`, so the condition in the `while` statement will eventually become `false` and terminate the loop. After this statement executes, the program continues by testing the condition in the `while` statement in line 23. If the condition is still true, the statements in lines 27–36 repeat. Otherwise the program continues execution with the first statement in sequence after the body of the loop (i.e., line 40).

Line 40 assigns the results of the average calculation to variable `average`. Lines 43–44 write a line of XHTML text in the document that displays the string `"Class average is "` followed by the value of variable `average` as an `<h1>` element in the browser.

Execute the script in a web browser by double clicking the XHTML document (from Windows Explorer). This script parses any user input as an integer. In the sample program execution in Fig. 5.5, the sum of the values entered (100, 88, 93, 55, 68, 77, 83, 95, 73 and 62) is 794. Although the treats all input as integers, the averaging calculation in the program does not produce an integer. Rather, the calculation produces a *floating-point number* (i.e., a number containing a decimal point). The average of the 10 integers input by the user in this example is 79.4.

Software Engineering Observation 5.5

If the string passed to parseInt contains a floating-point numeric value, parseInt simply truncates the floating-point part. For example, the string "27.95" results in the integer 27, and the string "–123.45" results in the integer –123. If the string passed to parseInt is not a numeric value, parseInt returns NaN (not a number).

JavaScript actually represents all numbers as floating-point numbers in memory. Floating-point numbers often develop through division, as shown in this example. When we divide 10 by 3, the result is 3.3333333..., with the sequence of 3s repeating infinitely. The computer allocates only a fixed amount of space to hold such a value, so the stored floating-point value can be only an approximation.

5.7 Formulating Algorithms: Sentinel-Controlled Repetition

Let us generalize the class-average problem. Consider the following problem:

> *Develop a class-averaging program that will process an arbitrary number of grades each time the program is run.*

In the first class-average example, the number of grades (10) was known in advance. In this example, no indication is given of how many grades the user will enter. The program must process an arbitrary number of grades. How can the program determine when to stop the input of grades? How will it know when to calculate and display the class average?

One way to solve this problem is to use a special value called a *sentinel value* (also called a *signal value*, a *dummy value* or a *flag value*) to indicate the end of data entry. The user types in grades until all legitimate grades have been entered. Then the user types the sentinel value to indicate that the last grade has been entered.

Clearly, one must choose a sentinel value that cannot be confused with an acceptable input value. −1 is an acceptable sentinel value for this problem because grades on a quiz are normally nonnegative integers from 0 to 100. Thus, an execution of the class-average program might process a stream of inputs such as 95, 96, 75, 74, 89 and −1. The program would compute and print the class average for the grades 95, 96, 75, 74 and 89 (−1 is the sentinel value, so it should not enter into the average calculation).

Figure 5.6 shows the JavaScript program and a sample execution. Although each grade is an integer, the averaging calculation is likely to produce a number with a decimal point (a real number).

```
1   <?xml version = "1.0" encoding = "utf-8"?>
2   <!DOCTYPE html PUBLIC "-//W3C//DTD XHTML 1.0 Strict//EN"
3      "http://www.w3.org/TR/xhtml11/DTD/xhtml11-strict.dtd">
4
5   <!-- Fig. 5.6: average2.html -->
6   <!-- Sentinel-controlled repetition to calculate a class average. -->
7   <html xmlns = "http://www.w3.org/1999/xhtml">
8      <head>
9         <title>Class Average Program: Sentinel-controlled Repetition</title>
10
11         <script type = "text/javascript">
12            <!--
13            var total; // sum of grades
14            var gradeCounter; // number of grades entered
15            var grade; // grade typed by user (as a string)
16            var gradeValue; // grade value (converted to integer)
17            var average; // average of all grades
18
19            // Initialization phase
20            total = 0; // clear total
21            gradeCounter = 0; // prepare to loop
22
23            // Processing phase
24            // prompt for input and read grade from user
25            grade = window.prompt(
26               "Enter Integer Grade, -1 to Quit:", "0" );
27
28            // convert grade from a string to an integer
29            gradeValue = parseInt( grade );
30
31            while ( gradeValue != -1 )
32            {
```

Fig. 5.6 | Sentinel-controlled repetition to calculate a class average. (Part 1 of 2.)

```
33              // add gradeValue to total
34              total = total + gradeValue;
35
36              // add 1 to gradeCounter
37              gradeCounter = gradeCounter + 1;
38
39              // prompt for input and read grade from user
40              grade = window.prompt(
41                  "Enter Integer Grade, -1 to Quit:", "0" );
42
43              // convert grade from a string to an integer
44              gradeValue = parseInt( grade );
45          } // end while
46
47          // Termination phase
48          if ( gradeCounter != 0 )
49          {
50              average = total / gradeCounter;
51
52              // display average of exam grades
53              document.writeln(
54                  "<h1>Class average is " + average + "</h1>" );
55          } // end if
56          else
57              document.writeln( "<p>No grades were entered</p>" );
58          // -->
59      </script>
60  </head>
61  <body>
62      <p>Click Refresh (or Reload) to run the script again</p>
63  </body>
64  </html>
```

This dialog is displayed four times. User input is 97, 88, 72 and –1.

Fig. 5.6 | Sentinel-controlled repetition to calculate a class average. (Part 2 of 2.)

In this example, we see that control statements may be stacked on top of one another (in sequence). The `while` statement (lines 31–45) is followed immediately by an `if...else` statement (lines 48–57) in sequence. Much of the code in this program is identical to the code in Fig. 5.5, so we concentrate in this example on the new features.

Line 21 initializes `gradeCounter` to 0, because no grades have been entered yet. Remember that the program uses sentinel-controlled repetition. To keep an accurate record of the number of grades entered, the script increments `gradeCounter` only after processing a valid grade value.

Note the block in the `while` loop in Fig. 5.6 (lines 32–45). Without the braces, the last three statements in the body of the loop would fall outside of the loop, causing the computer to interpret the code incorrectly, as follows:

```
while ( gradeValue != -1 )
   // add gradeValue to total
   total = total + gradeValue;

// add 1 to gradeCounter
gradeCounter = gradeCounter + 1;

// prompt for input and read grade from user
grade = window.prompt(
   "Enter Integer Grade, -1 to Quit:", "0" );

// convert grade from a string to an integer
gradeValue = parseInt( grade );
```

This interpretation would cause an infinite loop in the program if the user does not enter the sentinel -1 as the first input value in lines 25–26 (i.e., before the `while` statement).

Common Programming Error 5.7

Omitting the braces that delineate a block can lead to logic errors such as infinite loops.

5.8 Formulating Algorithms: Nested Control Statements

Consider the following problem statement:

A college offers a course that prepares students for the state licensing exam for real estate brokers. Last year, several of the students who completed this course took the licensing exam. Naturally, the college wants to know how well its students performed. You have been asked to write a program to summarize the results. You have been given a list of these 10 students. Next to each name is written a 1 if the student passed the exam and a 2 if the student failed.

Your program should analyze the results of the exam as follows:

1. *Input each test result (i.e., a 1 or a 2). Display the message "Enter result" on the screen each time the program requests another test result.*

2. *Count the number of test results of each type.*

3. *Display a summary of the test results indicating the number of students who passed and the number of students who failed.*

4. *If more than eight students passed the exam, print the message "Raise tuition."*

After reading the problem statement carefully, we make the following observations about the problem:

1. The program must process test results for 10 students. A counter-controlled loop will be used.

2. Each test result is a number—either a 1 or a 2. Each time the program reads a test result, the program must determine whether the number is a 1 or a 2. We test for a 1 in our algorithm. If the number is not a 1, we assume that it is a 2.

3. Two counters are used to keep track of the exam results—one to count the number of students who passed the exam and one to count the number of students who failed the exam.

After the program processes all the results, it must decide whether more than eight students passed the exam. The JavaScript program and two sample executions are shown in Fig. 5.7.

```
 1   <?xml version = "1.0" encoding = "utf-8"?>
 2   <!DOCTYPE html PUBLIC "-//W3C//DTD XHTML 1.0 Strict//EN"
 3      "http://www.w3.org/TR/xhtml1/DTD/xhtml1-strict.dtd">
 4
 5   <!-- Fig. 5.7: analysis.html -->
 6   <!-- Examination-results calculation. -->
 7   <html xmlns = "http://www.w3.org/1999/xhtml">
 8      <head>
 9         <title>Analysis of Examination Results</title>
10         <script type = "text/javascript">
11            <!--
12            // initializing variables in declarations
13            var passes = 0; // number of passes
14            var failures = 0; // number of failures
15            var student = 1; // student counter
16            var result; // one exam result
17
18            // process 10 students; counter-controlled loop
19            while ( student <= 10 )
20            {
21               result = window.prompt( "Enter result (1=pass,2=fail)", "0" );
22
23               if ( result == "1" )
24                  passes = passes + 1;
25               else
26                  failures = failures + 1;
27
28               student = student + 1;
29            } // end while
30
31            // termination phase
32            document.writeln( "<h1>Examination Results</h1>" );
```

Fig. 5.7 | Examination-results calculation. (Part 1 of 2.)

```
33              document.writeln(
34                 "Passed: " + passes + "<br />Failed: " + failures );
35
36           if ( passes > 8 )
37              document.writeln( "<br />Raise Tuition" );
38           // -->
39        </script>
40     </head>
41     <body>
42        <p>Click Refresh (or Reload) to run the script again</p>
43     </body>
44  </html>
```

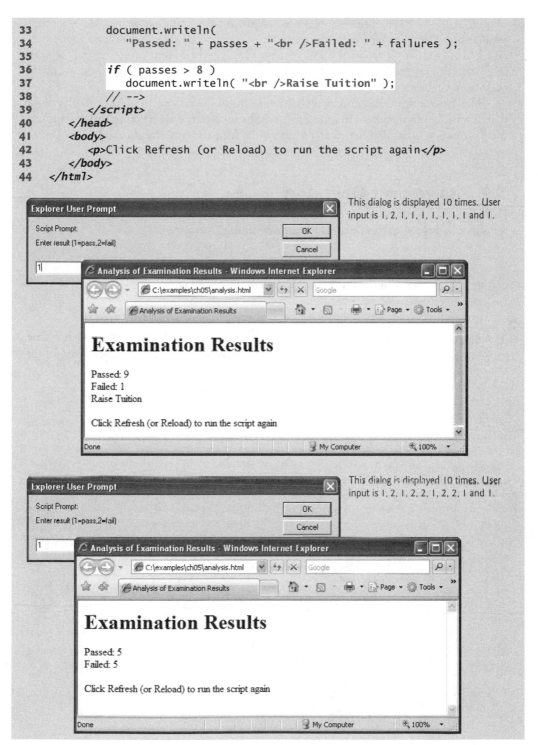

Fig. 5.7 | Examination-results calculation. (Part 2 of 2.)

Lines 13–16 declare the variables used to process the examination results. Note that JavaScript allows variable initialization to be incorporated into declarations (passes is assigned 0, failures is assigned 0 and student is assigned 1). Some programs may require reinitialization at the beginning of each repetition; such reinitialization would normally occur in assignment statements.

The processing of the exam results occurs in the while statement in lines 19–29. Note that the if...else statement in lines 23–26 in the loop tests only whether the exam result was 1; it assumes that all other exam results are 2. Normally, you should validate the values input by the user (i.e., determine whether the values are correct).

5.9 Assignment Operators

JavaScript provides several assignment operators (called *compound assignment operators*) for abbreviating assignment expressions. For example, the statement

```
c = c + 3;
```

can be abbreviated with the *addition assignment operator*, +=, as

```
c += 3;
```

The += operator adds the value of the expression on the right of the operator to the value of the variable on the left of the operator and stores the result in the variable on the left of the operator. Any statement of the form

variable = variable operator expression;

where *operator* is one of the binary operators +, -, *, / or % (or others we'll discuss later in the text), can be written in the form

variable operator = expression;

Thus, the assignment c += 3 adds 3 to c. Figure 5.8 shows the arithmetic assignment operators, sample expressions using these operators and explanations of the meaning of the operators.

Assignment operator	Initial value of variable	Sample expression	Explanation	Assigns
+=	c = 3	c += 7	c = c + 7	10 to c
-=	d = 5	d -= 4	d = d – 4	1 to d
*=	e = 4	e *= 5	e = e * 5	20 to e
/=	f = 6	f /= 3	f = f / 3	2 to f
%=	g = 12	g %= 9	g = g % 9	3 to g

Fig. 5.8 | Arithmetic assignment operators.

Performance Tip 5.1

Programmers can write programs that execute a bit faster when the arithmetic assignment operators are used, because the variable on the left side of the assignment does not have to be evaluated twice.

Performance Tip 5.2

Many of the performance tips we mention in this text result in only nominal improvements, so you may be tempted to ignore them. Significant performance improvement often is realized when a supposedly nominal improvement is placed in a loop that may repeat a large number of times.

5.10 Increment and Decrement Operators

JavaScript provides the unary *increment operator* (++) and *decrement operator* (--) (summarized in Fig. 5.9). If a variable c is incremented by 1, the increment operator, ++, can be used rather than the expression c = c + 1 or c += 1. If an increment or decrement operator is placed before a variable, it is referred to as the *preincrement* or *predecrement operator*, respectively. If an increment or decrement operator is placed after a variable, it is referred to as the *postincrement* or *postdecrement operator*, respectively.

Error-Prevention Tip 5.1

The predecrement and postdecrement JavaScript operators cause the W3C XHTML Validator to incorrectly report errors. The validator attempts to interpret the decrement operator as part of an XHTML comment tag (<!-- or -->). You can avoid this problem by using the subtraction assignment operator (-=) to subtract one from a variable. Note that the validator may report many more (nonexistent) errors once it improperly parses the decrement operator.

Preincrementing (or predecrementing) a variable causes the program to increment (decrement) the variable by 1, then use the new value of the variable in the expression in which it appears. Postincrementing (postdecrementing) the variable causes the program to use the current value of the variable in the expression in which it appears, then increment (decrement) the variable by 1.

Operator	Example	Called	Explanation
++	++a	preincrement	Increment a by 1, then use the new value of a in the expression in which a resides.
++	a++	postincrement	Use the current value of a in the expression in which a resides, then increment a by 1.
--	--b	predecrement	Decrement b by 1, then use the new value of b in the expression in which b resides.
--	b--	postdecrement	Use the current value of b in the expression in which b resides, then decrement b by 1.

Fig. 5.9 | Increment and decrement operators.

The script in Fig. 5.10 demonstrates the difference between the preincrementing version and the postincrementing version of the ++ increment operator. Postincrementing the variable c causes it to be incremented after it is used in the document.writeln method call (line 18). Preincrementing the variable c causes it to be incremented before it is used in the document.writeln method call (line 25). The program displays the value of c before and after the ++ operator is used. The decrement operator (--) works similarly.

 Good Programming Practice 5.3

For readability, unary operators should be placed next to their operands, with no intervening spaces.

The three assignment statements in Fig. 5.7 (lines 24, 26 and 28, respectively),

```
passes = passes + 1;
failures = failures + 1;
student = student + 1;
```

can be written more concisely with assignment operators as

```
passes += 1;
failures += 1;
student += 1;
```

```
1   <?xml version = "1.0" encoding = "utf-8"?>
2   <!DOCTYPE html PUBLIC "-//W3C//DTD XHTML 1.0 Strict//EN"
3       "http://www.w3.org/TR/xhtml11/DTD/xhtml11-strict.dtd">
4
5   <!-- Fig. 5.10: increment.html -->
6   <!-- Preincrementing and Postincrementing. -->
7   <html xmlns = "http://www.w3.org/1999/xhtml">
8       <head>
9           <title>Preincrementing and Postincrementing</title>
10          <script type = "text/javascript">
11              <!--
12              var c;
13
14              c = 5;
15              document.writeln( "<h3>Postincrementing</h3>" );
16              document.writeln( c ); // prints 5
17              // prints 5 then increments
18              document.writeln( "<br />" + c++ );
19              document.writeln( "<br />" + c ); // prints 6
20
21              c = 5;
22              document.writeln( "<h3>Preincrementing</h3>" );
23              document.writeln( c ); // prints 5
24              // increments then prints 6
25              document.writeln( "<br />" + ++c );
26              document.writeln( "<br />" + c ); // prints 6
27              // -->
28          </script>
29      </head><body></body>
30  </html>
```

Fig. 5.10 | Preincrementing and postincrementing. (Part 1 of 2.)

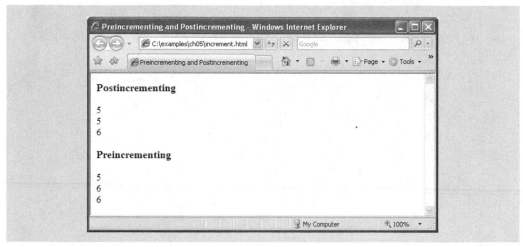

Fig. 5.10 | Preincrementing and postincrementing. (Part 2 of 2.)

with preincrement operators as

```
++passes;
++failures;
++student;
```

or with postincrement operators as

```
passes++;
failures++;
student++;
```

It is important to note here that when incrementing or decrementing a variable in a statement by itself, the preincrement and postincrement forms have the same effect, and the predecrement and postdecrement forms have the same effect. It is only when a variable appears in the context of a larger expression that preincrementing the variable and postincrementing the variable have different effects. Predecrementing and postdecrementing behave similarly.

Common Programming Error 5.8

*Attempting to use the increment or decrement operator on an expression other than a **left-hand-side expression**—commonly called an **lvalue**—is a syntax error. A left-hand-side expression is a variable or expression that can appear on the left side of an assignment operation. For example, writing ++(x + 1) is a syntax error, because (x + 1) is not a left-hand-side expression.*

Figure 5.11 lists the precedence and associativity of the operators introduced to this point. The operators are shown top to bottom in decreasing order of precedence. The second column describes the associativity of the operators at each level of precedence. Notice that the conditional operator (?:), the unary operators increment (++) and decrement (--) and the assignment operators =, +=, -=, *=, /= and %= associate from right to left. All other operators in the operator precedence table (Fig. 5.11) associate from left to right. The third column names the groups of operators.

Operator	Associativity	Type
++ --	right to left	unary
* / %	left to right	multiplicative
+ -	left to right	additive
< <= > >=	left to right	relational
== !=	left to right	equality
?:	right to left	conditional
= += -= *= /= %=	right to left	assignment

Fig. 5.11 | Precedence and associativity of the operators discussed so far.

5.11 Web Resources

www.deitel.com/javascript/

The Deitel JavaScript Resource Center contains links to some of the best JavaScript resources on the web. There you'll find categorized links to JavaScript tutorials, tools, code generators, forums, books, libraries, frameworks and more. Be sure to visit the related Resource Centers on XHTML (www.deitel.com/xhtml/) and CSS 2.1 (www.deitel.com/css21/).

6

JavaScript: Control Statements II

Not everything that can be counted counts, and not every thing that counts can be counted.
—Albert Einstein

Who can control his fate?
—William Shakespeare

The used key is always bright.
—Benjamin Franklin

Intelligence ... is the faculty of making artificial objects, especially tools to make tools.
—Henri Bergson

Every advantage in the past is judged in the light of the final issue.
—Demosthenes

OBJECTIVES

In this chapter you'll learn:

- The essentials of counter-controlled repetition.

- To use the `for` and `do...while` repetition statements to execute statements in a program repeatedly.

- To perform multiple selection using the `switch` selection statement.

- To use the `break` and `continue` program-control statements

- To use the logical operators.

6.1 Introduction

Chapter 5 began our introduction to control statements. In this chapter, we introduce JavaScript's remaining control statements (with the exception of for...in, which is presented in Chapter 8). In later chapters, you'll see that control structures are helpful in manipulating objects.

6.2 Essentials of Counter-Controlled Repetition

Counter-controlled repetition requires:

1. The *name* of a control variable (or loop counter).

2. The *initial value* of the control variable.

3. The *increment* (or *decrement*) by which the control variable is modified each time through the loop (also known as *each iteration of the loop*).

4. The condition that tests for the *final value* of the control variable to determine whether looping should continue.

To see the four elements of counter-controlled repetition, consider the simple script shown in Fig. 6.1, which displays lines of XHTML text that illustrate the seven different font sizes supported by XHTML. The declaration in line 12 *names* the control variable (counter), reserves space for it in memory and sets it to an *initial value* of 1. The declaration and initialization of counter could also have been accomplished by the following declaration and assignment statement:

```
var counter; // declare counter
counter = 1; // initialize counter to 1
```

```
1   <?xml version = "1.0" encoding = "utf-8"?>
2   <!DOCTYPE html PUBLIC "-//W3C//DTD XHTML 1.0 Strict//EN"
3      "http://www.w3.org/TR/xhtml1/DTD/xhtml1-strict.dtd">
4
5   <!-- Fig. 6.1: WhileCounter.html -->
6   <!-- Counter-controlled repetition. -->
```

Fig. 6.1 | Counter-controlled repetition. (Part 1 of 2.)

```
 7    <html xmlns = "http://www.w3.org/1999/xhtml">
 8      <head>
 9        <title>Counter-Controlled Repetition</title>
10        <script type = "text/javascript">
11          <!--
12          var counter = 1; // initialization
13
14          while ( counter <= 7 ) // repetition condition
15          {
16            document.writeln( "<p style = \"font-size: " +
17              counter + "ex\">XHTML font size " + counter +
18              "ex</p>" );
19            ++counter; // increment
20          } //end while
21          // -->
22        </script>
23      </head><body></body>
24    </html>
```

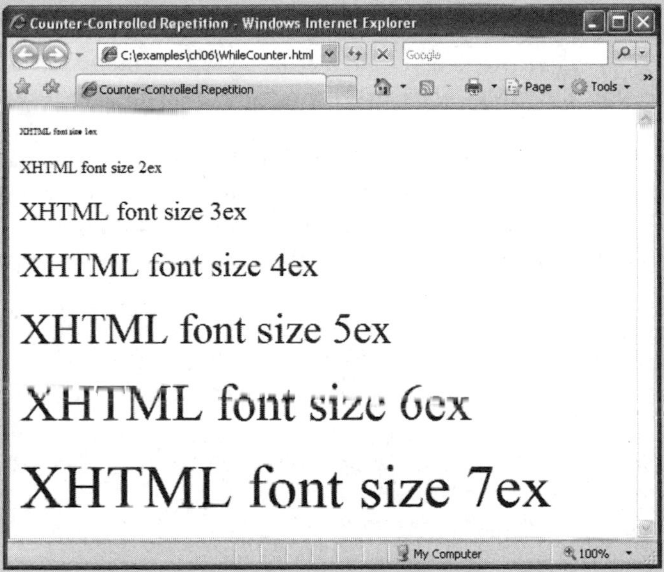

Fig. 6.1 | Counter-controlled repetition. (Part 2 of 2.)

Lines 16–18 in the while statement write a paragraph element consisting of the string "XHTML font size" concatenated with the control variable counter's value, which represents the font size. An inline CSS style attribute sets the font-size property to the value of counter concatenated to ex. Note the use of the escape sequence \", which is placed around attribute style's value. Because the double-quote character delimits the beginning and end of a string literal in JavaScript, it cannot be used in the contents of the string unless it is preceded by a \ to create the escape sequence \". For example, if counter is 5, the preceding statement produces the markup

```
<p style = "font-size: 5ex">XHTML font size 5ex</p>
```

XHTML allows either single quotes (') or double quotes (") to be placed around the value specified for an attribute. JavaScript allows single quotes to be placed in a string literal. Thus, we could have placed single quotes around the font-size property to produce equivalent XHTML output without the use of escape sequences.

 Common Programming Error 6.1

Placing a double-quote (") character inside a string literal that is delimited by double quotes causes a runtime error when the script is interpreted. To be displayed as part of a string literal, a double-quote (") character must be preceded by a \ to form the escape sequence \".

Line 19 in the while statement *increments* the control variable by 1 for each iteration of the loop (i.e., each time the body of the loop is performed). The loop-continuation condition (line 14) in the while statement tests whether the value of the control variable is less than or equal to 7 (the *final value* for which the condition is true). Note that the body of this while statement executes even when the control variable is 7. The loop terminates when the control variable exceeds 7 (i.e., counter becomes 8).

6.3 for Repetition Statement

The *for repetition statement* handles all the details of counter-controlled repetition. Figure 6.2 illustrates the power of the for statement by reimplementing the script of Fig. 6.1.

When the for statement begins executing (line 15), the control variable counter is declared and is initialized to 1 (i.e., the first statement of the for statement declares the control variable's *name* and provides the control variable's *initial value*). Next, the loop-continuation condition, counter <= 7, is checked. The condition contains the *final value*

```
1   <?xml version = "1.0" encoding = "utf-8"?>
2   <!DOCTYPE html PUBLIC "-//W3C//DTD XHTML 1.0 Strict//EN"
3      "http://www.w3.org/TR/xhtml1/DTD/xhtml1-strict.dtd">
4
5   <!-- Fig. 6.2: ForCounter.html -->
6   <!-- Counter-controlled repetition with the for statement. -->
7   <html xmlns = "http://www.w3.org/1999/xhtml">
8      <head>
9         <title>Counter-Controlled Repetition</title>
10        <script type = "text/javascript">
11           <!--
12           // Initialization, repetition condition and
13           // incrementing are all included in the for
14           // statement header.
15           for ( var counter = 1; counter <= 7; ++counter )
16              document.writeln( "<p style = \"font-size: " +
17                 counter + "ex\">XHTML font size " + counter +
18                 "ex</p>" );
19           // -->
20        </script>
21     </head><body></body>
22  </html>
```

Fig. 6.2 | Counter-controlled repetition with the for statement. (Part 1 of 2.)

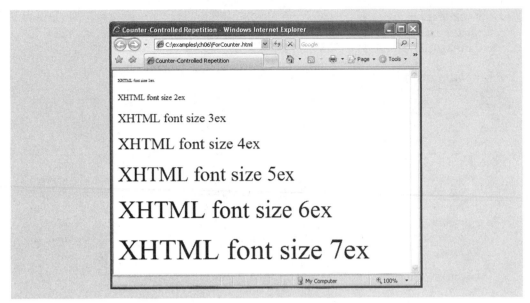

Fig. 6.2 | Counter-controlled repetition with the for statement. (Part 2 of 2.)

(7) of the control variable. The initial value of counter is 1. Therefore, the condition is satisfied (i.e., true), so the body statement (lines 16–18) writes a paragraph element in the XHTML document. Then, variable counter is incremented in the expression ++counter and the loop continues execution with the loop-continuation test. The control variable is now equal to 2, so the final value is not exceeded and the program performs the body statement again (i.e., performs the next iteration of the loop). This process continues until the control variable counter becomes 8, at which point the loop-continuation test fails and the repetition terminates.

The program continues by performing the first statement after the for statement. (In this case, the script terminates, because the interpreter reaches the end of the script.)

Figure 6.3 takes a closer look at the for statement at line 15 of Fig. 6.2. The for statement's first line (including the keyword for and everything in parentheses after for) is often called the ***for statement header***. Note that the for statement "does it all"—it specifies each of the items needed for counter-controlled repetition with a control variable.

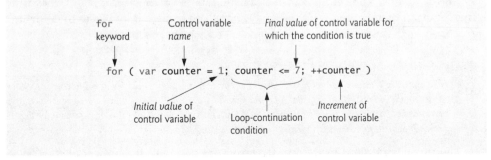

Fig. 6.3 | for statement header components.

Note that Fig. 6.3 uses the loop-continuation condition counter <= 7. If you incorrectly write counter < 7, the loop will execute only six times. This is an example of the common logic error called an *off-by-one error.*

Common Programming Error 6.2

Using an incorrect relational operator or an incorrect final value of a loop counter in the condition of a while, for or do...while statement can cause an off-by-one error or an infinite loop.

Error-Prevention Tip 6.1

*Using the final value in the condition of a while or for statement and using the <= relational operator will help avoid off-by-one errors. For a loop used to print the values 1 to 10, for example, the initial value of counter should be 1, and the loop-continuation condition should be counter <= 10 rather than counter < 10 (which is an off-by-one error) or counter < 11 (which is correct). Many programmers, however, prefer so-called **zero-based counting**, in which, to count 10 times through the loop, counter would be initialized to zero and the loop-continuation test would be counter < 10.*

The general format of the for statement is

> **for** (*initialization*; *loopContinuationTest*; *increment*)
>   *statements*

where the *initialization* expression names the loop's control variable and provides its initial value, *loopContinuationTest* is the expression that tests the loop-continuation condition (containing the final value of the control variable for which the condition is true), and *increment* is an expression that increments the control variable. The for statement can be represented by an equivalent while statement, with *initialization, loopContinuationTest* and *increment* placed as follows (Section 6.7 discusses an exception to this rule):

> *initialization*;
>
> **while** (*loopContinuationTest*)
> {
>   *statements*
>   *increment*;
> }

If the *initialization* expression in the for statement's header is the first definition of the control variable, the control variable can still be used after the for statement in the script. The part of a script in which a variable name can be used is known as the variable's *scope*. Scope is discussed in detail in Chapter 7, JavaScript: Functions.

Good Programming Practice 6.1

Place only expressions involving the control variable in the initialization and increment sections of a for statement. Manipulations of other variables should appear either before the loop (if they execute only once, like initialization statements) or in the loop body (if they execute once per iteration of the loop, like incrementing or decrementing statements).

The three expressions in the for statement are optional. If *loopContinuationTest* is omitted, JavaScript assumes that the loop-continuation condition is true, thus creating an infinite loop. One might omit the *initialization* expression if the control variable is initialized before the loop. One might omit the *increment* expression if the increment is calculated by statements in the body of the for statement or if no increment is needed. The increment expression in the for statement acts like a stand-alone statement at the end of the body of the for statement. Therefore, the expressions

```
counter = counter + 1
counter += 1
++counter
counter++
```

are all equivalent in the incrementing portion of the for statement. Many programmers prefer the form counter++. This is because the incrementing of the control variable occurs after the body of the loop is executed, and therefore the postincrementing form seems more natural. Preincrementing and postincrementing both have the same effect in our example, because the variable being incremented does not appear in a larger expression. The two semicolons in the for statement header are required.

Common Programming Error 6.3

Using commas instead of the two required semicolons in the header of a for statement is a syntax error.

Common Programming Error 6.4

Placing a semicolon immediately to the right of the right parenthesis of the header of a for statement makes the body of that for statement an empty statement. This code is normally a logic error.

The "increment" may be negative, in which case the loop counts downward. If the loop-continuation condition initially is false, the for statement's body is not performed. Instead, execution proceeds with the statement following the for statement.

The control variable frequently is printed or used in calculations in the body of a for statement, but it does not have to be. Other times, the control variable is used for controlling repetition but never mentioned in the body of the for statement.

Error-Prevention Tip 6.2

Although the value of the control variable can be changed in the body of a for statement, avoid changing it, because doing so can lead to subtle errors.

The for statement is flowcharted much like the while statement. For example, Fig. 6.4 shows the flowchart of the for statement

```
for ( var counter = 1; counter <= 7; ++counter )
   document.writeln( "<p style = \"font-size: " +
      counter + "ex\">XHTML font size " + counter +
      "ex</p>" );
```

This flowchart makes it clear that the initialization occurs only once and that incrementing occurs *after* each execution of the body statement. Note that, besides small circles and arrows, the flowchart contains only rectangle symbols and a diamond symbol.

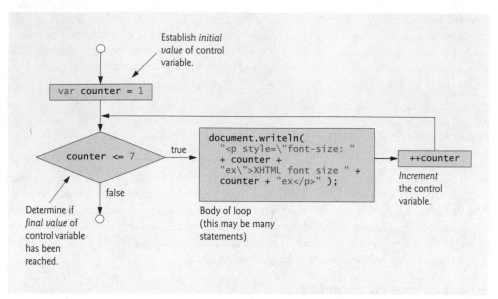

Fig. 6.4 | for repetition statement flowchart.

6.4 Examples Using the for Statement

The examples in this section show methods of varying the control variable in a for statement. In each case, we write the appropriate for header. Note the change in the relational operator for loops that decrement the control variable.

a) Vary the control variable from 1 to 100 in increments of 1.

```
for ( var i = 1; i <= 100; ++i )
```

b) Vary the control variable from 100 to 1 in increments of -1 (i.e., decrements of 1).

```
for ( var i = 100; i >= 1; --i )
```

c) Vary the control variable from 7 to 77 in steps of 7.

```
for ( var i = 7; i <= 77; i += 7 )
```

d) Vary the control variable from 20 to 2 in steps of -2.

```
for ( var i = 20; i >= 2; i -= 2 )
```

e) Vary the control variable over the following sequence of values: 2, 5, 8, 11, 14, 17, 20.

```
for ( var j = 2; j <= 20; j += 3 )
```

f) Vary the control variable over the following sequence of values: 99, 88, 77, 66, 55, 44, 33, 22, 11, 0.

```
for ( var j = 99; j >= 0; j -= 11 )
```

Common Programming Error 6.5

Not using the proper relational operator in the loop-continuation condition of a loop that counts downward (e.g., using i <= 1 in a loop that counts down to 1) is usually a logic error that will yield incorrect results when the program runs.

The next two scripts demonstrate the for repetition statement. Figure 6.5 uses the for statement to sum the even integers from 2 to 100. Note that the increment expression adds 2 to the control variable number after the body executes during each iteration of the loop. The loop terminates when number has the value 102 (which is not added to the sum).

Note that the body of the for statement in Fig. 6.5 actually could be merged into the rightmost (increment) portion of the for header by using a comma, as follows:

```
for ( var number = 2; number <= 100; sum += number, number += 2)
   ;
```

Similarly, the initialization sum = 0 could be merged into the initialization section of the for statement.

```
1   <?xml version = "1.0" encoding = "utf-8"?>
2   <!DOCTYPE html PUBLIC "-//W3C//DTD XHTML 1.0 Strict//EN"
3      "http://www.w3.org/TR/xhtml1/DTD/xhtml1-strict.dtd">
4
5   <!-- Fig. 6.5: Sum.html -->
6   <!-- Summation with the for repetition structure. -->
7   <html xmlns = "http://www.w3.org/1999/xhtml">
8      <head>
9         <title>Sum the Even Integers from 2 to 100</title>
10        <script type = "text/javascript">
11           <!--
12           var sum = 0;
13
14           for ( var number = 2; number <= 100; number += 2 )
15              sum += number;
16
17           document.writeln( "The sum of the even integers " +
18              "from 2 to 100 is " + sum );
19           // -->
20        </script>
21     </head><body></body>
22  </html>
```

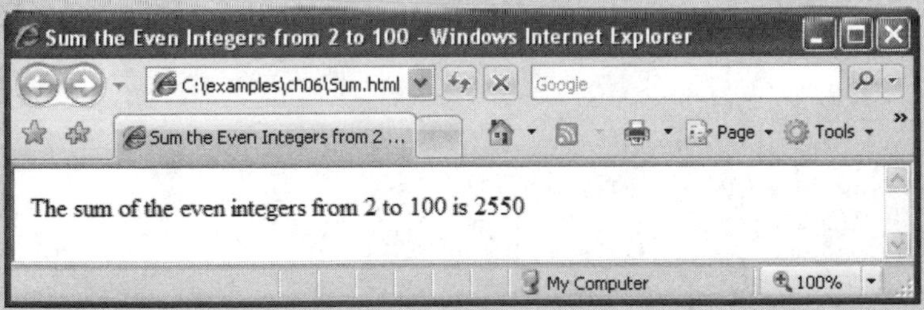

Fig. 6.5 | Summation with the for repetition structure.

Good Programming Practice 6.2

Although statements preceding a for *statement and in the body of a* for *statement can often be merged into the* for *header, avoid doing so, because it makes the program more difficult to read.*

Good Programming Practice 6.3

For clarity, limit the size of control-statement headers to a single line, if possible.

The next example computes compound interest (compounded yearly) using the for statement. Consider the following problem statement:

A person invests $1000.00 in a savings account yielding 5 percent interest. Assuming that all the interest is left on deposit, calculate and print the amount of money in the account at the end of each year for 10 years. Use the following formula to determine the amounts:

$$a = p\,(1 + r)^n$$

where

p is the original amount invested (i.e., the principal)
r is the annual interest rate
n is the number of years
a is the amount on deposit at the end of the nth year.

This problem involves a loop that performs the indicated calculation for each of the 10 years the money remains on deposit. Figure 6.6 presents the solution to this problem, displaying the results in a table.

```
1   <?xml version = "1.0" encoding = "utf-8"?>
2   <!DOCTYPE html PUBLIC "-//W3C//DTD XHTML 1.0 Strict//EN"
3      "http://www.w3.org/TR/xhtml1/DTD/xhtml1-strict.dtd">
4
5   <!-- Fig. 6.6: Interest.html -->
6   <!-- Compound interest calculation with a for loop. -->
7   <html xmlns = "http://www.w3.org/1999/xhtml">
8      <head>
9         <title>Calculating Compound Interest</title>
10        <style type = "text/css">
11           table { width: 100% }
12           th    { text-align: left }
13        </style>
14        <script type = "text/javascript">
15           <!--
16           var amount; // current amount of money
17           var principal = 1000.0; // principal amount
18           var rate = .05; // interest rate
19
20           document.writeln(
21              "<table border = \"1\">" ); // begin the table
22           document.writeln(
23              "<caption>Calculating Compound Interest</caption>" );
```

Fig. 6.6 | Compound interest calculation with a for loop. (Part 1 of 2.)

```
24          document.writeln(
25             "<thead><tr><th>Year</th>" ); // year column heading
26          document.writeln(
27             "<th>Amount on deposit</th>" ); // amount column heading
28          document.writeln( "</tr></thead><tbody>" );
29
30          // output a table row for each year
31          for ( var year = 1; year <= 10; ++year )
32          {
33             amount = principal * Math.pow( 1.0 + rate, year );
34             document.writeln( "<tr><td>" + year +
35                "</td><td>" + amount.toFixed(2) +
36                "</td></tr>" );
37          } //end for
38
39          document.writeln( "</tbody></table>" );
40          // -->
41       </script>
42    </head><body></body>
43 </html>
```

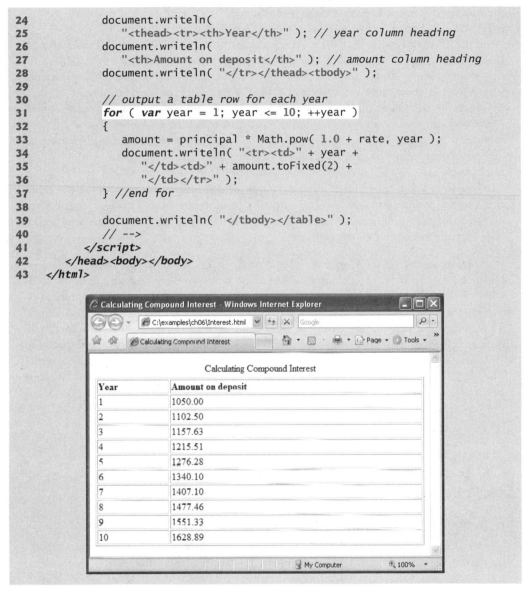

Fig. 6.6 | Compound interest calculation with a for loop. (Part 2 of 2.)

Lines 16–18 declare three variables and initialize principal to 1000.0 and rate to .05. Lines 20–21 write an XHTML <table> tag, and lines 22–23 write the caption that summarizes the table's content. Lines 24–25 create the table's header section (<thead>), a row (<tr>) and a column heading (<th>) containing "Year." Lines 26–28 create a table heading for "Amount on deposit" and write the closing </tr> and </thead> tags.

The for statement (lines 31–37) executes its body 10 times, incrementing control variable year from 1 to 10 (note that year represents *n* in the problem statement). Java-Script does not include an exponentiation operator. Instead, we use the Math object's pow method for this purpose. Math.pow(x, y) calculates the value of x raised to the yth power. Method Math.pow takes two numbers as arguments and returns the result.

Line 33 performs the calculation using the formula given in the problem statement. Lines 34–36 write a line of XHTML markup that creates another row in the table. The first column is the current year value. The second column displays the value of amount. Line 39 writes the closing </tbody> and </table> tags after the loop terminates.

Line 35 introduces the **Number object** and its **toFixed method**. The variable amount contains a numerical value, so JavaScript represents it as a Number object. The toFixed method of a Number object formats the value by rounding it to the specified number of decimal places. In line 35, amount.toFixed(2) outputs the value of amount with two decimal places.

Variables amount, principal and rate represent numbers in this script. Remember that JavaScript represents all numbers as floating-point numbers. This feature is convenient in this example, because we are dealing with fractional parts of dollars and need a type that allows decimal points in its values.

A Caution about Using Floating Point Numbers for Monetary Amounts

Unfortunately, floating-point numbers can cause trouble. Here is a simple example of what can go wrong when using floating-point numbers to represent dollar amounts (assuming that dollar amounts are displayed with two digits to the right of the decimal point): Two dollar amounts stored in the machine could be 14.234 (which would normally be rounded to 14.23 for display purposes) and 18.673 (which would normally be rounded to 18.67 for display purposes). When these amounts are added, they produce the internal sum 32.907, which would normally be rounded to 32.91 for display purposes. Thus your printout could appear as

```
    14.23
  + 18.67
  _____
    32.91
```

but a person adding the individual numbers as printed would expect the sum to be 32.90. You have been warned!

6.5 switch Multiple-Selection Statement

Occasionally, an algorithm will contain a series of decisions in which a variable or expression is tested separately for each of the values it may assume, and different actions are taken for each value. JavaScript provides the switch multiple-selection statement to handle such decision making. The script in Fig. 6.7 demonstrates three different CSS list formats determined by the value the user enters.

```
1   <?xml version = "1.0" encoding = "utf-8"?>
2   <!DOCTYPE html PUBLIC "-//W3C//DTD XHTML 1.0 Strict//EN"
3      "http://www.w3.org/TR/xhtml1/DTD/xhtml1-strict.dtd">
4
5   <!-- Fig. 6.7: SwitchTest.html -->
6   <!-- Using the switch multiple-selection statement. -->
```

Fig. 6.7 | Using the switch multiple-selection statement. (Part 1 of 4.)

```
7   <html xmlns = "http://www.w3.org/1999/xhtml">
8     <head>
9       <title>Switching between XHTML List Formats</title>
10      <script type = "text/javascript">
11        <!--
12        var choice; // user's choice
13        var startTag; // starting list item tag
14        var endTag; // ending list item tag
15        var validInput = true; // indicates if input is valid
16        var listType; // type of list as a string
17
18        choice = window.prompt( "Select a list style:\n" +
19           "1 (numbered), 2 (lettered), 3 (roman)", "1" );
20
21        switch ( choice )
22        {
23          case "1":
24            startTag = "<ol>";
25            endTag = "</ol>";
26            listType = "<h1>Numbered List</h1>";
27            break;
28          case "2":
29            startTag = "<ol style = \"list-style-type: upper-alpha\">";
30            endTag = "</ol>";
31            listType = "<h1>Lettered List</h1>";
32            break;
33          case "3":
34            startTag = "<ol style = \"list-style-type: upper-roman\">";
35            endTag = "</ol>";
36            listType = "<h1>Roman Numbered List</h1>";
37            break;
38          default:
39            validInput = false;
40        } //end switch
41
42        if ( validInput == true )
43        {
44          document.writeln( listType + startTag );
45
46          for ( var i = 1; i <= 3; ++i )
47            document.writeln( "<li>List item " + i + "</li>" );
48
49          document.writeln( endTag );
50        } //end if
51        else
52          document.writeln( "Invalid choice: " + choice );
53        // -->
54      </script>
55    </head>
56    <body>
57      <p>Click Refresh (or Reload) to run the script again</p>
58    </body>
59  </html>
```

Fig. 6.7 | Using the switch multiple-selection statement. (Part 2 of 4.)

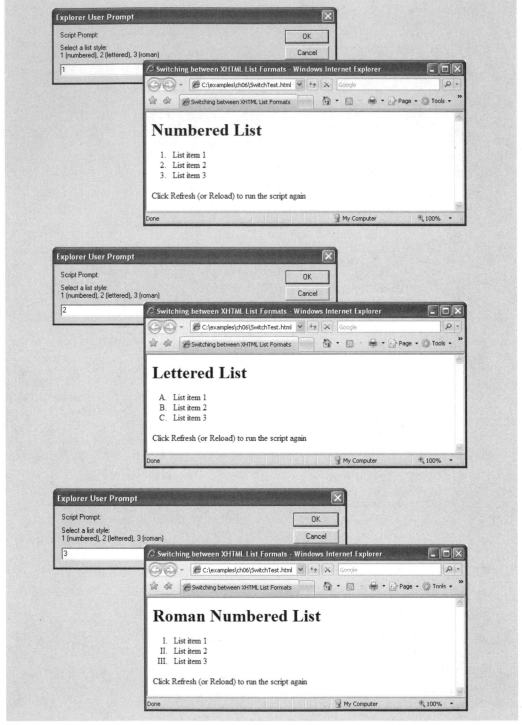

Fig. 6.7 | Using the switch multiple-selection statement. (Part 3 of 4.)

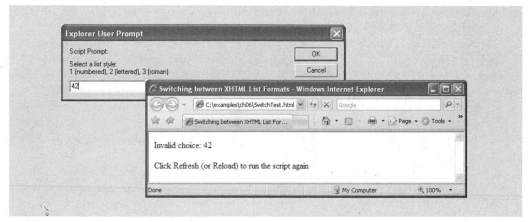

Fig. 6.7 | Using the switch multiple-selection statement. (Part 4 of 4.)

Line 12 in the script declares the variable choice. This variable stores the user's choice, which determines what type of XHTML list to display. Lines 13–14 declare variables startTag and endTag, which will store the XHTML tags that will be used to create the list element. Line 15 declares variable validInput and initializes it to true. The script uses this variable to determine whether the user made a valid choice (indicated by the value of true). If a choice is invalid, the script sets validInput to false. Line 16 declares variable listType, which will store an h1 element indicating the list type. This heading appears before the list in the XHTML document.

Lines 18–19 prompt the user to enter a 1 to display a numbered list, a 2 to display a lettered list and a 3 to display a list with roman numerals. Lines 21–40 define a *switch statement* that assigns to the variables startTag, endTag and listType values based on the value input by the user in the prompt dialog. We create these different lists using the CSS property *list-style-type*, which allows us to set the numbering system for the list. Possible values include decimal (numbers—the default), lower-roman (lowercase Roman numerals), upper-roman (uppercase Roman numerals), lower-alpha (lowercase letters), upper-alpha (uppercase letters), and several others.

The switch statement consists of a series of *case labels* and an optional *default case*. When the flow of control reaches the switch statement, the script evaluates the *controlling expression* (choice in this example) in the parentheses following keyword switch. The value of this expression is compared with the value in each of the case labels, starting with the first case label. Assume that the user entered 2. Remember that the value typed by the user in a prompt dialog is returned as a string. So, the string 2 is compared to the string in each case in the switch statement. If a match occurs (case "2":), the statements for that case execute. For the string 2 (lines 29–32), we set startTag to an opening ol tag with the style property list-style-type set to upper-alpha, set endTag to "</ol>" to indicate the end of an ordered list and set listType to "<h1>Lettered List</h1>". If no match occurs between the controlling expression's value and a case label, the default case executes and sets variable validInput to false.

The break statement in line 32 causes program control to proceed with the first statement after the switch statement. The break statement is used because the cases in a switch statement would otherwise run together. If break is not used anywhere in a switch statement, then each time a match occurs in the statement, the statements for all the remaining cases execute.

Next, the flow of control continues with the if statement in line 42, which tests variable validInput to determine whether its value is true. If so, lines 44–49 write the listType, the startTag, three list items (<li>) and the endTag. Otherwise, the script writes text in the XHTML document indicating that an invalid choice was made (line 52).

Each case can have multiple actions (statements). The switch statement is different from others in that braces are not required around multiple actions in a case of a switch. The general switch statement (i.e., using a break in each case) is flowcharted in Fig. 6.8. [*Note:* As an exercise, flowchart the general switch statement without break statements.]

The flowchart makes it clear that each break statement at the end of a case causes control to exit from the switch statement immediately. The break statement is not required for the last case in the switch statement (or the default case, when it appears last), because program control automatically continues with the next statement after the switch statement.

Common Programming Error 6.6

Forgetting a break statement when one is needed in a switch statement is a logic error.

Software Engineering Observation 6.1

Provide a default case in switch statements. Cases not explicitly tested in a switch statement without a default case are ignored. Including a default case focuses you on processing exceptional conditions. However, there are situations in which no default processing is needed.

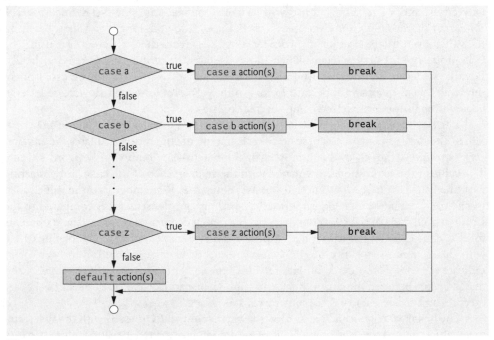

Fig. 6.8 | switch multiple-selection statement.

Good Programming Practice 6.4

Although the case *clauses and the* default *case clause in a* switch *statement can occur in any order, it is clearer (and more common) to place the* default *clause last.*

Good Programming Practice 6.5

In a switch *statement, when the* default *clause is listed last, its* break *statement is not required. Some programmers include this* break *for clarity and for symmetry with other* cases.

Note that having several case labels listed together (e.g., case 1: case 2: with no statements between the cases) performs the same set of actions for each case.

6.6 do...while Repetition Statement

The *do...while repetition statement* is similar to the while statement. In the while statement, the loop-continuation test occurs at the beginning of the loop, before the body of the loop executes. The do...while statement tests the loop-continuation condition *after* the loop body executes—therefore, *the loop body always executes at least once.* When a do...while terminates, execution continues with the statement after the while clause. Note that it is not necessary to use braces in a do...while statement if there is only one statement in the body. However, the braces usually are included, to avoid confusion between the while and do...while statements. For example,

> **while** (*condition*)

normally is regarded as the header to a while statement. A do...while statement with no braces around a single-statement body appears as

> **do**
>   *statement*
> **while** (*condition*);

which can be confusing. The last line—while(*condition*);—may be misinterpreted as a while statement containing an empty statement (the semicolon by itself). Thus, to avoid confusion, the do...while statement with a one-statement body is often written as follows:

> **do**
> {
>   *statement*
> } **while** (*condition*);

Good Programming Practice 6.6

Some programmers always include braces in a do...while statement even if they are not necessary. This helps eliminate ambiguity between the while statement and the do...while statement containing a one-statement body.

Error-Prevention Tip 6.3

Infinite loops are caused when the loop-continuation condition never becomes false *in a* while, *for or* do...while *statement. To prevent this, make sure that there is not a semicolon immediately after the header of a* while *or* for *statement. In a counter-controlled loop, make sure that the control variable is incremented (or decremented) in the body of the loop. In a sentinel-controlled loop, make sure that the sentinel value is eventually input.*

The script in Fig. 6.9 uses a do...while statement to display each of the six different XHTML heading types (h1 through h6). Line 12 declares control variable counter and initializes it to 1. Upon entering the do...while statement, lines 15–17 write a line of XHTML text in the document. The value of control variable counter is used to create the starting and ending header tags (e.g., <h1> and </h1>) and to create the line of text to display (e.g., This is an h1 level head). Line 18 increments the counter before the loop-continuation test occurs at the bottom of the loop.

The do...while flowchart in Fig. 6.10 makes it clear that the loop-continuation test does not occur until the action executes at least once.

```
1   <?xml version = "1.0" encoding = "utf-8"?>
2   <!DOCTYPE html PUBLIC "-//W3C//DTD XHTML 1.0 Strict//EN"
3      "http://www.w3.org/TR/xhtml1/DTD/xhtml1-strict.dtd">
4
5   <!-- Fig. 6.9: DoWhileTest.html -->
6   <!-- Using the do...while repetition statement. -->
7   <html xmlns = "http://www.w3.org/1999/xhtml">
8      <head>
9         <title>Using the do...while Repetition Statement</title>
10        <script type = "text/javascript">
11           <!--
12           var counter = 1;
13
14           do {
15              document.writeln( "<h" + counter + ">This is " +
16                 "an h" + counter + " level head" + "</h" +
17                 counter + ">" );
18              ++counter;
19           } while ( counter <= 6 );
20           // -->
21        </script>
22
23     </head><body></body>
24  </html>
```

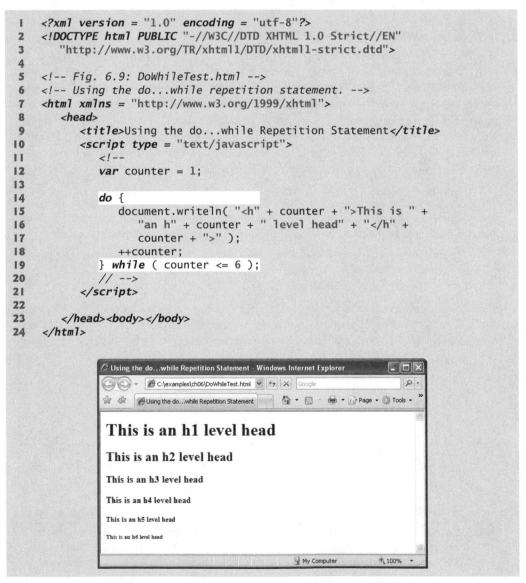

Fig. 6.9 | Using the do...while repetition statement.

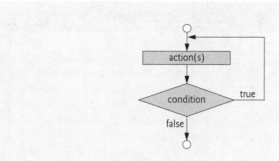

Fig. 6.10 | do...while repetition statement flowchart.

6.7 break and continue Statements

The ***break*** and ***continue*** *statements* alter the flow of control. The break statement, when executed in a while, for, do...while or switch statement, causes immediate exit from the statement. Execution continues with the first statement after the structure. The break statement is commonly used to escape early from a loop or to skip the remainder of a switch statement (as in Fig. 6.7). Figure 6.11 demonstrates the break statement in a for repetition statement.

```
1   <?xml version = "1.0" encoding = "utf-8"?>
2   <!DOCTYPE html PUBLIC "-//W3C//DTD XHTML 1.0 Strict//EN"
3      "http://www.w3.org/TR/xhtml1/DTD/xhtml1-strict.dtd">
4
5   <!-- Fig. 6.11: BreakTest.html -->
6   <!-- Using the break statement in a for statement. -->
7   <html xmlns = "http://www.w3.org/1999/xhtml">
8      <head>
9         <title>
10           Using the break Statement in a for Statement
11        </title>
12        <script type = "text/javascript">
13           <!--
14           for ( var count = 1; count <= 10; ++count )
15           {
16              if ( count == 5 )
17                 break; // break loop only if count == 5
18
19              document.writeln( "Count is: " + count + "<br />" );
20           } //end for
21
22           document.writeln(
23              "Broke out of loop at count = " + count );
24           // -->
25        </script>
26     </head><body></body>
27  </html>
```

Fig. 6.11 | Using the break statement in a for statement. (Part 1 of 2.)

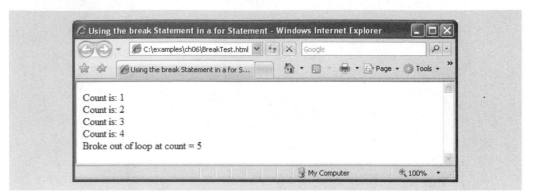

Fig. 6.11 | Using the break statement in a for statement. (Part 2 of 2.)

During each iteration of the for statement in lines 14–20, the script writes the value of count in the XHTML document. When the if statement in line 16 detects that count is 5, the break in line 17 executes. This statement terminates the for statement, and the program proceeds to line 22 (the next statement in sequence immediately after the for statement), where the script writes the value of count when the loop terminated (i.e., 5). The loop executes line 19 only four times.

The continue statement, when executed in a while, for or do...while statement, skips the remaining statements in the body of the statement and proceeds with the next iteration of the loop. In while and do...while statements, the loop-continuation test evaluates immediately after the continue statement executes. In for statements, the increment expression executes, then the loop-continuation test evaluates. This is the one case in which for and while differ. Improper placement of continue before the increment in a while may result in an infinite loop.

Figure 6.12 uses continue in a for statement to skip the document.writeln statement in line 20 when the if statement in line 17 determines that the value of count is 5. When the continue statement executes, the script skips the remainder of the for statement's body. Program control continues with the increment of the for statement's control variable, followed by the loop-continuation test to determine whether the loop should continue executing.

```
1   <?xml version = "1.0" encoding = "utf-8"?>
2   <!DOCTYPE html PUBLIC "-//W3C//DTD XHTML 1.0 Strict//EN"
3       "http://www.w3.org/TR/xhtml1/DTD/xhtml1-strict.dtd">
4
5   <!-- Fig. 6.12: ContinueTest.html -->
6   <!-- Using the continue statement in a for statement. -->
7   <html xmlns = "http://www.w3.org/1999/xhtml">
8       <head>
9           <title>
10              Using the continue Statement in a for Statement
11          </title>
12
```

Fig. 6.12 | Using the continue statement in a for statement. (Part 1 of 2.)

```
13      <script type = "text/javascript">
14        <!--
15        for ( var count = 1; count <= 10; ++count )
16        {
17           if ( count == 5 )
18              continue; // skip remaining loop code only if count == 5
19
20           document.writeln( "Count is: " + count + "<br />" );
21        } //end for
22
23        document.writeln( "Used continue to skip printing 5" );
24        // -->
25      </script>
26
27    </head><body></body>
28 </html>
```

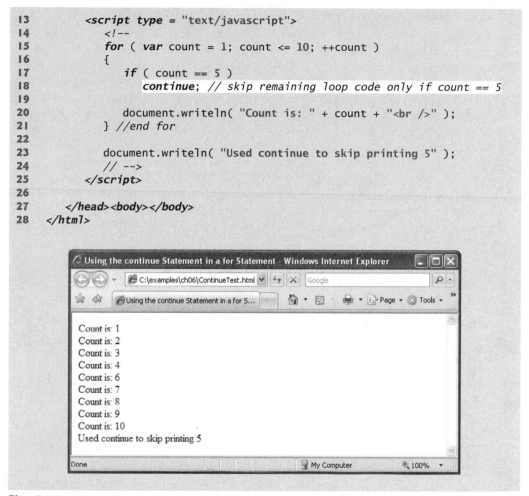

Fig. 6.12 | Using the continue statement in a for statement. (Part 2 of 2.)

Software Engineering Observation 6.2

Some programmers feel that break and continue violate structured programming. They do not use break and continue, because the effects of these statements can be achieved by structured programming techniques.

Performance Tip 6.1

The break and continue statements, when used properly, perform faster than the corresponding structured techniques.

Software Engineering Observation 6.3

There is a tension between achieving quality software engineering and achieving the best-performing software. Often, one of these goals is achieved at the expense of the other. For all but the most performance-intensive situations, the following rule of thumb should be followed: First make your code simple, readable and correct; then make it fast and small, but only if necessary.

6.8 Labeled break and continue Statements

The break statement can break out of an immediately enclosing while, for, do...while or switch statement. To break out of a nested set of structures, you can use the *labeled break statement*. This statement, when executed in a while, for, do...while or switch statement, causes immediate exit from that statement and any number of enclosing repetition statements; program execution resumes with the first statement after the enclosing *labeled statement* (a statement preceded by a label). The labeled statement can be a block (a set of statements enclosed in curly braces, {}). Labeled break statements commonly are used to terminate nested looping structures containing while, for, do...while or switch statements. Figure 6.13 demonstrates the labeled break in a nested for statement.

The labeled block (lines 12–28) begins with a *label* (an identifier followed by a colon). Here, we use the label stop:. The block is enclosed between the braces at the end of line 12 and in line 28, and includes both the nested for statement starting in line 13 and the document.writeln statement in line 27. When the if statement in line 17 detects that row

```
 1   <?xml version = "1.0" encoding = "utf-8"?>
 2   <!DOCTYPE html PUBLIC "-//W3C//DTD XHTML 1.0 Strict//EN"
 3      "http://www.w3.org/TR/xhtml1/DTD/xhtml1-strict.dtd">
 4
 5   <!-- Fig. 6.13: BreakLabelTest.html -->
 6   <!-- Labeled break statement in a nested for statement. -->
 7   <html xmlns = "http://www.w3.org/1999/xhtml">
 8      <head>
 9         <title>Using the break Statement with a Label</title>
10         <script type = "text/javascript">
11            <!--
12            stop: { // labeled block
13               for ( var row = 1; row <= 10; ++row )
14               {
15                  for ( var column = 1; column <= 5 ; ++column )
16                  {
17                     if ( row == 5 )
18                        break stop; // jump to end of stop block
19
20                     document.write( "* " );
21                  } //end for
22
23                  document.writeln( "<br />" );
24               } //end for
25
26               // the following line is skipped
27               document.writeln( "This line should not print" );
28            } // end block labeled stop
29
30            document.writeln( "End of script" );
31            // -->
32         </script>
33      </head><body></body>
34   </html>
```

Fig. 6.13 | Labeled break statement in a nested for statement. (Part 1 of 2.)

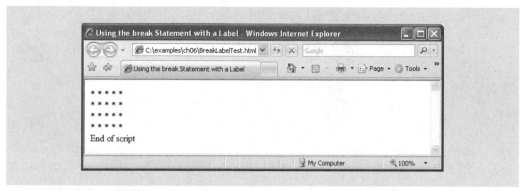

Fig. 6.13 | Labeled break statement in a nested for statement. (Part 2 of 2.)

is equal to 5, the statement in line 18 executes. This statement terminates both the for statement in line 15 and its enclosing for statement in line 13, and the program proceeds to the statement in line 30 (the first statement in sequence after the labeled block). The inner for statement executes its body only four times. Note that the document.writeln statement in line 27 never executes, because it is included in the labeled block and the outer for statement never completes.

The continue statement proceeds with the next iteration (repetition) of the immediately enclosing while, for or do...while statement. The *labeled continue statement*, when executed in a repetition statement (while, for or do...while), skips the remaining statements in the structure's body and any number of enclosing repetition statements, then proceeds with the next iteration of the enclosing *labeled repetition statement* (a repetition statement preceded by a label). In labeled while and do...while statements, the loop-continuation test evaluates immediately after the continue statement executes. In a labeled for statement, the increment expression executes, then the loop-continuation test evaluates. Figure 6.14 uses the labeled continue statement in a nested for statement to cause execution to continue with the next iteration of the outer for statement.

```
1    <?xml version = "1.0" encoding = "utf-8"?>
2    <!DOCTYPE html PUBLIC "-//W3C//DTD XHTML 1.0 Strict//EN"
3       "http://www.w3.org/TR/xhtml1/DTD/xhtml1-strict.dtd">
4
5    <!-- Fig. 6.14: ContinueLabelTest.html -->
6    <!-- Labeled continue statement in a nested for statement. -->
7    <html xmlns = "http://www.w3.org/1999/xhtml">
8       <head>
9          <title>Using the continue Statement with a Label</title>
10         <script type = "text/javascript">
11            <!--
12            nextRow: // target label of continue statement
13               for ( var row = 1; row <= 5; ++row )
14               {
15                  document.writeln( "<br />" );
16
```

Fig. 6.14 | Labeled continue statement in a nested for statement. (Part 1 of 2.)

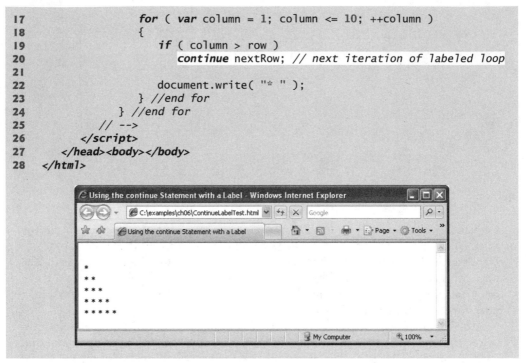

```
17                      for ( var column = 1; column <= 10; ++column )
18                      {
19                          if ( column > row )
20                              continue nextRow; // next iteration of labeled loop
21
22                          document.write( "* " );
23                      } //end for
24                  } //end for
25              // -->
26          </script>
27      </head><body></body>
28  </html>
```

Fig. 6.14 | Labeled `continue` statement in a nested `for` statement. (Part 2 of 2.)

The labeled `for` statement (lines 13–24) starts with the `nextRow` label in line 12. When the `if` statement in line 19 in the inner `for` statement detects that `column` is greater than `row`, line 20 executes and program control continues with the increment of the control variable of the outer `for` statement. Even though the inner `for` statement counts from 1 to 10, the number of * characters output on a row never exceeds the value of `row`.

6.9 Logical Operators

So far, we have studied only such *simple conditions* as `count <= 10`, `total > 1000` and `number != sentinelValue`. These conditions were expressed in terms of the relational operators `>`, `<`, `>=` and `<=`, and in terms of the equality operators `==` and `!=`. Each decision tested one condition. To make a decision based on multiple conditions, we performed these tests in separate statements or in nested `if` or `if...else` statements.

JavaScript provides *logical operators* that can be used to form more complex conditions by combining simple conditions. The logical operators are *&& (logical AND)*, *|| (logical OR)* and *! (logical NOT*, also called *logical negation)*. We consider examples of each of these operators.

Suppose that, at some point in a program, we wish to ensure that two conditions are *both* true before we choose a certain path of execution. In this case, we can use the logical `&&` operator, as follows:

```
if ( gender == 1 && age >= 65 )
    ++seniorFemales;
```

This if statement contains two simple conditions. The condition gender == 1 might be evaluated to determine, for example, whether a person is a female. The condition age >= 65 is evaluated to determine whether a person is a senior citizen. The if statement then considers the combined condition

```
gender == 1 && age >= 65
```

This condition is true *if and only if* both of the simple conditions are true. Finally, if this combined condition is indeed true, the count of seniorFemales is incremented by 1. If either or both of the simple conditions are false, the program skips the incrementing and proceeds to the statement following the if statement. The preceding combined condition can be made more readable by adding redundant parentheses:

```
( gender == 1 ) && ( age >= 65 )
```

The table in Fig. 6.15 summarizes the && operator. The table shows all four possible combinations of false and true values for *expression1* and *expression2*. Such tables are often called **truth tables**. JavaScript evaluates to false or true all expressions that include relational operators, equality operators and/or logical operators.

expression1	expression2	expression1 && expression2
false	false	false
false	true	false
true	false	false
true	true	true

Fig. 6.15 | Truth table for the && (logical AND) operator.

Now let us consider the || (logical OR) operator. Suppose we wish to ensure that either *or* both of two conditions are true before we choose a certain path of execution. In this case, we use the || operator, as in the following program segment:

```
if ( semesterAverage >= 90 || finalExam >= 90 )
    document.writeln( "Student grade is A" );
```

This statement also contains two simple conditions. The condition semesterAverage >= 90 is evaluated to determine whether the student deserves an "A" in the course because of a solid performance throughout the semester. The condition finalExam >= 90 is evaluated to determine whether the student deserves an "A" in the course because of an outstanding performance on the final exam. The if statement then considers the combined condition

```
semesterAverage >= 90 || finalExam >= 90
```

and awards the student an "A" if either or both of the simple conditions are true. Note that the message "Student grade is A" is *not* printed only when both of the simple conditions are false. Figure 6.16 is a truth table for the logical OR operator (||).

expression1	expression2	expression1 || expression2
false	false	false
false	true	true
true	false	true
true	true	true

Fig. 6.16 | Truth table for the \|\| (logical OR) operator.

The **&&** operator has a higher precedence than the **\|\|** operator. Both operators associate from left to right. An expression containing **&&** or **\|\|** operators is evaluated only until truth or falsity is known. Thus, evaluation of the expression

```
gender == 1 && age >= 65
```

stops immediately if `gender` is not equal to 1 (i.e., the entire expression is `false`) and continues if `gender` is equal to 1 (i.e., the entire expression could still be `true` if the condition `age >= 65` is true). Similarly, the **\|\|** operator immediately returns `true` if the first operand is `true`. This performance feature for evaluation of logical AND and logical OR expressions is called *short-circuit evaluation*.

JavaScript provides the **!** (logical negation) operator to enable a programmer to "reverse" the meaning of a condition (i.e., a `true` value becomes `false`, and a `false` value becomes `true`). Unlike the logical operators **&&** and **\|\|**, which combine two conditions (i.e., they are binary operators), the logical negation operator has only a single condition as an operand (i.e., it is a unary operator). The logical negation operator is placed before a condition to choose a path of execution if the original condition (without the logical negation operator) is `false`, as in the following program segment:

```
if ( ! ( grade == sentinelValue ) )
    document.writeln( "The next grade is " + grade );
```

The parentheses around the condition `grade == sentinelValue` are needed, because the logical negation operator has a higher precedence than the equality operator. Figure 6.17 is a truth table for the logical negation operator.

expression	!expression
false	true
true	false

Fig. 6.17 | Truth table for operator ! (logical negation).

In most cases, you can avoid using logical negation by expressing the condition differently with an appropriate relational or equality operator. For example, the preceding statement may also be written as follows:

```
if ( grade != sentinelValue )
    document.writeln( "The next grade is " + grade );
```

The script in Fig. 6.18 demonstrates all the logical operators by producing their truth tables. The script produces an XHTML table containing the results.

In the output of Fig. 6.18, the strings "false" and "true" indicate false and true for the operands in each condition. The result of the condition is shown as true or false. Note that when you use the concatenation operator with a boolean value and a string, JavaScript automatically converts the boolean value to string "false" or "true". Lines 16–39 build an XHTML table containing the results.

```
1   <?xml version = "1.0" encoding = "utf-8"?>
2   <!DOCTYPE html PUBLIC "-//W3C//DTD XHTML 1.0 Strict//EN"
3      "http://www.w3.org/TR/xhtml1/DTD/xhtml1-strict.dtd">
4
5   <!-- Fig. 6.18: LogicalOperators.html -->
6   <!-- Demonstrating logical operators. -->
7   <html xmlns = "http://www.w3.org/1999/xhtml">
8      <head>
9         <title>Demonstrating the Logical Operators</title>
10        <style type = "text/css">
11           table  { width: 100% }
12           td.left { width: 25% }
13        </style>
14        <script type = "text/javascript">
15           <!--
16           document.writeln(
17              "<table border = \"1\"" );
18           document.writeln(
19              "<caption>Demonstrating Logical " +
20                 "Operators</caption>" );
21           document.writeln(
22              "<tr><td class = \"left\">Logical AND (&&)</td>" +
23              "<td>false && false: " + ( false && false ) +
24              "<br />false && true: " + ( false && true ) +
25              "<br />true && false: " + ( true && false ) +
26              "<br />true && true: " + ( true && true ) +
27              "</td></tr>" );
28           document.writeln(
29              "<tr><td class = \"left\">Logical OR (||)</td>" +
30              "<td>false || false: " + ( false || false ) +
31              "<br />false || true: " + ( false || true ) +
32              "<br />true || false: " + ( true || false ) +
33              "<br />true || true: " + ( true || true ) +
34              "</td></tr>" );
35           document.writeln(
36              "<tr><td class = \"left\">Logical NOT (!)</td>" +
37              "<td>!false: " + ( !false ) +
38              "<br />!true: " + ( !true ) + "</td></tr>" );
39           document.writeln( "</table>" );
40           // -->
41        </script>
42     </head><body></body>
43  </html>
```

Fig. 6.18 | Demonstrating logical operators. (Part 1 of 2.)

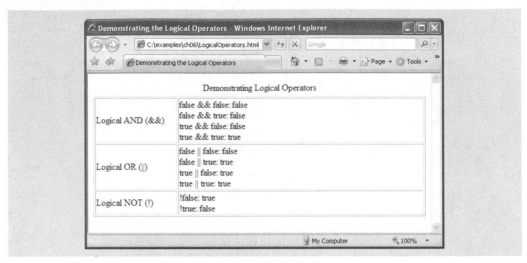

Fig. 6.18 | Demonstrating logical operators. (Part 2 of 2.)

An interesting feature of JavaScript is that most nonboolean values can be converted to boolean `true` or `false` values. Nonzero numeric values are considered to be `true`. The numeric value zero is considered to be `false`. Any string that contains characters is considered to be `true`. The empty string (i.e., the string containing no characters) is considered to be `false`. The value `null` and variables that have been declared but not initialized are considered to be `false`. All objects (e.g., the browser's `document` and `window` objects and JavaScript's `Math` object) are considered to be `true`.

Figure 6.19 shows the precedence and associativity of the JavaScript operators introduced up to this point. The operators are shown top to bottom in decreasing order of precedence.

Operator						Associativity	Type
++	--	!				right to left	unary
*	/	%				left to right	multiplicative
+	-					left to right	additive
<	<=	>	>=			left to right	relational
==	!=					left to right	equality
&&						left to right	logical AND
||						left to right	logical OR
?:						right to left	conditional
=	+=	-=	*=	/=	%=	right to left	assignment

Fig. 6.19 | Precedence and associativity of the operators discussed so far.

7

JavaScript: Functions

Form ever follows function.
—Louis Sullivan

E pluribus unum.
(One composed of many.)
—Virgil

O! call back yesterday, bid
time return.
—William Shakespeare

Call me Ishmael.
—Herman Melville

When you call me that,
smile.
—Owen Wister

OBJECTIVES

In this chapter you'll learn:

■ How to create new functions.

■ How to pass information between functions.

■ Simulation techniques that use random number generation.

■ How the visibility of identifiers is limited to specific regions of programs.

■ To use JavaScript's global functions.

■ To use recursive functions.

■ To compare recursion vs. iteration.

7.1 Introduction

Most computer programs that solve real-world problems are much larger than the programs presented in the first few chapters of this book. Experience has shown that the best way to develop and maintain a large program is to construct it from small, simple pieces, or *modules*. This technique is called *divide and conquer*. This chapter describes many key features of JavaScript that facilitate the design, implementation, operation and maintenance of large scripts.

7.2 Functions

Modules in JavaScript are called *functions*. JavaScript programs are written by combining new functions that you write with "prepackaged" functions and objects available in JavaScript. The prepackaged functions that belong to JavaScript objects (such as `Math.pow` and `Math.round`, introduced previously) are called *methods*. The term method implies that the function belongs to a particular object. We refer to functions that belong to a particular JavaScript object as methods; all others are referred to as functions.

JavaScript provides several objects that have a rich collection of methods for performing common mathematical calculations, string manipulations, date and time manipulations, and manipulations of collections of data called arrays. These objects provide many of the capabilities you'll frequently need. Some common predefined objects of JavaScript and their methods are discussed in Chapter 8, JavaScript: Arrays, and Chapter 9, JavaScript: Objects.

Software Engineering Observation 7.1

Avoid reinventing the wheel. Use existing JavaScript objects, methods and functions instead of writing new ones. This reduces script-development time and helps avoid introducing errors.

Portability Tip 7.1

Using the methods built into JavaScript objects helps make scripts more portable.

You can write functions to define specific tasks that may be used at many points in a script. These functions are referred to as *programmer-defined functions*. The actual statements defining the function are written only once and are hidden from other functions.

Functions are invoked by writing the name of the function, followed by a left parenthesis, followed by a comma-separated list of zero or more arguments, followed by a right parenthesis. For example, a programmer desiring to convert a string stored in variable `inputValue` to a floating-point number and add it to variable `total` might write

```
total += parseFloat( inputValue );
```

When this statement executes, JavaScript function ***parseFloat*** converts the string in the `inputValue` variable to a floating-point value and adds that value to `total`. Variable `inputValue` is function `parseFloat`'s argument. Function `parseFloat` takes a string representation of a floating-point number as an argument and returns the corresponding floating-point numeric value. Function arguments may be constants, variables or expressions.

Methods are called in the same way, but require the name of the object to which the method belongs and a dot preceding the method name. For example, we've already seen the syntax `document.writeln("Hi there.");`. This statement calls the `document` object's `writeln` method to output the text.

7.3 Programmer-Defined Functions

Functions allow you to modularize a program. All variables declared in function definitions are *local variables*—they can be accessed only in the function in which they are defined. Most functions have a list of *parameters* that provide the means for communicating information between functions via function calls. A function's parameters are also considered to be local variables. When a function is called, the arguments in the function call are assigned to the corresponding parameters in the function definition.

Software Engineering Observation 7.2

If a function's task cannot be expressed concisely, perhaps the function is performing too many different tasks. It is usually best to break such a function into several smaller functions.

7.4 Function Definitions

Each script we've presented thus far in the text has consisted of a series of statements and control structures in sequence. These scripts have been executed as the browser loads the web page and evaluates the `<head>` section of the page. We now consider how you can write your own customized functions and call them in a script.

Programmer-Defined Function square

Consider a script (Fig. 7.1) that uses a function `square` to calculate the squares of the integers from 1 to 10. [*Note:* We continue to show many examples in which the `body` element of the XHTML document is empty and the document is created directly by JavaScript. In later chapters, we show many examples in which JavaScripts interact with the elements in the `body` of a document.]

The `for` statement in lines 15–17 outputs XHTML that displays the results of squaring the integers from 1 to 10. Each iteration of the loop calculates the `square` of the current value of control variable x and outputs the result by writing a line in the XHTML document. Function `square` is invoked, or called, in line 17 with the expression

```
1   <?xml version = "1.0" encoding = "utf-8"?>
2   <!DOCTYPE html PUBLIC "-//W3C//DTD XHTML 1.0 Strict//EN"
3      "http://www.w3.org/TR/xhtml1/DTD/xhtml1-strict.dtd">
4
5   <!-- Fig. 7.1: SquareInt.html -->
6   <!-- Programmer-defined function square. -->
7   <html xmlns = "http://www.w3.org/1999/xhtml">
8      <head>
9         <title>A Programmer-Defined square Function</title>
10        <script type = "text/javascript">
11           <!--
12           document.writeln( "<h1>Square the numbers from 1 to 10</h1>" );
13
14           // square the numbers from 1 to 10
15           for ( var x = 1; x <= 10; x++ )
16              document.writeln( "The square of " + x + " is " +
17                 square( x ) + "<br />" );
18
19           // The following square function definition is executed
20           // only when the function is explicitly called.
21
22           // square function definition
23           function square( y )
24           {
25              return y * y;
26           } // end function square
27           // -->
28        </script>
29     </head><body></body>
30  </html>
```

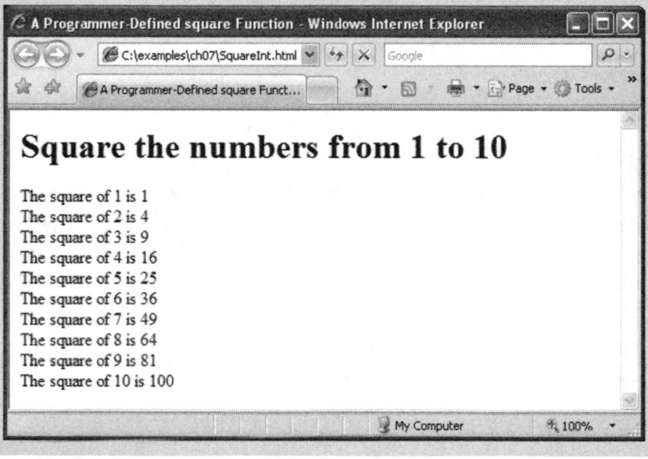

Square the numbers from 1 to 10

The square of 1 is 1
The square of 2 is 4
The square of 3 is 9
The square of 4 is 16
The square of 5 is 25
The square of 6 is 36
The square of 7 is 49
The square of 8 is 64
The square of 9 is 81
The square of 10 is 100

Fig. 7.1 | Programmer-defined function square.

square(x). When program control reaches this expression, the program calls function square (defined in lines 23–26). The parentheses () represent the *function-call operator*, which has high precedence. At this point, the program makes a copy of the value of x (the argument) and program control transfers to the first line of function square. Function square receives the copy of the value of x and stores it in the parameter y. Then square calculates y * y. The result is passed back (returned) to the point in line 17 where square was invoked. Lines 16–17 concatenate "The square of ", the value of x, the string " is ", the value returned by function square and a <br /> tag and write that line of text in the XHTML document. This process is repeated 10 times.

The definition of function square (lines 23–26) shows that square expects a single parameter y. Function square uses this name in its body to manipulate the value passed to square from line 17. The *return statement* in square passes the result of the calculation y * y back to the calling function. Note that JavaScript keyword var is not used to declare variables in the parameter list of a function.

Common Programming Error 7.1

Using the JavaScript var keyword to declare a variable in a function parameter list results in a JavaScript runtime error.

In this example, function square follows the rest of the script. When the for statement terminates, program control does *not* flow sequentially into function square. A function must be called explicitly for the code in its body to execute. Thus, when the for statement terminates in this example, the script terminates.

Software Engineering Observation 7.3

Statements that are enclosed in the body of a function definition are not executed by the JavaScript interpreter unless the function is invoked explicitly.

The format of a function definition is

```
function function-name( parameter-list )
{
    declarations and statements
}
```

The *function-name* is any valid identifier. The *parameter-list* is a comma-separated list containing the names of the parameters received by the function when it is called. There should be one argument in the function call for each parameter in the function definition. If a function does not receive any values, the *parameter-list* is empty (i.e., the function name is followed by an empty set of parentheses). The *declarations* and *statements* in braces form the *function body.*

Common Programming Error 7.2

Forgetting to return a value from a function that is supposed to return a value is a logic error.

Common Programming Error 7.3

Placing a semicolon after the right parenthesis enclosing the parameter list of a function definition results in a JavaScript runtime error.

Common Programming Error 7.4

Redefining a function parameter as a local variable in the function is a logic error.

Common Programming Error 7.5

Passing to a function an argument that is not compatible with the corresponding parameter's expected type is a logic error and may result in a JavaScript runtime error.

Good Programming Practice 7.1

Although it is not incorrect to do so, do not use the same name for an argument passed to a function and the corresponding parameter in the function definition. Using different names avoids ambiguity.

Software Engineering Observation 7.4

To promote software reusability, every function should be limited to performing a single, well-defined task, and the name of the function should express that task effectively. Such functions make programs easier to write, debug, maintain and modify.

There are three ways to return control to the point at which a function was invoked. If the function does not return a result, control returns when the program reaches the function-ending right brace or by executing the statement

    return;

If the function does return a result, the statement

    return *expression*;

returns the value of *expression* to the caller. When a return statement is executed, control returns immediately to the point at which the function was invoked.

Programmer-Defined Function maximum
The script in our next example (Fig. 7.2) uses a programmer-defined function called max-imum to determine and return the largest of three floating-point values.

```
 1   <?xml version = "1.0" encoding = "utf-8"?>
 2   <!DOCTYPE html PUBLIC "-//W3C//DTD XHTML 1.0 Strict//EN"
 3      "http://www.w3.org/TR/xhtml/DTD/xhtml1-strict.dtd">
 4
 5   <!-- Fig. 7.2: maximum.html -->
 6   <!-- Programmer-Defined maximum function. -->
 7   <html xmlns = "http://www.w3.org/1999/xhtml">
 8      <head>
 9         <title>Finding the Maximum of Three Values</title>
10         <script type = "text/javascript">
11            <!--
12            var input1 = window.prompt( "Enter first number", "0" );
13            var input2 = window.prompt( "Enter second number", "0" );
14            var input3 = window.prompt( "Enter third number", "0" );
15
16            var value1 = parseFloat( input1 );
17            var value2 = parseFloat( input2 );
18            var value3 = parseFloat( input3 );
```

Fig. 7.2 | Programmer-defined maximum function. (Part 1 of 2.)

```
19
20              var maxValue = maximum( value1, value2, value3 );
21
22              document.writeln( "First number: " + value1 +
23                 "<br />Second number: " + value2 +
24                 "<br />Third number: " + value3 +
25                 "<br />Maximum is: " + maxValue );
26
27              // maximum function definition (called from line 20)
28              function maximum( x, y, z )
29              {
30                 return Math.max( x, Math.max( y, z ) );
31              } // end function maximum
32              // -->
33           </script>
34        </head>
35        <body>
36           <p>Click Refresh (or Reload) to run the script again</p>
37        </body>
38     </html>
```

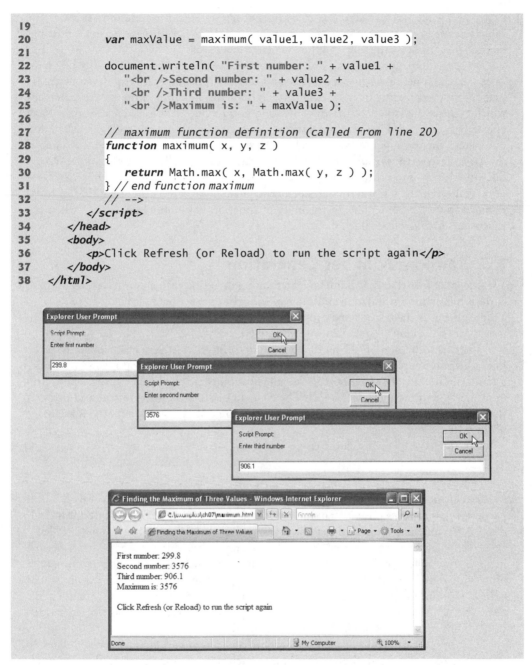

Fig. 7.2 | Programmer-defined `maximum` function. (Part 2 of 2.)

The three floating-point values are input by the user via `prompt` dialogs (lines 12–14). Lines 16–18 use function `parseFloat` to convert the strings entered by the user to floating-point values. The statement in line 20 passes the three floating-point values to function `maximum` (defined in lines 28–31), which determines the largest floating-point value. This value is returned to line 20 by the return statement in function maximum. The value returned is assigned to variable maxValue. Lines 22–25 display the three floating-point values input by the user and the calculated maxValue.

Note the implementation of the function maximum (lines 28–31). The first line indicates that the function's name is maximum and that the function takes three parameters (x, y and z) to accomplish its task. Also, the body of the function contains the statement which returns the largest of the three floating-point values, using two calls to the Math object's max method. First, method Math.max is invoked with the values of variables y and z to determine the larger of the two values. Next, the value of variable x and the result of the first call to Math.max are passed to method Math.max. Finally, the result of the second call to Math.max is returned to the point at which maximum was invoked (i.e., line 20). Note once again that the script terminates before sequentially reaching the definition of function maximum. The statement in the body of function maximum executes only when the function is invoked from line 20.

7.5 Random Number Generation

We now take a brief and, it is hoped, entertaining diversion into a popular programming application, namely simulation and game playing. In this section and the next, we develop a nicely structured game-playing program that includes multiple functions. The program uses most of the control statements we've studied.

There is something in the air of a gambling casino that invigorates people, from the high rollers at the plush mahogany-and-felt craps tables to the quarter poppers at the one-armed bandits. It is the *element of chance*, the possibility that luck will convert a pocketful of money into a mountain of wealth. The element of chance can be introduced through the Math object's *random method*. (Remember, we are calling random a method because it belongs to the Math object.)

Consider the following statement:

```
var randomValue = Math.random();
```

Method random generates a floating-point value from 0.0 up to, but not including, 1.0. If random truly produces values at random, then every value from 0.0 up to, but not including, 1.0 has an equal *chance* (or *probability*) of being chosen each time random is called.

The range of values produced directly by random is often different than what is needed in a specific application. For example, a program that simulates coin tossing might require only 0 for heads and 1 for tails. A program that simulates rolling a six-sided die would require random integers in the range from 1 to 6. A program that randomly predicts the next type of spaceship, out of four possibilities, that will fly across the horizon in a video game might require random integers in the range 0–3 or 1–4.

To demonstrate method random, let us develop a program (Fig. 7.3) that simulates 20 rolls of a six-sided die and displays the value of each roll. We use the multiplication operator (*) with random as follows:

```
Math.floor( 1 + Math.random() * 6 )
```

First, the preceding expression multiplies the result of a call to Math.random() by 6 to produce a number in the range 0.0 up to, but not including, 6.0. This is called *scaling* the

```
 1  <?xml version = "1.0" encoding = "utf-8"?>
 2  <!DOCTYPE html PUBLIC "-//W3C//DTD XHTML 1.0 Strict//EN"
 3     "http://www.w3.org/TR/xhtml1/DTD/xhtml1-strict.dtd">
 4
 5  <!-- Fig. 7.3: RandomInt.html -->
 6  <!-- Random integers, shifting and scaling. -->
 7  <html xmlns = "http://www.w3.org/1999/xhtml">
 8     <head>
 9        <title>Shifted and Scaled Random Integers</title>
10        <style type = "text/css">
11           table { width: 50%;
12                   border: 1px solid gray;
13                   text-align: center }
14        </style>
15        <script type = "text/javascript">
16           <!--
17           var value;
18
19           document.writeln( "<table>" );
20           document.writeln( "<caption>Random Numbers</caption><tr>" );
21
22           for ( var i = 1; i <= 20; i++ )
23           {
24              value = Math.floor( 1 + Math.random() * 6 );
25              document.writeln( "<td>" + value + "</td>" );
26
27              // start a new table row every 5 entries
28              if ( i % 5 == 0 && i != 20 )
29                 document.writeln( "</tr><tr>" );
30           } // end for
31
32           document.writeln( "</tr></table>" );
33           // -->
34        </script>
35     </head>
36     <body>
37        <p>Click Refresh (or Reload) to run the script again</p>
38     </body>
39  </html>
```

Fig. 7.3 | Random integers, shifting and scaling. (Part 1 of 2.)

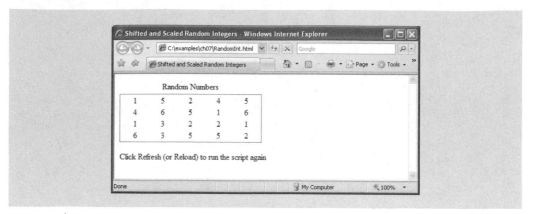

Fig. 7.3 | Random integers, shifting and scaling. (Part 2 of 2.)

range of the random numbers. Next, we add 1 to the result to shift the range of numbers to produce a number in the range 1.0 up to, but not including, 7.0. Finally, we use method **Math.floor** to *round* the result down to the closest integer not greater than the argument's value—for example, 1.75 is rounded to 1. Figure 7.3 confirms that the results are in the range 1 to 6.

To show that these numbers occur with approximately equal likelihood, let us simulate 6000 rolls of a die with the program in Fig. 7.4. Each integer from 1 to 6 should appear approximately 1000 times. Use your browser's **Refresh** (or **Reload**) button to execute the script again.

As the output of the program shows, we used Math method random and the scaling and shifting techniques of the previous example to simulate the rolling of a six-sided die. Note that we used nested control statements to determine the number of times each side of the six-sided die occurred. Lines 12–17 declare and initialize counters to keep track of the number of times each of the six die values appears. Line 18 declares a variable to store the face value of the die. The for statement in lines 21–46 iterates 6000 times. During

```
 1   <?xml version = "1.0" encoding = "utf-8"?>
 2   <!DOCTYPE html PUBLIC "-//W3C//DTD XHTML 1.0 Strict//EN"
 3      "http://www.w3.org/TR/xhtml1/DTD/xhtml1-strict.dtd">
 4
 5   <!-- Fig. 7.4: RollDie.html -->
 6   <!-- Rolling a Six-Sided Die 6000 times. -->
 7   <html xmlns = "http://www.w3.org/1999/xhtml">
 8      <head>
 9         <title>Roll a Six-Sided Die 6000 Times</title>
10         <script type = "text/javascript">
11            <!--
12            var frequency1 = 0;
13            var frequency2 = 0;
14            var frequency3 = 0;
15            var frequency4 = 0;
16            var frequency5 = 0;
```

Fig. 7.4 | Rolling a six-sided die 6000 times. (Part 1 of 3.)

```
17            var frequency6 = 0;
18            var face;
19
20            // roll die 6000 times and accumulate results
21            for ( var roll = 1; roll <= 6000; roll++ )
22            {
23                face = Math.floor( 1 + Math.random() * 6 );
24
25                switch ( face )
26                {
27                    case 1:
28                        ++frequency1;
29                        break;
30                    case 2:
31                        ++frequency2;
32                        break;
33                    case 3:
34                        ++frequency3;
35                        break;
36                    case 4:
37                        ++frequency4;
38                        break;
39                    case 5:
40                        ++frequency5;
41                        break;
42                    case 6:
43                        ++frequency6;
44                        break;
45                } // end switch
46            } // end for
47
48            document.writeln( "<table border = \"1\">" );
49            document.writeln( "<thead><th>Face</th>" +
50                "<th>Frequency</th></thead>" );
51            document.writeln( "<tbody><tr><td>1</td><td>" +
52                frequency1 + "</td></tr>" );
53            document.writeln( "<tr><td>2</td><td>" + frequency2 +
54                "</td></tr>" );
55            document.writeln( "<tr><td>3</td><td>" + frequency3 +
56                "</td></tr>" );
57            document.writeln( "<tr><td>4</td><td>" + frequency4 +
58                "</td></tr>" );
59            document.writeln( "<tr><td>5</td><td>" + frequency5 +
60                "</td></tr>" );
61            document.writeln( "<tr><td>6</td><td>" + frequency6 +
62                "</td></tr></tbody></table>" );
63            // -->
64        </script>
65    </head>
66    <body>
67        <p>Click Refresh (or Reload) to run the script again</p>
68    </body>
69 </html>
```

Fig. 7.4 | Rolling a six-sided die 6000 times. (Part 2 of 3.)

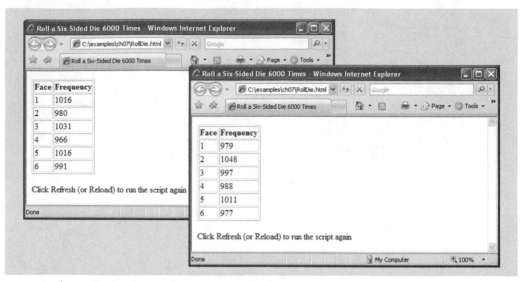

Fig. 7.4 | Rolling a six-sided die 6000 times. (Part 3 of 3.)

each iteration of the loop, line 23 produces a value from 1 to 6, which is stored in `face`. The nested `switch` statement in lines 25–45 uses the `face` value that was randomly chosen as its controlling expression. Based on the value of `face`, the program increments one of the six counter variables during each iteration of the loop. Note that no `default` case is provided in this `switch` statement, because the statement in line 23 produces only the values 1, 2, 3, 4, 5 and 6. In this example, the `default` case would never execute. After we study Arrays in Chapter 8, we discuss a way to replace the entire `switch` statement in this program with a single-line statement.

Run the program several times, and observe the results. Note that the program produces different random numbers each time the script executes, so the results should vary.

The values returned by `random` are always in the range

```
0.0 ≤Math.random() < 1.0
```

Previously, we demonstrated the statement

```
face = Math.floor( 1 + Math.random() * 6 );
```

which simulates the rolling of a six-sided die. This statement always assigns an integer (at random) to variable `face`, in the range 1 ≤face ≤6. Note that the width of this range (i.e., the number of consecutive integers in the range) is 6, and the starting number in the range is 1. Referring to the preceding statement, we see that the width of the range is determined by the number used to scale `random` with the multiplication operator (6 in the preceding statement) and that the starting number of the range is equal to the number (1 in the preceding statement) added to `Math.random() * 6`. We can generalize this result as

```
face = Math.floor( a + Math.random() * b );
```

where a is the *shifting value* (which is equal to the first number in the desired range of consecutive integers) and b is the *scaling factor* (which is equal to the width of the desired range of consecutive integers).

7.6 Example: Game of Chance

One of the most popular games of chance is a dice game known as craps, which is played in casinos and back alleys throughout the world. The rules of the game are straightforward:

> *A player rolls two dice. Each die has six faces. These faces contain one, two, three, four, five and six spots, respectively. After the dice have come to rest, the sum of the spots on the two upward faces is calculated. If the sum is 7 or 11 on the first throw, the player wins. If the sum is 2, 3 or 12 on the first throw (called "craps"), the player loses (i.e., the "house" wins). If the sum is 4, 5, 6, 8, 9 or 10 on the first throw, that sum becomes the player's "point." To win, you must continue rolling the dice until you "make your point" (i.e., roll your point value). You lose by rolling a 7 before making the point.*

Figure 7.5 simulates the game of craps. The player must roll two dice on the first and all subsequent rolls. When you execute the script, click the **Roll Dice** button to play the game. A message below the **Roll Dice** button displays the status of the game after each roll.

```
1   <?xml version = "1.0" encoding = "utf-8"?>
2   <!DOCTYPE html PUBLIC "-//W3C//DTD XHTML 1.0 Strict//EN"
3      "http://www.w3.org/TR/xhtml1/DTD/xhtml1-strict.dtd">
4
5   <!-- Fig. 7.5: Craps.html -->
6   <!-- Craps game simulation. -->
7   <html xmlns = "http://www.w3.org/1999/xhtml">
8      <head>
9         <title>Program that Simulates the Game of Craps</title>
10        <style type = "text/css">
11           table   { text-align: right }
12           body    { font-family: arial, sans-serif }
13           div.red { color: red }
14        </style>
15        <script type = "text/javascript">
16           <!--
17           // variables used to test the state of the game
18           var WON = 0;
19           var LOST = 1;
20           var CONTINUE_ROLLING = 2;
21
22           // other variables used in program
23           var firstRoll = true; // true if current roll is first
24           var sumOfDice = 0; // sum of the dice
25           var myPoint = 0; // point if no win/loss on first roll
26           var gameStatus = CONTINUE_ROLLING; // game not over yet
27
28           // process one roll of the dice
29           function play()
30           {
31              // get the point field on the page
32              var point = document.getElementById( "pointfield" );
33
34              // get the status div on the page
35              var statusDiv = document.getElementById( "status" );
```

Fig. 7.5 | Craps game simulation. (Part 1 of 4.)

```
36              if ( firstRoll ) // first roll of the dice
37              {
38                  sumOfDice = rollDice();
39
40                  switch ( sumOfDice )
41                  {
42                      case 7: case 11: // win on first roll
43                          gameStatus = WON;
44                          // clear point field
45                          point.value = "";
46                          break;
47                      case 2: case 3: case 12: // lose on first roll
48                          gameStatus = LOST;
49                          // clear point field
50                          point.value = "";
51                          break;
52                      default:                    // remember point
53                          gameStatus = CONTINUE_ROLLING;
54                          myPoint = sumOfDice;
55                          point.value = myPoint;
56                          firstRoll = false;
57                  } // end switch
58              } // end if
59              else
60              {
61                  sumOfDice = rollDice();
62
63                  if ( sumOfDice == myPoint ) // win by making point
64                      gameStatus = WON;
65                  else
66                      if ( sumOfDice == 7 )     // lose by rolling 7
67                          gameStatus = LOST;
68              } // end else
69
70              if ( gameStatus == CONTINUE_ROLLING )
71                  statusDiv.innerHTML = "Roll again";
72              else
73              {
74                  if ( gameStatus == WON )
75                      statusDiv.innerHTML = "Player wins. " +
76                          "Click Roll Dice to play again.";
77                  else
78                      statusDiv.innerHTML = "Player loses. " +
79                          "Click Roll Dice to play again.";
80
81                  firstRoll = true;
82              } // end else
83          } // end function play
84
85          // roll the dice
86          function rollDice()
87          {
88              var die1;
```

Fig. 7.5 | Craps game simulation. (Part 2 of 4.)

```
 89            var die2;
 90            var workSum;
 91
 92            die1 = Math.floor( 1 + Math.random() * 6 );
 93            die2 = Math.floor( 1 + Math.random() * 6 );
 94            workSum = die1 + die2;
 95
 96            document.getElementById( "die1field" ).value = die1;
 97            document.getElementById( "die2field" ).value = die2;
 98            document.getElementById( "sumfield" ).value = workSum;
 99
100            return workSum;
101         } // end function rollDice
102         // -->
103      </script>
104   </head>
105   <body>
106      <form action = "">
107         <table>
108         <caption>Craps</caption>
109         <tr><td>Die 1</td>
110            <td><input id = "die1field" type = "text" />
111            </td></tr>
112         <tr><td>Die 2</td>
113            <td><input id = "die2field" type = "text" />
114            </td></tr>
115         <tr><td>Sum</td>
116            <td><input id = "sumfield" type = "text" />
117            </td></tr>
118         <tr><td>Point</td>
119            <td><input id = "pointfield" type = "text" />
120            </td></tr>
121         <tr><td /><td><input type = "button" value = "Roll Dice"
122            onclick = "play()" /></td></tr>
123         </table>
124         <div id = "status" class = "red">
125            Click the Roll Dice button to play</div>
126      </form>
127   </body>
128 </html>
```

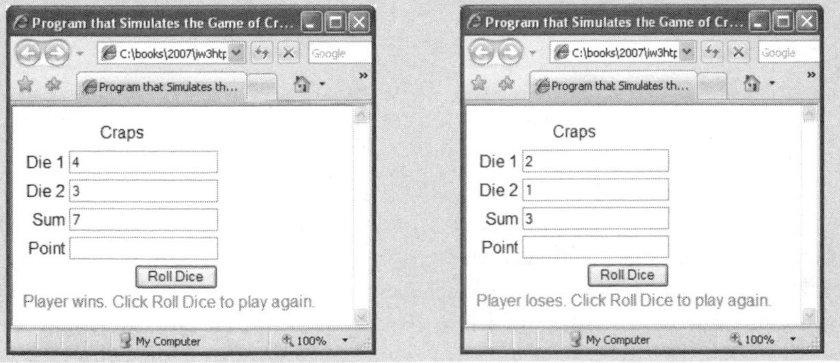

Fig. 7.5 | Craps game simulation. (Part 3 of 4.)

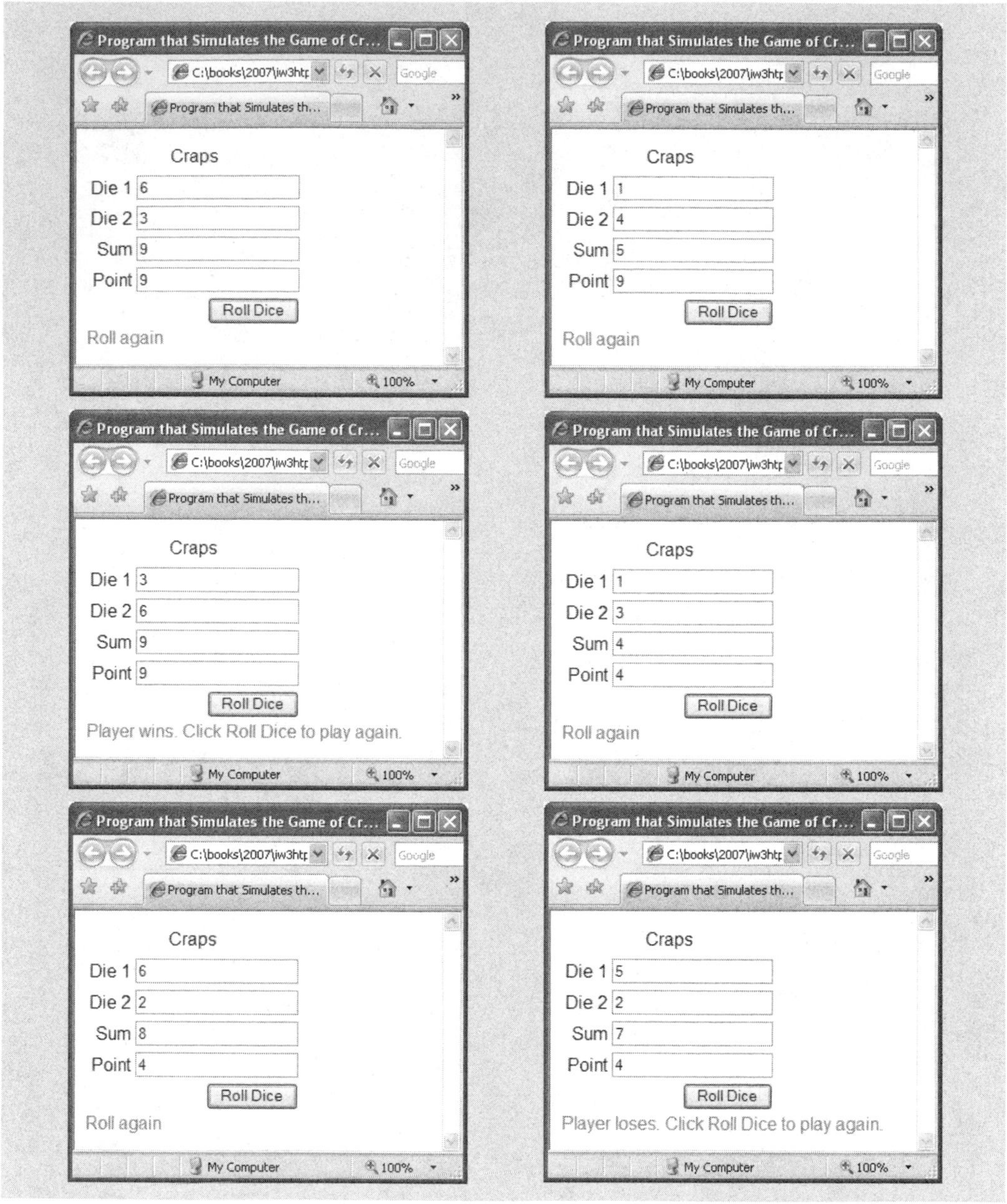

Fig. 7.5 | Craps game simulation. (Part 4 of 4.)

Until now, all user interactions with scripts have been through either a prompt dialog (in which the user types an input value for the program) or an alert dialog (in which a message is displayed to the user, and the user can click **OK** to dismiss the dialog). Although these dialogs are valid ways to receive input from a user and to display messages, they are fairly limited in their capabilities. A prompt dialog can obtain only one value at a time from the user, and a message dialog can display only one message.

XHTML Forms

More frequently, multiple inputs are received from the user at once via an XHTML form (such as one in which the user enters name and address information) or to display many pieces of data at once (e.g., the values of the dice, the sum of the dice and the point in this example). To begin our introduction to more elaborate user interfaces, this program uses an XHTML form (discussed in Chapter 2) and a new graphical user interface concept—GUI *event handling*. This is our first example in which the JavaScript executes in response to the user's interaction with a GUI component in an XHTML form. This interaction causes an event. Scripts are often used to respond to events.

Before we discuss the script code, we discuss the XHTML document's body element (lines 105–126). The GUI components in this section are used extensively in the script.

Line 106 begins the definition of an XHTML form element. The XHTML standard requires that every form contain an action attribute, but because this form does not post its information to a web server, the empty string ("") is used.

In this example, we have decided to place the form's GUI components in an XHTML table element, so line 107 begins the definition of the XHTML table. Lines 109–120 create four table rows. Each row contains a left cell with a text label and an input element in the right cell.

Four input fields (lines 110, 113, 116 and 119) are created to display the value of the first die, the second die, the sum of the dice and the current point value, if any. Their id attributes are set to die1field, die2field, sumfield, and pointfield, respectively. The id attribute can be used to apply CSS styles and to enable script code to refer to an element in an XHTML document. Because the id attribute, if specified, must have a unique value, JavaScript can reliably refer to any single element via its id attribute. We see how this is done in a moment.

Lines 121–122 create a fifth row with an empty cell in the left column before the **Roll Dice** button. The button's *onclick attribute* indicates the action to take when the user of the XHTML document clicks the **Roll Dice** button. In this example, clicking the button causes a call to function play.

Event-Driven Programming

This style of programming is known as *event-driven programming*—the user interacts with a GUI component, the script is notified of the event and the script processes the event. The user's interaction with the GUI "drives" the program. The button click is known as the *event*. The function that is called when an event occurs is known as an *event-handling function* or *event handler*. When a GUI event occurs in a form, the browser calls the specified event-handling function. Before any event can be processed, each GUI component must know which event-handling function will be called when a particular event occurs. Most XHTML GUI components have several different event types. The event model is discussed in detail in Chapter 11, JavaScript: Events. By specifying onclick = "play()" for the **Roll Dice** button, we instruct the browser to *listen for events* (button-click events in particular). This *registers the event handler* for the GUI component, causing the browser to begin listening for the click event on the component. If no event handler is specified for the **Roll Dice** button, the script will not respond when the user presses the button.

Lines 123–125 end the table and form elements, respectively. After the table, a div element is created with an id attribute of "status". This element will be updated by the script to display the result of each roll to the user. A style declaration in line 13 colors the text contained in this div red.

Discussing the Game's Script Code

The game is reasonably involved. The player may win or lose on the first roll, or may win or lose on any subsequent roll. Lines 18–20 create variables that define the three game states—game won, game lost and continue rolling the dice. Unlike many other programming languages, JavaScript does not provide a mechanism to define a *constant* (i.e., a variable whose value cannot be modified). For this reason, we use all capital letters for these variable names, to indicate that we do not intend to modify their values and to make them stand out in the code—a common industry practice for genuine constants.

Good Programming Practice 7.2

Use only uppercase letters (with underscores between words) in the names of variables that should be used as constants. This format makes such variables stand out in a program.

Good Programming Practice 7.3

Use meaningfully named variables rather than literal values (such as 2) to make programs more readable.

Lines 23–26 declare several variables that are used throughout the script. Variable firstRoll indicates whether the next roll of the dice is the first roll in the current game. Variable sumOfDice maintains the sum of the dice from the last roll. Variable myPoint stores the point if the player does not win or lose on the first roll. Variable gameStatus keeps track of the current state of the game (WON, LOST or CONTINUE_ROLLING).

We define a function rollDice (lines 86–101) to roll the dice and to compute and display their sum. Function rollDice is defined once, but is called from two places in the program (lines 38 and 61). Function rollDice takes no arguments, so it has an empty parameter list. Function rollDice returns the sum of the two dice.

The user clicks the **Roll Dice** button to roll the dice. This action invokes function play (lines 29–83) of the script. Lines 32 and 35 create two new variables with objects representing elements in the XHTML document using the document object's ***getElementById method***. The getElementById method, given an id as an argument, finds the XHTML element with a matching id attribute and returns a JavaScript object representing the element. Line 32 stores an object representing the pointfield input element (line 119) in the variable point. Line 35 gets an object representing the status div from line 124. In a moment, we show how you can use these objects to manipulate the XHTML document.

Function play checks the variable firstRoll (line 36) to determine whether it is true or false. If true, the roll is the first roll of the game. Line 38 calls rollDice, which picks two random values from 1 to 6, displays the value of the first die, the value of the second die and the sum of the dice in the first three text fields and returns the sum of the dice. (We discuss function rollDice in detail shortly.) After the first roll (if firstRoll is false), the nested switch statement in lines 40–57 determines whether the game is won or lost, or whether it should continue with another roll. After the first roll, if the game is not over, sumOfDice is saved in myPoint and displayed in the text field point in the XHTML form.

Note how the text field's value is changed in lines 45, 50 and 55. The object stored in the variable point allows access to the pointfield text field's contents. The expression `point.value` accesses the ***value** property* of the text field referred to by `point`. The `value` property specifies the text to display in the text field. To access this property, we specify the object representing the text field (`point`), followed by a ***dot*** (.) and the name of the property to access (`value`). This technique for accessing properties of an object (also used to access methods as in `Math.pow`) is called ***dot notation***. We discuss using scripts to access elements in an XHTML page in more detail in Chapter 10.

The program proceeds to the nested `if...else` statement in lines 70–82, which uses the `statusDiv` variable to update the `div` that displays the game status. Using the object's ***innerHTML** property*, we set the text inside the `div` to reflect the most recent status. Lines 71, 75–76 and 78–79 set the `div`'s `innerHTML` to

> `Roll again.`

if `gameStatus` is equal to `CONTINUE_ROLLING`, to

> `Player wins. Click Roll Dice to play again.`

if `gameStatus` is equal to `WON` and to

> `Player loses. Click Roll Dice to play again.`

If `gameStatus` is equal to `LOST`. If the game is won or lost, line 81 sets `firstRoll` to `true` to indicate that the next roll of the dice begins the next game.

The program then waits for the user to click the button **Roll Dice** again. Each time the user clicks **Roll Dice**, the program calls function `play`, which, in turn, calls the `rollDice` function to produce a new value for `sumOfDice`. If `sumOfDice` matches `myPoint`, `gameStatus` is set to `WON`, the `if...else` statement in lines 70–82 executes and the game is complete. If sum is equal to 7, `gameStatus` is set to `LOST`, the `if...else` statement in lines 70–82 executes and the game is complete. Clicking the **Roll Dice** button starts a new game. The program updates the four text fields in the XHTML form with the new values of the dice and the sum on each roll, and updates the text field `point` each time a new game begins.

Function `rollDice` (lines 86–101) defines its own local variables `die1`, `die2` and `workSum` (lines 88–90). Lines 92–93 pick two random values in the range 1 to 6 and assign them to variables `die1` and `die2`, respectively. Lines 96–98 once again use the `document`'s `getElementById` method to find and update the correct `input` elements with the values of `die1`, `die2` and `workSum`. Note that the integer values are converted automatically to strings when they are assigned to each text field's `value` property. Line 100 returns the value of `workSum` for use in function `play`.

Error-Prevention Tip 7.1

Initializing variables when they are declared in functions helps avoid incorrect results and interpreter messages warning of uninitialized data.

7.7 Another Example: Random Image Generator

Web content that varies randomly adds dynamic, interesting effects to a page. In the next example, we build a *random image generator*, a script that displays a randomly selected image every time the page that contains the script is loaded.

For the script in Fig. 7.6 to function properly, the directory containing the file RandomPicture.html must also contain seven images with integer filenames (i.e., 1.gif, 2.gif, ..., 7.gif). The web page containing this script displays one of these seven images, selected at random, each time the page loads.

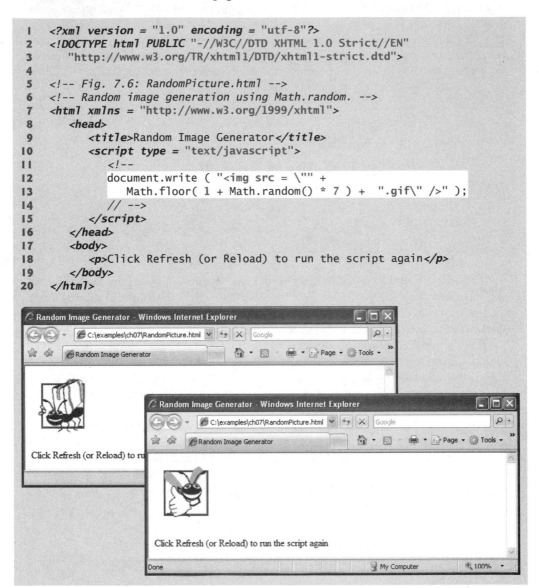

```
 1   <?xml version = "1.0" encoding = "utf-8"?>
 2   <!DOCTYPE html PUBLIC "-//W3C//DTD XHTML 1.0 Strict//EN"
 3      "http://www.w3.org/TR/xhtml1/DTD/xhtml1-strict.dtd">
 4
 5   <!-- Fig. 7.6: RandomPicture.html -->
 6   <!-- Random image generation using Math.random. -->
 7   <html xmlns = "http://www.w3.org/1999/xhtml">
 8      <head>
 9         <title>Random Image Generator</title>
10         <script type = "text/javascript">
11            <!--
12            document.write ( "<img src = \"" +
13               Math.floor( 1 + Math.random() * 7 ) +  ".gif\" />" );
14            // -->
15         </script>
16      </head>
17      <body>
18         <p>Click Refresh (or Reload) to run the script again</p>
19      </body>
20   </html>
```

Fig. 7.6 | Random image generation using Math.random.

Lines 12–13 randomly select an image to display on a web page. This document.write statement creates an image tag in the web page with the src attribute set to a random integer from 1 to 7, concatenated with ".gif". Thus, the script dynamically sets the source of the image tag to the name of one of the image files in the current directory.

7.8 Scope Rules

Chapters 4–6 used identifiers for variable names. The attributes of variables include name, value and data type (e.g., string, number or boolean). We also use identifiers as names for user-defined functions. Each identifier in a program also has a scope.

The *scope* of an identifier for a variable or function is the portion of the program in which the identifier can be referenced. *Global variables* or *script-level variables* that are declared in the head element are accessible in any part of a script and are said to have *global scope*. Thus every function in the script can potentially use the variables.

Identifiers declared inside a function have *function* (or *local*) *scope* and can be used only in that function. Function scope begins with the opening left brace ({) of the function in which the identifier is declared and ends at the terminating right brace (}) of the function. Local variables of a function and function parameters have function scope. If a local variable in a function has the same name as a global variable, the global variable is "hidden" from the body of the function.

Good Programming Practice 7.4

Avoid local-variable names that hide global-variable names. This can be accomplished by simply avoiding the use of duplicate identifiers in a script.

The script in Fig. 7.7 demonstrates the *scope rules* that resolve conflicts between global variables and local variables of the same name. This example also demonstrates the *onload event* (line 52), which calls an event handler (start) when the <body> of the XHTML document is completely loaded into the browser window.

```
1   <?xml version = "1.0" encoding = "utf-8"?>
2   <!DOCTYPE html PUBLIC "-//W3C//DTD XHTML 1.0 Strict//EN"
3      "http://www.w3.org/TR/xhtml1/DTD/xhtml1-strict.dtd">
4
5   <!-- Fig. 7.7: scoping.html -->
6   <!-- Scoping example. -->
7   <html xmlns = "http://www.w3.org/1999/xhtml">
8      <head>
9         <title>A Scoping Example</title>
10        <script type = "text/javascript">
11           <!--
12           var x = 1; // global variable
13
14           function start()
15           {
16              var x = 5; // variable local to function start
17
18              document.writeln( "local x in start is " + x );
19
20              functionA(); // functionA has local x
21              functionB(); // functionB uses global variable x
22              functionA(); // functionA reinitializes local x
23              functionB(); // global variable x retains its value
24
```

Fig. 7.7 | Scoping example. (Part 1 of 2.)

```
25              document.writeln(
26                 "<p>local x in start is " + x + "</p>" );
27           } // end function start
28
29           function functionA()
30           {
31              var x = 25; // initialized each time
32                          // functionA is called
33
34              document.writeln( "<p>local x in functionA is " +
35                                x + " after entering functionA" );
36              ++x;
37              document.writeln( "<br />local x in functionA is " +
38                 x + " before exiting functionA" + "</p>" );
39           } // end functionA
40
41           function functionB()
42           {
43              document.writeln( "<p>global variable x is " + x +
44                 " on entering functionB" );
45              x *= 10;
46              document.writeln( "<br />global variable x is " +
47                 x + " on exiting functionB"  + "</p>" );
48           } // end functionB
49           // -->
50        </script>
51     </head>
52     <body onload = "start()"></body>
53  </html>
```

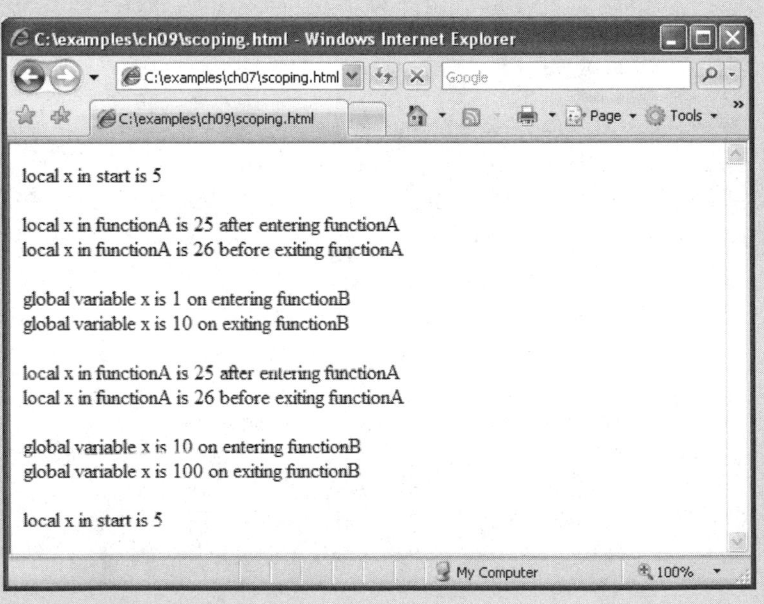

Fig. 7.7 | Scoping example. (Part 2 of 2.)

Global variable x (line 12) is declared and initialized to 1. This global variable is hidden in any block (or function) that declares a variable named x. Function start (line 14–27) declares a local variable x (line 16) and initializes it to 5. This variable is output in a line of XHTML text to show that the global variable x is hidden in start. The script defines two other functions—functionA and functionB—that each take no arguments and return nothing. Each function is called twice from function start.

Function functionA defines local variable x (line 31) and initializes it to 25. When functionA is called, the variable is output in a line of XHTML text to show that the global variable x is hidden in functionA; then the variable is incremented and output in a line of XHTML text again before the function is exited. Each time this function is called, local variable x is re-created and initialized to 25.

Function functionB does not declare any variables. Therefore, when it refers to variable x, the global variable x is used. When functionB is called, the global variable is output in a line of XHTML text, multiplied by 10 and output in a line of XHTML text again before the function is exited. The next time function functionB is called, the global variable has its modified value, 10, which again gets multiplied by 10, and 100 is output. Finally, the program outputs local variable x in start in a line of XHTML text again, to show that none of the function calls modified the value of x in start, because the functions all referred to variables in other scopes.

7.9 JavaScript Global Functions

JavaScript provides seven global functions. We have already used two of these functions—parseInt and parseFloat. The global functions are summarized in Fig. 7.8.

Actually, the global functions in Fig. 7.8 are all part of JavaScript's *Global object*. The Global object contains all the global variables in the script, all the user-defined functions in the script and all the functions listed in Fig. 7.8. Because global functions and user-defined functions are part of the Global object, some JavaScript programmers refer to these functions as methods. We use the term method only when referring to a function that is called for a particular object (e.g., Math.random()). As a JavaScript programmer, you do not need to use the Global object directly; JavaScript references it for you.

Global function	Description
escape	Takes a string argument and returns a string in which all spaces, punctuation, accent characters and any other character that is not in the ASCII character set are encoded in a hexadecimal format that can be represented on all platforms.
eval	Takes a string argument representing JavaScript code to execute. The JavaScript interpreter evaluates the code and executes it when the eval function is called. This function allows JavaScript code to be stored as strings and executed dynamically. [*Caution:* It is considered a serious security risk to use eval to process any data entered by a user because a malicious user could exploit this to run dangerous code.]

Fig. 7.8 | JavaScript global functions. (Part 1 of 2.)

Global function	Description
isFinite	Takes a numeric argument and returns true if the value of the argument is not NaN, Number.POSITIVE_INFINITY or Number.NEGATIVE_INFINITY (values that are not numbers or numbers outside the range that JavaScript supports)—otherwise, the function returns false.
isNaN	Takes a numeric argument and returns true if the value of the argument is not a number; otherwise, it returns false. The function is commonly used with the return value of parseInt or parseFloat to determine whether the result is a proper numeric value.
parseFloat	Takes a string argument and attempts to convert the beginning of the string into a floating-point value. If the conversion is unsuccessful, the function returns NaN; otherwise, it returns the converted value (e.g., parseFloat("abc123.45") returns NaN, and parseFloat("123.45abc") returns the value 123.45).
parseInt	Takes a string argument and attempts to convert the beginning of the string into an integer value. If the conversion is unsuccessful, the function returns NaN; otherwise, it returns the converted value (e.g., parseInt("abc123") returns NaN, and parseInt("123abc") returns the integer value 123). This function takes an optional second argument, from 2 to 36, specifying the *radix* (or *base*) of the number. Base 2 indicates that the first argument string is in *binary* format, base 8 indicates that the first argument string is in *octal* format and base 16 indicates that the first argument string is in *hexadecimal* format.
unescape	Takes a string as its argument and returns a string in which all characters previously encoded with escape are decoded.

Fig. 7.8 | JavaScript global functions. (Part 2 of 2.)

7.10 Recursion

The programs we have discussed thus far are generally structured as functions that call one another in a disciplined, hierarchical manner. A *recursive function* is a function that calls *itself*, either directly, or indirectly through another function. In this section, we present a simple example of recursion.

We consider recursion conceptually first; then we examine several programs containing recursive functions. Recursive problem-solving approaches have a number of elements in common. A recursive function is called to solve a problem. The function actually knows how to solve only the simplest case(s), or *base case(s)*. If the function is called with a base case, the function returns a result. If the function is called with a more complex problem, it divides the problem into two conceptual pieces—a piece that the function knows how to process (the base case) and a piece that the function does not know how to process. To make recursion feasible, the latter piece must resemble the original problem, but be a simpler or smaller version of it. Because this new problem looks like the original problem, the function invokes (calls) a fresh copy of itself to go to work on the smaller problem; this invocation is referred to as a ***recursive call***, or the ***recursion step***. The recursion step also normally includes the keyword `return`, because its result will be combined with the portion of the problem the function knew how to solve to form a result that will be passed back to the original caller.

The recursion step executes while the original call to the function is still open (i.e., it has not finished executing). The recursion step can result in many more recursive calls as the function divides each new subproblem into two conceptual pieces. For the recursion eventually to terminate, each time the function calls itself with a simpler version of the original problem, the sequence of smaller and smaller problems must converge on the base case. At that point, the function recognizes the base case, returns a result to the previous copy of the function, and a sequence of returns ensues up the line until the original function call eventually returns the final result to the caller.

As an example of these concepts at work, let us write a recursive program to perform a popular mathematical calculation. The factorial of a nonnegative integer n, written $n!$ (and pronounced "n factorial"), is the product

$$n \cdot (n-1) \cdot (n-2) \cdot \ldots \cdot 1$$

where 1! is equal to 1 and 0! is defined as 1. For example, 5! is the product $5 \cdot 4 \cdot 3 \cdot 2 \cdot 1$, which is equal to 120.

The factorial of an integer (number in the following example) greater than or equal to zero can be calculated *iteratively* (nonrecursively) using a `for` statement, as follows:

```
var factorial = 1;

for ( var counter = number; counter >= 1; --counter )
   factorial *= counter;
```

A recursive definition of the factorial function is arrived at by observing the following relationship:

$$n! = n \cdot (n-1)!$$

For example, 5! is clearly equal to 5 * 4!, as is shown by the following equations:

$$5! = 5 \cdot 4 \cdot 3 \cdot 2 \cdot 1$$
$$5! = 5 \cdot (4 \cdot 3 \cdot 2 \cdot 1)$$
$$5! = 5 \cdot (4!)$$

The evaluation of 5! would proceed as shown in Fig. 7.9. Figure 7.9 (a) shows how the succession of recursive calls proceeds until 1! is evaluated to be 1, which terminates the recursion. Figure 7.9 (b) shows the values returned from each recursive call to its caller until the final value is calculated and returned.

Figure 7.10 uses recursion to calculate and print the factorials of the integers 0 to 10. The recursive function `factorial` first tests (line 24) whether a terminating condition is true, i.e., whether `number` is less than or equal to 1. If so, `factorial` returns 1, no further recursion is necessary and the function returns. If `number` is greater than 1, line 27 expresses the problem as the product of `number` and the value returned by a recursive call to `factorial` evaluating the factorial of `number - 1`. Note that `factorial( number - 1 )` is a simpler problem than the original calculation, `factorial( number )`.

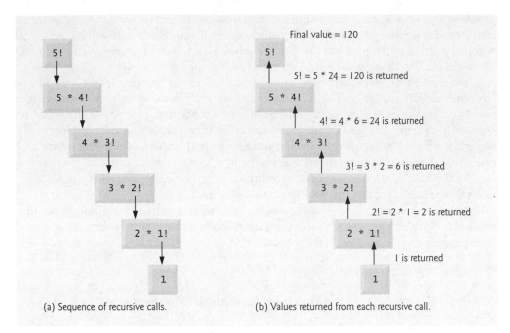

(a) Sequence of recursive calls.   (b) Values returned from each recursive call.

Fig. 7.9 | Recursive evaluation of 5!.

Function `factorial` (lines 22–28) receives as its argument the value for which to calculate the factorial. As can be seen in the screen capture in Fig. 7.10, factorial values become large quickly.

 Common Programming Error 7.6

Forgetting to return a value from a recursive function when one is needed results in a logic error.

```
1   <?xml version = "1.0" encoding = "utf-8"?>
2   <!DOCTYPE html PUBLIC "-//W3C//DTD XHTML 1.0 Strict//EN"
3      "http://www.w3.org/TR/xhtml1/DTD/xhtml1-strict.dtd">
4
5   <!-- Fig. 7.10: FactorialTest.html -->
6   <!-- Factorial calculation with a recursive function. -->
7   <html xmlns = "http://www.w3.org/1999/xhtml">
8      <head>
9         <title>Recursive Factorial Function</title>
10        <script type = "text/javascript">
11        <!--
12           document.writeln( "<h1>Factorials of 1 to 10</h1>" );
13           document.writeln( "<table>" );
14
15           for ( var i = 0; i <= 10; i++ )
16              document.writeln( "<tr><td>" + i + "!</td><td>" +
17                 factorial( i ) + "</td></tr>" );
```

Fig. 7.10 | Factorial calculation with a recursive function. (Part 1 of 2.)

```
18
19          document.writeln( "</table>" );
20
21          // Recursive definition of function factorial
22          function factorial( number )
23          {
24             if ( number <= 1 )  // base case
25                return 1;
26             else
27                return number * factorial( number - 1 );
28          } // end function factorial
29          // -->
30       </script>
31    </head><body></body>
32 </html>
```

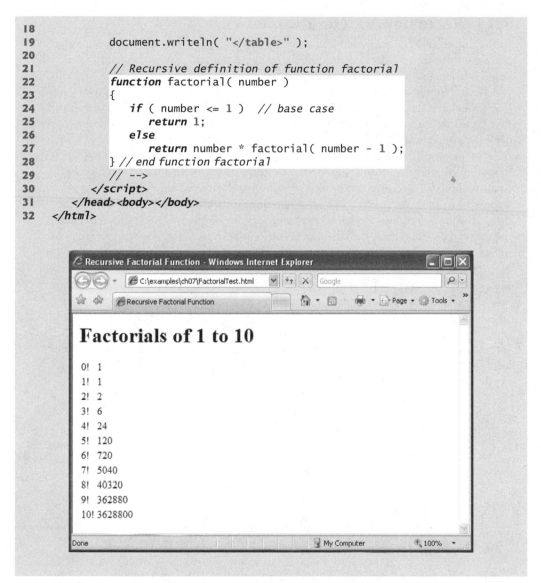

Fig. 7.10 | Factorial calculation with a recursive function. (Part 2 of 2.)

Common Programming Error 7.7

Omitting the base case and writing the recursion step incorrectly so that it does not converge on the base case are both errors that cause infinite recursion, eventually exhausting memory. This situation is analogous to the problem of an infinite loop in an iterative (nonrecursive) solution.

Error-Prevention Tip 7.2

Internet Explorer displays an error message when a script seems to be going into infinite recursion. Firefox simply terminates the script after detecting the problem. This allows the user of the web page to recover from a script that contains an infinite loop or infinite recursion.

7.11 Recursion vs. Iteration

In the preceding section, we studied a function that can easily be implemented either recursively or iteratively. In this section, we compare the two approaches and discuss why you might choose one approach over the other in a particular situation.

Both iteration and recursion are based on a control statement: Iteration uses a repetition statement (e.g., `for`, `while` or `do...while`); recursion uses a selection statement (e.g., `if`, `if...else` or `switch`). Both iteration and recursion involve repetition: Iteration explicitly uses a repetition statement; recursion achieves repetition through repeated function calls. Iteration and recursion each involve a termination test: Iteration terminates when the loop-continuation condition fails; recursion terminates when a base case is recognized. Iteration both with counter-controlled repetition and with recursion gradually approaches termination: Iteration keeps modifying a counter until the counter assumes a value that makes the loop-continuation condition fail; recursion keeps producing simpler versions of the original problem until the base case is reached. Both iteration and recursion can occur infinitely: An infinite loop occurs with iteration if the loop-continuation test never becomes false; infinite recursion occurs if the recursion step does not reduce the problem each time via a sequence that converges on the base case or if the base case is incorrect.

One negative aspect of recursion is that function calls require a certain amount of time and memory space not directly spent on executing program instructions. This is known as function-call overhead. Because recursion uses repeated function calls, this overhead greatly affects the performance of the operation. In many cases, using repetition statements in place of recursion is more efficient. However, some problems can be solved more elegantly (and more easily) with recursion.

Software Engineering Observation 7.5

Any problem that can be solved recursively can also be solved iteratively (nonrecursively). A recursive approach is normally chosen in preference to an iterative approach when the recursive approach more naturally mirrors the problem and results in a program that is easier to understand and debug. Another reason to choose a recursive solution is that an iterative solution may not be apparent.

Performance Tip 7.1

Avoid using recursion in performance-oriented situations. Recursive calls take time and consume additional memory.

In addition to the factorial function example (Fig. 7.10), Fig. 12.26 uses recursion to traverse an XML document tree.

8

JavaScript: Arrays

*With sobs and tears he sorted
out
Those of the largest size . . .*
—Lewis Carroll

*Attempt the end, and never
stand to doubt;
Nothing's so hard, but search
will find it out.*
—Robert Herrick

*Now go, write it before them
in a table,
and note it in a book.*
—Isaiah 30:8

*'Tis in my memory lock'd,
And you yourself shall keep
the key of it.*
—William Shakespeare

OBJECTIVES

In this chapter you'll learn:

■ To use arrays to store lists and tables of values.

■ To declare an array, initialize an array and refer to individual elements of an array.

■ To pass arrays to functions.

■ To sort an array.

■ To declare and manipulate multidimensional arrays.

8.1 Introduction

Arrays are data structures consisting of related data items (sometimes called *collections* of data items). JavaScript arrays are "dynamic" entities in that they can change size after they are created. Many of the techniques demonstrated in this chapter are used frequently in Chapters 10–11 as we introduce the collections that allow a script programmer to manipulate every element of an XHTML document dynamically.

8.2 Arrays

An array is a group of memory locations that all have the same name and normally are of the same type (although this attribute is not required in JavaScript). To refer to a particular location or element in the array, we specify the name of the array and the position number of the particular element in the array.

Figure 8.1 shows an array of integer values named c. This array contains 12 *elements*. Any one of these elements may be referred to by giving the name of the array followed by the position number of the element in square brackets ([]). The first element in every array is the *zeroth element*. Thus, the first element of array c is referred to as c[0], the second element of array c is referred to as c[1], the seventh element of array c is referred to as c[6] and, in general, the *i*th element of array c is referred to as c[i-1]. Array names follow the same conventions as other identifiers.

The position number in square brackets is called a *subscript* (or an *index*). A subscript must be an integer or an integer expression. Note that a subscripted array name is a left-hand-side expression—it can be used on the left side of an assignment to place a new value into an array element. It can also be used on the right side of an assignment to assign its value to another left-hand side expression.

Let us examine array c in Fig. 8.1 more closely. The array's *name* is c. The *length* of array c is 12 and can be found using by the following expression:

```
c.length
```

Every array in JavaScript knows its own length. The array's 12 elements are referred to as c[0], c[1], c[2], ..., c[11]. The *value* of c[0] is -45, the value of c[1] is 6, the value of c[2] is 0, the value of c[7] is 62 and the value of c[11] is 78.

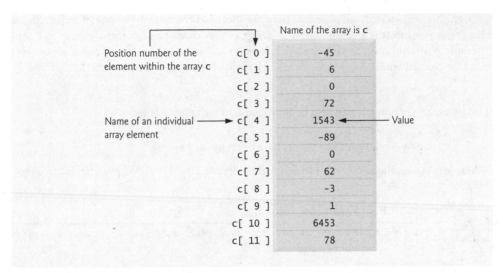

Fig. 8.1 | Array with 12 elements.

The brackets that enclose the array subscript are a JavaScript operator. Brackets have the same level of precedence as parentheses. The chart in Fig. 8.2 shows the precedence and associativity of the operators introduced so far. They are shown from top to bottom in decreasing order of precedence, alongside their associativity and type.

Operators	Associativity	Type
() [] .	left to right	highest
++ -- !	right to left	unary
* / %	left to right	multiplicative
+ -	left to right	additive
< <= > >=	left to right	relational
== !=	left to right	equality
&&	left to right	logical AND
||	left to right	logical OR
?:	right to left	conditional
= += -= *= /= %=	right to left	assignment

Fig. 8.2 | Precedence and associativity of the operators discussed so far.

8.3 Declaring and Allocating Arrays

Arrays occupy space in memory. Actually, an array in JavaScript is an *Array object*. You use *operator new* to dynamically allocate (request memory for) the number of elements required by each array. Operator new creates an object as the program executes by obtaining enough memory to store an object of the type specified to the right of new. The process of creating new objects is also known as *creating an instance* or *instantiating an object,* and operator new is known as the *dynamic memory allocation operator.* Arrays are objects must be created with new. To allocate 12 elements for integer array c, use the statement

```
var c = new Array( 12 );
```

The preceding statement can also be performed in two steps, as follows:

```
var c; // declares the array
c = new Array( 12 ); // allocates the array
```

When arrays are allocated, the elements are not initialized—they have the value unde-fined.

Common Programming Error 8.1

Assuming that the elements of an array are initialized when the array is allocated may result in logic errors.

8.4 Examples Using Arrays

This section presents several examples of creating and manipulating arrays.

Creating and Initializing Arrays

The script in Fig. 8.3 uses operator new to allocate an Array of five elements and an empty array. The script demonstrates initializing an Array of existing elements and also shows that an Array can grow dynamically to accommodate new elements. The Array's values are displayed in XHTML tables.

```
1   <?xml version = "1.0" encoding = "utf-8"?>
2   <!DOCTYPE html PUBLIC "-//W3C//DTD XHTML 1.0 Strict//EN"
3      "http://www.w3.org/TR/xhtml1/DTD/xhtml1-strict.dtd">
4
5   <!-- Fig. 8.3: InitArray.html -->
6   <!-- Initializing the elements of an array. -->
7   <html xmlns = "http://www.w3.org/1999/xhtml">
8      <head>
9         <title>Initializing an Array</title>
10        <style type = "text/css">
11           table { width: 10em }
12           th    { text-align: left }
13        </style>
14        <script type = "text/javascript">
15           <!--
16           // create (declare) two new arrays
17           var n1 = new Array( 5 ); // allocate five-element Array
18           var n2 = new Array(); // allocate empty Array
19
20           // assign values to each element of Array n1
21           for ( var i = 0; i < n1.length; ++i )
22              n1[ i ] = i;
```

Fig. 8.3 | Initializing the elements of an array. (Part 1 of 2.)

```
23
24          // create and initialize five elements in Array n2
25          for ( i = 0; i < 5; ++i )
26             n2[ i ] = i;
27
28          outputArray( "Array n1:", n1 );
29          outputArray( "Array n2:", n2 );
30
31          // output the heading followed by a two-column table
32          // containing subscripts and elements of "theArray"
33          function outputArray( heading, theArray )
34          {
35             document.writeln( "<h2>" + heading + "</h2>" );
36             document.writeln( "<table border = \"1\"" );
37             document.writeln( "<thead><th>Subscript</th>" +
38                "<th>Value</th></thead><tbody>" );
39
40             // output the subscript and value of each array element
41             for ( var i = 0; i < theArray.length; i++ )
42                document.writeln( "<tr><td>" + i + "</td><td>" +
43                   theArray[ i ] + "</td></tr>" );
44
45             document.writeln( "</tbody></table>" );
46          } // end function outputArray
47          // -->
48       </script>
49    </head><body></body>
50 </html>
```

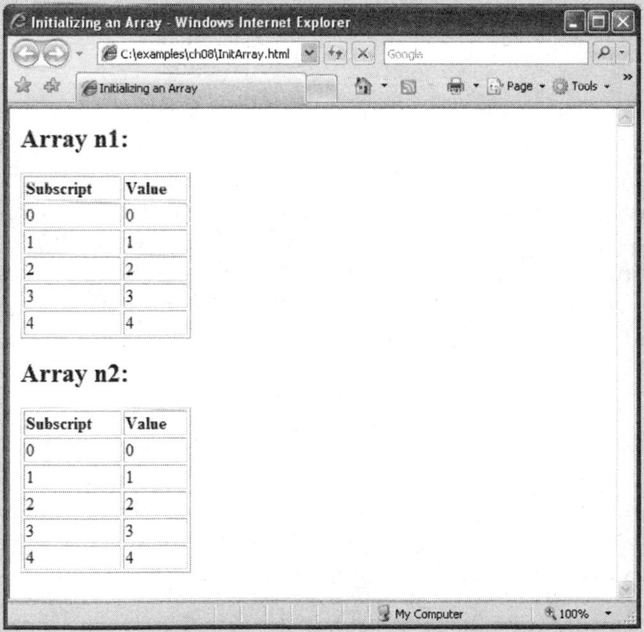

Fig. 8.3 | Initializing the elements of an array. (Part 2 of 2.)

Line 17 creates Array n1 as an array of five elements. Line 18 creates Array n2 as an empty array. Lines 21–22 use a for statement to initialize the elements of n1 to their subscript numbers (0 to 4). Note the use of the expression n1.length in the condition for the for statement to determine the length of the array. In this example, the length of the array is 5, so the loop continues executing as long as the value of control variable i is less than 5. For a five-element array, the subscript values are 0 through 4, so using the less than operator, <, guarantees that the loop does not attempt to access an element beyond the end of the array. Zero-based counting is usually used to iterate through arrays.

Lines 25–26 use a for statement to add five elements to the Array n2 and initialize each element to its subscript number (0 to 4). Note that Array n2 grows dynamically to accommodate the values assigned to each element of the array.

Software Engineering Observation 8.1

JavaScript automatically reallocates an Array when a value is assigned to an element that is outside the bounds of the original Array. Elements between the last element of the original Array and the new element have undefined values.

Lines 28–29 invoke function outputArray (defined in lines 33–46) to display the contents of each array in an XHTML table. Function outputArray receives two arguments—a string to be output before the XHTML table that displays the contents of the array and the array to output. Lines 41–43 use a for statement to output XHTML text that defines each row of the table.

Common Programming Error 8.2

Referring to an element outside the Array bounds is normally a logic error.

If the values of an Array's elements are known in advance, the elements can be allocated and initialized in the declaration of the array. There are two ways in which the initial values can be specified. The statement

    var n = [10, 20, 30, 40, 50];

uses a comma-separated *initializer list* enclosed in square brackets ([and]) to create a five-element Array with subscripts of 0, 1, 2, 3 and 4. The array size is determined by the number of values in the initializer list. Note that the preceding declaration does not require the new operator to create the Array object—this functionality is provided by the interpreter when it encounters an array declaration that includes an initializer list. The statement

    var n = *new* Array(10, 20, 30, 40, 50);

also creates a five-element array with subscripts of 0, 1, 2, 3 and 4. In this case, the initial values of the array elements are specified as arguments in the parentheses following new Array. The size of the array is determined by the number of values in parentheses. It is also possible to reserve a space in an Array for a value to be specified later by using a comma as a place holder in the initializer list. For example, the statement

    var n = [10, 20, , 40, 50];

creates a five-element array with no value specified for the third element (n[2]).

Initializing Arrays with Initializer Lists

The script in Fig. 8.4 creates three Array objects to demonstrate initializing arrays with initializer lists (lines 18–20) and displays each array in an XHTML table using the same function outputArray discussed in Fig. 8.3. Note that when Array integers2 is displayed in the web page, the elements with subscripts 1 and 2 (the second and third elements of

```
1   <?xml version = "1.0" encoding = "utf-8"?>
2   <!DOCTYPE html PUBLIC "-//W3C//DTD XHTML 1.0 Strict//EN"
3      "http://www.w3.org/TR/xhtml1/DTD/xhtml1-strict.dtd">
4
5   <!-- Fig. 8.4: InitArray2.html -->
6   <!-- Declaring and initializing arrays. -->
7   <html xmlns = "http://www.w3.org/1999/xhtml">
8      <head>
9         <title>Initializing an Array with a Declaration</title>
10        <style type = "text/css">
11           table { width: 15em }
12           th    { text-align: left }
13        </style>
14        <script type = "text/javascript">
15           <!--
16           // Initializer list specifies the number of elements and
17           // a value for each element.
18           var colors = new Array( "cyan", "magenta","yellow", "black" );
19           var integers1 = [ 2, 4, 6, 8 ];
20           var integers2 = [ 2, , , 8 ];
21
22           outputArray( "Array colors contains", colors );
23           outputArray( "Array integers1 contains", integers1 );
24           outputArray( "Array integers2 contains", integers2 );
25
26           // output the heading followed by a two-column table
27           // containing the subscripts and elements of theArray
28           function outputArray( heading, theArray )
29           {
30              document.writeln( "<h2>" + heading + "</h2>" );
31              document.writeln( "<table border = \"1\"" );
32              document.writeln( "<thead><th>Subscript</th>" +
33                 "<th>Value</th></thead><tbody>" );
34
35              // output the subscript and value of each array element
36              for ( var i = 0; i < theArray.length; i++ )
37                 document.writeln( "<tr><td>" + i + "</td><td>" +
38                    theArray[ i ] + "</td></tr>" );
39
40              document.writeln( "</tbody></table>" );
41           } // end function outputArray
42           // -->
43        </script>
44     </head><body></body>
45  </html>
```

Fig. 8.4 | Declaring and initializing arrays. (Part 1 of 2.)

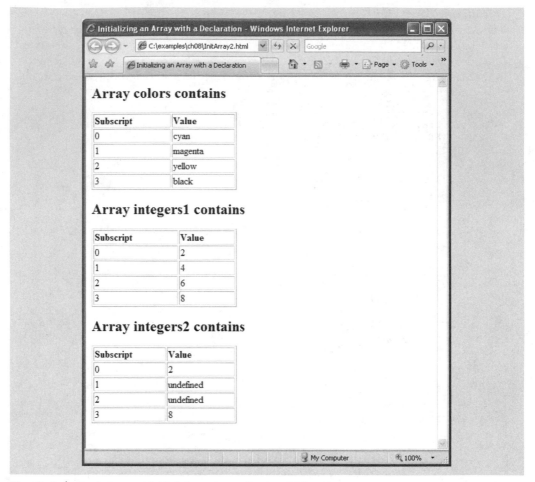

Fig. 8.4 | Declaring and initializing arrays. (Part 2 of 2.)

the array) appear in the web page as undefined. These are the two elements for which we did not supply values in the declaration in line 20 in the script.

Summing the Elements of an Array with for and for...in

The script in Fig. 8.5 sums the values contained in theArray, the 10-element integer array declared, allocated and initialized in line 13. The statement in line 19 in the body of the first for statement does the totaling. Note that the values supplied as initializers for array theArray could be read into the program using an XHTML form.

In this example, we introduce JavaScript's **for...in statement**, which enables a script to perform a task for each element in an array (or, as we'll see in Chapters 10–11, for each element in a collection). Lines 25-26 show the syntax of a for...in statement. Inside the parentheses, we declare the element variable used to select each element in the object to the right of keyword in (theArray in this case). When using for...in, JavaScript automatically determines the number of elements in the array. As the JavaScript interpreter iterates over theArray's elements, variable element is assigned a value that can be used as a sub-

```
1   <?xml version = "1.0" encoding = "utf-8"?>
2   <!DOCTYPE html PUBLIC "-//W3C//DTD XHTML 1.0 Strict//EN"
3       "http://www.w3.org/TR/xhtml1/DTD/xhtml1-strict.dtd">
4
5   <!-- Fig. 8.5: SumArray.html -->
6   <!-- Summing elements of an array. -->
7   <html xmlns = "http://www.w3.org/1999/xhtml">
8      <head>
9         <title>Sum the Elements of an Array</title>
10
11        <script type = "text/javascript">
12           <!--
13           var theArray = [ 1, 2, 3, 4, 5, 6, 7, 8, 9, 10 ];
14           var total1 = 0, total2 = 0;
15
16           // iterates through the elements of the array in order and adds
17           // each element's value to total1
18           for ( var i = 0; i < theArray.length; i++ )
19              total1 += theArray[ i ];
20
21           document.writeln( "Total using subscripts: " + total1 );
22
23           // iterates through the elements of the array using a for... in
24           // statement to add each element's value to total2
25           for ( var element in theArray )
26              total2 += theArray[ element ];
27
28           document.writeln( "<br />Total using for...in: " + total2 );
29           // -->
30        </script>
31     </head><body></body>
32  </html>
```

Total using subscripts: 55
Total using for...in: 55

Fig. 8.5 | Summing elements of an array.

script for theArray. In the case of an Array, the value assigned is a subscript in the range from 0 up to, but not including, theArray.length. Each value is added to total2 to produce the sum of the elements in the array.

Error-Prevention Tip 8.1

When iterating over all the elements of an Array, use a for...in statement to ensure that you manipulate only the existing elements of the Array. Note that a for...in statement skips any undefined elements in the array.

Using the Elements of an Array as Counters

In Chapter 7, we indicated that there is a more elegant way to implement the dice-rolling program in Fig. 7.4. The program rolled a single six-sided die 6000 times and used a `switch` statement to total the number of times each value was rolled. An array version of this script is shown in Fig. 8.6. The `switch` statement in Fig. 7.4 is replaced by line 24 of this program. This line uses the random `face` value as the subscript for the array `frequency` to determine which element to increment during each iteration of the loop. Because the random number calculation in line 23 produces numbers from 1 to 6 (the values for a six-sided die), the `frequency` array must be large enough to allow subscript values of 1 to 6. The smallest number of elements required for an array to have these subscript values is seven elements (subscript values from 0 to 6). In this program, we ignore element 0 of array `frequency` and use only the elements that correspond to values on the sides of a die. Also, lines 32–34 of this program use a loop to generate the table that was written one line at a time in Fig. 7.4. Because we can loop through array `frequency` to help produce the output, we do not have to enumerate each XHTML table row as we did in Fig. 7.4.

```
1   <?xml version = "1.0" encoding = "utf-8"?>
2   <!DOCTYPE html PUBLIC "-//W3C//DTD XHTML 1.0 Strict//EN"
3       "http://www.w3.org/TR/xhtml1/DTD/xhtml1-strict.dtd">
4
5   <!-- Fig. 8.6: RollDie.html -->
6   <!-- Dice-rolling program using an array instead of a switch. -->
7   <html xmlns = "http://www.w3.org/1999/xhtml">
8      <head>
9         <title>Roll a Six-Sided Die 6000 Times</title>
10        <style type = "text/css">
11           table { width: 15em }
12           th    { text-align: left }
13        </style>
14        <script type = "text/javascript">
15           <!--
16           var face;
17           var frequency = [ , 0, 0, 0, 0, 0, 0 ]; // leave frequency[0]
18                                                   // uninitialized
19
20           // summarize results
21           for ( var roll = 1; roll <= 6000; ++roll )
22           {
23              face = Math.floor( 1 + Math.random() * 6 );
24              ++frequency[ face ];
25           } // end for
26
27           document.writeln( "<table border = \"1\"><thead>" );
28           document.writeln( "<th>Face</th>" +
29              "<th>Frequency</th></thead><tbody>" );
30
31           // generate entire table of frequencies for each face
32           for ( face = 1; face < frequency.length; ++face )
33              document.writeln( "<tr><td>" + face + "</td><td>" +
34                 frequency[ face ] + "</td></tr>" );
```

Fig. 8.6 | Dice-rolling program using an array instead of a `switch`. (Part 1 of 2.)

```
35
36              document.writeln( "</tbody></table>" );
37           // -->
38        </script>
39     </head>
40     <body>
41        <p>Click Refresh (or Reload) to run the script again</p>
42     </body>
43  </html>
```

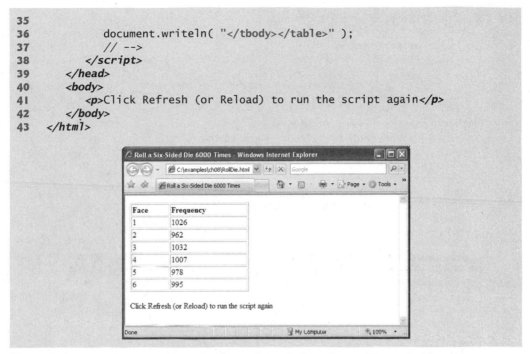

Fig. 8.6 | Dice-rolling program using an array instead of a `switch`. (Part 2 of 2.)

8.5 Random Image Generator Using Arrays

In Chapter 7, we created a random image generator that required image files to be named 1.gif, 2.gif, ..., 7.gif. In this example (Fig. 8.7), we create a more elegant random image generator that does not require the image filenames to be integers. This version of the random image generator uses an array pictures to store the names of the image files as strings. The script generates a random integer and uses it as a subscript into the pictures array. The script outputs an XHTML img element whose src attribute contains the image filename located in the randomly selected position in the pictures array.

```
1   <?xml version = "1.0" encoding = "utf-8"?>
2   <!DOCTYPE html PUBLIC "-//W3C//DTD XHTML 1.0 Strict//EN"
3      "http://www.w3.org/TR/xhtml1/DTD/xhtml1-strict.dtd">
4
5   <!-- Fig. 8.7: RandomPicture2.html -->
6   <!-- Random image generation using arrays. -->
7   <html xmlns = "http://www.w3.org/1999/xhtml">
8      <head>
9         <title>Random Image Generator</title>
10        <style type = "text/css">
11           table { width: 15em }
12           th    { text-align: left }
13        </style>
```

Fig. 8.7 | Random image generation using arrays. (Part 1 of 2.)

```
14        <script type = "text/javascript">
15           <!--
16           var pictures =
17              [ "CPE", "EPT", "GPP", "GUI", "PERF", "PORT", "SEO" ];
18
19           // pick a random image from the pictures array and displays by
20           // creating an img tag and appending the src attribute to the
21           // filename
22           document.write ( "<img src = \"" +
23              pictures[ Math.floor( Math.random() * 7 ) ] + ".gif\" />" );
24           // -->
25        </script>
26     </head>
27     <body>
28        <p>Click Refresh (or Reload) to run the script again</p>
29     </body>
30  </html>
```

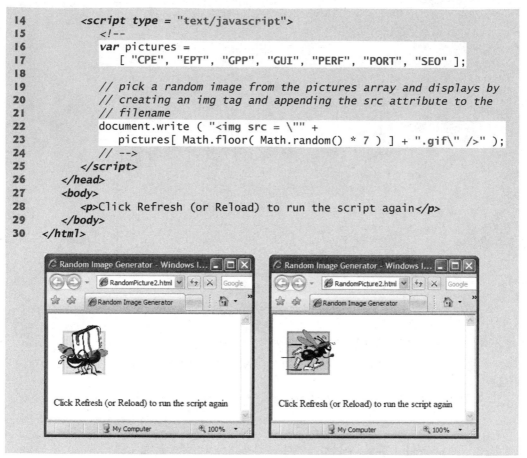

Fig. 8.7 | Random image generation using arrays. (Part 2 of 2.)

The script declares the array `pictures` in lines 16–17 and initializes it with the names of seven image files. Lines 22–23 create the `img` tag that displays the random image on the web page. Line 22 opens the `img` tag and begins the `src` attribute. Line 23 generates a random integer from 0 to 6 as an index into the `pictures` array, the result of which is a randomly selected image filename. The expression

```
pictures[ Math.floor( Math.random() * 7 ) ]
```

evaluates to a string from the `pictures` array, which then is written to the document (line 23). Line 23 completes the `img` tag with the extension of the image file (`.gif`).

8.6 References and Reference Parameters

Two ways to pass arguments to functions (or methods) in many programming languages are *pass-by-value* and *pass-by-reference*. When an argument is passed to a function by value, a *copy* of the argument's value is made and is passed to the called function. In JavaScript, numbers, boolean values and strings are passed to functions by value.

With pass-by-reference, the caller gives the called function direct access to the caller's data and allows it to modify the data if it so chooses. This procedure is accomplished by passing to the called function the address of the location in memory where the data resides. Pass-by-reference can improve performance because it can eliminate the overhead of copying large amounts of data, but it can weaken security because the called function can access the caller's data. In JavaScript, all objects (and thus all Arrays) are passed to functions by reference.

Error-Prevention Tip 8.2

With pass-by-value, changes to the copy of the called function do not affect the original variable's value in the calling function. This prevents the accidental side effects that so greatly hinder the development of correct and reliable software systems.

Software Engineering Observation 8.2

Unlike some other languages, JavaScript does not allow you to choose whether to pass each argument by value or by reference. Numbers, boolean values and strings are passed by value. Objects are passed to functions by reference. When a function receives a reference to an object, the function can manipulate the object directly.

Software Engineering Observation 8.3

When returning information from a function via a return statement, numbers and boolean values are always returned by value (i.e., a copy is returned), and objects are always returned by reference. Note that, in the pass-by-reference case, it is not necessary to return the new value, since the object is already modified.

To pass a reference to an object into a function, simply specify the reference name in the function call. Normally, the reference name is the identifier that the program uses to manipulate the object. Mentioning the reference by its parameter name in the body of the called function actually refers to the original object in memory, which can be accessed directly by the called function. In the next section, we demonstrate pass-by-value and pass-by-reference, using arrays.

8.7 Passing Arrays to Functions

To pass an array argument to a function (Fig. 8.8), specify the name of the array (a reference to the array) without brackets. For example, if array hourlyTemperatures has been declared as

```
var hourlyTemperatures = new Array( 24 );
```

then the function call

```
modifyArray( hourlyTemperatures );
```

passes array hourlyTemperatures to function modifyArray. As stated in Section 8.2, every array object in JavaScript knows its own size (via the length attribute). Thus, when we pass an array object into a function, we do not pass the size of the array separately as an argument. Figure 8.3 illustrated this concept when we passed Arrays n1 and n2 to function outputArray to display each Array's contents.

```
 1    <?xml version = "1.0" encoding = "utf-8"?>
 2    <!DOCTYPE html PUBLIC "-//W3C//DTD XHTML 1.0 Strict//EN"
 3       "http://www.w3.org/TR/xhtml1/DTD/xhtml1-strict.dtd">
 4
 5    <!-- Fig. 8.8: PassArray.html -->
 6    <!-- Passing arrays and individual array elements to functions. -->
 7    <html xmlns = "http://www.w3.org/1999/xhtml">
 8       <head>
 9          <title>Passing arrays and individual array
10             elements to functions</title>
11          <script type = "text/javascript">
12             <!--
13             var a = [ 1, 2, 3, 4, 5 ];
14
15             document.writeln( "<h2>Effects of passing entire " +
16                "array by reference</h2>" );
17             outputArray( "Original array: ", a );
18
19             modifyArray( a );  // array a passed by reference
20
21             outputArray( "Modified array: ", a );
22
23             document.writeln( "<h2>Effects of passing array " +
24                "element by value</h2>" +
25                "a[3] before modifyElement: " + a[ 3 ] );
26
27             modifyElement( a[ 3 ] ); // array element a[3] passed by value
28
29             document.writeln( "<br />a[3] after modifyElement: " + a[ 3 ] );
30
31             // outputs heading followed by the contents of "theArray"
32             function outputArray( heading, theArray )
33             {
34                document.writeln(
35                   heading + theArray.join( " " ) + "<br />" );
36             } // end function outputArray
37
38             // function that modifies the elements of an array
39             function modifyArray( theArray )
40             {
41                for ( var j in theArray )
42                   theArray[ j ] *= 2;
43             } // end function modifyArray
44
45             // function that modifies the value passed
46             function modifyElement( e )
47             {
48                e *= 2; // scales element e only for the duration of the
49                        // function
50                document.writeln( "<br />value in modifyElement: " + e );
51             } // end function modifyElement
52             // -->
```

Fig. 8.8 | Passing arrays and individual array elements to functions. (Part 1 of 2.)

```
53          </script>
54      </head><body></body>
55  </html>
```

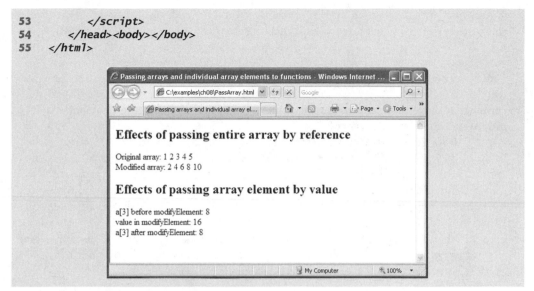

Fig. 8.8 | Passing arrays and individual array elements to functions. (Part 2 of 2.)

Although entire arrays are passed by reference, *individual numeric and boolean array elements* are passed *by value* exactly as simple numeric and boolean variables are passed (the objects referred to by individual elements of an Array of objects are still passed by reference). Such simple single pieces of data are called *scalars*. To pass an array element to a function, use the subscripted name of the element as an argument in the function call.

For a function to receive an Array through a function call, the function's parameter list must specify a parameter that will refer to the Array in the body of the function. Unlike other programming languages, JavaScript does not provide a special syntax for this purpose. JavaScript simply requires that the identifier for the Array be specified in the parameter list. For example, the function header for function modifyArray might be written as

> *function* modifyArray(b)

indicating that modifyArray expects to receive a parameter named b (the argument supplied in the calling function must be an Array). Arrays are passed by reference, and therefore when the called function uses the array name b, it refers to the actual array in the caller (array hourlyTemperatures in the preceding call). The script in Fig. 8.8 demonstrates the difference between passing an entire array and passing an array element.

Software Engineering Observation 8.4

JavaScript does not check the number of arguments or types of arguments that are passed to a function. It is possible to pass any number of values to a function. JavaScript will attempt to perform conversions when the values are used.

The statement in line 17 invokes function outputArray to display the contents of array a before it is modified. Function outputArray (defined in lines 32–36) receives a string to output and the array to output. The statement in lines 34–35 uses Array method *join* to create a string containing all the elements in theArray. Method join takes as its argument a string containing the *separator* that should be used to separate the elements of the array in the string that is returned. If the argument is not specified, the empty string is used as the separator.

Line 19 invokes function modifyArray (lines 39–43) and passes it array a. The modifyArray function multiplies each element by 2. To illustrate that array a's elements were modified, the statement in line 21 invokes function outputArray again to display the contents of array a after it is modified. As the screen capture shows, the elements of a are indeed modified by modifyArray.

To show the value of a[3] before the call to modifyElement, line 25 outputs the value of a[3]. Line 27 invokes modifyElement (lines 46–51) and passes a[3] as the argument. Remember that a[3] actually is one integer value in the array a. Also remember that numeric values and boolean values are always passed to functions by value. Therefore, a copy of a[3] is passed. Function modifyElement multiplies its argument by 2 and stores the result in its parameter e. The parameter of function modifyElement is a local variable in that function, so when the function terminates, the local variable is no longer accessible. Thus, when control is returned to the main script, the unmodified value of a[3] is displayed by the statement in line 29.

8.8 Sorting Arrays

The Array object in JavaScript has a built-in method *sort* for sorting arrays. Figure 8.9 demonstrates the Array object's sort method.

```
1   <?xml version = "1.0" encoding = "utf-8"?>
2   <!DOCTYPE html PUBLIC "-//W3C//DTD XHTML 1.0 Strict//EN"
3      "http://www.w3.org/TR/xhtml1/DTD/xhtml1-strict.dtd">
4
5   <!-- Fig. 8.9: Sort.html -->
6   <!-- Sorting an array with sort. -->
7   <html xmlns = "http://www.w3.org/1999/xhtml">
8      <head>
9         <title>Sorting an Array with Array Method sort</title>
10        <script type = "text/javascript">
11           <!--
12           var a = [ 10, 1, 9, 2, 8, 3, 7, 4, 6, 5 ];
13
14           document.writeln( "<h1>Sorting an Array</h1>" );
15           outputArray( "Data items in original order: ", a );
16           a.sort( compareIntegers );   // sort the array
17           outputArray( "Data items in ascending order: ", a );
18
19           // output the heading followed by the contents of theArray
20           function outputArray( heading, theArray )
21           {
22              document.writeln( "<p>" + heading +
23                 theArray.join( " " ) + "</p>" );
24           } // end function outputArray
25
```

Fig. 8.9 | Sorting an array with Array method sort. (Part 1 of 2.)

```
26              // comparison function for use with sort
27              function compareIntegers( value1, value2 )
28              {
29                  return parseInt( value1 ) - parseInt( value2 );
30              } // end function compareIntegers
31              // -->
32          </script>
33      </head><body></body>
34  </html>
```

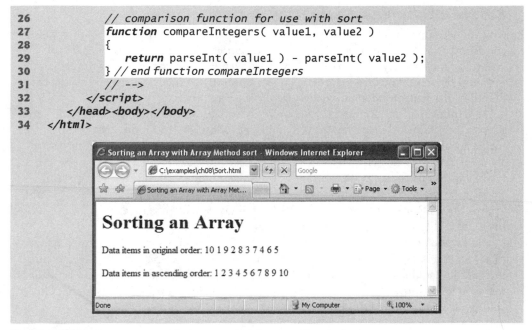

Fig. 8.9 | Sorting an array with `Array` method `sort`. (Part 2 of 2.)

By default, `Array` method `sort` (with no arguments) uses string comparisons to determine the sorting order of the `Array` elements. The strings are compared by the ASCII values of their characters. [*Note:* String comparison is discussed in more detail in Chapter 9, JavaScript: Objects.] In this example, we'd like to sort an array of integers.

Method `sort` takes as its optional argument the name of a function (called the *comparator function*) that compares its two arguments and returns one of the following:

- a negative value if the first argument is less than the second argument
- zero if the arguments are equal, or
- a positive value if the first argument is greater than the second argument

This example uses function `compareIntegers` (defined in lines 27–30) as the comparator function for method `sort`. It calculates the difference between the integer values of its two arguments (function `parseInt` ensures that the arguments are handled properly as integers). If the first argument is less than the second argument, the difference will be a negative value. If the arguments are equal, the difference will be zero. If the first argument is greater than the second argument, the difference will be a positive value.

Line 16 invokes `Array` object `a`'s `sort` method and passes the name of function `compareIntegers` as an argument. Method `sort` receives function `compareIntegers` as an argument, then uses the function to compare elements of the `Array` `a` to determine their sorting order.

Software Engineering Observation 8.5

Functions in JavaScript are considered to be data. Therefore, functions can be assigned to variables, stored in `Arrays` and passed to functions just like other data types.

8.9 Multidimensional Arrays

Multidimensional arrays with two subscripts are often used to represent tables of values consisting of information arranged in *rows* and *columns*. To identify a particular table element, we must specify the two subscripts; by convention, the first identifies the element's row, and the second identifies the element's column. Arrays that require two subscripts to identify a particular element are called *two-dimensional arrays*.

Multidimensional arrays can have more than two dimensions. JavaScript does not support multidimensional arrays directly, but does allow you to specify arrays whose elements are also arrays, thus achieving the same effect. When an array contains one-dimensional arrays as its elements, we can imagine these one-dimensional arrays as rows of a table, and the positions in these arrays as columns. Figure 8.10 illustrates a two-dimensional array named a that contains three rows and four columns (i.e., a three-by-four array—three one-dimensional arrays, each with 4 elements). In general, an array with m rows and n columns is called an *m-by-n array*.

Every element in array a is identified in Fig. 8.10 by an element name of the form a[i][j]; a is the name of the array, and i and j are the subscripts that uniquely identify the row and column, respectively, of each element in a. Note that the names of the elements in the first row all have a first subscript of 0; the names of the elements in the fourth column all have a second subscript of 3.

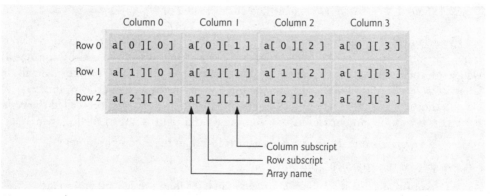

Fig. 8.10 | Two-dimensional array with three rows and four columns.

Arrays of One-Dimensional Arrays

Multidimensional arrays can be initialized in declarations like a one-dimensional array. Array b with two rows and two columns could be declared and initialized with the statement

> *var* b = [[1, 2], [3, 4]];

The values are grouped by row in square brackets. The array [1, 2] initializes element b[0], and the array [3, 4] initializes element b[1]. So 1 and 2 initialize b[0][0] and b[0][1], respectively. Similarly, 3 and 4 initialize b[1][0] and b[1][1], respectively. The interpreter determines the number of rows by counting the number of sub initializer lists—arrays nested within the outermost array. The interpreter determines the number of columns in each row by counting the number of values in the sub-array that initializes the row.

Two-Dimensional Arrays with Rows of Different Lengths

The rows of a two-dimensional array can vary in length. The declaration

```
var b = [ [ 1, 2 ], [ 3, 4, 5 ] ];
```

creates array b with row 0 containing two elements (1 and 2) and row 1 containing three elements (3, 4 and 5).

Creating Two-Dimensional Arrays with new

A multidimensional array in which each row has a different number of columns can be allocated dynamically, as follows:

```
var b;
b = new Array( 2 ); // allocate rows
b[ 0 ] = new Array( 5 ); // allocate columns for row 0
b[ 1 ] = new Array( 3 ); // allocate columns for row 1
```

The preceding code creates a two-dimensional array with two rows. Row 0 has five columns, and row 1 has three columns.

Two-Dimensional Array Example: Displaying Element Values

Figure 8.11 initializes two-dimensional arrays in declarations and uses nested for...in loops to *traverse the arrays* (i.e., manipulate every element of the array).

```
1   <?xml version = "1.0" encoding = "utf-8"?>
2   <!DOCTYPE html PUBLIC "-//W3C//DTD XHTML 1.0 Strict//EN"
3      "http://www.w3.org/TR/xhtml1/DTD/xhtml1-strict.dtd">
4
5   <!-- Fig. 8.11: InitArray3.html -->
6   <!-- Initializing multidimensional arrays. -->
7   <html xmlns = "http://www.w3.org/1999/xhtml">
8      <head>
9         <title>Initializing Multidimensional Arrays</title>
10        <script type = "text/javascript">
11           <!--
12           var array1 = [ [ 1, 2, 3 ], // first row
13                          [ 4, 5, 6 ] ]; // second row
14           var array2 = [ [ 1, 2 ], // first row
15                          [ 3 ], // second row
16                          [ 4, 5, 6 ] ]; // third row
17
18           outputArray( "Values in array1 by row", array1 );
19           outputArray( "Values in array2 by row", array2 );
20
21           function outputArray( heading, theArray )
22           {
23              document.writeln( "<h2>" + heading + "</h2><pre>" );
24
25              // iterates through the set of one-dimensional arrays
26              for ( var i in theArray )
27              {
```

Fig. 8.11 | Initializing multidimensional arrays. (Part 1 of 2.)

```
28              // iterates through the elements of each one-dimensional
29              // array
30              for ( var j in theArray[ i ] )
31                 document.write( theArray[ i ][ j ] + " " );
32
33              document.writeln( "<br />" );
34           } // end for
35
36           document.writeln( "</pre>" );
37        } // end function outputArray
38        // -->
39     </script>
40  </head><body></body>
41 </html>
```

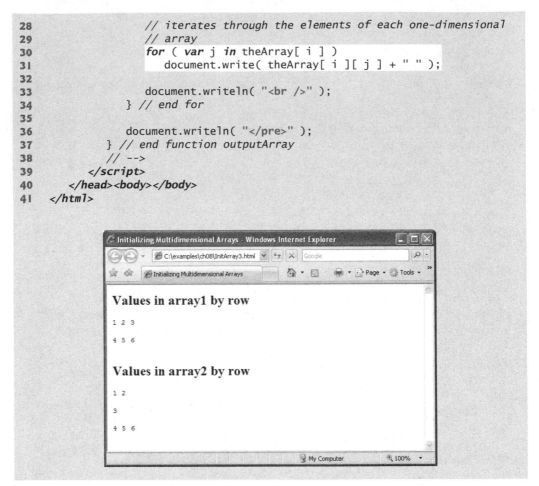

Fig. 8.11 | Initializing multidimensional arrays. (Part 2 of 2.)

The program declares two arrays in main script (in the XHTML head element). The declaration of array1 (lines 12–13 provides six initializers in two sublists. The first sublist initializes the first row of the array to the values 1, 2 and 3; the second sublist initializes the second row of the array to the values 4, 5 and 6. The declaration of array2 (lines 14–16) provides six initializers in three sublists. The sublist for the first row explicitly initializes the first row to have two elements, with values 1 and 2, respectively. The sublist for the second row initializes the second row to have one element, with value 3. The sublist for the third row initializes the third row to the values 4, 5 and 6.

The script calls function outputArray from lines 18–19 to display each array's elements in the web page. Function outputArray (lines 21–37) receives two arguments—a string heading to output before the array and the array to output (called theArray). Note the use of a nested for...in statement to output the rows of each two-dimensional array. The outer for...in statement iterates over the rows of the array. The inner for...in statement iterates over the columns of the current row being processed. The nested for...in statement in this example could have been written with for statements, as follows:

```
for ( var i = 0; i < theArray.length; ++i )
{
    for ( var j = 0; j < theArray[ i ].length; ++j )
        document.write( theArray[ i ][ j ] + " " );

    document.writeln( "<br />" );
}
```

In the outer for statement, the expression theArray.length determines the number of rows in the array. In the inner for statement, the expression theArray[i].length determines the number of columns in each row of the array. This condition enables the loop to determine, for each row, the exact number of columns.

Common Multidimensional-Array Manipulations with for *and* for... in *Statements*

Many common array manipulations use for or for...in statements. For example, the following for statement sets all the elements in the third row of array a in Fig. 8.10 to zero:

```
for ( var col = 0; col < a[ 2 ].length; ++col )
    a[ 2 ][ col ] = 0;
```

We specified the *third* row; therefore, we know that the first subscript is always 2 (0 is the first row and 1 is the second row). The for loop varies only the second subscript (i.e., the column subscript). The preceding for statement is equivalent to the statements

```
a[ 2 ][ 0 ] = 0;
a[ 2 ][ 1 ] = 0;
a[ 2 ][ 2 ] = 0;
a[ 2 ][ 3 ] = 0;
```

The following for...in statement is also equivalent to the preceding for statement:

```
for ( var col in a[ 2 ] )
    a[ 2 ][ col ] = 0;
```

The following nested for statement determines the total of all the elements in array a:

```
var total = 0;

for ( var row = 0; row < a.length; ++row )

    for ( var col = 0; col < a[ row ].length; ++col )
        total += a[ row ][ col ];
```

The for statement totals the elements of the array, one row at a time. The outer for statement begins by setting the row subscript to 0, so that the elements of the first row may be totaled by the inner for statement. The outer for statement then increments row to 1, so that the elements of the second row can be totaled. Then the outer for statement increments row to 2, so that the elements of the third row can be totaled. The result can be displayed when the nested for statement terminates. The preceding for statement is equivalent to the following for...in statement:

```
var total = 0;

for ( var row in a )

    for ( var col in a[ row ] )
        total += a[ row ][ col ];
```

8.10 Building an Online Quiz

Online quizzes and polls are popular web applications often used for educational purposes or just for fun. Web developers typically build quizzes using simple XHTML forms and process the results with JavaScript. Arrays allow a programmer to represent several possible answer choices in a single data structure. Figure 8.12 contains an online quiz consisting of one question. The quiz page contains one of the tip icons used throughout this book and an XHTML form in which the user identifies the type of tip the image represents by selecting one of four radio buttons. After the user selects one of the radio button choices and submits the form, the script determines whether the user selected the correct type of tip to match the mystery image. The JavaScript function that checks the user's answer combines several of the concepts from the current chapter and previous chapters in a concise and useful script.

```
1   <?xml version = "1.0" encoding = "utf-8"?>
2   <!DOCTYPE html PUBLIC "-//W3C//DTD XHTML 1.0 Strict//EN"
3      "http://www.w3.org/TR/xhtml1/DTD/xhtml1-strict.dtd">
4
5   <!-- Fig. 8.12: quiz.html -->
6   <!-- Online quiz graded with JavaScript. -->
7   <html xmlns = "http://www.w3.org/1999/xhtml">
8      <head>
9         <title>Online Quiz</title>
10        <script type = "text/JavaScript">
11           <!--
12           function checkAnswers()
13           {
14              var myQuiz = document.getElementById( "myQuiz" );
15
16              // determine whether the answer is correct
17              if ( myQuiz.elements[ 1 ].checked )
18                 alert( "Congratulations, your answer is correct" );
19              else // if the answer is incorrect
20                 alert( "Your answer is incorrect. Please try again" );
21           } // end function checkAnswers
22           -->
23        </script>
24     </head>
25     <body>
26        <form id = "myQuiz" onsubmit = "checkAnswers()" action = "">
27           <p>Select the name of the tip that goes with the
28              image shown:<br />
29              <img src="EPT.gif" alt="mystery tip"/>
30              <br />
31
32              <input type = "radio" name = "radiobutton" value = "CPE" />
33              <label>Common Programming Error</label>
34
35              <input type = "radio" name = "radiobutton" value = "EPT" />
36              <label>Error-Prevention Tip</label>
37
```

Fig. 8.12 | Online quiz graded with JavaScript. (Part 1 of 2.)

```
38              <input type = "radio" name = "radiobutton" value = "PERF" />
39              <label>Performance Tip</label>
40
41              <input type = "radio" name = "radiobutton" value = "PORT" />
42              <label>Portability Tip</label><br />
43
44              <input type = "submit" name = "submit" value = "Submit" />
45              <input type = "reset" name = "reset" value = "Reset" />
46          </p>
47      </form>
48  </body>
49 </html>
```

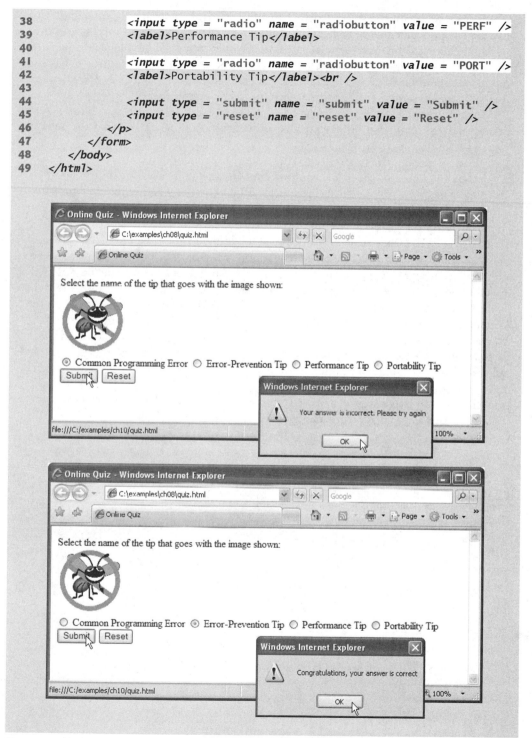

Fig. 8.12 | Online quiz graded with JavaScript. (Part 2 of 2.)

Before we discuss the script code, we first discuss the body element (lines 25–48) of the XHTML document. The body's GUI components play an important role in the script.

Lines 26–47 define the form that presents the quiz to users. Line 26 begins the form element and specifies the onsubmit attribute to "checkAnswers()", indicating that the interpreter should execute the JavaScript function checkAnswers (lines 12–21) when the user submits the form (i.e., clicks the **Submit** button or presses *Enter*).

Line 29 adds the tip image to the page. Lines 32–42 display the radio buttons and corresponding labels that display possible answer choices. Lines 44–45 add the submit and reset buttons to the page.

We now examine the script used to check the answer submitted by the user. Lines 12–21 declare the function checkAnswers that contains all the JavaScript required to grade the quiz. The if...else statement in lines 17–20 determines whether the user answered the question correctly. The image that the user is asked to identify is the Error-Prevention Tip icon. Thus the correct answer to the quiz corresponds to the second radio button.

An XHTML form's elements can be accessed individually using getElementById or through the *elements property* of the containing form object. The elements property contains an array of all the form's controls. The radio buttons are part of the XHTML form myQuiz, so we access the elements array in line 17 using dot notation (myQuiz.elements[1]). The array element myQuiz.elements[1] corresponds to the correct answer (i.e., the second radio button). Finally, line 17 determines whether the property *checked* of the second radio button is true. Property checked of a radio button is true when the radio button is selected, and it is false when the radio button is not selected. Recall that only one radio button may be selected at any given time. If property myQuiz.elements[1].checked is true, indicating that the correct answer is selected, the script alerts a congratulatory message. If property checked of the radio button is false, then the script alerts an alternate message (line 20).

JavaScript: Objects

*My object all sublime
I shall achieve in time.*
—W. S. Gilbert

*Is it a world to hide virtues
in?*
—William Shakespeare

*Good as it is to inherit a
library, it is better to collect
one.*
—Augustine Birrell

OBJECTIVES

In this chapter you'll learn:

- Object-based programming terminology and concepts.
- The concepts of encapsulation and data hiding.
- The value of object orientation.
- To use the JavaScript objects Math, String, Date, Boolean and Number.
- To use the browser's document and window objects.
- To use cookies.
- To represent objects simply using JSON.

9.1 Introduction

This chapter presents a more formal treatment of *objects*. We begin by briefly introducing the concepts of object orientation. The remainder of the chapter overviews several of Java-Script's built-in objects and demonstrates many of their capabilities. We also provide a brief introduction to JavaScript Object Notation (JSON)—a human-readable data format that is typically used to transmit data between clients and web servers and is also used to create objects in JavaScript. In the coming chapters on the Document Object Model and events we discuss the objects provided by the browser that enable scripts to interact with the elements of an XHTML document.

9.2 Introduction to Object Technology

This section provides a general introduction to object orientation. The terminology and technologies discussed here support the upcoming chapters. Here, you'll learn that objects are a natural way of thinking about the world and about scripts that manipulate XHTML documents. In Chapters 4–8, we used built-in JavaScript objects—`Math` and `Array`—and objects provided by the web browser—`document` and `window`—to perform tasks in our scripts. JavaScript uses objects to perform many tasks and therefore is referred to as an *object-based programming language*. Our goal is to help you develop an object-oriented way of thinking. Technologies such as CSS, JavaScript and Ajax are based on at least some of the concepts introduced in this section.

Basic Object-Technology Concepts

We begin our introduction to object technology with some key terminology. Everywhere you look in the real world you see objects—people, animals, plants, cars, planes, buildings, computers, monitors and so on. Humans think in terms of objects. Telephones, houses, traffic lights, microwave ovens and water coolers are just a few more common objects we see around us.

We sometimes divide objects into two categories: animate and inanimate. Animate objects are "alive" in some sense—they move around and do things. Inanimate objects do not move on their own. Objects of both types, however, have some things in common. They all have *attributes* (e.g., size, shape, color and weight), and they all exhibit *behaviors* (e.g., a ball rolls, bounces, inflates and deflates; a baby cries, sleeps, crawls, walks and blinks; a car accelerates, brakes and turns; a towel absorbs water). We'll study the kinds of attributes and behaviors that software objects have.

Humans learn about existing objects by studying their attributes and observing their behaviors. Different objects can have similar attributes and can exhibit similar behaviors. Comparisons can be made, for example, between babies and adults, and between humans and chimpanzees.

Object-oriented design (OOD) models software in terms similar to those that people use to describe real-world objects. It takes advantage of class relationships, where objects of a certain class, such as a class of vehicles, have the same characteristics—cars, trucks, little red wagons and roller skates have much in common. OOD takes advantage of *inheritance* relationships, where new classes of objects are derived by absorbing characteristics of existing classes and adding unique characteristics of their own. An object of class "convertible" certainly has the characteristics of the more general class "automobile," but more specifically, the roof goes up and down.

Object-oriented design provides a natural and intuitive way to view the software design process—namely, modeling objects by their attributes, behaviors and interrelationships, just as we describe real-world objects. OOD also models communication between objects. Just as people send messages to one another (e.g., a sergeant commands a soldier to stand at attention), objects also communicate via messages. A bank account object may receive a message to decrease its balance by a certain amount because the customer has withdrawn that amount of money.

OOD *encapsulates* (i.e., wraps) attributes and *operations* (behaviors) into objects—an object's attributes and operations are intimately tied together. Objects have the property of *information hiding*. This means that objects may know how to communicate with one another across well-defined *interfaces,* but normally they are not allowed to know how other objects are implemented—implementation details are hidden within the objects themselves. We can drive a car effectively, for instance, without knowing the details of how engines, transmissions, brakes and exhaust systems work internally—as long as we know how to use the accelerator pedal, the brake pedal, the steering wheel and so on. Information hiding, as we'll see, is crucial to good software engineering.

Like the designers of an automobile, the designers of web browsers have defined a set of objects that encapsulate an XHTML document's elements and expose to a JavaScript programmer the attributes and behaviors that enable a JavaScript program to interact with (or script) those elements (objects). You'll soon see that the browser's document object contains attributes and behaviors that provide access to every element of an XHTML document. Similarly, JavaScript provides objects that encapsulate various capabilities in a script. For example, the JavaScript Array object provides attributes and behaviors that enable a script to manipulate a collection of data. The Array object's length property (attribute) contains the number of elements in the Array. The Array object's sort method (behavior) orders the elements of the Array.

Some programming languages—like Java, Visual Basic, C# and C++—are *object oriented*. Programming in such a language is called *object-oriented programming (OOP)*, and it allows computer programmers to implement object-oriented designs as working software systems. Languages like C, on the other hand, are *procedural*, so programming tends to be *action oriented*. In procedural languages, the unit of programming is the *function*. In object-oriented languages, the unit of programming is the *class* from which objects are eventually *instantiated* (an OOP term for "created"). Classes contain functions that implement operations and data that comprises attributes.

Procedural programmers concentrate on writing functions. Programmers group actions that perform some common task into functions, and group functions to form programs. Data is certainly important in procedural languages, but the view is that data exists primarily in support of the actions that functions perform. The *verbs* in a system specification help a procedural programmer determine the set of functions that work together to implement the system.

Classes, Properties and Methods

Object-oriented programmers concentrate on creating their own *user-defined types* called *classes*. Each class contains data as well as the set of functions that manipulate that data and provide services to *clients* (i.e., other classes or functions that use the class). The data components of a class are called properties. For example, a bank account class might include an account number and a balance. The function components of a class are called methods. For example, a bank account class might include methods to make a deposit (increasing the balance), make a withdrawal (decreasing the balance) and inquire what the current balance is. You use built-in types (and other user-defined types) as the "building blocks" for constructing new user-defined types (classes). The *nouns* in a system specification help you determine the set of classes from which objects are created that work together to implement the system.

Classes are to objects as blueprints are to houses—a class is a "plan" for building an object of the class. Just as we can build many houses from one blueprint, we can instantiate (create) many objects from one class. You cannot cook meals in the kitchen of a blueprint; you can cook meals in the kitchen of a house. You cannot sleep in the bedroom of a blueprint; you can sleep in the bedroom of a house.

Classes can have relationships with other classes. For example, in an object-oriented design of a bank, the "bank teller" class needs to relate to other classes, such as the "customer" class, the "cash drawer" class, the "safe" class, and so on. These relationships are called *associations*.

Packaging software as classes makes it possible for future software systems to *reuse* the classes. Groups of related classes are often packaged as reusable *components*. Just as realtors often say that the three most important factors affecting the price of real estate are "location, location and location," some people in the software development community say that the three most important factors affecting the future of software development are "reuse, reuse and reuse."

Indeed, with object technology, you can build much of the new software you'll need by combining existing classes, just as automobile manufacturers combine interchangeable parts. Each new class you create will have the potential to become a valuable software asset that you and other programmers can reuse to speed and enhance the quality of future software development efforts.

9.3 Math Object

The Math object's methods allow you to perform many common mathematical calculations. As shown previously, an object's methods are called by writing the name of the object followed by a dot (.) and the name of the method. In parentheses following the method name is the argument (or a comma-separated list of arguments) to the method. For example, to calculate and display the square root of 900.0 you might write

```
document.writeln( Math.sqrt( 900.0 ) );
```

which calls method Math.sqrt to calculate the square root of the number contained in the parentheses (900.0), then outputs the result. The number 900.0 is the argument of the Math.sqrt method. The preceding statement would display 30.0. Some *Math* object methods are summarized in Fig. 9.1.

Method	Description	Examples
abs(x)	absolute value of x	abs(7.2) is 7.2 abs(0.0) is 0.0 abs(-5.6) is 5.6
ceil(x)	rounds x to the smallest integer not less than x	ceil(9.2) is 10.0 ceil(-9.8) is -9.0
cos(x)	trigonometric cosine of x (x in radians)	cos(0.0) is 1.0
exp(x)	exponential method e^x	exp(1.0) is 2.71828 exp(2.0) is 7.38906
floor(x)	rounds x to the largest integer not greater than x	floor(9.2) is 9.0 floor(-9.8) is -10.0
log(x)	natural logarithm of x (base e)	log(2.718282) is 1.0 log(7.389056) is 2.0
max(x, y)	larger value of x and y	max(2.3, 12.7) is 12.7 max(-2.3, -12.7) is -2.3
min(x, y)	smaller value of x and y	min(2.3, 12.7) is 2.3 min(-2.3, -12.7) is -12.7
pow(x, y)	x raised to power y (x^y)	pow(2.0, 7.0) is 128.0 pow(9.0, .5) is 3.0
round(x)	rounds x to the closest integer	round(9.75) is 10 round(9.25) is 9
sin(x)	trigonometric sine of x (x in radians)	sin(0.0) is 0.0
sqrt(x)	square root of x	sqrt(900.0) is 30.0 sqrt(9.0) is 3.0
tan(x)	trigonometric tangent of x (x in radians)	tan(0.0) is 0.0

Fig. 9.1 | Math object methods.

Common Programming Error 9.1

Forgetting to invoke a Math method by preceding the method name with the object name Math and a dot (.) is an error.

Software Engineering Observation 9.1

The primary difference between invoking a standalone function and invoking a method of an object is that an object name and a dot are not required to call a standalone function.

The Math object defines several commonly used mathematical constants, summarized in Fig. 9.2. [*Note:* By convention, the names of constants are written in all uppercase letters so they stand out in a program.]

Good Programming Practice 9.1

Use the mathematical constants of the Math object rather than explicitly typing the numeric value of the constant.

Constant	Description	Value
Math.E	Base of a natural logarithm (*e*).	Approximately 2.718
Math.LN2	Natural logarithm of 2	Approximately 0.693
Math.LN10	Natural logarithm of 10	Approximately 2.302
Math.LOG2E	Base 2 logarithm of *e*	Approximately 1.442
Math.LOG10E	Base 10 logarithm of *e*	Approximately 0.434
Math.PI	π—the ratio of a circle's circumference to its diameter	Approximately 3.141592653589793
Math.SQRT1_2	Square root of 0.5	Approximately 0.707
Math.SQRT2	Square root of 2.0	Approximately 1.414

Fig. 9.2 | Constants of the Math object.

9.4 String Object

In this section, we introduce JavaScript's string- and character-processing capabilities. The techniques discussed here are appropriate for processing names, addresses, telephone numbers, and similar items.

9.4.1 Fundamentals of Characters and Strings

Characters are the fundamental building blocks of JavaScript programs. Every program is composed of a sequence of characters grouped together meaningfully that is interpreted by the computer as a series of instructions used to accomplish a task.

A string is a series of characters treated as a single unit. A string may include letters, digits and various ***special characters***, such as +, -, *, /, and $. JavaScript supports the set of characters called ***Unicode***®, which represents a large portion of the world's languages. A string is an object of type **String**. *String literals* or ***string constants*** (often called ***anonymous String objects***) are written as a sequence of characters in double quotation marks or single quotation marks, as follows:

```
"John Q. Doe"              (a name)
'9999 Main Street'        (a street address)
"Waltham, Massachusetts"  (a city and state)
'(201) 555-1212'          (a telephone number)
```

A String may be assigned to a variable in a declaration. The declaration

```
var color = "blue";
```

initializes variable color with the String object containing the string "blue". Strings can be compared via the relational (<, <=, > and >=) and equality operators (== and !=). Strings are compared using the Unicode values of the corresponding characters. For example, the expression "hello" < "Hello" evaluates to false because lowercase letters have higher Unicode values.

9.4.2 Methods of the String Object

The String object encapsulates the attributes and behaviors of a string of characters. It provides many methods (behaviors) that accomplish useful tasks such as selecting characters from a string, combining strings (called *concatenation*), obtaining substrings of a string, searching for substrings within a string, tokenizing strings (i.e., splitting strings into individual words) and converting strings to all uppercase or lowercase letters. The String object also provides several methods that generate XHTML tags. Figure 9.3 summarizes many String methods. Figures 9.4–9.7 demonstrate some of these methods.

Method	Description
charAt(*index*)	Returns a string containing the character at the specified *index*. If there is no character at the *index*, charAt returns an empty string. The first character is located at *index* 0.
charCodeAt(*index*)	Returns the Unicode value of the character at the specified *index*, or NaN (not a number) if there is no character at that *index*.
concat(*string*)	Concatenates its argument to the end of the string that invokes the method. The string invoking this method is not modified; instead a new String is returned. This method is the same as adding two strings with the string-concatenation operator + (e.g., s1.concat(s2) is the same as s1 + s2).
fromCharCode(*value1*, *value2*, ...)	Converts a list of Unicode values into a string containing the corresponding characters.
indexOf(*substring*, *index*)	Searches for the first occurrence of *substring* starting from position *index* in the string that invokes the method. The method returns the starting index of *substring* in the source string or –1 if *substring* is not found. If the *index* argument is not provided, the method begins searching from index 0 in the source string.

Fig. 9.3 | Some String object methods. (Part I of 2.)

Method	Description
lastIndexOf(*substring*, *index*)	Searches for the last occurrence of *substring* starting from position *index* and searching toward the beginning of the string that invokes the method. The method returns the starting index of *substring* in the source string or −1 if *substring* is not found. If the *index* argument is not provided, the method begins searching from the end of the source string.
replace(*searchString*, *replaceString*)	Searches for the substring *searchString*, and replaces the first occurrence with *replaceString* and returns the modified string, or the original string if no replacement was made.
slice(*start*, *end*)	Returns a string containing the portion of the string from index *start* through index *end*. If the *end* index is not specified, the method returns a string from the *start* index to the end of the source string. A negative *end* index specifies an offset from the end of the string, starting from a position one past the end of the last character (so −1 indicates the last character position in the string).
split(*string*)	Splits the source string into an array of strings (tokens), where its *string* argument specifies the delimiter (i.e., the characters that indicate the end of each token in the source string).
substr(*start*, *length*)	Returns a string containing *length* characters starting from index *start* in the source string. If *length* is not specified, a string containing characters from *start* to the end of the source string is returned.
substring(*start*, *end*)	Returns a string containing the characters from index *start* up to but not including index *end* in the source string.
toLowerCase()	Returns a string in which all uppercase letters are converted to lowercase letters. Nonletter characters are not changed.
toUpperCase()	Returns a string in which all lowercase letters are converted to uppercase letters. Nonletter characters are not changed.
Methods that generate XHTML tags	
anchor(*name*)	Wraps the source string in an anchor element (<a></a>) with *name* as the anchor name.
fixed()	Wraps the source string in a <tt></tt> element.
link(*url*)	Wraps the source string in an anchor element (<a></a>) with *url* as the hyperlink location.
strike()	Wraps the source string in a <strike></strike> element.
sub()	Wraps the source string in a element.
sup()	Wraps the source string in a element.

Fig. 9.3 | Some String object methods. (Part 2 of 2.)

9.4.3 Character-Processing Methods

The script in Fig. 9.4 demonstrates some of the String object's character-processing methods, including *charAt* (returns the character at a specific position), *charCodeAt* (returns the Unicode value of the character at a specific position), *fromCharCode* (returns a string created from a series of Unicode values), *toLowerCase* (returns the lowercase version of a string) and *toUpperCase* (returns the uppercase version of a string).

Lines 16–17 display the first character in String s ("ZEBRA") using String method charAt. Method *charAt* returns a string containing the character at the specified index (0 in this example). Indices for the characters in a string start at 0 (the first character) and go up to (but do not include) the string's length (i.e., if the string contains five characters, the indices are 0 through 4). If the index is outside the bounds of the string, the method returns an empty string.

Lines 18–19 display the character code for the first character in String s ("ZEBRA") by calling String method charCodeAt. Method charCodeAt returns the Unicode value of

```
1   <?xml version = "1.0" encoding = "utf-8"?>
2   <!DOCTYPE html PUBLIC "-//W3C//DTD XHTML 1.0 Strict//EN"
3      "http://www.w3.org/TR/xhtml1/DTD/xhtml1-strict.dtd">
4
5   <!-- Fig. 9.4: CharacterProcessing.html -->
6   <!-- String methods charAt, charCodeAt, fromCharCode, toLowercase and
7      toUpperCase. -->
8   <html xmlns = "http://www.w3.org/1999/xhtml">
9      <head>
10         <title>Character Processing Methods</title>
11         <script type = "text/javascript">
12            <!--
13            var s = "ZEBRA";
14            var s2 = "AbCdEfG";
15
16            document.writeln( "<p>Character at index 0 in '" +
17               s + "' is " + s.charAt( 0 ) );
18            document.writeln( "<br />Character code at index 0 in '"
19               + s + "' is " + s.charCodeAt( 0 ) + "</p>" );
20
21            document.writeln( "<p>'" +
22               String.fromCharCode( 87, 79, 82, 68 ) +
23               "' contains character codes 87, 79, 82 and 68</p>" )
24
25            document.writeln( "<p>'" + s2 + "' in lowercase is '" +
26               s2.toLowerCase() + "'" );
27            document.writeln( "<br />'" + s2 + "' in uppercase is '"
28               + s2.toUpperCase() + "'</p>" );
29            // -->
30         </script>
31      </head><body></body>
32   </html>
```

Fig. 9.4 | String methods charAt, charCodeAt, fromCharCode, toLowercase and toUpperCase. (Part 1 of 2.)

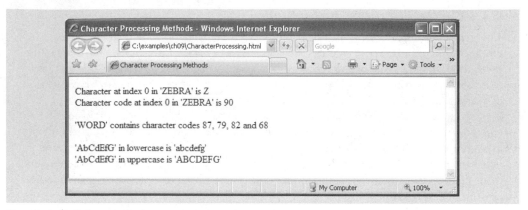

Fig. 9.4 | String methods `charAt`, `charCodeAt`, `fromCharCode`, `toLowercase` and `toUpperCase`. (Part 2 of 2.)

the character at the specified index (0 in this example). If the index is outside the bounds of the string, the method returns `NaN`.

`String` method `fromCharCode` receives as its argument a comma-separated list of Unicode values and builds a string containing the character representation of those Unicode values. Lines 21–23 display the string `"WORD"`, which consists of the character codes 87, 79, 82 and 68. Note that the `String` object calls method `fromCharCode`, rather than a specific `String` variable.

The statements in lines 25–26 and 27–28 use `String` methods ***toLowerCase*** and ***toUpperCase*** to display versions of `String` `s2` (`"AbCdEfG"`) in all lowercase letters and all uppercase letters, respectively.

9.4.4 Searching Methods

Being able to search for a character or a sequence of characters in a string is often useful. For example, if you are creating your own word processor, you may want to provide a capability for searching through the document. The script in Fig. 9.5 demonstrates the `String` object methods ***indexOf*** and ***lastIndexOf*** that search for a specified substring in a string. All the searches in this example are performed on the global string `letters` (initialized in line 14 with `"abcdefghijklmnopqrstuvwxyzabcdefghijklm"` in the script).

The user types a substring in the XHTML form `searchForm`'s `inputVal` text field and presses the **Search** button to search for the substring in `letters`. Clicking the **Search** button calls function `buttonPressed` (defined in lines 16–29) to respond to the `onclick` event and perform the searches. The results of each search are displayed in the appropriate text field of `searchForm`.

Lines 21–22 use `String` method `indexOf` to determine the location of the first occurrence in string `letters` of the string `inputVal.value` (i.e., the string the user typed in the `inputVal` text field). If the substring is found, the index at which the first occurrence of the substring begins is returned; otherwise, −1 is returned.

Lines 23–24 use `String` method `lastIndexOf` to determine the location of the last occurrence in `letters` of the string in `inputVal`. If the substring is found, the index at which the last occurrence of the substring begins is returned; otherwise, −1 is returned.

```
 1    <?xml version = "1.0" encoding = "utf-8"?>
 2    <!DOCTYPE html PUBLIC "-//W3C//DTD XHTML 1.0 Strict//EN"
 3       "http://www.w3.org/TR/xhtml1/DTD/xhtml1-strict.dtd">
 4
 5    <!-- Fig. 9.5: SearchingStrings.html -->
 6    <!-- String searching with indexOf and lastIndexOf. -->
 7    <html xmlns = "http://www.w3.org/1999/xhtml">
 8       <head>
 9          <title>
10             Searching Strings with indexOf and lastIndexOf
11          </title>
12          <script type = "text/javascript">
13             <!--
14             var letters = "abcdefghijklmnopqrstuvwxyzabcdefghijklm";
15
16             function buttonPressed()
17             {
18                var searchForm = document.getElementById( "searchForm" );
19                var inputVal = document.getElementById( "inputVal" );
20
21                searchForm.elements[2].value =
22                   letters.indexOf( inputVal.value );
23                searchForm.elements[3].value =
24                   letters.lastIndexOf( inputVal.value );
25                searchForm.elements[4].value =
26                   letters.indexOf( inputVal.value, 12 );
27                searchForm.elements[5].value =
28                   letters.lastIndexOf( inputVal.value, 12 );
29             } // end function buttonPressed
30             // -->
31          </script>
32       </head>
33       <body>
34          <form id = "searchForm" action = "">
35             <h1>The string to search is:<br />
36                abcdefghijklmnopqrstuvwxyzabcdefghijklm</h1>
37             <p>Enter substring to search for
38             <input id = "inputVal" type = "text" />
39             <input id = "search" type = "button" value = "Search"
40                onclick = "buttonPressed()" /><br /></p>
41
42             <p>First occurrence located at index
43             <input id = "first" type = "text" size = "5" />
44             <br />Last occurrence located at index
45             <input id = "last" type = "text" size = "5" />
46             <br />First occurrence from index 12 located at index
47             <input id = "first12" type = "text" size = "5" />
48             <br />Last occurrence from index 12 located at index
49             <input id = "last12" type = "text" size = "5" /></p>
50          </form>
51       </body>
52    </html>
```

Fig. 9.5 | String searching with indexOf and lastIndexOf. (Part 1 of 2.)

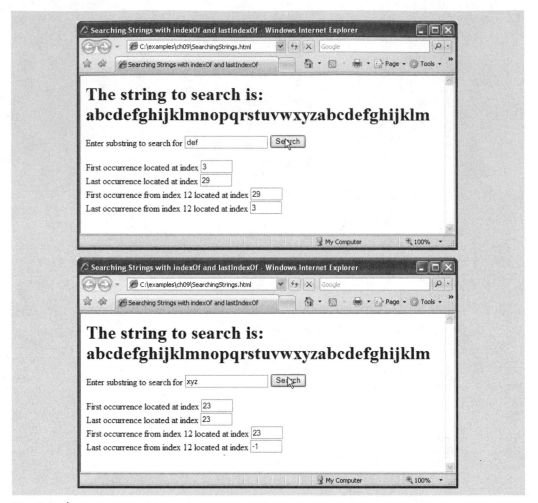

Fig. 9.5 | String searching with indexOf and lastIndexOf. (Part 2 of 2.)

Lines 25–26 use String method indexOf to determine the location of the first occurrence in string letters of the string in the inputVal text field, starting from index 12 in letters. If the substring is found, the index at which the first occurrence of the substring (starting from index 12) begins is returned; otherwise, –1 is returned.

Lines 27–28 use String method lastIndexOf to determine the location of the last occurrence in letters of the string in the inputVal text field, starting from index 12 in letters and moving toward the beginning of the input. If the substring is found, the index at which the first occurrence of the substring (if one appears before index 12) begins is returned; otherwise, –1 is returned.

Software Engineering Observation 9.2

String methods indexOf and lastIndexOf, with their optional second argument (the starting index from which to search), are particularly useful for continuing a search through a large amount of text.

9.4.5 Splitting Strings and Obtaining Substrings

When you read a sentence, your mind breaks it into individual words, or *tokens*, each of which conveys meaning to you. The process of breaking a string into tokens is called *tokenization*. Interpreters also perform tokenization. They break up statements into such individual pieces as keywords, identifiers, operators and other elements of a programming language. Figure 9.6 demonstrates String method *split*, which breaks a string into its component tokens. Tokens are separated from one another by *delimiters*, typically whitespace characters such as blanks, tabs, newlines and carriage returns. Other characters may also be used as delimiters to separate tokens. The XHTML document displays a form containing a text field where the user types a sentence to tokenize. The results of the tokenization process are displayed in an XHTML textarea GUI component. The script also demonstrates String method *substring*, which returns a portion of a string.

```
 1   <?xml version = "1.0" encoding = "utf-8"?>
 2   <!DOCTYPE html PUBLIC "-//W3C//DTD XHTML 1.0 Strict//EN"
 3      "http://www.w3.org/TR/xhtml1/DTD/xhtml1-strict.dtd">
 4
 5   <!-- Fig. 9.6: SplitAndSubString.html -->
 6   <!-- String object methods split and substring. -->
 7   <html xmlns = "http://www.w3.org/1999/xhtml">
 8      <head>
 9         <title>String Methods split and substring</title>
10         <script type = "text/javascript">
11            <!--
12            function splitButtonPressed()
13            {
14               var inputString = document.getElementById( "inputVal" ).value;
15               var tokens = inputString.split( " " );
16               document.getElementById( "output" ).value =
17                  tokens.join( "\n" ) ;
18
19               document.getElementById( "outputSubstring" ).value =
20                  inputString.substring( 0, 10 );
21            } // end function splitButtonPressed
22            // -->
23         </script>
24      </head>
25      <body>
26         <form action = "">
27            <p>Enter a sentence to split into words<br />
28            <input id = "inputVal" type = "text" size = "40" />
29            <input type = "button" value = "Split"
30               onclick = "splitButtonPressed()" /></p>
31
32            <p>The sentence split into words is<br />
33            <textarea id = "output" rows = "8" cols = "34">
34            </textarea></p>
35
36            <p>The first 10 characters of the input string are
```

Fig. 9.6 | String object methods split and substring. (Part I of 2.)

```
37                  <input id = "outputSubstring" type = "text"
38                     size = "15" /></p>
39          </form>
40       </body>
41    </html>
```

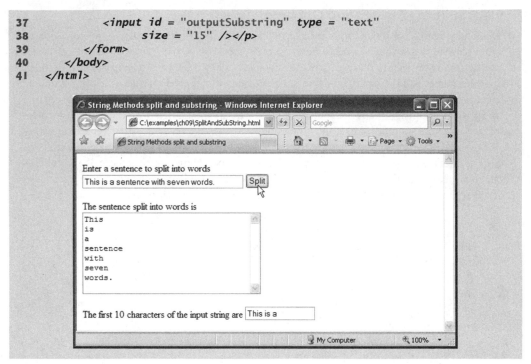

Fig. 9.6 | String object methods split and substring. (Part 2 of 2.)

The user types a sentence into the text field with id inputVal text field and presses the **Split** button to tokenize the string. Function splitButtonPressed (lines 12–21) handles the button's onclick event.

Line 14 gets the value of the input field and stores it in variable inputString. Line 15 calls String method split to tokenize inputString. The argument to method split is the *delimiter string*—the string that determines the end of each token in the original string. In this example, the space character delimits the tokens. The delimiter string can contain multiple characters that should be used as delimiters. Method split returns an array of strings containing the tokens. Line 17 uses Array method join to combine the tokens in array tokens and separate each token with a newline character (\n). The resulting string is assigned to the value property of the XHTML form's output GUI component (an XHTML textarea).

Lines 19–20 use String method substring to obtain a string containing the first 10 characters of the string the user entered (still stored in inputString). The method returns the substring from the *starting index* (0 in this example) up to but not including the *ending index* (10 in this example). If the ending index is greater than the length of the string, the substring returned includes the characters from the starting index to the end of the original string.

9.4.6 XHTML Markup Methods

The script in Fig. 9.7 demonstrates the String object's methods that generate XHTML markup tags. When a String object invokes a markup method, the method wraps the

`String`'s contents in the appropriate XHTML tag. These methods are particularly useful for generating XHTML dynamically during script processing.

```
 1   <?xml version = "1.0" encoding = "utf-8"?>
 2   <!DOCTYPE html PUBLIC "-//W3C//DTD XHTML 1.0 Strict//EN"
 3      "http://www.w3.org/TR/xhtml1/DTD/xhtml1-strict.dtd">
 4
 5   <!-- Fig. 9.7: MarkupMethods.html -->
 6   <!-- String object XHTML markup methods. -->
 7   <html xmlns = "http://www.w3.org/1999/xhtml">
 8      <head>
 9         <title>XHTML Markup Methods of the String Object</title>
10         <script type = "text/javascript">
11            <!--
12            var anchorText = "This is an anchor";
13            var fixedText = "This is monospaced text";
14            var linkText = "Click here to go to anchorText";
15            var strikeText = "This is strike out text";
16            var subText = "subscript";
17            var supText = "superscript";
18
19            document.writeln( anchorText.anchor( "top" ) );
20            document.writeln( "<br />" + fixedText.fixed() );
21            document.writeln( "<br />" + strikeText.strike() );
22            document.writeln(
23               "<br />This is text with a " + subText.sub() );
24            document.writeln(
25               "<br />This is text with a " + supText.sup() );
26            document.writeln( "<br />" + linkText.link( "#top" ) );
27            // -->
28         </script>
29      </head><body></body>
30   </html>
```

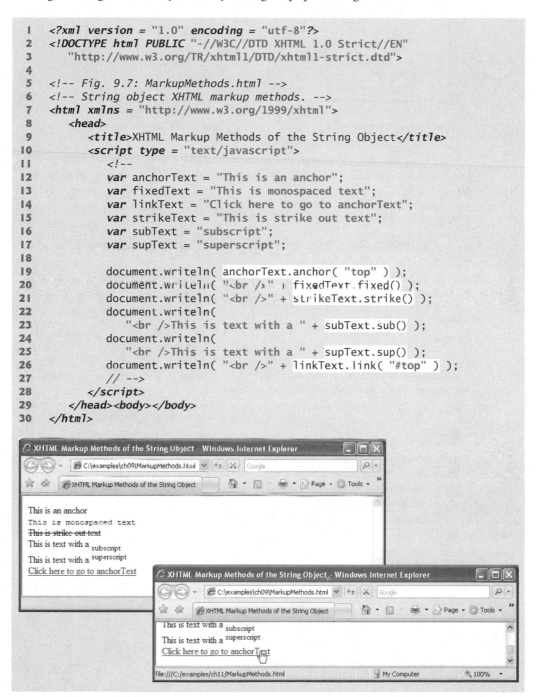

Fig. 9.7 | String object XHTML markup methods. (Part 1 of 2.)

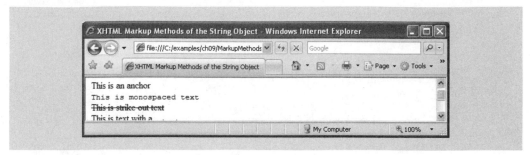

Fig. 9.7 | String object XHTML markup methods. (Part 2 of 2.)

Lines 12–17 define the strings that call each of the XHTML markup methods of the String object. Line 19 uses String method **anchor** to format the string in variable anchorText ("This is an anchor") as

> **<a name** = "top">This is an anchor**</a>**

The name of the anchor is the argument to the method. This anchor will be used later in the example as the target of a hyperlink.

Line 20 uses String method **fixed** to display text in a fixed-width font by formatting the string in variable fixedText ("This is monospaced text") as

> **<tt>**This is monospaced text**</tt>**

Line 21 uses String method **strike** to display text with a line through it by formatting the string in variable strikeText ("This is strike out text") as

> **<strike>**This is strike out text**</strike>**

Lines 22–23 use String method **sub** to display subscript text by formatting the string in variable subText ("subscript") as

> **_{**subscript**}**

Note that the resulting line in the XHTML document displays the word subscript smaller than the rest of the line and slightly below the line.

Lines 24–25 call String method **sup** to display superscript text by formatting the string in variable supText ("superscript") as

> **^{**superscript**}**

Note that the resulting line in the XHTML document displays the word superscript smaller than the rest of the line and slightly above the line.

Line 26 uses String method **link** to create a hyperlink by formatting the string in variable linkText ("Click here to go to anchorText") as

> **<a href** = "#top">Click here to go to anchorText**</a>**

The target of the hyperlink (#top in this example) is the argument to the method and can be any URL. In this example, the hyperlink target is the anchor created in line 19. If you make your browser window short and scroll to the bottom of the web page, then click this link, the browser will reposition to the top of the web page.

9.5 Date Object

JavaScript's *Date* object provides methods for date and time manipulations. Date and time processing can be performed based on the computer's *local time zone* or based on World Time Standard's *Coordinated Universal Time* (abbreviated *UTC*)—formerly called *Greenwich Mean Time (GMT)*. Most methods of the Date object have a local time zone and a UTC version. The methods of the Date object are summarized in Fig. 9.8.

Method	Description
getDate() getUTCDate()	Returns a number from 1 to 31 representing the day of the month in local time or UTC.
getDay() getUTCDay()	Returns a number from 0 (Sunday) to 6 (Saturday) representing the day of the week in local time or UTC.
getFullYear() getUTCFullYear()	Returns the year as a four-digit number in local time or UTC.
getHours() getUTCHours()	Returns a number from 0 to 23 representing hours since midnight in local time or UTC.
getMilliseconds() getUTCMilliSeconds()	Returns a number from 0 to 999 representing the number of milliseconds in local time or UTC, respectively. The time is stored in hours, minutes, seconds and milliseconds.
getMinutes() getUTCMinutes()	Returns a number from 0 to 59 representing the minutes for the time in local time or UTC.
getMonth() getUTCMonth()	Returns a number from 0 (January) to 11 (December) representing the month in local time or UTC.
getSeconds() getUTCSeconds()	Returns a number from 0 to 59 representing the seconds for the time in local time or UTC.
getTime()	Returns the number of milliseconds between January 1, 1970, and the time in the Date object.
getTimezoneOffset()	Returns the difference in minutes between the current time on the local computer and UTC (Coordinated Universal Time).
setDate(*val*) setUTCDate(*val*)	Sets the day of the month (1 to 31) in local time or UTC.
setFullYear(*y*, *m*, *d*) setUTCFullYear(*y*, *m*, *d*)	Sets the year in local time or UTC. The second and third arguments representing the month and the date are optional. If an optional argument is not specified, the current value in the Date object is used.

Fig. 9.8 | Date object methods. (Part 1 of 2.)

Method	Description
setHours(*h*, *m*, *s*, *ms*) setUTCHours(*h*, *m*, *s*, *ms*)	Sets the hour in local time or UTC. The second, third and fourth arguments, representing the minutes, seconds and milliseconds, are optional. If an optional argument is not specified, the current value in the Date object is used.
setMilliSeconds(*ms*) setUTCMilliseconds(*ms*)	Sets the number of milliseconds in local time or UTC.
setMinutes(*m*, *s*, *ms*) setUTCMinutes(*m*, *s*, *ms*)	Sets the minute in local time or UTC. The second and third arguments, representing the seconds and milliseconds, are optional. If an optional argument is not specified, the current value in the Date object is used.
setMonth(*m*, *d*) setUTCMonth(*m*, *d*)	Sets the month in local time or UTC. The second argument, representing the date, is optional. If the optional argument is not specified, the current date value in the Date object is used.
setSeconds(*s*, *ms*) setUTCSeconds(*s*, *ms*)	Sets the second in local time or UTC. The second argument, representing the milliseconds, is optional. If this argument is not specified, the current millisecond value in the Date object is used.
setTime(*ms*)	Sets the time based on its argument—the number of elapsed milliseconds since January 1, 1970.
toLocaleString()	Returns a string representation of the date and time in a form specific to the computer's locale. For example, September 13, 2007, at 3:42:22 PM is represented as *09/13/07 15:47:22* in the United States and *13/09/07 15:47:22* in Europe.
toUTCString()	Returns a string representation of the date and time in the form: *15 Sep 2007 15:47:22 UTC*
toString()	Returns a string representation of the date and time in a form specific to the locale of the computer (*Mon Sep 17 15:47:22 EDT 2007* in the United States).
valueOf()	The time in number of milliseconds since midnight, January 1, 1970. (Same as getTime.)

Fig. 9.8 | Date object methods. (Part 2 of 2.)

The script of Fig. 9.9 demonstrates many of the local time zone methods in Fig. 9.8. Line 12 creates a new Date object. The new operator allocates the memory for the Date object. The empty parentheses indicate a call to the Date object's *constructor* with no arguments. A constructor is an initializer method for an object. Constructors are called automatically when an object is allocated with new. The Date constructor with no arguments initializes the Date object with the local computer's current date and time.

```
 1    <?xml version = "1.0" encoding = "utf-8"?>
 2    <!DOCTYPE html PUBLIC "-//W3C//DTD XHTML 1.0 Strict//EN"
 3       "http://www.w3.org/TR/xhtml1/DTD/xhtml1-strict.dtd">
 4
 5    <!-- Fig. 9.9: DateTime.html -->
 6    <!-- Date and time methods of the Date object. -->
 7    <html xmlns = "http://www.w3.org/1999/xhtml">
 8       <head>
 9          <title>Date and Time Methods</title>
10          <script type = "text/javascript">
11             <!--
12             var current = new Date();
13
14             document.writeln(
15                "<h1>String representations and valueOf</h1>" );
16             document.writeln( "toString: " + current.toString() +
17                "<br />toLocaleString: " + current.toLocaleString() +
18                "<br />toUTCString: " + current.toUTCString() +
19                "<br />valueOf: " + current.valueOf() );
20
21             document.writeln(
22                "<h1>Get methods for local time zone</h1>" );
23             document.writeln( "getDate: " + current.getDate() +
24                "<br />getDay: " + current.getDay() +
25                "<br />getMonth: " + current.getMonth() +
26                "<br />getFullYear: " + current.getFullYear() +
27                "<br />getTime: " + current.getTime() +
28                "<br />getHours: " + current.getHours() +
29                "<br />getMinutes: " + current.getMinutes() +
30                "<br />getSeconds: " + current.getSeconds() +
31                "<br />getMilliseconds: " + current.getMilliseconds() +
32                "<br />getTimezoneOffset: " + current.getTimezoneOffset() );
33
34             document.writeln(
35                "<h1>Specifying arguments for a new Date</h1>" );
36             var anotherDate = new Date( 2007, 2, 18, 1, 5, 0, 0 );
37             document.writeln( "Date: " + anotherDate );
38
39             document.writeln( "<h1>Set methods for local time zone</h1>" );
40             anotherDate.setDate( 31 );
41             anotherDate.setMonth( 11 );
42             anotherDate.setFullYear( 2007 );
43             anotherDate.setHours( 23 );
44             anotherDate.setMinutes( 59 );
45             anotherDate.setSeconds( 59 );
46             document.writeln( "Modified date: " + anotherDate );
47             // -->
48          </script>
49       </head><body></body>
50    </html>
```

Fig. 9.9 | Date and time methods of the Date object. (Part 1 of 2.)

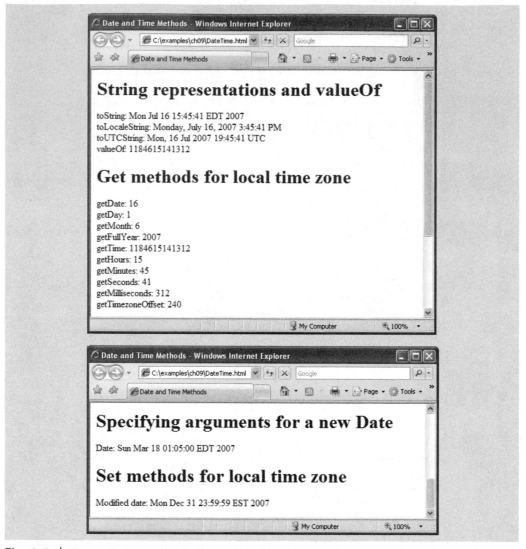

Fig. 9.9 | Date and time methods of the Date object. (Part 2 of 2.)

Software Engineering Observation 9.3

When an object is allocated with new, the object's constructor is called automatically to initialize the object before it is used in the program.

Lines 16–19 demonstrate the methods toString, toLocaleString, toUTCString and valueOf. Note that method valueOf returns a large integer value representing the total number of milliseconds between midnight, January 1, 1970, and the date and time stored in Date object current.

Lines 23–32 demonstrate the Date object's *get* methods for the local time zone. Note that method getFullYear returns the year as a four-digit number. Note as well that method getTimeZoneOffset returns the difference in minutes between the local time zone and UTC time (i.e., a difference of four hours in our time zone when this example was executed).

Line 36 demonstrates creating a new Date object and supplying arguments to the Date constructor for *year*, *month*, *date*, *hours*, *minutes*, *seconds* and *milliseconds*. Note that the *hours*, *minutes*, *seconds* and *milliseconds* arguments are all optional. If any one of these arguments is not specified, a zero is supplied in its place. For the *hours*, *minutes* and *seconds* arguments, if the argument to the right of any of these arguments is specified, it too must be specified (e.g., if the *minutes* argument is specified, the *hours* argument must be specified; if the *milliseconds* argument is specified, all the arguments must be specified).

Lines 40–45 demonstrate the Date object *set* methods for the local time zone. Date objects represent the month internally as an integer from 0 to 11. These values are off by one from what you might expect (i.e., 1 for January, 2 for February, ..., and 12 for December). When creating a Date object, you must specify 0 to indicate January, 1 to indicate February, ..., and 11 to indicate December.

Common Programming Error 9.2

Assuming that months are represented as numbers from 1 to 12 leads to off-by-one errors when you are processing Dates.

The Date object provides two other methods that can be called without creating a new Date object—**Date.parse** and **Date.UTC**. Method Date.parse receives as its argument a string representing a date and time, and returns the number of milliseconds between midnight, January 1, 1970, and the specified date and time. This value can be converted to a Date object with the statement

var theDate = *new* Date(*numberOfMilliseconds*);

which passes to the Date constructor the number of milliseconds since midnight, January 1, 1970, for the Date object.

Method parse converts the string using the following rules:

- Short dates can be specified in the form MM-DD-YY, MM-DD-YYYY, MM/DD/YY or MM/DD/YYYY. The month and day are not required to be two digits.

- Long dates that specify the complete month name (e.g., "January"), date and year can specify the month, date and year in any order.

- Text in parentheses within the string is treated as a comment and ignored. Commas and white-space characters are treated as delimiters.

- All month and day names must have at least two characters. The names are not required to be unique. If the names are identical, the name is resolved as the last match (e.g., "Ju" represents "July" rather than "June").

- If the name of the day of the week is supplied, it is ignored.

- All standard time zones (e.g., EST for Eastern Standard Time), Coordinated Universal Time (UTC) and Greenwich Mean Time (GMT) are recognized.

- When specifying hours, minutes and seconds, separate each by colons.

- When using a 24-hour-clock format, "PM" should not be used for times after 12 noon.

Date method UTC returns the number of milliseconds between midnight, January 1, 1970, and the date and time specified as its arguments. The arguments to the UTC method include the required *year, month* and *date*, and the optional *hours, minutes, seconds* and *milliseconds*. If any of the *hours, minutes, seconds* or *milliseconds* arguments is not specified, a zero is supplied in its place. For the *hours, minutes* and *seconds* arguments, if the argument to the right of any of these arguments in the argument list is specified, that argument must also be specified (e.g., if the *minutes* argument is specified, the *hours* argument must be specified; if the *milliseconds* argument is specified, all the arguments must be specified). As with the result of Date.parse, the result of Date.UTC can be converted to a Date object by creating a new Date object with the result of Date.UTC as its argument.

9.6 Boolean and Number Objects

JavaScript provides the *Boolean* and *Number* objects as object *wrappers* for boolean true/false values and numbers, respectively. These wrappers define methods and properties useful in manipulating boolean values and numbers. Wrappers provide added functionality for working with simple data types.

When a JavaScript program requires a boolean value, JavaScript automatically creates a Boolean object to store the value. JavaScript programmers can create Boolean objects explicitly with the statement

```
var b = new Boolean( booleanValue );
```

The constructor argument *booleanValue* specifies whether the value of the Boolean object should be true or false. If *booleanValue* is false, 0, null, Number.NaN or an empty string (""), or if no argument is supplied, the new Boolean object contains false. Otherwise, the new Boolean object contains true. Figure 9.10 summarizes the methods of the Boolean object.

JavaScript automatically creates Number objects to store numeric values in a JavaScript program. JavaScript programmers can create a Number object with the statement

```
var n = new Number( numericValue );
```

The constructor argument *numericValue* is the number to store in the object. Although you can explicitly create Number objects, normally the JavaScript interpreter creates them as needed. Figure 9.11 summarizes the methods and properties of the Number object.

Method	Description
toString()	Returns the string "true" if the value of the Boolean object is true; otherwise, returns the string "false".
valueOf()	Returns the value true if the Boolean object is true; otherwise, returns false.

Fig. 9.10 | Boolean object methods.

Method or property	Description
toString(*radix*)	Returns the string representation of the number. The optional *radix* argument (a number from 2 to 36) specifies the number's base. For example, radix 2 results in the binary representation of the number, 8 results in the octal representation, 10 results in the decimal representation and 16 results in the hexadecimal representation.
valueOf()	Returns the numeric value.
Number.MAX_VALUE	This property represents the largest value that can be stored in a JavaScript program—approximately 1.79E+308.
Number.MIN_VALUE	This property represents the smallest value that can be stored in a JavaScript program—approximately 5.00E–324.
Number.NaN	This property represents *not a number*—a value returned from an arithmetic expression that does not result in a number (e.g., the expression parseInt("hello") cannot convert the string "hello" into a number, so parseInt would return Number.NaN. To determine whether a value is NaN, test the result with function isNaN, which returns true if the value is NaN; otherwise, it returns false.
Number.NEGATIVE_INFINITY	This property represents a value less than -Number.MAX_VALUE.
Number.POSITIVE_INFINITY	This property represents a value greater than Number.MAX_VALUE.

Fig. 9.11 | Number object methods and properties.

9.7 document Object

The *document* object is used to manipulate the document that is currently visible in the browser window. The document object has many properties and methods, such as methods document.write and document.writeln, which have both been used in prior JavaScript examples. Figure 9.12 shows the methods and properties of the document objects that are used in this chapter. You can learn more about the properties and methods of the document object in our JavaScript Resource Center (www.deitel.com/javascript).

Method or property	Description
getElementById(*id*)	Returns the DOM node representing the XHTML element whose id attribute matches *id*.

Fig. 9.12 | Important document object methods and properties. (Part 1 of 2.)

Method or property	Description
write(*string*)	Writes the string to the XHTML document as XHTML code.
writeln(*string*)	Writes the string to the XHTML document as XHTML code and adds a newline character at the end.
cookie	A string containing the values of all the cookies stored on the user's computer for the current document. See Section 9.9, Using Cookies.
lastModified	The date and time that this document was last modified.

Fig. 9.12 | Important **document** object methods and properties. (Part 2 of 2.)

9.8 **window Object**

The *window* object provides methods for manipulating browser windows. The following script shows many of the commonly used properties and methods of the window object and uses them to create a website that spans multiple browser windows. Figure 9.13 allows the user to create a new, fully customized browser window by completing an XHTML form and clicking the **Submit** button. The script also allows the user to add text to the new window and navigate the window to a different URL.

The script starts in line 10. Line 12 declares a variable to refer to the new window. We refer to the new window as the *child window* because it is created and controlled by the main, or *parent*, window in this script. Lines 14–50 define the createChildWindow function, which determines the features that have been selected by the user and creates a child window with those features (but does not add any content to the window). Lines 18–20 declare several variables to store the status of the checkboxes on the page. Lines 23–38 set each variable to "yes" or "no" based on whether the corresponding checkbox is checked or unchecked.

```
1   <?xml version = "1.0" encoding = "utf-8"?>
2   <!DOCTYPE html PUBLIC "-//W3C//DTD XHTML 1.0 Strict//EN"
3      "http://www.w3.org/TR/xhtml1/DTD/xhtml1-strict.dtd">
4
5   <!-- Fig. 9.13: window.html -->
6   <!-- Using the window object to create and modify child windows. -->
7   <html xmlns = "http://www.w3.org/1999/xhtml">
8   <head>
9   <title>Using the Window Object</title>
10  <script type = "text/javascript">
11     <!--
12     var childWindow; // variable to control the child window
13
14     function createChildWindow()
15     {
```

Fig. 9.13 | Using the window object to create and modify child windows. (Part 1 of 4.)

```
16         // these variables all contain either "yes" or "no"
17         // to enable or disable a feature in the child window
18         var toolBar;
19         var menuBar;
20         var scrollBars;
21
22         // determine whether the Tool Bar checkbox is checked
23         if ( document.getElementById( "toolBarCheckBox" ).checked )
24            toolBar = "yes";
25         else
26            toolBar = "no";
27
28         // determine whether the Menu Bar checkbox is checked
29         if ( document.getElementById( "menuBarCheckBox" ).checked )
30            menuBar = "yes";
31         else
32            menuBar = "no";
33
34         // determine whether the Scroll Bar checkbox is checked
35         if ( document.getElementById( "scrollBarsCheckBox" ).checked )
36            scrollBars = "yes";
37         else
38            scrollBars = "no";
39
40         //display window with selected features
41         childWindow = window.open( "", "",
42            ",toolbar = " + toolBar +
43            ",menubar = " + menuBar +
44            ",scrollbars = " + scrollBars );
45
46         // disable buttons
47         document.getElementById( "closeButton" ).disabled = false;
48         document.getElementById( "modifyButton" ).disabled = false;
49         document.getElementById( "setURLButton" ).disabled = false;
50      } // end function createChildWindow
51
52      // insert text from the textbox in the child window
53      function modifyChildWindow()
54      {
55         if ( childWindow.closed )
56            alert( "You attempted to interact with a closed window" );
57         else
58            childWindow.document.write(
59               document.getElementById( "textForChild" ).value );
60      } // end function modifyChildWindow
61
62      // close the child window
63      function closeChildWindow()
64      {
65         if ( childWindow.closed )
66            alert( "You attempted to interact with a closed window" );
```

Fig. 9.13 | Using the window object to create and modify child windows. (Part 2 of 4.)

```
67        else
68            childWindow.close();
69
70        document.getElementById( "closeButton" ).disabled = true;
71        document.getElementById( "modifyButton" ).disabled = true;
72        document.getElementById( "setURLButton" ).disabled = true;
73    } // end function closeChildWindow
74
75    // set the URL of the child window to the URL
76    // in the parent window's myChildURL
77    function setChildWindowURL()
78    {
79        if ( childWindow.closed )
80            alert( "You attempted to interact with a closed window" );
81        else
82            childWindow.location =
83                document.getElementById( "myChildURL" ).value;
84    } // end function setChildWindowURL
85    //-->
86  </script>
87  </head>
88  <body>
89    <h1>Hello, this is the main window</h1>
90    <p>Please check the features to enable for the child window<br/>
91    <input id = "toolBarCheckBox" type = "checkbox" value = ""
92        checked = "checked" />
93        <label>Tool Bar</label>
94    <input id = "menuBarCheckBox" type = "checkbox" value = ""
95        checked = "checked" />
96        <label>Menu Bar</label>
97    <input id = "scrollBarsCheckBox" type = "checkbox" value = ""
98        checked = "checked" />
99        <label>Scroll Bars</label></p>
100
101    <p>Please enter the text that you would like to display
102    in the child window<br/>
103    <input id = "textForChild" type = "text"
104        value = "<h1>Hello, I am a child window.</h1> " />
105    <input id = "createButton" type = "button"
106        value = "Create Child Window" onclick = "createChildWindow()" />
107    <input id= "modifyButton" type = "button" value = "Modify Child Window"
108        onclick = "modifyChildWindow()" disabled = "disabled" />
109    <input id = "closeButton" type = "button" value = "Close Child Window"
110        onclick = "closeChildWindow()" disabled = "disabled" /></p>
111
112    <p>The other window's URL is: <br/>
113    <input id = "myChildURL" type = "text" value = "./" />
114    <input id = "setURLButton" type = "button" value = "Set Child URL"
115        onclick = "setChildWindowURL()" disabled = "disabled" /></p>
116  </body>
117  </html>
```

Fig. 9.13 | Using the window object to create and modify child windows. (Part 3 of 4.)

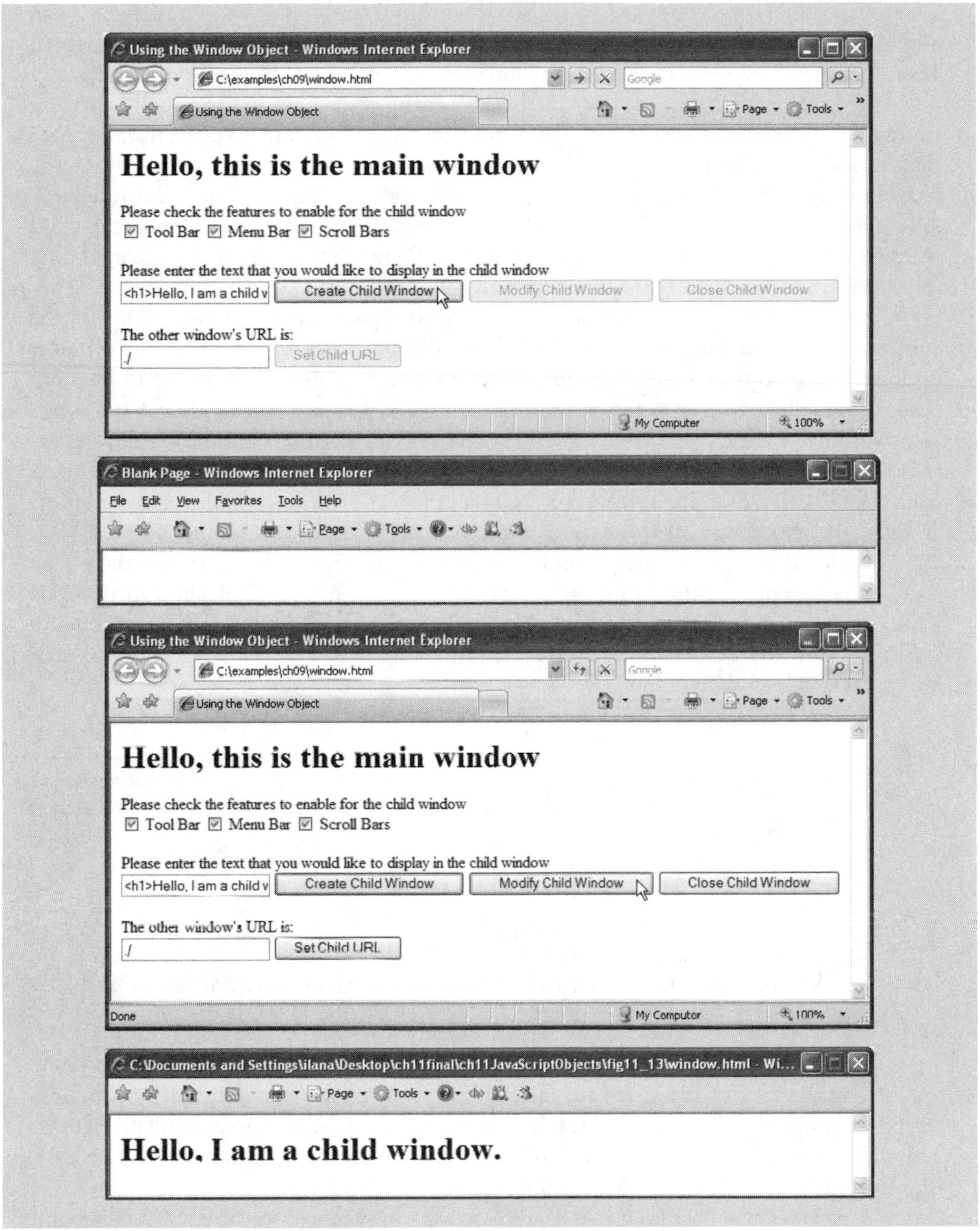

Fig. 9.13 | Using the window object to create and modify child windows. (Part 4 of 4.)

Lines 41–44 use the window object's open method to create the child window. Method open has three parameters. The first parameter is the URL of the page to open in the new window, and the second parameter is the name of the window. If you specify the target attribute of an a (anchor) element to correspond to the name of a window, the href of the link will be opened in the window. In our example, we pass `window.open` empty strings as the first two parameter values because we want the new window to open a blank page, and we use a different method to manipulate the child window's URL.

The third parameter of the open method is a string of comma-separated, all-lowercase feature names, each followed by an = sign and either "yes" or "no" to determine whether that feature should be displayed in the new window. If these parameters are omitted, the browser defaults to a new window containing an empty page, no title and all features visible. [*Note:* If your menu bar is normally hidden in IE7, it will not appear in the child window. Press the *Alt* key to display it.] Lines 47–49 enable the buttons for manipulating the child window—these are initially disabled when the page loads.

Lines 53–60 define the function `modifyChildWindow`, which adds a line of text to the content of the child window. In line 55, the script determines whether the child window is closed. Function `modifyChildWindow` uses property `childWindow.closed` to obtain a boolean value that is `true` if `childWindow` is closed and `false` if the window is still open. If the window is closed, an alert box is displayed notifying the user that the window is currently closed and cannot be modified. If the child window is open, lines 58–59 obtain text from the `textForChild` input (lines 103–104) in the XHTML form in the parent window and uses the child's `document.write` method to write this text to the child window.

Function `closeChildWindow` (lines 63–73) also determines whether the child window is closed before proceeding. If the child window is closed, the script displays an alert box telling the user that the window is already closed. If the child window is open, line 68 closes it using the `childWindow.close` method. Lines 70–72 disable the buttons that interact with the child window.

Look-and-Feel Observation 9.1

Popup windows should be used sparingly. Many users dislike websites that open additional windows, or that resize or reposition the browser. Some users have popup blockers that will prevent new windows from opening.

Software Engineering Observation 9.4

`window.location` is a property that always contains a string representation of the URL displayed in the current window. Typically, web browsers will allow a script to retrieve the `window.location` property of another window only if the script belongs to the same website as the page in the other window.

Function `setChildWindowURL` (lines 77–84) copies the contents of the `myChildURL` text field to the `location` property of the child window. If the child window is open, lines 81–82 set property `location` of the child window to the string in the `myChildURL` textbox. This action changes the URL of the child window and is equivalent to typing a new URL into the window's address bar and clicking **Go** (or pressing *Enter*).

The script ends in line 86. Lines 88–116 contain the body of the XHTML document, comprising a form that contains checkboxes, buttons, textboxes and form field labels. The script uses the form elements defined in the body to obtain input from the user. Lines 106, 108, 110, and 115 specify the `onclick` attributes of XHTML buttons. Each button is set to call a corresponding JavaScript function when clicked.

Figure 9.14 contains a list of some commonly used methods and properties of the `window` object.

Method or property	Description
`open( url, name, options )`	Creates a new window with the URL of the window set to *url*, the name set to *name* to refer to it in the script, and the visible features set by the string passed in as *option*.
`prompt( prompt, default )`	Displays a dialog box asking the user for input. The text of the dialog is *prompt*, and the default value is set to *default*.
`close()`	Closes the current window and deletes its object from memory.
`focus()`	This method gives focus to the window (i.e., puts the window in the foreground, on top of any other open browser windows).
`blur()`	This method takes focus away from the window (i.e., puts the window in the background).
`window.document`	This property contains the `document` object representing the document currently inside the window.
`window.closed`	This property contains a boolean value that is set to true if the window is closed, and false if it is not.
`window.opener`	This property contains the `window` object of the window that opened the current window, if such a window exists.

Fig. 9.14 | Important `window` object methods and properties.

9.9 Using Cookies

Cookies provide web developers with a tool for personalizing web pages. A *cookie* is a piece of data that is stored on the user's computer to maintain information about the client during and between browser sessions. A website may store a cookie on the client's computer to record user preferences or other information that the website can retrieve during the client's subsequent visits. For example, a website can retrieve the user's name from a cookie and use it to display a personalized greeting.

Microsoft Internet Explorer and Mozilla Firefox store cookies as small text files on the client's hard drive. When a user visits a website, the browser locates any cookies written by scripts on that site and makes them available to any scripts located on the site. Note that cookies may be accessed only by scripts belonging to the same website from which they originated (i.e., a cookie set by a script on amazon.com can be read only by other scripts on amazon.com).

Cookies are accessible in JavaScript through the document object's *cookie* property. JavaScript treats a cookie as a string of text. Any standard string function or method can manipulate a cookie. A cookie has the syntax "*identifier=value*," where *identifier* is any valid JavaScript variable identifier, and *value* is the value of the cookie variable. When multiple cookies exist for one website, *identifier-value* pairs are separated by semicolons in the document.cookie string.

Cookies differ from ordinary strings in that each cookie has an expiration date, after which the web browser deletes it. This date can be defined by setting the *expires* property in the cookie string. If a cookie's expiration date is not set, then the cookie expires by default after the user closes the browser window. A cookie can be deleted immediately by setting the `expires` property to a date and time in the past.

The assignment operator does not overwrite the entire list of cookies, but appends a cookie to the end of it. Thus, if we set two cookies

```
document.cookie = "name1=value1;";
document.cookie = "name2=value2;";
```

`document.cookie` will contain `"name1=value1; name2=value2"`.

Figure 9.15 uses a cookie to store the user's name and displays a personalized greeting. This example improves upon the functionality in the dynamic welcome page example of Fig. 4.11 by requiring the user to enter a name only during the first visit to the web page. On each subsequent visit, the script can display the user name that is stored in the cookie.

Line 10 begins the script. Lines 12–13 declare the variables needed to obtain the time, and line 14 declares the variable that stores the name of the user. Lines 16–27 contain the same `if...else` statement used in Fig. 4.11 to display a time-sensitive greeting.

Lines 30–66 contain the code used to manipulate the cookie. Line 30 determines whether a cookie exists on the client computer. The expression `document.cookie` evaluates to `true` if a cookie exists. If a cookie does not exist, then the script prompts the user to enter a name (line 45). The script creates a cookie containing the string `"name="`, followed by a copy of the user's name produced by the built-in JavaScript function ***escape*** (line 49). The function `escape` converts any non-alphanumeric characters, such as spaces and semicolons, in a string to their equivalent ***hexadecimal escape sequences*** of the form "%*XX*," where *XX* is the two-digit hexadecimal ASCII value of a special character. For example, if name contains the value `"David Green"`, the statement `escape( name )` evaluates to `"David%20Green"`, because the hexadecimal ASCII value of a blank space is 20. It

```
1   <?xml version = "1.0" encoding = "utf-8"?>
2   <!DOCTYPE html PUBLIC "-//W3C//DTD XHTML 1.0 Strict//EN"
3      "http://www.w3.org/TR/xhtml1/DTD/xhtml1-strict.dtd">
4
5   <!-- Fig. 9.15: cookie.html -->
6   <!-- Using cookies to store user identification data. -->
7   <html xmlns = "http://www.w3.org/1999/xhtml">
8      <head>
9         <title>Using Cookies</title>
10        <script type = "text/javascript">
11           <!--
12           var now = new Date(); // current date and time
13           var hour = now.getHours(); // current hour (0-23)
14           var name;
15
16           if ( hour < 12 ) // determine whether it is morning
17              document.write( "<h1>Good Morning, " );
18           else
19           {
20              hour = hour - 12; // convert from 24-hour clock to PM time
21
```

Fig. 9.15 | Using cookies to store user identification data. (Part 1 of 3.)

```
22              // determine whether it is afternoon or evening
23              if ( hour < 6 )
24                  document.write( "<h1>Good Afternoon, " );
25              else
26                  document.write( "<h1>Good Evening, " );
27          } // end else
28
29          // determine whether there is a cookie
30          if ( document.cookie )
31          {
32              // convert escape characters in the cookie string to their
33              // English notation
34              var myCookie = unescape( document.cookie );
35
36              // split the cookie into tokens using = as delimiter
37              var cookieTokens = myCookie.split( "=" );
38
39              // set name to the part of the cookie that follows the = sign
40              name = cookieTokens[ 1 ];
41          } // end if
42          else
43          {
44              // if there was no cookie, ask the user to input a name
45              name = window.prompt( "Please enter your name", "Paul" );
46
47              // escape special characters in the name string
48              // and add name to the cookie
49              document.cookie = "name=" + escape( name );
50          } // end else
51
52          document.writeln(
53              name + ", welcome to JavaScript programming!</h1>" );
54          document.writeln( "<a href = 'javascript:wrongPerson()'> " +
55              "Click here if you are not " + name + "</a>" );
56
57          // reset the document's cookie if wrong person
58          function wrongPerson()
59          {
60              // reset the cookie
61              document.cookie= "name=null;" +
62                  " expires=Thu, 01-Jan-95 00:00:01 GMT";
63
64              // reload the page to get a new name after removing the cookie
65              location.reload();
66          } // end function wrongPerson
67
68          // -->
69      </script>
70  </head>
71  <body>
72      <p>Click Refresh (or Reload) to run the script again</p>
73  </body>
74 </html>
```

Fig. 9.15 | Using cookies to store user identification data. (Part 2 of 3.)

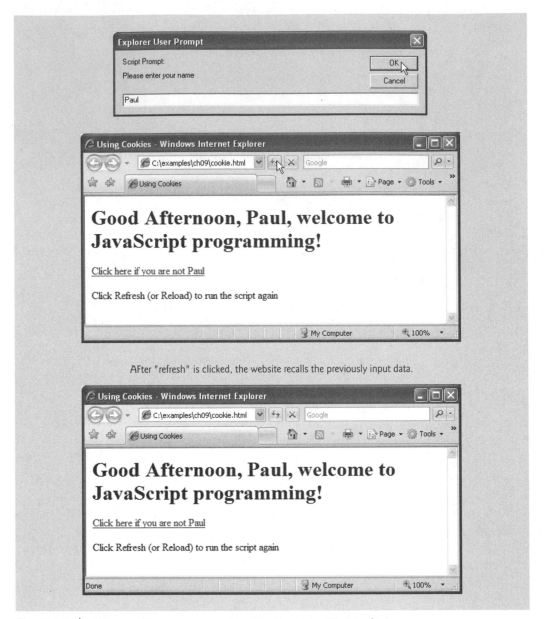

Fig. 9.15 | Using cookies to store user identification data. (Part 3 of 3.)

is a good idea to always escape cookie values before writing them to the client. This conversion prevents any special characters in the cookie from being misinterpreted as having a special meaning in the code, rather than being a character in a cookie value. For instance, a semicolon in a cookie value could be misinterpreted as a semicolon separating two adjacent *identifier-value* pairs. Applying the function **unescape** to cookies when they are read out of the document.cookie string converts the hexadecimal escape sequences back to English characters for display in a web page.

```
12    var now = new Date(); // current date and time
13    var hour = now.getHours(); // current hour
14
15    // array with names of the images that will be randomly selected
16    var pictures =
17       [ "CPE", "EPT", "GPP", "GUI", "PERF", "PORT", "SEO" ];
18
19    // array with the quotes that will be randomly selected
20    var quotes = [ "Form ever follows function.<br/>" +
21       " Louis Henri Sullivan", "E pluribus unum." +
22       " (One composed of many.) <br/> Virgil", "Is it a" +
23       " world to hide virtues in?<br/> William Shakespeare" ];
24
25    // write the current date and time to the web page
26    document.write( "<p>" + now.toLocaleString() + "<br/></p>" );

      // determine whether it is morning
      if ( hour < 12 )
         document.write( "<h2>Good Morning, " );
      else
      {
         hour = hour - 12; // convert from 24-hour clock to PM time

         // determine whether it is afternoon or evening
         if ( hour < 6 )
            document.write( "<h2>Good Afternoon, " );
         else
            document.write( "<h2>Good Evening, " );
      } // end else

      // determine whether there is a cookie
      if ( document.cookie )
      {
         // convert escape characters in the cookie string to their
         // English notation
         var myCookie = unescape( document.cookie );

         // split the cookie into tokens using = as delimiter
         var cookieTokens = myCookie.split( "=" );

         // set name to the part of the cookie that follows the = sign
         name = cookieTokens[ 1 ];
      } // end if
      else
      {
         // if there was no cookie, ask the user to input a name
         name = window.prompt( "Please enter your name", "Paul" );

         // escape special characters in the name string
         // and add name to the cookie
         document.cookie = "name =" + escape( name );
      } // end else
```

ch welcome page using several JavaScript concepts. (Part 2 of 5.)

Good Programming Practice 9.2

Always store values in cookies with self-documenting identifiers. Do not forget to identifier followed by an = sign before the value being stored.

If a cookie exists (i.e., the user has been to the page before), then the scrip user name out of the cookie string and stores it in a local variable. Parsing ge to the act of splitting a string into smaller, more useful components. Line 34 Script function unescape to replace all the escape sequences in the cookie wi alent English-language characters. The script stores the unescaped cook variable myCookie (line 34) and uses the JavaScript function split (line in Section 9.4.5, to break the cookie into identifier and value tokens. At script, myCookie contains a string of the form "name=*value*". We call sp with = as the delimiter to obtain the cookieTokens array, with the firs the name of the identifier and the second element equal to the value of 40 assigns the value of the second element in the cookieTokens array (stored in the cookie) to the variable name. Lines 52–53 add the pers the web page, using the user's name stored in the cookie.

The script allows the user to reset the cookie, which is useful i using the computer. Lines 54–55 create a hyperlink that, when clic function wrongPerson (lines 58–66). Lines 61–62 set the cooki expires property to January 1, 1995 (though any date in the p Explorer detects that the expires property is set to a date in the p from the user's computer. The next time this page loads, no *reload* method of the location object forces the page to refre find an existing cookie, the script prompts the user to enter a

9.10 Multipage HTML and JavaScript

The past few chapters have explored many JavaScript con plied on the web. The next JavaScript example combines single web page. Figure 9.16 uses functions, cookies, arr window object and the document object to create a sam personalized greeting, a short quiz, a random image ar seen all of these concepts before, but this example illu one web page.

```
1   <?xml version = "1.0" encoding = "utf-8"?
2   <!DOCTYPE html PUBLIC "-//W3C//DTD XHTML
3       "http://www.w3.org/TR/xhtml1/DTD/xhtm
4
5   <!-- Fig. 9.16: final.html -->
6   <!-- Rich welcome page using several J
7   <html xmlns = "http://www.w3.org/1999/
8       <head>
9           <title>Putting It All Together
10          <script type = "text/javascrip
11              <!--
```

Fig. 9.16 | Rich welcome page using several Jav

```
64
65        // write the greeting to the page
66        document.writeln(
67           name + ", welcome to JavaScript programming!</h2>" );
68
69        // write the link for deleting the cookie to the page
70        document.writeln( "<a href = \"javascript:wrongPerson()\" > " +
71           "Click here if you are not " + name + "</a><br/>" );
72
73        // write the random image to the page
74        document.write ( "<img src = \"" +
75           pictures[ Math.floor( Math.random() * 7 ) ] +
76           ".gif\" /> <br/>" );
77
78        // write the random quote to the page
79        document.write ( quotes[ Math.floor( Math.random() * 3 ) ] );
80
81        // create a window with all the quotes in it
82        function allQuotes()
83        {
84           // create the child window for the quotes
85           var quoteWindow = window.open( "", "", "resizable=yes, " +
86              "toolbar=no, menubar=no, status=no, location=no," +
87              " scrollBars=yes" );
88           quoteWindow.document.write( "<p>" )
89
90           // loop through all quotes and write them in the new window
91           for ( var i = 0; i < quotes.length; i++ )
92              quoteWindow.document.write( ( i + 1 ) + ".) " +
93                 quotes[ i ] + "<br/><br/>");
94
95           // write a close link to the new window
96           quoteWindow.document.write( "</p><br/><a href = " +
97              "\"javascript:window.close()\">Close this window</a>" );
98        } // end function allQuotes
99
100       // reset the document's cookie if wrong person
101       function wrongPerson()
102       {
103          // reset the cookie
104          document.cookie= "name=null;" +
105             " expires=Thu, 01-Jan-95 00:00:01 GMT";
106
107          // reload the page to get a new name after removing the cookie
108          location.reload();
109       } // end function wrongPerson
110
111       // open a new window with the quiz2.html file in it
112       function openQuiz()
113       {
114          window.open( "quiz2.html", "", "toolbar = no, " +
115             "menubar = no, scrollBars = no" );
116       } // end function openQuiz
```

Fig. 9.16 | Rich welcome page using several JavaScript concepts. (Part 3 of 5.)

```
117        // -->
118        </script>
119   </head>
120   <body>
121      <p><a href = "javascript:allQuotes()">View all quotes</a></p>
122
123      <p id = "quizSpot">
124         <a href = "javascript:openQuiz()">Please take our quiz</a></p>
125
126      <script type = "text/javascript">
127         // variable that gets the last modification date and time
128         var modDate = new Date( document.lastModified );
129
130         // write the last modified date and time to the page
131         document.write ( "This page was last modified " +
132            modDate.toLocaleString() );
133      </script>
134   </body>
135 </html>
```

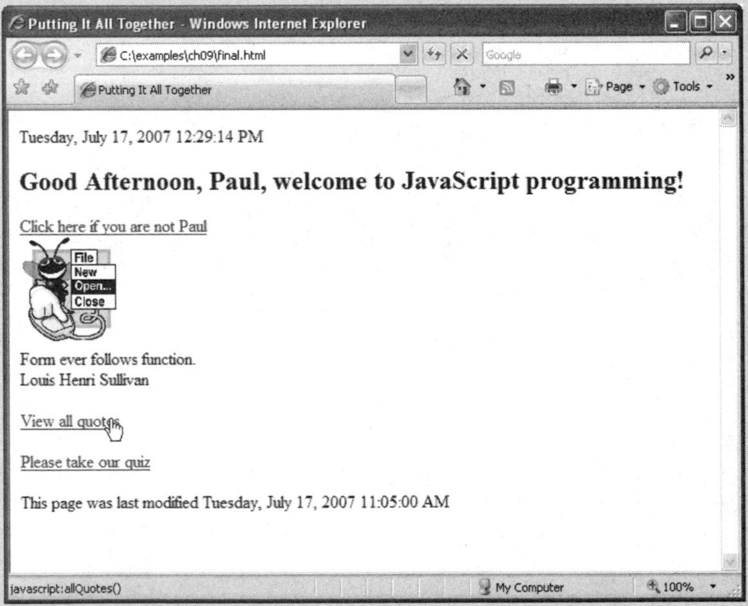

Fig. 9.16 | Rich welcome page using several JavaScript concepts. (Part 4 of 5.)

Good Programming Practice 9.2

Always store values in cookies with self-documenting identifiers. Do not forget to include the identifier followed by an = sign before the value being stored.

If a cookie exists (i.e., the user has been to the page before), then the script *parses* the user name out of the cookie string and stores it in a local variable. Parsing generally refers to the act of splitting a string into smaller, more useful components. Line 34 uses the Java-Script function unescape to replace all the escape sequences in the cookie with their equivalent English-language characters. The script stores the unescaped cookie value in the variable myCookie (line 34) and uses the JavaScript function split (line 37), introduced in Section 9.4.5, to break the cookie into identifier and value tokens. At this point in the script, myCookie contains a string of the form "name=*value*". We call split on myCookie with = as the delimiter to obtain the cookieTokens array, with the first element equal to the name of the identifier and the second element equal to the value of the identifier. Line 40 assigns the value of the second element in the cookieTokens array (i.e., the actual value stored in the cookie) to the variable name. Lines 52–53 add the personalized greeting to the web page, using the user's name stored in the cookie.

The script allows the user to reset the cookie, which is useful in case someone new is using the computer. Lines 54–55 create a hyperlink that, when clicked, calls the JavaScript function wrongPerson (lines 58–66). Lines 61–62 set the cookie name to null and the expires property to January 1, 1995 (though any date in the past will suffice). Internet Explorer detects that the expires property is set to a date in the past and deletes the cookie from the user's computer. The next time this page loads, no cookie will be found. The *reload* method of the location object forces the page to refresh (line 65), and, unable to find an existing cookie, the script prompts the user to enter a new name.

9.10 Multipage HTML and JavaScript Application

The past few chapters have explored many JavaScript concepts and how they can be applied on the web. The next JavaScript example combines many of these concepts into a single web page. Figure 9.16 uses functions, cookies, arrays, loops, the Date object, the window object and the document object to create a sample welcome screen containing a personalized greeting, a short quiz, a random image and a random quotation. We have seen all of these concepts before, but this example illustrates how they work together on one web page.

```
1    <?xml version = "1.0" encoding = "utf-8"?>
2    <!DOCTYPE html PUBLIC "-//W3C//DTD XHTML 1.0 Strict//EN"
3       "http://www.w3.org/TR/xhtml1/DTD/xhtml1-strict.dtd">
4
5    <!-- Fig. 9.16: final.html -->
6    <!-- Rich welcome page using several JavaScript concepts. -->
7    <html xmlns = "http://www.w3.org/1999/xhtml">
8       <head>
9          <title>Putting It All Together</title>
10         <script type = "text/javascript">
11            <!--
```

Fig. 9.16 | Rich welcome page using several JavaScript concepts. (Part 1 of 5.)

```
12          var now = new Date(); // current date and time
13          var hour = now.getHours(); // current hour
14
15          // array with names of the images that will be randomly selected
16          var pictures =
17             [ "CPE", "EPT", "GPP", "GUI", "PERF", "PORT", "SEO" ];
18
19          // array with the quotes that will be randomly selected
20          var quotes = [ "Form ever follows function.<br/>" +
21             " Louis Henri Sullivan", "E pluribus unum." +
22             " (One composed of many.) <br/> Virgil", "Is it a" +
23             " world to hide virtues in?<br/> William Shakespeare" ];
24
25          // write the current date and time to the web page
26          document.write( "<p>" + now.toLocaleString() + "<br/></p>" );
27
28          // determine whether it is morning
29          if ( hour < 12 )
30             document.write( "<h2>Good Morning, " );
31          else
32          {
33             hour = hour - 12; // convert from 24-hour clock to PM time
34
35             // determine whether it is afternoon or evening
36             if ( hour < 6 )
37                document.write( "<h2>Good Afternoon, " );
38             else
39                document.write( "<h2>Good Evening, " );
40          } // end else
41
42          // determine whether there is a cookie
43          if ( document.cookie )
44          {
45             // convert escape characters in the cookie string to their
46             // English notation
47             var myCookie = unescape( document.cookie );
48
49             // split the cookie into tokens using = as delimiter
50             var cookieTokens = myCookie.split( "=" );
51
52             // set name to the part of the cookie that follows the = sign
53             name = cookieTokens[ 1 ];
54          } // end if
55          else
56          {
57             // if there was no cookie, ask the user to input a name
58             name = window.prompt( "Please enter your name", "Paul" );
59
60             // escape special characters in the name string
61             // and add name to the cookie
62             document.cookie = "name =" + escape( name );
63          } // end else
```

Fig. 9.16 | Rich welcome page using several JavaScript concepts. (Part 2 of 5.)

```
64
65          // write the greeting to the page
66          document.writeln(
67             name + ", welcome to JavaScript programming!</h2>" );
68
69          // write the link for deleting the cookie to the page
70          document.writeln( "<a href = \"javascript:wrongPerson()\" > " +
71             "Click here if you are not " + name + "</a><br/>" );
72
73          // write the random image to the page
74          document.write ( "<img src = \"" +
75             pictures[ Math.floor( Math.random() * 7 ) ] +
76             ".gif\" /> <br/>" );
77
78          // write the random quote to the page
79          document.write ( quotes[ Math.floor( Math.random() * 3 ) ] );
80
81          // create a window with all the quotes in it
82          function allQuotes()
83          {
84             // create the child window for the quotes
85             var quoteWindow = window.open( "", "", "resizable=yes, " +
86                "toolbar=no, menubar=no, status=no, location=no," +
87                " scrollBars=yes" );
88             quoteWindow.document.write( "<p>" )
89
90             // loop through all quotes and write them in the new window
91             for ( var i = 0; i < quotes.length; i++ )
92                quoteWindow.document.write( ( i + 1 ) + ".) " +
93                   quotes[ i ] + "<br/><br/>");
94
95             // write a close link to the new window
96             quoteWindow.document.write( "</p><br/><a href = " +
97                "\"javascript:window.close()\">Close this window</a>" );
98          } // end function allQuotes
99
100         // reset the document's cookie if wrong person
101         function wrongPerson()
102         {
103            // reset the cookie
104            document.cookie= "name=null;" +
105               " expires=Thu, 01-Jan-95 00:00:01 GMT";
106
107            // reload the page to get a new name after removing the cookie
108            location.reload();
109         } // end function wrongPerson
110
111         // open a new window with the quiz2.html file in it
112         function openQuiz()
113         {
114            window.open( "quiz2.html", "", "toolbar = no, " +
115               "menubar = no, scrollBars = no" );
116         } // end function openQuiz
```

Fig. 9.16 | Rich welcome page using several JavaScript concepts. (Part 3 of 5.)

```
117        // -->
118      </script>
119   </head>
120   <body>
121      <p><a href = "javascript:allQuotes()">View all quotes</a></p>
122
123      <p id = "quizSpot">
124         <a href = "javascript:openQuiz()">Please take our quiz</a></p>
125
126      <script type = "text/javascript">
127         // variable that gets the last modification date and time
128         var modDate = new Date( document.lastModified );
129
130         // write the last modified date and time to the page
131         document.write ( "This page was last modified " +
132            modDate.toLocaleString() );
133      </script>
134   </body>
135 </html>
```

Explorer User Prompt

Script Prompt:
Please enter your name

OK   Cancel

Paul

Putting It All Together - Windows Internet Explorer

C:\examples\ch09\final.html   Google

Putting It All Together   Page ▾ Tools ▾

Tuesday, July 17, 2007 12:29:14 PM

Good Afternoon, Paul, welcome to JavaScript programming!

Click here if you are not Paul

File
New
Open...
Close

Form ever follows function.
Louis Henri Sullivan

View all quotes

Please take our quiz

This page was last modified Tuesday, July 17, 2007 11:05:00 AM

javascript:allQuotes()   My Computer   100%

Fig. 9.16 | Rich welcome page using several JavaScript concepts. (Part 4 of 5.)

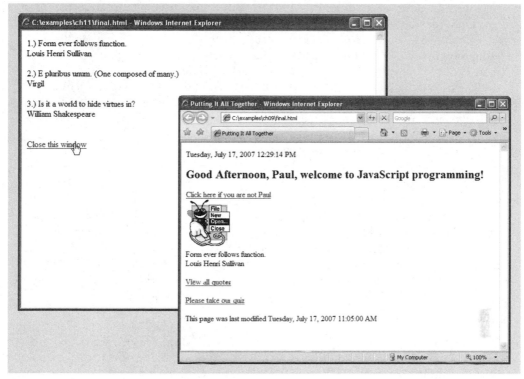

Fig. 9.16 | Rich welcome page using several JavaScript concepts. (Part 5 of 5.)

The script that builds most of this page starts in line 10. Lines 12–13 declare variables needed for determining the time of day. Lines 16–23 create two arrays from which content is randomly selected. This web page contains both an image (whose filename is randomly selected from the pictures array) and a quote (whose text is randomly selected from the quotes array). Line 26 writes the user's local date and time to the web page using the Date object's toLocaleString method. Lines 29–40 display a time-sensitive greeting using the same code as Fig. 4.11. The script either uses an existing cookie to obtain the user's name (lines 43–54) or prompts the user for a name, which the script then stores in a new cookie (lines 55–63). Lines 66–67 write the greeting to the web page, and lines 70–71 produce the link for resetting the cookie. This is the same code used in Fig. 9.15 to manipulate cookies. Lines 74–79 write the random image and random quote to the web page. The script chooses each by randomly selecting an index into each array. This code is similar to the code used in Fig. 8.7 to display a random image using an array.

Function allQuotes (lines 82–98) uses the window object and a for loop to open a new window containing all the quotes in the quotes array. Lines 85–87 create a new window called quoteWindow. The script does not assign a URL or a name to this window, but it does specify the window features to display. Line 88 opens a new paragraph in quoteWindow. A for loop (lines 91–93) traverses the quotes array and writes each quote to quoteWindow. Lines 96–97 close the paragraph in quoteWindow, insert a new line and add a link at the bottom of the page that allows the user to close the window. Note that allQuotes generates a web page and opens it in an entirely new window with JavaScript.

Function `wrongPerson` (lines 101–109) resets the cookie storing the user's name. This function is identical to function `wrongPerson` in Fig. 9.15.

Function `openQuiz` (lines 112–116) opens a new window to display a sample quiz. Using the `window.open` method, the script creates a new window containing `quiz2.html` (lines 114–115). We discuss `quiz2.html` later in this section.

The primary script ends in line 118, and the body of the XHTML document begins in line 120. Line 121 creates the link that calls function `allQuotes` when clicked. Lines 123–124 create a paragraph element containing the attribute `id = "quizSpot"`. This paragraph contains a link that calls function `openQuiz`.

Lines 126–133 contain a second script. This script appears in the XHTML document's `body` because it adds a dynamic footer to the page, which must appear after the static XHTML content contained in the first part of the body. This script creates another instance of the `Date` object, but the date is set to the last modified date and time of the XHTML document, rather than the current date and time (line 128). The script obtains the last modified date and time using property `document.lastModified`. Lines 131–132 add this information to the web page. Note that the last modified date and time appear at the bottom of the page, after the rest of the body content. If this script were in the `head` element, this information would be displayed before the entire body of the XHTML document. Lines 133–135 close the `script`, the body and the XHTML document.

The Quiz Page

The quiz used in this example is in a separate XHTML document named `quiz2.html` (Fig. 9.17). This document is similar to `quiz.html` in Fig. 8.12. The quiz in this example differs from the quiz in Fig. 8.12 in that it shows the result in the main window in the example, whereas the earlier quiz example alerts the result. After the **Submit** button in the quiz window is clicked, the main window changes to reflect that the quiz was taken, and the quiz window closes.

Lines 15–22 of this script check the user's answer and output the result to the main window. Lines 16–17 use `window.opener` to write to the main window. The property *window.opener* always contains a reference to the window that opened the current window, if such a window exists. Lines 16–17 write to property `window.opener.document.getElementById("quizSpot").innerHTML`. Recall that `quizSpot` is the `id` of the paragraph in the main window that contains the link to open the quiz. Property *innerHTML* refers to the HTML code inside the `quizSpot` paragraph (i.e., the code between `<p>` and `</p>`). Modifying the `innerHTML` property dynamically changes the XHTML code in the paragraph. Thus, when lines 16–17 execute, the link in the main window disappears, and the string `"Congratulations, your answer is correct."` appears. Lines 19–22 modify `window.opener.document.getElementById("quizSpot").innerHTML`. Lines 19–22 use the same technique to display `"Your answer is incorrect. Please try again"`, followed by a link to try the quiz again.

```
1    <?xml version = "1.0" encoding = "utf-8"?>
2    <!DOCTYPE html PUBLIC "-//W3C//DTD XHTML 1.0 Strict//EN"
3        "http://www.w3.org/TR/xhtml1/DTD/xhtml1-strict.dtd">
```

Fig. 9.17 | Online quiz in a child window. (Part 1 of 3.)

```
 4
 5      <!-- Fig. 9.17: quiz2.html -->
 6      <!-- Online quiz in a child window. -->
 7      <html xmlns = "http://www.w3.org/1999/xhtml">
 8         <head>
 9            <title>Online Quiz</title>
10            <script type = "text/JavaScript">
11               <!--
12               function checkAnswers()
13               {
14                  // determine whether the answer is correct
15                  if ( document.getElementById( "myQuiz" ).elements[1].checked )
16                     window.opener.document.getElementById( "quizSpot" ).
17                        innerHTML = "Congratulations, your answer is correct";
18                  else // if the answer is incorrect
19                     window.opener.document.getElementById( "quizSpot" ).
20                        innerHTML = "Your answer is incorrect. " +
21                        "Please try again <br /> <a href = " +
22                        \"javascript:openQuiz()\">Please take our quiz</a>";
23
24                  window.opener.focus();
25                  window.close();
26               } // end function checkAnswers
27               //-->
28            </script>
29         </head>
30         <body>
31            <form id = "myQuiz" action = "javascript:checkAnswers()">
32               <p>Select the name of the tip that goes with the
33                  image shown:<br />
34                  <img src = "EPT.gif" alt = "mystery tip"/>
35                  <br />
36
37                  <input type = "radio" name = "radiobutton" value = "CPE" />
38                  <label>Common Programming Error</label>
39
40                  <input type = "radio" name = "radiobutton" value = "EPT" />
41                  <label>Error-Prevention Tip</label>
42
43                  <input type = "radio" name = "radiobutton" value = "PERF" />
44                  <label>Performance Tip</label>
45
46                  <input type = "radio" name = "radiobutton" value = "PORT" />
47                  <label>Portability Tip</label><br />
48
49                  <input type = "submit" name = "Submit" value = "Submit" />
50                  <input type = "reset" name = "reset" value = "Reset" />
51               </p>
52            </form>
53         </body>
54      </html>
```

Fig. 9.17 | Online quiz in a child window. (Part 2 of 3.)

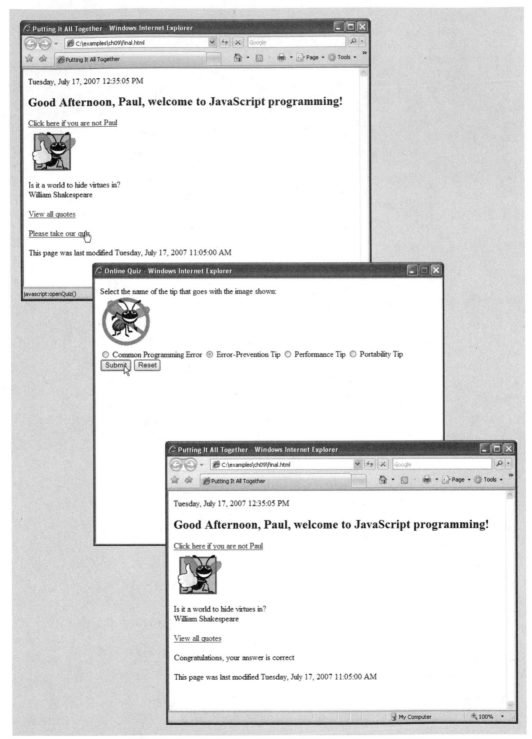

Fig. 9.17 | Online quiz in a child window. (Part 3 of 3.)

After checking the quiz answer, the script gives focus to the main window (i.e., puts the main window in the foreground, on top of any other open browser windows), using the method *focus* of the main window's window object. The property window.opener references the main window, so window.opener.focus() (line 24) gives the main window focus, allowing the user to see the changes made to the text of the main window's quiz-Spot paragraph. Finally, the script closes the quiz window, using method window.close (line 25).

Lines 28–29 close the script and head elements of the XHTML document. Line 30 opens the body of the XHTML document. The body contains the form, image, text labels and radio buttons that comprise the quiz. Lines 52–54 close the form, the body and the XHTML document.

9.11 Using JSON to Represent Objects

JSON (JavaScript Object Notation)—a simple way to represent JavaScript objects as strings—is an alternative to XML as a data-exchange technique. JSON has gained acclaim due to its simple format, making objects easy to read, create and parse. Each JSON object is represented as a list of property names and values contained in curly braces, in the following format:

> { *propertyName1* : *value1*, *propertyName2* : *value2* }

Arrays are represented in JSON with square brackets in the following format:

> [*value1*, *value2*, *value3*]

Each value can be a string, a number, a JSON object, true, false or null. To appreciate the simplicity of JSON data, examine this representation of an array of address-book entries:

```
[ { first: 'Cheryl', last: 'Black' },
  { first: 'James', last: 'Blue' },
  { first: 'Mike', last: 'Brown' },
  { first: 'Meg', last: 'Gold' } ]
```

JSON provides a straightforward way to manipulate objects in JavaScript, and many other programming languages now support this format. In addition to simplifying object creation, JSON allows programs to manipulate data easily and to efficiently transmit data across the Internet. JSON integrates well with Ajax applications—see Section 13.7 for a more detailed discussion of JSON and an Ajax-specific example. For more information on JSON, visit our JSON Resource Center at www.deitel.com/json.

10

Document Object Model (DOM): Objects and Collections

OBJECTIVES

In this chapter you'll learn:

- To use JavaScript and the W3C Document Object Model to create dynamic web pages.
- The concepts of DOM nodes and DOM trees.
- To traverse, edit and modify elements in an XHTML document.
- To change CSS styles dynamically.
- To create JavaScript animations.

10.1 **Introduction**

In this chapter we introduce the *Document Object Model (DOM)*. The DOM gives you access to all the elements on a web page. Inside the browser, the whole web page—paragraphs, forms, tables, etc.—is represented in an *object hierarchy*. Using JavaScript, you can create, modify and remove elements in the page dynamically.

Previously, both Internet Explorer and Netscape had different versions of Dynamic HTML, which provided similar functionality to the DOM. However, while they provided many of the same capabilities, these two models were incompatible with each other. In an effort to encourage cross-browser websites, the W3C created the standardized Document Object Model. Firefox, Internet Explorer 7, and many other major browsers implement *most* of the features of the W3C DOM.

This chapter begins by formally introducing the concept of DOM nodes and DOM trees. We then discuss properties and methods of DOM nodes and cover additional methods of the document object. We also discuss how to dynamically change style properties, which enables you to create many types of effects, such as user-defined background colors and animations. Then, we present a diagram of the extensive object hierarchy, with explanations of the various objects and properties, and we provide links to websites with further information on the topic.

Software Engineering Observation 10.1

With the DOM, XHTML elements can be treated as objects, and many attributes of XHTML elements can be treated as properties of those objects. Then, objects can be scripted (through their id *attributes) with JavaScript to achieve dynamic effects.*

10.2 **Modeling a Document: DOM Nodes and Trees**

As we saw in previous chapters, the document's getElementById method is the simplest way to access a specific element in a page. In this section and the next, we discuss more thoroughly the objects returned by this method.

The getElementById method returns objects called *DOM nodes*. Every element in an XHTML page is modeled in the web browser by a DOM node. All the nodes in a document make up the page's *DOM tree*, which describes the relationships among elements. Nodes are related to each other through child-parent relationships. An XHTML element inside another element is said to be a *child* of the containing element. The containing element is known as the *parent*. A node may have multiple children, but only one parent. Nodes with the same parent node are referred to as *siblings*.

Some browsers have tools that allow you to see a visual representation of the DOM tree of a document. When installing Firefox, you can choose to install a tool called the *DOM Inspector*, which allows you to view the DOM tree of an XHTML document. To inspect a document, Firefox users can access the **DOM Inspector** from the **Tools** menu of Firefox. If the DOM inspector is not in the menu, run the Firefox installer and choose **Custom** in the **Setup Type** screen, making sure the **DOM Inspector** box is checked in the **Optional Components** window.

Microsoft provides a *Developer Toolbar* for Internet Explorer that allows you to inspect the DOM tree of a document. The toolbar can be downloaded from Microsoft at go.microsoft.com/fwlink/?LinkId=92716. Once the toolbar is installed, restart the browser, then click the » icon at the right of the toolbar and choose **IE Developer Toolbar** from the menu. Figure 10.1 shows an XHTML document and its DOM tree displayed in Firefox's DOM Inspector and in IE's Web Developer Toolbar.

The XHTML document contains a few simple elements. We explain the example based on the Firefox DOM Inspector—the IE Toolbar displays the document with only minor differences. A node can be expanded and collapsed using the + and - buttons next to the node's name. Figure 10.1(b) shows all the nodes in the document fully expanded. The document node (shown as **#document**) at the top of the tree is called the *root node*, because it has no parent. Below the document node, the **HTML** node is indented from the document node to signify that the **HTML** node is a child of the **#document** node. The **HTML** node represents the html element (lines 7–24).

The **HEAD** and **BODY** nodes are siblings, since they are both children of the **HTML** node. The **HEAD** contains two **#comment** nodes, representing lines 5–6. The **TITLE** node

```
1   <?xml version = "1.0" encoding = "utf-8"?>
2   <!DOCTYPE html PUBLIC "-//W3C//DTD XHTML 1.0 Strict//EN"
3      "http://www.w3.org/TR/xhtml1/DTD/xhtml1-strict.dtd">
4
5   <!-- Fig. 10.1: domtree.html -->
6   <!-- Demonstration of a document's DOM tree. -->
7   <html xmlns = "http://www.w3.org/1999/xhtml">
8      <head>
9         <title>DOM Tree Demonstration</title>
10     </head>
11     <body>
12        <h1>An XHTML Page</h1>
13        <p>This page contains some basic XHTML elements. We use the Firefox
14           DOM Inspector and the IE Developer Toolbar to view the DOM tree
15           of the document, which contains a DOM node for every element in
16           the document.</p>
17        <p>Here's a list:</p>
18        <ul>
19           <li>One</li>
20           <li>Two</li>
21           <li>Three</li>
22        </ul>
23     </body>
24  </html>
```

Fig. 10.1 | Demonstration of a document's DOM tree. (Part 1 of 3.)

a) The XHTML document is rendered in Firefox.

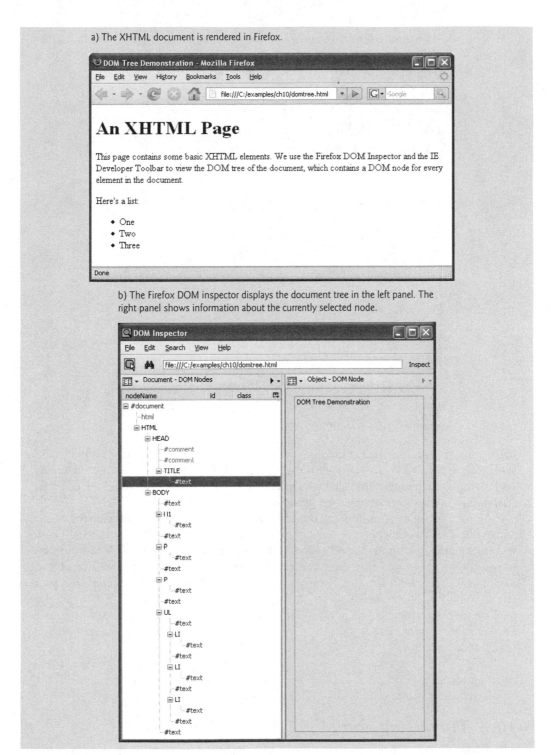

b) The Firefox DOM inspector displays the document tree in the left panel. The right panel shows information about the currently selected node.

Fig. 10.1 | Demonstration of a document's DOM tree. (Part 2 of 3.)

c) The Internet Explorer Web Developer Toolbar displays much of the same information as the DOM inspector in Firefox in a panel at the bottom of the browser window.

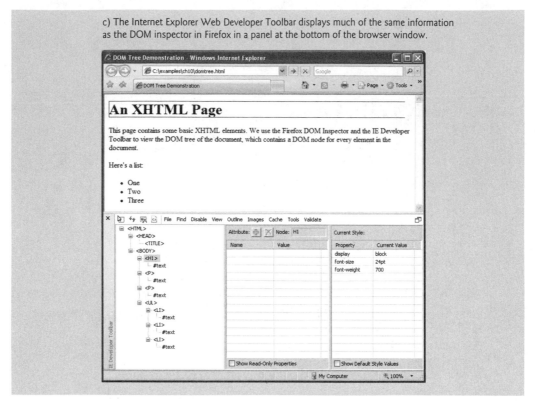

Fig. 10.1 | Demonstration of a document's DOM tree. (Part 3 of 3.)

has a child text node (**#text**) containing the text **DOM Tree Demonstration**, visible in the right pane of the DOM inspector when the text node is selected. The **BODY** node contains nodes representing each of the elements in the page. Note that the **LI** nodes are children of the **UL** node, since they are nested inside it.

Also, notice that, in addition to the text nodes representing the text inside the body, paragraphs and list elements, a number of other text nodes appear in the document. These text nodes contain nothing but white space. When Firefox parses an XHTML document into a DOM tree, the white space between sibling elements is interpreted as text and placed inside text nodes. Internet Explorer ignores white space and does not convert it into empty text nodes. If you run this example on your own computer, you will notice that the **BODY** node has a **#comment** child node not present above in both the Firefox and Internet Explorer DOM trees. This is a result of the copyright line at the end of the example file that you downloaded.

This section introduced the concept of DOM nodes and DOM trees. The next section considers DOM nodes in more detail, discussing methods and properties of DOM nodes that allow you to modify the DOM tree of a document using JavaScript.

10.3 Traversing and Modifying a DOM Tree

The DOM gives you access to the elements of a document, allowing you to modify the contents of a page dynamically using event-driven JavaScript. This section introduces properties and methods of all DOM nodes that enable you to traverse the DOM tree, modify nodes and create or delete content dynamically.

Figure 10.2 shows some of the functionality of DOM nodes, as well as two additional methods of the document object. The program allows you to highlight, modify, insert and remove elements.

Lines 117–132 contain basic XHTML elements and content. Each element has an id attribute, which is also displayed at the beginning of the element in square brackets. For example, the id of the h1 element in lines 117–118 is set to bigheading, and the heading text begins with [bigheading]. This allows the user to see the id of each element in the page. The body also contains an h3 heading, several p elements, and an unordered list.

A div element (lines 133–162) contains the remainder of the XHTML body. Line 134 begins a form element, assigning the empty string to the required action attribute (because we're not submitting to a server) and returning false to the onsubmit attribute. When a form's onsubmit handler returns false, the navigation to the address specified in the action attribute is aborted. This allows us to modify the page using JavaScript event handlers without reloading the original, unmodified XHTML.

```
 1   <?xml version = "1.0" encoding = "utf-8"?>
 2   <!DOCTYPE html PUBLIC "-//W3C//DTD XHTML 1.0 Strict//EN"
 3      "http://www.w3.org/TR/xhtml1/DTD/xhtml1-strict.dtd">
 4
 5   <!-- Fig. 10.2: dom.html -->
 6   <!-- Basic DOM functionality. -->
 7   <html xmlns = "http://www.w3.org/1999/xhtml">
 8      <head>
 9         <title>Basic DOM Functionality</title>
10         <style type = "text/css">
11            h1, h3       { text-align: center;
12                           font-family: tahoma, geneva, sans-serif }
13            p            { margin-left: 5%;
14                           margin-right: 5%;
15                           font-family: arial, helvetica, sans-serif }
16            ul           { margin-left: 10% }
17            a            { text-decoration: none }
18            a:hover      { text-decoration: underline }
19            .nav         { width: 100%;
20                           border-top: 3px dashed blue;
21                           padding-top: 10px }
22            .highlighted { background-color: yellow }
23            .submit      { width: 120px }
24         </style>
25         <script type = "text/javascript">
26            <!--
27            var currentNode; // stores the currently highlighted node
28            var idcount = 0; // used to assign a unique id to new elements
29
30            // get and highlight an element by its id attribute
31            function byId()
32            {
```

Fig. 10.2 | Basic DOM functionality. (Part 1 of 8.)

```
33          var id = document.getElementById( "gbi" ).value;
34          var target = document.getElementById( id );
35
36          if ( target )
37              switchTo( target );
38      } // end function byId
39
40      // insert a paragraph element before the current element
41      // using the insertBefore method
42      function insert()
43      {
44          var newNode = createNewNode(
45              document.getElementById( "ins" ).value );
46          currentNode.parentNode.insertBefore( newNode, currentNode );
47          switchTo( newNode );
48      } // end function insert
49
50      // append a paragraph node as the child of the current node
51      function appendNode()
52      {
53          var newNode = createNewNode(
54              document.getElementById( "append" ).value );
55          currentNode.appendChild( newNode );
56          switchTo( newNode );
57      } // end function appendNode
58
59      // replace the currently selected node with a paragraph node
60      function replaceCurrent()
61      {
62          var newNode = createNewNode(
63              document.getElementById( "replace" ).value );
64          currentNode.parentNode.replaceChild( newNode, currentNode );
65          switchTo( newNode );
66      } // end function replaceCurrent
67
68      // remove the current node
69      function remove()
70      {
71          if ( currentNode.parentNode == document.body )
72              alert( "Can't remove a top-level element." );
73          else
74          {
75              var oldNode = currentNode;
76              switchTo( oldNode.parentNode );
77              currentNode.removeChild( oldNode );
78          } // end else
79      } // end function remove
80
81      // get and highlight the parent of the current node
82      function parent()
83      {
84          var target = currentNode.parentNode;
85
```

Fig. 10.2 | Basic DOM functionality. (Part 2 of 8.)

```
86          if ( target != document.body )
87             switchTo( target );
88          else
89             alert( "No parent." );
90       } // end function parent
91
92       // helper function that returns a new paragraph node containing
93       // a unique id and the given text
94       function createNewNode( text )
95       {
96          var newNode = document.createElement( "p" );
97          nodeId = "new" + idcount;
98          ++idcount;
99          newNode.id = nodeId;
100         text = "[" + nodeId + "] " + text;
101         newNode.appendChild(document.createTextNode( text ) );
102         return newNode;
103      } // end function createNewNode
104
105      // helper function that switches to a new currentNode
106      function switchTo( newNode )
107      {
108         currentNode.className = "";  // remove old highlighting
109         currentNode = newNode;
110         currentNode.className = "highlighted"; // highlight new node
111         document.getElementById( "gbi" ).value = currentNode.id;
112      } // end function switchTo
113      // -->
114   </script>
115 </head>
116 <body onload = "currentNode = document.getElementById( 'bigheading' )">
117    <h1 id = "bigheading" class = "highlighted">
118       [bigheading] DHTML Object Model</h1>
119    <h3 id = "smallheading">[smallheading] Element Functionality</h3>
120    <p id = "para1">[para1] The Document Object Model (DOM) allows for
121       quick, dynamic access to all elements in an XHTML document for
122       manipulation with JavaScript.</p>
123    <p id = "para2">[para2] For more information, check out the
124       "JavaScript and the DOM" section of Deitel's
125       <a id = "link" href = "http://www.deitel.com/javascript">
126          [link] JavaScript Resource Center.</a></p>
127    <p id = "para3">[para3] The buttons below demonstrate:(list)</p>
128    <ul id = "list">
129       <li id = "item1">[item1] getElementById and parentNode</li>
130       <li id = "item2">[item2] insertBefore and appendChild</li>
131       <li id = "item3">[item3] replaceChild and removeChild </li>
132    </ul>
133    <div id = "nav" class = "nav">
134       <form onsubmit = "return false" action = "">
135          <table>
136             <tr>
137                <td><input type = "text" id = "gbi"
138                   value = "bigheading" /></td>
```

Fig. 10.2 | Basic DOM functionality. (Part 3 of 8.)

```
139                        <td><input type = "submit" value = "Get By id"
140                           onclick = "byId()" class = "submit" /></td>
141                     </tr><tr>
142                        <td><input type = "text" id = "ins" /></td>
143                        <td><input type = "submit" value = "Insert Before"
144                           onclick = "insert()" class = "submit" /></td>
145                     </tr><tr>
146                        <td><input type = "text" id = "append" /></td>
147                        <td><input type = "submit" value = "Append Child"
148                           onclick = "appendNode()" class = "submit" /></td>
149                     </tr><tr>
150                        <td><input type = "text" id = "replace" /></td>
151                        <td><input type = "submit" value = "Replace Current"
152                           onclick = "replaceCurrent()" class = "submit" /></td>
153                     </tr><tr><td />
154                        <td><input type = "submit" value = "Remove Current"
155                           onclick = "remove()" class = "submit" /></td>
156                     </tr><tr><td />
157                        <td><input type = "submit" value = "Get Parent"
158                           onclick = "parent()" class = "submit" /></td>
159                     </tr>
160                  </table>
161               </form>
162            </div>
163         </body>
164      </html>
```

a) This is the page when it first loads. It begins with the large heading highlighted.

Fig. 10.2 | Basic DOM functionality. (Part 4 of 8.)

b) This is the document after using the **Get By id** button to select para3.

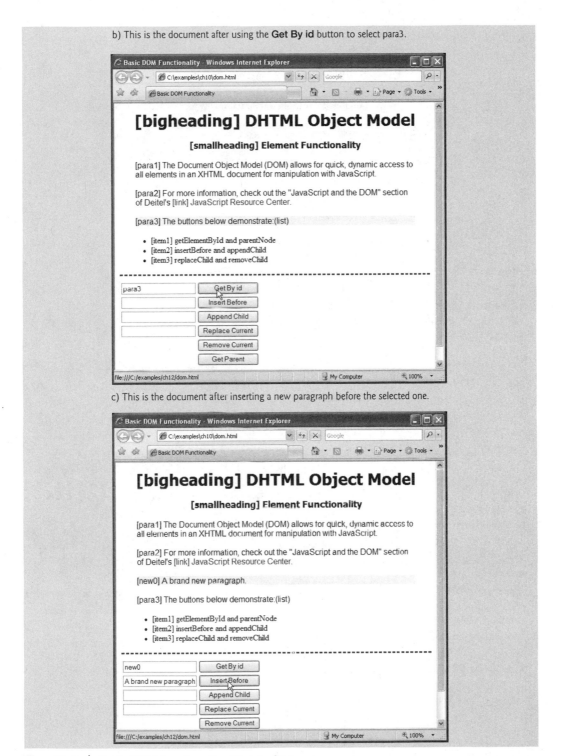

c) This is the document after inserting a new paragraph before the selected one.

Fig. 10.2 | Basic DOM functionality. (Part 5 of 8.)

d) Using the **Append Child** button, a child paragraph is created.

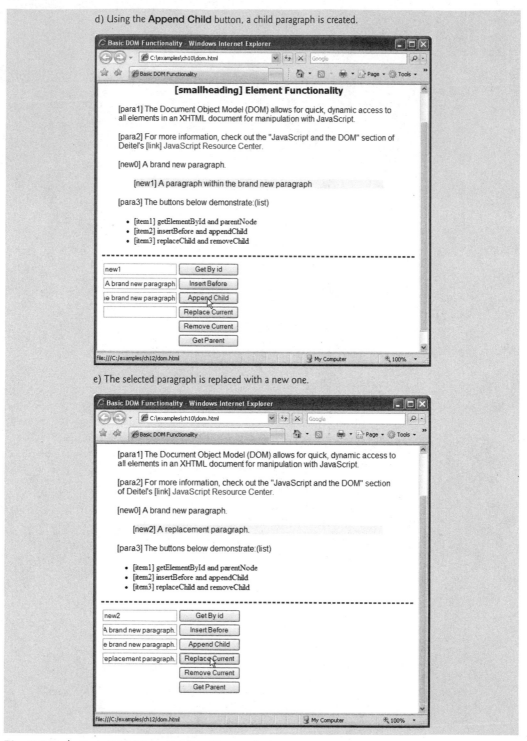

e) The selected paragraph is replaced with a new one.

Fig. 10.2 | Basic DOM functionality. (Part 6 of 8.)

f) The **Get Parent** button gets the parent of the selected node.

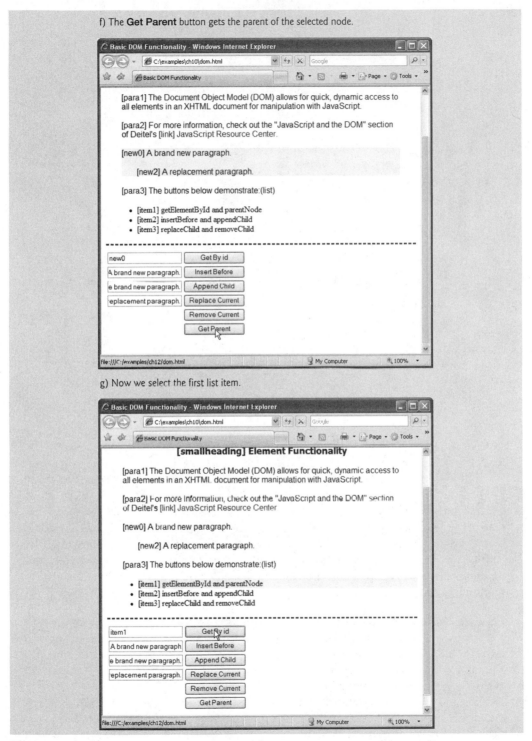

g) Now we select the first list item.

Fig. 10.2 | Basic DOM functionality. (Part 7 of 8.)

h) The **Remove Current** button removes the current node and selects its parent.

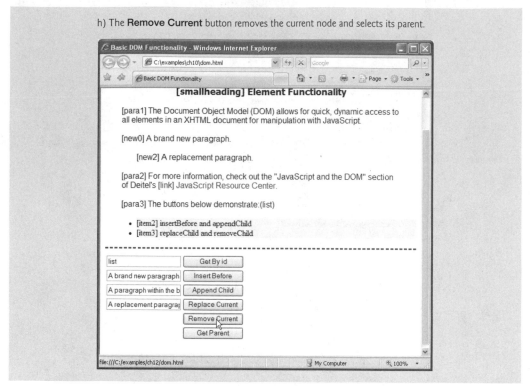

Fig. 10.2 | Basic DOM functionality. (Part 8 of 8.)

A `table` (lines 135–160) contains the controls for modifying and manipulating the elements on the page. Each of the six buttons calls its own event-handling function to perform the action described by its `value`.

The JavaScript code begins by declaring two variables. The variable `currentNode` (line 27) keeps track of the currently highlighted node, because the functionality of the buttons depends on which node is currently selected. The `body`'s `onload` attribute (line 116) initializes `currentNode` to the `h1` element with `id` `bigheading`. Variable `idcount` (line 28) is used to assign a unique `id` to any new elements that are created. The remainder of the JavaScript code contains event handling functions for the XHTML buttons and two helper functions that are called by the event handlers. We now discuss each button and its corresponding event handler in detail.

Finding and Highlighting an Element Using *getElementById* and *className*

The first row of the table (lines 136-141) allows the user to enter the `id` of an element into the text field (lines 137–138) and click the `Get By Id` button (lines 139–140) to find and highlight the element, as shown in Fig. 10.2(b) and (g). The `onclick` attribute sets the button's event handler to function `byId`.

The `byId` function is defined in lines 31–38. Line 33 uses `getElementById` to assign the contents of the text field to variable `id`. Line 34 uses `getElementById` again to find the element whose `id` attribute matches the contents of variable `id`, and assign it to variable `target`. If an element is found with the given `id`, `getElementById` returns an object representing that element. If no element is found, getElementById returns null. Line 36 checks whether target is an object—recall that any object used as a boolean expression is true, while null is false. If target evaluates to true, line 37 calls the switchTo function with target as its argument.

The switchTo function, defined in lines 106–112, is used throughout the program to highlight a new element in the page. The current element is given a yellow background using the style class highlighted, defined in line 22. Line 108 sets the current node's className property to the empty string. The *className property* allows you to change an XHTML element's class attribute. In this case, we clear the class attribute in order to remove the highlighted class from the currentNode before we highlight the new one.

Line 109 assigns the newNode object (passed into the function as a parameter) to variable currentNode. Line 110 adds the highlighted style class to the new currentNode using the className property.

Finally, line 111 uses the *id property* to assign the current node's id to the input field's value property. Just as className allows access to an element's class attribute, the id property controls an element's id attribute. While this isn't necessary when switchTo is called by byId, we will see shortly that other functions call switchTo. This line makes sure that the text field's value is consistent with the currently selected node's id. Having found the new element, removed the highlighting from the old element, updated the currentNode variable and highlighted the new element, the program has finished selecting a new node by a user-entered id.

Creating and Inserting Elements Using insertBefore and appendChild

The next two table rows allow the user to create a new element and insert it before the current node or as a child of the current node. The second row (lines 141–145) allows the user to enter text into the text field and click the Insert Before button. The text is placed in a new paragraph element, which is then inserted into the document before the currently selected element, as in Fig. 10.2(c). The button in lines 143–144 calls the insert function, defined in lines 42–48.

Lines 44–45 call the function createNewNode, passing it the value of the input field (whose id is ins) as an argument. Function createNewNode, defined in lines 94–103, creates a paragraph node containing the text passed to it. Line 96 creates a p element using the document object's *createElement method*. The createElement method creates a new DOM node, taking the tag name as an argument. Note that while createElement *creates* an element, it does not *insert* the element on the page.

Line 97 creates a unique id for the new element by concatenating "new" and the value of idcount before incrementing idcount in line 98. Line 99 assigns the id to the new element. Line 100 concatenates the element's id in square brackets to the beginning of text (the parameter containing the paragraph's text).

Line 101 introduces two new methods. The document's *createTextNode method* creates a node that can contain only text. Given a string argument, createTextNode inserts the string into the text node. In line 101, we create a new text node containing the contents of variable text. This new node is then used (still in line 101) as the argument to the *appendChild method*, which is called on the paragraph node. Method appendChild is called on a parent node to insert a child node (passed as an argument) after any existing children.

After the p element is created, line 102 returns the node to the calling function insert, where it is assigned to variable newNode in lines 44–45. Line 46 inserts the newly created node before the currently selected node. The ***parentNode* property** of any DOM node contains the node's parent. In line 46, we use the parentNode property of current-Node to get its parent.

We call the insertBefore method (line 46) on the parent with newNode and currentNode as its arguments to insert newNode as a child of the parent directly before currentNode. The general syntax of the ***insertBefore* method** is

>   *parent*.insertBefore(*newChild*, *existingChild*);

The method is called on a parent with the new child and an existing child as arguments. The node *newChild* is inserted as a child of *parent* directly before *existingChild*. Line 47 uses the switchTo function (discussed earlier in this section) to update the currentNode to the newly inserted node and highlight it in the XHTML page.

The third table row (lines 145–149) allows the user to append a new paragraph node as a child of the current element, demonstrated in Fig. 10.2(d). This feature uses a similar procedure to the insertBefore functionality. Lines 53–54 in function appendNode create a new node, line 55 inserts it as a child of the current node, and line 56 uses switchTo to update currentNode and highlight the new node.

Replacing and Removing Elements Using replaceChild *and* removeChild

The next two table rows (lines 149–156) allow the user to replace the current element with a new p element or simply remove the current element. Lines 150–152 contain a text field and a button that replaces the currently highlighted element with a new paragraph node containing the text in the text field. This feature is demonstrated in Fig. 10.2(e).

The button in lines 151–152 calls function replaceCurrent, defined in lines 60–66. Lines 62–63 call createNewNode, in the same way as in insert and appendNode, getting the text from the correct input field. Line 64 gets the parent of currentNode, then calls the replaceChild method on the parent. The ***replaceChild* method** works as follows:

>   *parent*.replaceChild(*newChild*, *oldChild*);

The *parent*'s replaceChild method inserts *newChild* into its list of children in place of *old-Child*.

The Remove Current feature, shown in Fig. 10.2(h), removes the current element entirely and highlights the parent. No text field is required because a new element is not being created. The button in lines 154-155 calls the remove function, defined in lines 69–79. If the node's parent is the body element, line 72 alerts an error—the program does not allow the entire body element to be selected. Otherwise, lines 75–77 remove the current element. Line 75 stores the old currentNode in variable oldNode. We do this to maintain a reference to the node to be removed after we've changed the value of currentNode. Line 76 calls switchTo to highlight the parent node.

Line 77 uses the ***removeChild* method** to remove the oldNode (a child of the new currentNode) from its place in the XHTML document. In general,

>   *parent*.removeChild(*child*);

looks in *parent*'s list of children for *child* and removes it.

The final button (lines 157–158) selects and highlights the parent element of the currently highlighted element by calling the parent function, defined in lines 82–90. Function parent simply gets the parent node (line 84), makes sure it is not the body element, (line 86) and calls switchTo to highlight it (line 87). Line 89 alerts an error if the parent node is the body element. This feature is shown in Fig. 10.2(f).

This section introduced the basics of DOM tree traversal and manipulation. Next, we introduce the concept of collections, which give you access to multiple elements in a page.

10.4 DOM Collections

Included in the Document Object Model is the notion of *collections*, which are groups of related objects on a page. DOM collections are accessed as properties of DOM objects such as the document object or a DOM node. The document object has properties containing the *images collection*, *links collection*, *forms collection* and *anchors collection*. These collections contain all the elements of the corresponding type on the page. Figure 10.3 gives an example that uses the links collection to extract all of the links on a page and display them together at the bottom of the page.

```
1   <?xml version = "1.0" encoding = "utf-8"?>
2   <!DOCTYPE html PUBLIC "-//W3C//DTD XHTML 1.0 Strict//EN"
3      "http://www.w3.org/TR/xhtml11/DTD/xhtml11-strict.dtd">
4
5   <!-- Fig. 10.3: collections.html -->
6   <!-- Using the links collection. -->
7   <html xmlns = "http://www.w3.org/1999/xhtml">
8      <head>
9         <title>Using Links Collection</title>
10        <style type = "text/css">
11           body          { font-family: arial, helvetica, sans-serif }
12           h1            { font-family: tahoma, geneva, sans-serif;
13                           text-align: center }
14           p             { margin: 5% }
15           p a           { color: #aa0000 }
16           .links        { font-size: 14px;
17                           text-align: justify;
18                           margin-left: 10%;
19                           margin-right: 10% }
20           .link a       { text-decoration: none }
21           .link a:hover { text-decoration: underline }
22        </style>
23        <script type = "text/javascript">
24           <!--
25           function processlinks()
26           {
27              var linkslist = document.links; // get the document's links
28              var contents = "Links in this page:\n<br />| ";
29
30              // concatenate each link to contents
31              for ( var i = 0; i < linkslist.length; i++ )
32              {
```

Fig. 10.3 | Using the links collection. (Part 1 of 2.)

```
33                        var currentLink = linkslist[ i ];
34                        contents += "<span class = 'link'>" +
35                            currentLink.innerHTML.link( currentLink.href ) +
36                            "</span> | ";
37                    } // end for
38
39                    document.getElementById( "links" ).innerHTML = contents;
40                } // end function processlinks
41                // -->
42            </script>
43        </head>
44        <body onload = "processlinks()">
45            <h1>Deitel Resource Centers</h1>
46            <p><a href = "http://www.deitel.com/">Deitel's website</a> contains
47                a rapidly growing
48                <a href = "http://www.deitel.com/ResourceCenters.html">list of
49                Resource Centers</a> on a wide range of topics. Many Resource
50                centers related to topics covered in this book,
51                <a href = "http://www.deitel.com/iw3htp4">Internet and World Wide
52                Web How to Program, 4th Edition</a>. We have Resouce Centers on
53                <a href = "http://www.deitel.com/Web2.0">Web 2.0</a>,
54                <a href = "http://www.deitel.com/Firefox">Firefox</a> and
55                <a href = "http://www.deitel.com/IE7">Internet Explorer 7</a>,
56                <a href = "http://www.deitel.com/XHTML">XHTML</a>, and
57                <a href = "http://www.deitel.com/JavaScript">JavaScript</a>.
58                Watch the list of Deitel Resource Centers for related new
59                Resource Centers.</p>
60            <div id = "links" class = "links"></div>
61        </body>
62    </html>
```

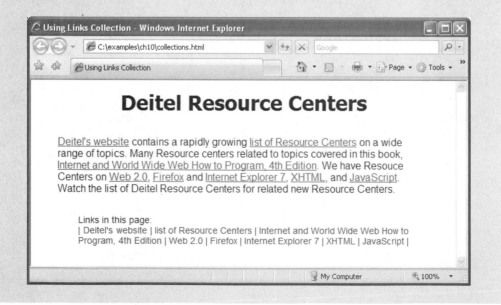

Fig. 10.3 | Using the links collection. (Part 2 of 2.)

The XHTML body contains a paragraph (lines 46–59) with links at various places in the text and an empty div (line 60) with id links. The body's onload attribute specifies that the processlinks method is called when the body finishes loading.

Method processlinks declares variable linkslist (line 27) to store the document's links collection, which is accessed as the links property of the document object. Line 28 creates the string (contents) that will contain all the document's links, to be inserted into the links div later. Line 31 begins a for statement to iterate through each link. To find the number of elements in the collection, we use the collection's *length property*.

Line 33 inside the for statement creates a variable (currentlink) that stores the current link. Note that we can access the collection stored in linkslist using indices in square brackets, just as we did with arrays. DOM collections are stored in objects which have only one property and two methods—the length property, the *item method* and the *namedItem method*. The item method—an alternative to the square bracketed indices—can be used to access specific elements in a collection by taking an index as an argument. The namedItem method takes a name as a parameter and finds the element in the collection, if any, whose id attribute or name attribute matches it.

Lines 34–36 add a span element to the contents string containing the current link. Recall that the link method of a string object returns the string as a link to the URL passed to the method. Line 35 uses the link method to create an a (anchor) element containing the proper text and href attribute.

Notice that variable currentLink (a DOM node representing an a element) has a specialized *href property* to refer to the link's href attribute. Many types of XHTML elements are represented by special types of nodes that extend the functionality of a basic DOM node. Line 39 inserts the contents into the empty div with id "links" (line 60) in order to show all the links on the page in one location.

Collections allow easy access to all elements of a single type in a page. This is useful for gathering elements into one place and for applying changes across an entire page. For example, the forms collection could be used to disable all form inputs after a submit button has been pressed to avoid multiple submissions while the next page loads. The next section discusses how to dynamically modify CSS styles using JavaScript and DOM nodes.

10.5 Dynamic Styles

An element's style can be changed dynamically. Often such a change is made in response to user events, which we discuss in Chapter 11. Such style changes can create many effects, including mouse hover effects, interactive menus, and animations. Figure 10.4 is a simple example that changes the background-color style property in response to user input.

```
1   <?xml version = "1.0" encoding = "utf-8"?>
2   <!DOCTYPE html PUBLIC "-//W3C//DTD XHTML 1.0 Strict//EN"
3      "http://www.w3.org/TR/xhtml1/DTD/xhtml1-strict.dtd">
4
5   <!-- Fig. 10.4: dynamicstyle.html -->
6   <!-- Dynamic styles. -->
7   <html xmlns = "http://www.w3.org/1999/xhtml">
8      <head>
```

Fig. 10.4 | Dynamic styles. (Part 1 of 2.)

```
 9          <title>Dynamic Styles</title>
10          <script type = "text/javascript">
11             <!--
12             function start()
13             {
14                var inputColor = prompt( "Enter a color name for the " +
15                   "background of this page", "" );
16                document.body.style.backgroundColor = inputColor;
17             } // end function start
18             // -->
19          </script>
20       </head>
21       <body id = "body" onload = "start()">
22          <p>Welcome to our website!</p>
23       </body>
24    </html>
```

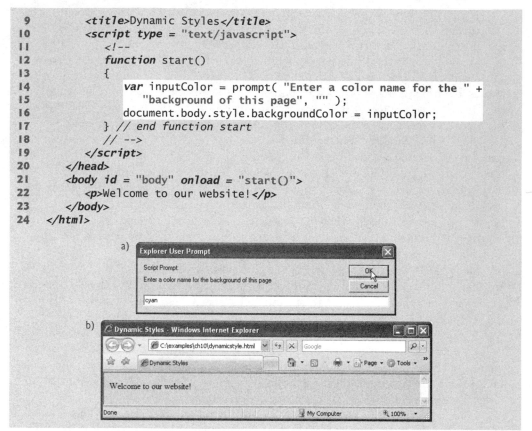

Fig. 10.4 | Dynamic styles. (Part 2 of 2.)

Function start (lines 12–17) prompts the user to enter a color name, then sets the background color to that value. [*Note:* An error occurs if the value entered is not a valid color.] We refer to the background color as document.body.style.backgroundColor— the **body** *property* of the document object refers to the body element. We then use the style property (a property of most XHTML elements) to set the background-color CSS property. This is referred to as backgroundColor in JavaScript—the hyphen is removed to avoid confusion with the subtraction (-) operator. This naming convention is consistent for most CSS properties. For example, borderWidth correlates to the border-width CSS property, and fontFamily correlates to the font-family CSS property. In general, CSS properties are accessed in the format *node*.style.*styleproperty*.

Figure 10.5 introduces the setInterval and clearInterval methods of the window object, combining them with dynamic styles to create animated effects. This example is a basic image viewer that allows you to select a Deitel book cover and view it in a larger size. When one of the thumbnail images on the right is clicked, the larger version grows from the top-left corner of the main image area.

The body (lines 66–85) contains two div elements, both floated left using styles defined in lines 14 and 17 in order to present them side by side. The left div contains the full-size image iw3htp4.jpg, which appears when the page loads. The right div contains six thumbnail images which respond to the click event by calling the `display` method and passing it the filename of the corresponding full-size image.

The `display` function (lines 46–62) dynamically updates the image in the left `div` to the one corresponding to the user's click. Lines 48–49 prevent the rest of the function from executing if `interval` is defined (i.e., an animation is in progress.) Line 51 gets the left `div` by its `id`, `imgCover`. Line 52 creates a new `img` element. Lines 53–55 set its `id` to `imgCover`, set its `src` to the correct image file in the `fullsize` directory, and set its required `alt` attribute. Lines 56–59 do some additional initialization before beginning the animation in line 61. To create the growing animation effect, lines 57–58 set the image `width` and `height` to 0. Line 59 replaces the current `bigImage` node with `newNode` (created in line 52), and line 60 sets `count`, the variable that controls the animation, to 0.

Line 61 introduces the `window` object's ***setInterval*** *method*, which starts the animation. This method takes two parameters—a statement to execute repeatedly, and an integer specifying how often to execute it, in milliseconds. We use `setInterval` to call

```
 1    <?xml version = "1.0" encoding = "utf-8"?>
 2    <!DOCTYPE html PUBLIC "-//W3C//DTD XHTML 1.0 Strict//EN"
 3        "http://www.w3.org/TR/xhtml1/DTD/xhtml1-strict.dtd">
 4
 5    <!-- Fig. 10.5: coverviewer.html -->
 6    <!-- Dynamic styles used for animation. -->
 7    <html xmlns = "http://www.w3.org/1999/xhtml">
 8       <head>
 9          <title>Deitel Book Cover Viewer</title>
10          <style type = "text/css">
11             .thumbs    { width: 192px;
12                          height: 370px;
13                          padding: 5px;
14                          float: left }
15             .mainimg   { width: 289px;
16                          padding: 5px;
17                          float: left }
18             .imgCover { height: 373px }
19             img        { border: 1px solid black }
20          </style>
21          <script type = "text/javascript">
22             <!--
23             var interval = null; // keeps track of the interval
24             var speed = 6; // determines the speed of the animation
25             var count = 0; // size of the image during the animation
26
27             // called repeatedly to animate the book cover
28             function run()
29             {
30                count += speed;
31
32                // stop the animation when the image is large enough
33                if ( count >= 375 )
34                {
```

Fig. 10.5 | Dynamic styles used for animation. (Part 1 of 4.)

```
35              window.clearInterval( interval );
36              interval = null;
37           } // end if
38
39           var bigImage = document.getElementById( "imgCover" );
40           bigImage.style.width = .7656 * count + "px";
41           bigImage.style.height = count + "px";
42        } // end function run
43
44        // inserts the proper image into the main image area and
45        // begins the animation
46        function display( imgfile )
47        {
48           if ( interval )
49              return;
50
51           var bigImage = document.getElementById( "imgCover" );
52           var newNode = document.createElement( "img" );
53           newNode.id = "imgCover";
54           newNode.src = "fullsize/" + imgfile;
55           newNode.alt = "Large image";
56           newNode.className = "imgCover";
57           newNode.style.width = "0px";
58           newNode.style.height = "0px";
59           bigImage.parentNode.replaceChild( newNode, bigImage );
60           count = 0; // start the image at size 0
61           interval = window.setInterval( "run()", 10 ); // animate
62        } // end function display
63        // -->
64     </script>
65  </head>
66  <body>
67     <div id = "mainimg" class = "mainimg">
68        <img id = "imgCover" src = "fullsize/iw3htp4.jpg"
69           alt = "Full cover image" class = "imgCover" />
70     </div>
71     <div id = "thumbs" class = "thumbs" >
72        <img src = "thumbs/iw3htp4.jpg" alt = "iw3htp4"
73           onclick = "display( 'iw3htp4.jpg' )" />
74        <img src = "thumbs/chtp5.jpg" alt = "chtp5"
75           onclick = "display( 'chtp5.jpg' )" />
76        <img src = "thumbs/cpphtp6.jpg" alt = "cpphtp6"
77           onclick = "display( 'cpphtp6.jpg' )" />
78        <img src = "thumbs/jhtp7.jpg" alt = "jhtp7"
79           onclick = "display( 'jhtp7.jpg' )" />
80        <img src = "thumbs/vbhtp3.jpg" alt = "vbhtp3"
81           onclick = "display( 'vbhtp3.jpg' )" />
82        <img src = "thumbs/vcsharphtp2.jpg" alt = "vcsharphtp2"
83           onclick = "display( 'vcsharphtp2.jpg' )" />
84     </div>
85  </body>
86 </html>
```

Fig. 10.5 | Dynamic styles used for animation. (Part 2 of 4.)

a) The cover viewer page loads with the cover of this book.

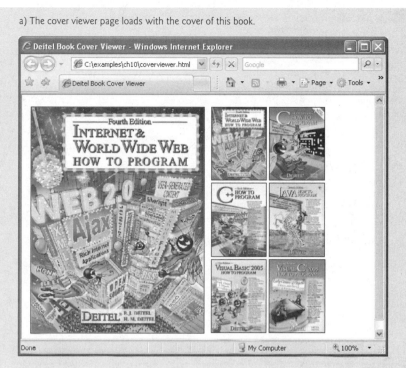

b) When the user clicks the thumbnail of *C How to Program*, the full-size image begins growing from the top-left corner of the window.

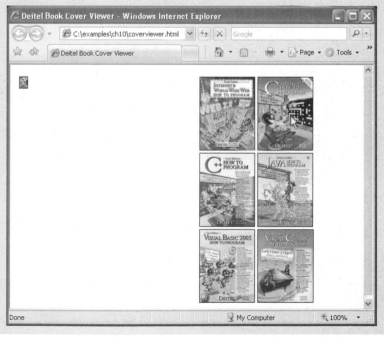

Fig. 10.5 | Dynamic styles used for animation. (Part 3 of 4.)

c) The cover continues to grow.

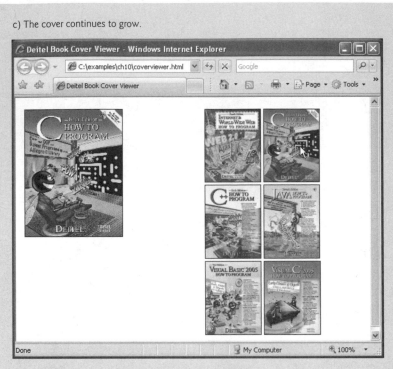

d) The animation finishes when the cover reaches its full size.

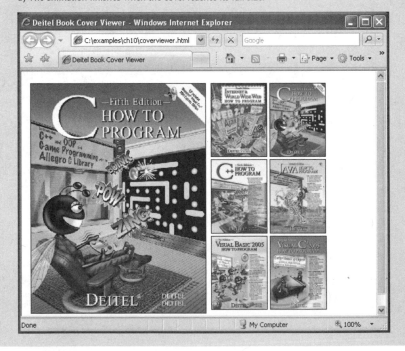

Fig. 10.5 | Dynamic styles used for animation. (Part 4 of 4.)

function run every 10 milliseconds. The setInterval method returns a unique identifier to keep track of that particular interval—we assign this identifier to the variable interval. We use this identifier to stop the animation when the image has finished growing.

The run function, defined in lines 28–42, increases the height of the image by the value of speed and updates its width accordingly to keep the aspect ratio consistent. Because the run function is called every 10 milliseconds, this increase happens repeatedly to create an animated growing effect. Line 30 adds the value of speed (declared and initialized to 6 in line 24) to count, which keeps track of the animation's progress and dictates the current size of the image. If the image has grown to its full height (375), line 35 uses the window's *clearInterval method* to stop the repetitive calls of the run method. We pass to clearInterval the interval identifier (stored in interval) that setInterval created in line 61. Although it seems unnecessary in this script, this identifier allows the script to keep track of multiple intervals running at the same time and to choose which interval to stop when calling clearInterval.

Line 39 gets the image and lines 40–41 set its width and height CSS properties. Note that line 40 multiplies count by a scaling factor of .7656 in order to keep the ratio of the image's dimensions consistent with the actual dimensions of the image. Run the code example and click on a thumbnail image to see the full animation effect.

This section demonstrated the concept of dynamically changing CSS styles using JavaScript and the DOM. We also discussed the basics of how to create scripted animations using setInterval and clearInterval.

10.6 Summary of the DOM Objects and Collections

As you've seen in the preceding sections, the objects and collections in the W3C DOM give you flexibility in manipulating the elements of a web page. We've shown how to access the objects in a page, how to access the objects in a collection, and how to change element styles dynamically.

The W3C DOM allows you to access every element in an XHTML document. Each element in a document is represented by a separate object. The diagram in Fig. 10.6 shows many of the important objects and collections provided by the W3C DOM. Figure 10.7 provides a brief description of each object and collection in Fig. 10.6.

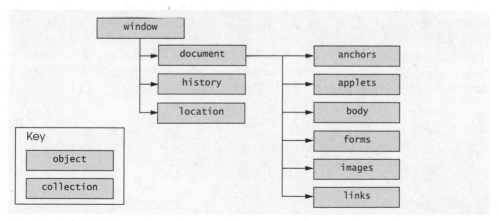

Fig. 10.6 | W3C Document Object Model.

Object or collection	Description
Objects	
window	Represents the browser window and provides access to the window's document object. Also contains history and location objects.
document	Represents the XHTML document rendered in a window. Provides access to every element in the document and allows dynamic modification of it. Contains collections for accessing all elements of a given type.
body	Provides access to the body element of an XHTML document.
history	Keeps track of the sites visited by the browser user. The object provides a script programmer with the ability to move forward and backward through the visited sites.
location	Contains the URL of the rendered document. When this object is set to a new URL, the browser immediately navigates to the new location.
Collections	
anchors	Collection contains all the anchor elements (a) that have a name or id attribute. The elements appear in the collection in the order in which they were defined in the XHTML document.
forms	Contains all the form elements in the XHTML document. The elements appear in the collection in the order in which they were defined in the XHTML document.
images	Contains all the img elements in the XHTML document. The elements appear in the collection in the order in which they were defined in the XHTML document.
links	Contains all the anchor elements (a) with an href property. The elements appear in the collection in the order in which they were defined in the XHTML document.

Fig. 10.7 | Objects and collections in the W3C Document Object Model.

For a complete reference on the W3C Document Object Model, see the DOM Level 3 recommendation from the W3C at http://www.w3.org/TR/DOM-Level-3-Core/. The DOM Level 2 HTML Specification (the most recent HTML DOM standard), available at http://www.w3.org/TR/DOM-Level-2-HTML/, describes additional DOM functionality specific to HTML, such as objects for various types of XHTML elements. Keep in mind that not all web browsers implement all features included in the specification.

JavaScript: Events

OBJECTIVES

In this chapter you'll learn:

- The concepts of events, event handlers and event hubbling.

- To create and register event handlers that respond to mouse and keyboard events.

- To use the event object to get information about an event.

- To recognize and respond to common events, including onload, onmousemove, onmouseover, onmouseout, onfocus, onblur, onsubmit and onreset.

11.1 Introduction

We've seen that XHTML pages can be controlled via scripting, and we've already used a few events to trigger scripts, such as the onclick and onsubmit events. This chapter goes into more detail on *JavaScript events*, which allow scripts to respond to user interactions and modify the page accordingly. Events allow scripts to respond to a user who is moving the mouse, entering form data or pressing keys. Events and event handling help make web applications more responsive, dynamic and interactive.

In this chapter, we discuss how to set up functions to react when an event *fires* (occurs). We give examples of event handling for nine common events, including mouse events and form-processing events. A the end of the chapter, we provide a table of the events covered in this chapter and other useful events.

11.2 Registering Event Handlers

Functions that handle events are called *event handlers*. Assigning an event handler to an event on a DOM node is called *registering an event handler*. Previously, we have registered event handlers using the *inline model*, treating events as attributes of XHTML elements (e.g., <p onclick = "myfunction()">). Another model, known as the *traditional model*, for registering event handlers is demonstrated alongside the inline model in Fig. 11.1.

In the earliest event-capable browsers, the inline model was the only way to handle events. Later, Netscape developed the traditional model and Internet Explorer adopted it. Since then, both Netscape and Microsoft have developed separate (incompatible) advanced event models with more functionality than either the inline or the traditional model. Netscape's advanced model was adapted by the W3C to create a DOM Events Specification. Most browsers support the W3C model, but Internet Explorer 7 does not.

```
1   <?xml version = "1.0" encoding = "utf-8"?>
2   <!DOCTYPE html PUBLIC "-//W3C//DTD XHTML 1.0 Strict//EN"
3      "http://www.w3.org/TR/xhtml1/DTD/xhtml1-strict.dtd">
4
5   <!-- Fig. 11.1: registering.html -->
6   <!-- Event registration models. -->
```

Fig. 11.1 | Event registration models. (Part 1 of 3.)

```
7   <html xmlns = "http://www.w3.org/1999/xhtml">
8      <head>
9         <title>Event Registration Models</title>
10        <style type = "text/css">
11           div { padding: 5px;
12                 margin: 10px;
13                 border: 3px solid #0000BB;
14                 width: 12em }
15        </style>
16        <script type = "text/javascript">
17           <!--
18           // handle the onclick event regardless of how it was registered
19           function handleEvent()
20           {
21              alert( "The event was successfully handled." );
22           } // end function handleEvent
23
24           // register the handler using the traditional model
25           function registerHandler()
26           {
27              var traditional = document.getElementById( "traditional" );
28              traditional.onclick = handleEvent;
29           } // end function registerHandler
30           // -->
31        </script>
32     </head>
33     <body onload = "registerHandler()">
34        <!-- The event handler is registered inline -->
35        <div id = "inline" onclick = "handleEvent()">
36           Inline registration model</div>
37
38        <!-- The event handler is registered by function registerHandler -->
39        <div id = "traditional">Traditional registration model</div>
40     </body>
41  </html>
```

a) The user clicks the **div** for which the event handler was registered using the inline model.

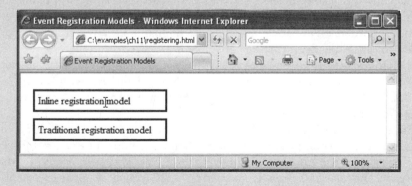

Fig. 11.1 | Event registration models. (Part 2 of 3.)

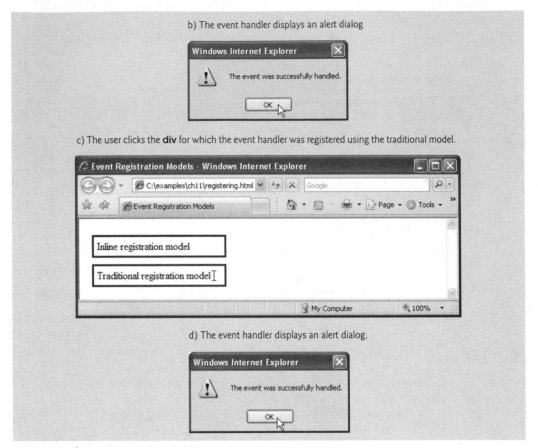

Fig. 11.1 | Event registration models. (Part 3 of 3.)

This means that to create cross-browser websites, we are mostly limited to the traditional and inline event models. While the advanced models provide more convenience and functionality, most of the features can be implemented with the traditional model.

Line 35 assigns "handleEvent()" to the onclick attribute of the div in lines 35–36. This is the inline model for event registration we've seen in previous examples. The div in line 39 is assigned an event handler using the traditional model. When the body element (lines 33–40) loads, the registerHandler function is called.

Function registerHandler (lines 25–29) uses JavaScript to register the function handleEvent as the event handler for the onclick event of the div with the id "traditional". Line 27 gets the div, and line 28 assigns the function handleEvent to the div's onclick property.

Notice that in line 28, we do not put handleEvent in quotes or include parentheses at the end of the function name, as we do in the inline model in line 35. In the inline model, the value of the XHTML attribute is a *JavaScript statement* to execute when the event occurs. The value of the onclick property of a DOM node is not an executable statement, but the name of a *function* to be called when the event occurs. Recall that JavaScript functions can be treated as data (i.e., passed into methods, assigned to variables, etc.).

Common Programming Error 11.1

Putting quotes around the function name when registering it using the inline model would assign a string to the onclick *property of the node—a string cannot be called.*

Common Programming Error 11.2

Putting parentheses after the function name when registering it using the inline model would call the function immediately and assign its return value to the onclick *property.*

Once the event handler is registered in line 28, the div in line 39 has the same behavior as the div in lines 35–36, because handleEvent (lines 19–22) is set to handle the onclick event for both divs. When either div is clicked, an alert will display "The event was successfully handled."

The traditional model allows us to register event handlers in JavaScript code. This has important implications for what we can do with JavaScript events. For example, traditional event-handler registration allows us to assign event handlers to many elements quickly and easily using repetition statements, instead of adding an inline event handler to each XHTML element. In the remaining examples in this chapter, we use both the inline and traditional registration models depending on which is more convenient.

11.3 Event onload

The onload event fires whenever an element finishes loading successfully (i.e., all its children are loaded). Frequently, this event is used in the body element to initiate a script after the page loads in the client's browser. Figure 11.2 uses the onload event for this purpose. The script called by the onload event updates a timer that indicates how many seconds have elapsed since the document was loaded.

```
1   <?xml version = "1.0" encoding = "utf-8"?>
2   <!DOCTYPE html PUBLIC "-//W3C//DTD XHTML 1.0 Strict//EN"
3       "http://www.w3.org/TR/xhtml1/DTD/xhtml1-strict.dtd">
4
5   <!-- Fig. 11.2: onload.html -->
6   <!-- Demonstrating the onload event. -->
7   <html xmlns = "http://www.w3.org/1999/xhtml">
8      <head>
9         <title>onload Event</title>
10        <script type = "text/javascript">
11           <!--
12           var seconds = 0;
13
14           // called when the page loads to begin the timer
15           function startTimer()
16           {
17              // 1000 milliseconds = 1 second
18              window.setInterval( "updateTime()", 1000 );
19           } // end function startTimer
20
```

Fig. 11.2 | Demonstrating the onload event. (Part 1 of 2.)

```
21              // called every 1000 ms to update the timer
22              function updateTime()
23              {
24                  ++seconds;
25                  document.getElementById( "soFar" ).innerHTML = seconds;
26              } // end function updateTime
27              // -->
28          </script>
29      </head>
30      <body onload = "startTimer()">
31          <p>Seconds you have spent viewing this page so far:
32          <strong id = "soFar">0</strong></p>
33      </body>
34  </html>
```

```
onload Event - Windows Internet Explorer
C:\examples\ch11\onload.html    Google
onload Event                    Page ▾  Tools ▾

Seconds you have spent viewing this page so far: 12

                              My Computer        100%
```

Fig. 11.2 | Demonstrating the `onload` event. (Part 2 of 2.)

Our use of the `onload` event occurs in line 30. After the `body` section loads, the browser triggers the `onload` event. This calls function `startTimer` (lines 15–19), which in turn uses method `window.setInterval` to specify that function `updateTime` (lines 22–26) should be called every 1000 milliseconds. The `updateTime` function increments variable `seconds` and updates the counter on the page.

Note that we could not have created this program without the onload event, because elements in the XHTML page cannot be accessed until the page has loaded. If a script in the head attempts to get a DOM node for an XHTML element in the body, `getElement-ById` returns `null` because the body has not yet loaded. Other uses of the `onload` event include opening a pop-up window once a page has loaded and triggering a script when an image or Java applet loads.

Common Programming Error 11.3

Trying to get an element in a page before the page has loaded is a common error. Avoid this by putting your script in a function using the `onload` event to call the function.

11.4 Event `onmousemove`, the event Object and `this`

This section introduces the `onmousemove` event, which fires repeatedly whenever the user moves the mouse over the web page. We also discuss the `event` object and the keyword `this`, which permit more advanced event-handling capabilities. Figure 11.3 uses `on-mousemove` and `this` to create a simple drawing program that allows the user to draw inside a box in red or blue by holding down the *Shift* or *Ctrl* keys.

The XHTML body has a table with a tbody containing one row that gives the user instructions on how to use the program. The body's onload attribute (line 61) calls function createCanvas, which initializes the program by filling in the table.

The createCanvas function (lines 23–41) fills in the table with a grid of cells. The CSS rule in lines 14–15 sets the width and height of every td element to 4px. Line 11

```
1   <?xml version = "1.0" encoding = "utf-8"?>
2   <!DOCTYPE html PUBLIC "-//W3C//DTD XHTML 1.0 Strict//EN"
3       "http://www.w3.org/TR/xhtml11/DTD/xhtml11-strict.dtd">
4
5   <!-- Fig. 11.3: draw.html -->
6   <!-- A simple drawing program. -->
7   <html xmlns = "http://www.w3.org/1999/xhtml">
8      <head>
9         <title>Simple Drawing Program</title>
10        <style type = "text/css">
11           #canvas { width: 400px;
12                     border: 1px solid #999999;
13                     border-collapse: collapse }
14           td      { width: 4px;
15                     height: 4px }
16           th.key  { font-family: arial, helvetica, sans-serif;
17                     font-size: 12px;
18                     border-bottom: 1px solid #999999 }
19        </style>
20        <script type = "text/javascript">
21           <!--
22           //initialization function to insert cells into the table
23           function createCanvas ()
24           {
25              var side = 100;
26              var tbody = document.getElementById( "tablebody" );
27
28              for ( var i = 0; i < side; i++ )
29              {
30                 var row = document.createElement( "tr" );
31
32                 for ( var j = 0; j < side; j++ )
33                 {
34                    var cell = document.createElement( "td" );
35                    cell.onmousemove = processMouseMove;
36                    row.appendChild( cell );
37                 } // end for
38
39                 tbody.appendChild( row );
40              } // end for
41           } // end function createCanvas
42
43           // processes the onmousemove event
44           function processMouseMove( e )
45           {
```

Fig. 11.3 | Simple drawing program. (Part 1 of 3.)

```
46              // get the event object from IE
47              if ( !e )
48                  var e = window.event;
49
50              // turn the cell blue if the Ctrl key is pressed
51              if ( e.ctrlKey )
52                  this.style.backgroundColor = "blue";
53
54              // turn the cell red if the Shift key is pressed
55              if ( e.shiftKey )
56                  this.style.backgroundColor = "red";
57          } // end function processMouseMove
58          // -->
59      </script>
60   </head>
61   <body onload = "createCanvas()">
62      <table id = "canvas" class = "canvas"><tbody id = "tablebody">
63      <tr><th class = "key" colspan = "100">Hold <tt>ctrl</tt>
64          to draw blue. Hold <tt>shift</tt> to draw red.</th></tr>
65      </tbody></table>
66   </body>
67 </html>
```

a) The page loads and fills with white cells. With no keys held down, moving the mouse does not draw anything.

b) The user holds the *Ctrl* key and moves the mouse to draw a blue line.

Fig. 11.3 | Simple drawing program. (Part 2 of 3.)

c) The user holds the *Shift* key and moves the mouse to draw a red line.

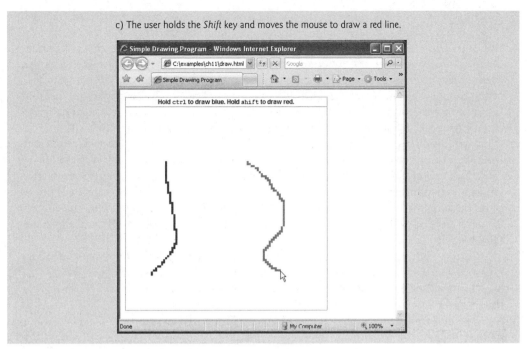

Fig. 11.3 | Simple drawing program. (Part 3 of 3.)

dictates that the table is 400px wide. Line 13 uses the border-collapse CSS property to eliminate space between the table cells.

Line 25 defines variable side, which determines the number of cells in each row and the number of rows created by the nested for statements in lines 28–40. We set side to 100 in order to fill the table with 10,000 4px cells. Line 26 stores the tbody element so that we can append rows to it as they are generated.

 Common Programming Error 11.4

Although you can omit the tbody element in an XHTML table, without it you cannot append tr elements as children of a table using JavaScript. While Firefox treats appended rows as members of the table body, Internet Explorer will not render any table cells that are dynamically added to a table outside a thead, tbody or tfoot element.

The nested for statements in lines 28–40 fill the table with a 100 × 100 grid of cells. The outer loop creates each table row, while the inner loop creates each cell. The inner loop uses the createElement method to create a table cell, assigns function process-MouseMove as the event handler for the cell's onmousemove event and appends the cell as a child of the row. The ***onmousemove event*** of an element fires whenever the user moves the mouse over that element.

At this point, the program is initialized and simply calls processMouseMove whenever the mouse moves over any table cell. The function processMouseMove (lines 44–57) colors the cell the mouse moves over, depending on the key that is pressed when the event occurs. Lines 44–48 get the ***event object***, which stores information about the event that called the event-handling function.

Internet Explorer and Firefox do not implement the same event models, so we need to account for some differences in how the event object can be handled and used. Firefox and other W3C-compliant browsers (e.g., Safari, Opera) pass the event object as an argument to the event-handling function. Internet Explorer, on the other hand, stores the event object in the event property of the window object. To get the event object regardless of the browser, we use a two-step process. Function processMouseMove takes the parameter e in line 44 to get the event object from Firefox. Then, if e is undefined (i.e., if the client is Internet Explorer), we assign the object in window.event to e in line 48.

In addition to providing different ways to access the event object, Firefox and Internet Explorer also implement different functionality in the event object itself. However, there are several event properties that both browsers implement with the same name, and some that both browsers implement with different names. In this book, we use properties that are implemented in both event models, or we write our code to use the correct property depending on the browser—all of our code runs properly in IE7 and Firefox 2 (and higher).

Once e contains the event object, we can use it to get information about the event. Lines 51–56 do the actual drawing. The event object's ***ctrlKey*** *property* contains a boolean which reflects whether the *Ctrl* key was pressed during the event. If ctrlKey is true, line 52 executes, changing the color of a table cell.

To determine which table cell to color, we introduce the ***this*** *keyword*. The meaning of this depends on its context. In an event-handling function, this refers to the DOM object on which the event occurred. Our function uses this to refer to the table cell over which the mouse moved. The this keyword allows us to use one event handler to apply a change to one of many DOM elements, depending on which one received the event.

Lines 51–52 change the background color of this table cell to blue if the *Ctrl* key is pressed during the event. Similarly, lines 55–56 color the cell red if the *Shift* key is pressed. To determine this, we use the ***shiftKey*** *property* of the event object. This simple function allows the user to draw inside the table on the page in red and blue.

This example demonstrated the ctrlKey and shiftKey properties of the event object. Figure 11.4 lists some important cross-browser properties of the event object.

This section introduced the event onmousemove and the keyword this. We also discussed more advanced event handling using the event object to get information about the event. The next section continues our introduction of events with the onmouseover and onmouseout events.

Property	Description
altKey	This value is true if the *Alt* key was pressed when the event fired.
cancelBubble	Set to true to prevent the event from bubbling. Defaults to false. (See Section 11.8, Event Bubbling.)
clientX and clientY	The coordinates of the mouse cursor inside the client area (i.e., the active area where the web page is displayed, excluding scrollbars, navigation buttons, etc.).

Fig. 11.4 | Some event object properties. (Part 1 of 2.)

Property	Description
`ctrlKey`	This value is true if the *Ctrl* key was pressed when the event fired.
`keyCode`	The ASCII code of the key pressed in a keyboard event.
`screenX` and `screenY`	The coordinates of the mouse cursor on the screen coordinate system.
`shiftKey`	This value is true if the *Shift* key was pressed when the event fired.
`type`	The name of the event that fired, without the prefix "on".

Fig. 11.4 | Some event object properties. (Part 2 of 2.)

11.5 Rollovers with onmouseover and onmouseout

Two more events fired by mouse movements are onmouseover and onmouseout. When the mouse cursor moves into an element, an ***onmouseover event*** occurs for that element. When the cursor leaves the element, an ***onmouseout event*** occurs. Figure 11.5 uses these events to achieve a *rollover effect* that updates text when the mouse cursor moves over it. We also introduce a technique for creating rollover images.

```
1   <?xml version = "1.0" encoding = "utf-8"?>
2   <!DOCTYPE html PUBLIC "-//W3C//DTD XHTML 1.0 Strict//EN"
3      "http://www.w3.org/TR/xhtml1/DTD/xhtml1-strict.dtd">
4
5   <!-- Fig. 11.5: onmouseoverout.html -->
6   <!-- Events onmouseover and onmouseout. -->
7   <html xmlns = "http://www.w3.org/1999/xhtml">
8      <head>
9         <title>Events onmouseover and onmouseout</title>
10        <style type = "text/css">
11           body  { background-color: wheat }
12           table { border-style: groove;
13                   text-align: center;
14                   font-family: monospace;
15                   font-weight: bold }
16           td    { width: 6em }
17        </style>
18        <script type = "text/javascript">
19           <!--
20           image1 = new Image();
21           image1.src = "heading1.gif";
22           image2 = new Image();
23           image2.src = "heading2.gif";
24
25           function mouseOver( e )
26           {
27              if ( !e )
28                 var e = window.event;
```

Fig. 11.5 | Events onmouseover and onmouseout. (Part 1 of 4.)

```
29
30              var target = getTarget( e );
31
32              // swap the image when the mouse moves over it
33              if ( target.id == "heading" )
34              {
35                  target.src = image2.src;
36                  return;
37              } // end if
38
39              // if an element's id is defined, assign the id to its color
40              // to turn hex code's text the corresponding color
41              if ( target.id )
42                  target.style.color = target.id;
43          } // end function mouseOver
44
45          function mouseOut( e )
46          {
47              if ( !e )
48                  var e = window.event;
49
50              var target = getTarget( e );
51
52              // put the original image back when the mouse moves away
53              if ( target.id == "heading" )
54              {
55                  target.src = image1.src;
56                  return;
57              } // end if
58
59              // if an element's id is defined, assign id to innerHTML
60              // to display the color name
61              if ( target.id )
62                  target.innerHTML = target.id;
63          } // end function mouseOut
64
65          // return either e.srcElement or e.target, whichever exists
66          function getTarget( e )
67          {
68              if ( e.srcElement )
69                  return e.srcElement;
70              else
71                  return e.target;
72          } // end function getTarget
73
74          document.onmouseover = mouseOver;
75          document.onmouseout = mouseOut;
76          // -->
77      </script>
78  </head>
79  <body>
80      <img src = "heading1.gif" id = "heading" alt = "Heading Image" />
```

Fig. 11.5 | Events onmouseover and onmouseout. (Part 2 of 4.)

```
81      <p>Can you tell a color from its hexadecimal RGB code
82      value? Look at the hex code, guess its color. To see
83      what color it corresponds to, move the mouse over the
84      hex code. Moving the mouse out of the hex code's table
85      cell will display the color name.</p>
86      <table>
87         <tr>
88            <td id = "Black">#000000</td>
89            <td id = "Blue">#0000FF</td>
90            <td id = "Magenta">#FF00FF</td>
91            <td id = "Gray">#808080</td>
92         </tr>
93         <tr>
94            <td id = "Green">#008000</td>
95            <td id = "Lime">#00FF00</td>
96            <td id = "Maroon">#800000</td>
97            <td id = "Navy">#000080</td>
98         </tr>
99         <tr>
100           <td id = "Olive">#808000</td>
101           <td id = "Purple">#800080</td>
102           <td id = "Red">#FF0000</td>
103           <td id = "Silver">#C0C0C0</td>
104        </tr>
105        <tr>
106           <td id = "Cyan">#00FFFF</td>
107           <td id = "Teal">#008080</td>
108           <td id = "Yellow">#FFFF00</td>
109           <td id = "White">#FFFFFF</td>
110        </tr>
111     </table>
112  </body>
113 </html>
```

a) The page loads with the blue heading image and all the hex codes in black.

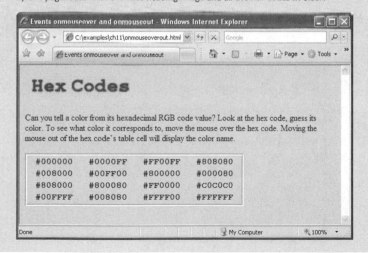

Fig. 11.5 | Events onmouseover and onmouseout. (Part 3 of 4.)

b) The heading image switches to an image with green text when the mouse rolls over it.

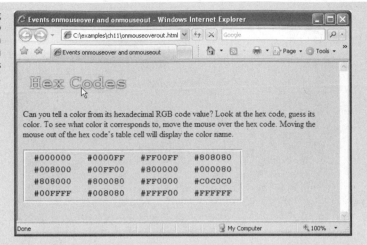

c) When mouse rolls over a hex code, the text color changes to the color represented by the hex code. Notice that the heading image has become blue again because the mouse is no longer over it.

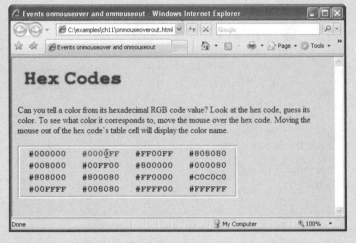

d) When the mouse leaves the hex code's table cell, the text changes to the name of the color.

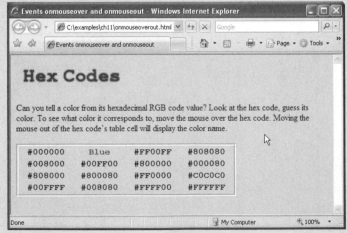

Fig. 11.5 | Events onmouseover and onmouseout. (Part 4 of 4.)

To create a rollover effect for the image in the heading, lines 20–23 create two new JavaScript Image objects—image1 and image2. Image image2 displays when the mouse hovers over the image. Image image1 displays when the mouse is outside the image. The script sets the src properties of each Image in lines 21 and 23, respectively. Creating Image objects preloads the images (i.e., loads the images in advance), so the browser does not need to download the rollover image the first time the script displays the image. If the image is large or the connection is slow, downloading would cause a noticeable delay in the image update.

Performance Tip 11.1

Preloading images used in rollover effects prevents a delay the first time an image is displayed.

Functions mouseOver and mouseOut are set to process the onmouseover and onmouseout events, respectively, in lines 74–75. Both functions begin (lines 25–28 and 45–48) by getting the event object and using function getTarget to find the element that received the action. Because of browser event model differences, we need getTarget (defined in lines 66–72) to return the DOM node targeted by the action. In Internet Explorer, this node is stored in the event object's ***srcElement property***. In Firefox, it is stored in the event object's ***target property***. Lines 68–71 return the node using the correct property to hide the browser differences from the rest of our program. We must use function getTarget instead of this because we do not define an event handler for each specific element in the document. In this case, using this would return the entire document. In both mouseOver and mouseOut, we assign the return value of getTarget to variable target (lines 30 and 50).

Lines 33–37 in the mouseOver function handle the onmouseover event for the heading image by setting its src attribute (target.src) to the src property of the appropriate Image object (image2.src). The same task occurs with image1 in the mouseOut function (lines 53–57).

The script handles the onmouseover event for the table cells in lines 41–42. This code tests whether an id is specified, which is true only for our hex code table cells and the heading image in this example. If the element receiving the action has an id, the code changes the color of the element to match the color name stored in the id. As you can see in the code for the table (lines 86–111), each td element containing a color code has an id attribute set to one of the 16 basic XHTML colors. Lines 61–62 handle the onmouseout event by changing the text in the table cell the mouse cursor just left to match the color that it represents.

11.6 Form Processing with `onfocus` and `onblur`

The onfocus and onblur events are particularly useful when dealing with form elements that allow user input (Fig. 11.6). The onfocus event fires when an element gains focus (i.e., when the user clicks a form field or uses the *Tab* key to move between form elements), and onblur fires when an element loses focus, which occurs when another control gains the focus. In lines 31–32, the script changes the text inside the div below the form (line 58) based on the messageNum passed to function helpText (lines 29–33). Each of the elements of the form, such as the name input in lines 40–41, passes a different value to the helpText function when it gains focus (and its onfocus event fires). These values are used as indices for `helpArray`, which is declared and initialized in lines 17–27 and stores help messages. When elements lose focus, they all pass the value 6 to `helpText` to clear the `tip` div (note that the empty string "" is stored in the last element of the array).

```
1   <?xml version = "1.0" encoding = "utf-8"?>
2   <!DOCTYPE html PUBLIC "-//W3C//DTD XHTML 1.0 Strict//EN"
3      "http://www.w3.org/TR/xhtml1/DTD/xhtml1-strict.dtd">
4
5   <!-- Fig. 11.6: onfocusblur.html -->
6   <!-- Demonstrating the onfocus and onblur events. -->
7   <html xmlns = "http://www.w3.org/1999/xhtml">
8      <head>
9         <title>A Form Using onfocus and onblur</title>
10        <style type = "text/css">
11           .tip { font-family: sans-serif;
12                  color: blue;
13                  font-size: 12px }
14        </style>
15        <script type = "text/javascript">
16           <!--
17           var helpArray =
18              [ "Enter your name in this input box.", // element 0
19                "Enter your e-mail address in this input box, " +
20                "in the format user@domain.", // element 1
21                "Check this box if you liked our site.", // element 2
22                "In this box, enter any comments you would " +
23                "like us to read.", // element 3
24                "This button submits the form to the " +
25                "server-side script.", // element 4
26                "This button clears the form.", // element 5
27                "" ]; // element 6
28
29           function helpText( messageNum )
30           {
31              document.getElementById( "tip" ).innerHTML =
32                 helpArray[ messageNum ];
33           } // end function helpText
34           // -->
35        </script>
36     </head>
37     <body>
38        <form id = "myForm" action = "">
39           <div>
40           Name: <input type = "text" name = "name"
41              onfocus = "helpText(0)" onblur = "helpText(6)" /><br />
42           E-mail: <input type = "text" name = "e-mail"
43              onfocus = "helpText(1)" onblur = "helpText(6)" /><br />
44           Click here if you like this site
45           <input type = "checkbox" name = "like" onfocus =
46              "helpText(2)" onblur = "helpText(6)" /><br /><hr />
47
48           Any comments?<br />
```

Fig. 11.6 | Demonstrating the onfocus and onblur events. (Part 1 of 2.)

```
49            <textarea name = "comments" rows = "5" cols = "45"
50               onfocus = "helpText(3)" onblur = "helpText(6)"></textarea>
51            <br />
52            <input type = "submit" value = "Submit" onfocus =
53               "helpText(4)" onblur = "helpText(6)" />
54            <input type = "reset" value = "Reset" onfocus =
55               "helpText(5)" onblur = "helpText(6)" />
56         </div>
57      </form>
58      <div id = "tip" class = "tip"></div>
59   </body>
60 </html>
```

a) The blue message at the bottom of the page instructs the user to enter an e-mail when the e-mail field has focus.

b) The message changes depending on which field has focus. Now it gives instructions for the comments box.

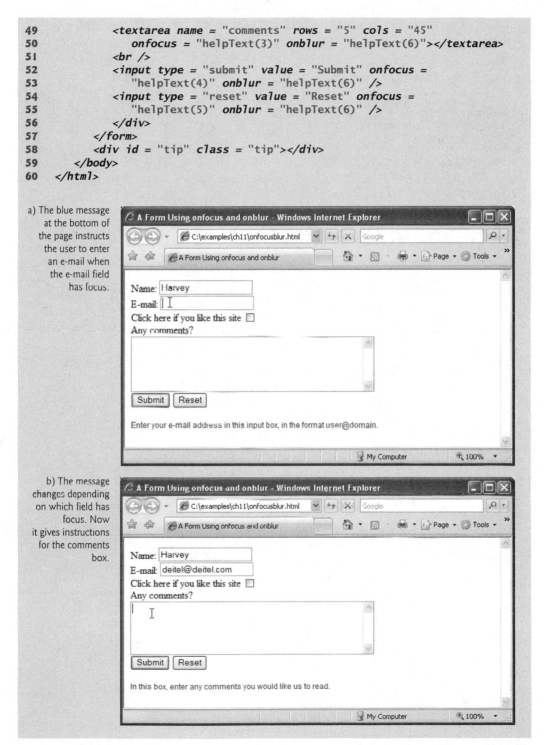

Fig. 11.6 | Demonstrating the `onfocus` and `onblur` events. (Part 2 of 2.)

11.7 Form Processing with onsubmit and onreset

Two more useful events for processing forms are onsubmit and onreset. These events fire when a form is submitted or reset, respectively (Fig. 11.7). Function registerEvents (lines 35–46) registers the event handlers for the form after the body has loaded.

```
1   <?xml version = "1.0" encoding = "utf-8"?>
2   <!DOCTYPE html PUBLIC "-//W3C//DTD XHTML 1.0 Strict//EN"
3      "http://www.w3.org/TR/xhtml11/DTD/xhtml1-strict.dtd">
4
5   <!-- Fig. 11.7: onsubmitreset.html -->
6   <!-- Demonstrating the onsubmit and onreset events. -->
7   <html xmlns = "http://www.w3.org/1999/xhtml">
8      <head>
9         <title>A Form Using onsubmit and onreset</title>
10        <style type = "text/css">
11           .tip { font-family: sans-serif;
12                  color: blue;
13                  font-size: 12px }
14        </style>
15        <script type = "text/javascript">
16           <!--
17           var helpArray =
18              [ "Enter your name in this input box.",
19                "Enter your e-mail address in this input box, " +
20                "in the format user@domain.",
21                "Check this box if you liked our site.",
22                "In this box, enter any comments you would " +
23                "like us to read.",
24                "This button submits the form to the " +
25                "server-side script.",
26                "This button clears the form.",
27                "" ];
28
29           function helpText( messageNum )
30           {
31              document.getElementById( "tip" ).innerHTML =
32                 helpArray[ messageNum ];
33           } // end function helpText
34
35           function registerEvents()
36           {
37              document.getElementById( "myForm" ).onsubmit = function()
38              {
39                 return confirm( "Are you sure you want to submit?" );
40              } // end anonymous function
41
42              document.getElementById( "myForm" ).onreset = function()
43              {
44                 return confirm( "Are you sure you want to reset?" );
45              } // end anonymous function
46           } // end function registerEvents
```

Fig. 11.7 | Demonstrating the onsubmit and onreset events. (Part 1 of 2.)

```
47              // -->
48          </script>
49      </head>
50      <body onload = "registerEvents()">
51          <form id = "myForm" action = "">
52              <div>
53              Name: <input type = "text" name = "name"
54                  onfocus = "helpText(0)" onblur = "helpText(6)" /><br />
55              E-mail: <input type = "text" name = "e-mail"
56                  onfocus = "helpText(1)" onblur = "helpText(6)" /><br />
57              Click here if you like this site
58              <input type = "checkbox" name = "like" onfocus =
59                  "helpText(2)" onblur = "helpText(6)" /><br /><hr />
60
61              Any comments?<br />
62              <textarea name = "comments" rows = "5" cols = "45"
63                  onfocus = "helpText(3)" onblur = "helpText(6)"></textarea>
64              <br />
65              <input type = "submit" value = "Submit" onfocus =
66                  "helpText(4)" onblur = "helpText(6)" />
67              <input type = "reset" value = "Reset" onfocus =
68                  "helpText(5)" onblur = "helpText(6)" />
69              </div>
70          </form>
71          <div id = "tip" class = "tip"></div>
72      </body>
73  </html>
```

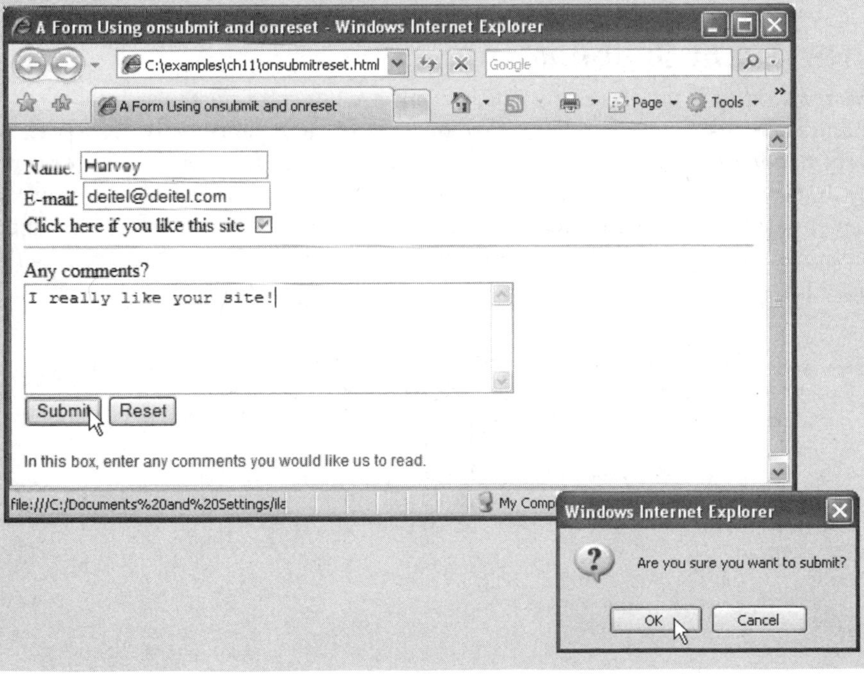

Fig. 11.7 | Demonstrating the onsubmit and onreset events. (Part 2 of 2.)

Lines 37–40 and 42–45 introduce several new concepts. Line 37 gets the form element ("myForm", lines 51–70), then lines 37–40 assign an *anonymous function* to its onsubmit property. An anonymous function is defined with no name—it is created in nearly the same way as any other function, but with no identifier after the keyword function. This notation is useful when creating a function for the sole purpose of assigning it to an event handler. We never call the function ourselves, so we don't need to give it a name, and it's more concise to create the function and register it as an event handler at the same time.

The anonymous function (lines 37–40) assigned to the onsubmit property of myForm executes in response to the user submitting the form (i.e., clicking the **Submit** button or pressing the *Enter* key). Line 39 introduces the *confirm method* of the window object. As with alert, we do not need to prefix the call with the object name window and the dot (.) operator. The confirm dialog asks the users a question, presenting them with an **OK** button and a **Cancel** button. If the user clicks **OK**, confirm returns true; otherwise, confirm returns false.

Our event handlers for the form's onsubmit and onreset events simply return the value of the confirm dialog, which asks the users if they are sure they want to submit or reset (lines 39 and 44, respectively). By returning either true or false, the event handlers dictate whether the default action for the event—in this case submitting or resetting the form—is taken. (Recall that we also returned false from some event-handling functions to prevent forms from submitting in Chapter 10.) Other default actions, such as following a hyperlink, can be prevented by returning false from an onclick event handler on the link. If an event handler returns true or does not return a value, the default action is taken once the event handler finishes executing.

11.8 Event Bubbling

Event bubbling is the process by which events fired in child elements "bubble" up to their parent elements. When an event is fired on an element, it is first delivered to the element's event handler (if any), then to the parent element's event handler (if any). This might result in event handling that was not intended. If you intend to handle an event in a child element alone, you should cancel the bubbling of the event in the child element's event-handling code by using the *cancelBubble property* of the event object, as shown in Fig. 11.8.

```
1   <?xml version = "1.0" encoding = "utf-8"?>
2   <!DOCTYPE html PUBLIC "-//W3C//DTD XHTML 1.0 Strict//EN"
3      "http://www.w3.org/TR/xhtml1/DTD/xhtml1-strict.dtd">
4
5   <!-- Fig. 11.8: bubbling.html -->
6   <!-- Canceling event bubbling. -->
7   <html xmlns = "http://www.w3.org/1999/xhtml">
8      <head>
9         <title>Event Bubbling</title>
10        <script type = "text/javascript">
11           <!--
```

Fig. 11.8 | Canceling event bubbling. (Part 1 of 3.)

```
12              function documentClick()
13              {
14                 alert( "You clicked in the document." );
15              } // end function documentClick
16
17              function bubble( e )
18              {
19                 if ( !e )
20                    var e = window.event;
21
22                 alert( "This will bubble." );
23                 e.cancelBubble = false;
24              } // end function bubble
25
26              function noBubble( e )
27              {
28                 if ( !e )
29                    var e = window.event;
30
31                 alert( "This will not bubble." );
32                 e.cancelBubble = true;
33              } // end function noBubble
34
35              function registerEvents()
36              {
37                 document.onclick = documentClick;
38                 document.getElementById( "bubble" ).onclick = bubble;
39                 document.getElementById( "noBubble" ).onclick = noBubble;
40              } // end function registerEvents
41              // -->
42           </script>
43        </head>
44        <body onload = "registerEvents()">
45           <p id = "bubble">Bubbling enabled.</p>
46           <p id = "noBubble">Bubbling disabled.</p>
47        </body>
48     </html>
```

a) The user clicks the first paragraph, for which bubbling is enabled.

Fig. 11.8 | Canceling event bubbling. (Part 2 of 3.)

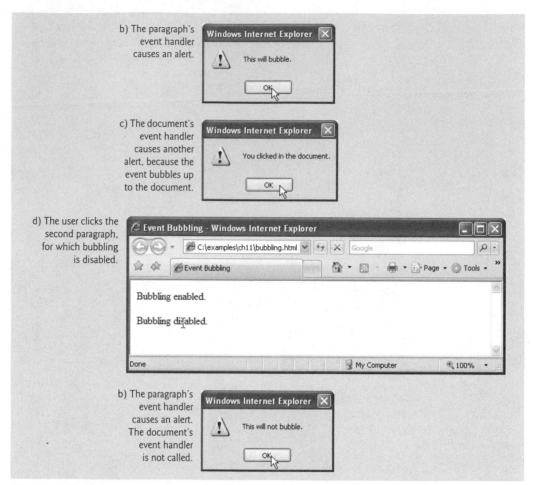

b) The paragraph's event handler causes an alert.

c) The document's event handler causes another alert, because the event bubbles up to the document.

d) The user clicks the second paragraph, for which bubbling is disabled.

b) The paragraph's event handler causes an alert. The document's event handler is not called.

Fig. 11.8 | Canceling event bubbling. (Part 3 of 3.)

Clicking the first p element (line 45) triggers a call to bubble. Then, because line 37 registers the document's onclick event, documentClick is also called. This occurs because the onclick event bubbles up to the document. This is probably not the desired result. Clicking the second p element (line 46) calls noBubble, which disables the event bubbling for this event by setting the cancelBubble property of the event object to true. [*Note:* The default value of cancelBubble is false, so the statement in line 23 is unnecessary.]

Common Programming Error 11.5

Forgetting to cancel event bubbling when necessary may cause unexpected results in your scripts.

11.9 More Events

The events we covered in this chapter are among the most commonly used. A list of some events supported by both Firefox and Internet Explorer is given with descriptions in Fig. 11.9.

Event	Fires when
onabort	Image transfer has been interrupted by user.
onchange	A new choice is made in a select element, or when a text input is changed and the element loses focus.
onclick	The user clicks using the mouse.
ondblclick	The mouse is double clicked.
onfocus	A form element gains focus.
onkeydown	The user pushes down a key.
onkeypress	The user presses then releases a key.
onkeyup	The user releases a key.
onload	An element and all its children have loaded.
onmousedown	A mouse button is pressed down.
onmousemove	The mouse moves.
onmouseout	The mouse leaves an element.
onmouseover	The mouse enters an element.
onmouseup	A mouse button is released.
onreset	A form resets (i.e., the user clicks a reset button).
onresize	The size of an object changes (i.e., the user resizes a window or frame).
onselect	A text selection begins (applies to input or textarea).
onsubmit	A form is submitted.
onunload	A page is about to unload.

Fig. 11.9 | Cross-browser events.

11.10 Web Resources

http://www.quirksmode.org/js/introevents.html
An introduction and reference site for JavaScript events. Includes comprehensive information on history of events, the different event models, and making events work across multiple browsers.

wsabstract.com/dhtmltutors/domevent1.shtml
This *JavaScript Kit* tutorial introduces event handling and discusses the W3C DOM advanced event model.

http://www.w3schools.com/jsref/jsref_events.asp
The W3 School's JavaScript Event Reference site has a comprehensive list of JavaScript events, a description of their usage and their browser compatibilities.

http://www.brainjar.com/dhtml/events/
BrainJar.com's DOM Event Model site provdes a comprehensive introduction to the DOM event model, and has example code to demonstrate several different ways of assigning and using events.

12

XML and RSS

OBJECTIVES

In this chapter you'll learn:

- To mark up data using XML.
- How XML namespaces help provide unique XML element and attribute names.
- To create DTDs and schemas for specifying and validating the structure of an XML document.
- To create and use simple XSL style sheets to render XML document data.
- To retrieve and manipulate XML data programmatically using JavaScript.
- RSS and how to programmatically apply an XSL transformation to an RSS document using JavaScript.

12.1 Introduction

The *Extensible Markup Language (XML)* was developed in 1996 by the *World Wide Web Consortium's (W3C's)* XML Working Group. XML is a widely supported *open technology* (i.e., nonproprietary technology) for describing data that has become the standard format for data exchanged between applications over the Internet.

Web applications use XML extensively and web browsers provide many XML-related capabilities. Sections 12.2–12.7 introduce XML and XML-related technologies—XML namespaces for providing unique XML element and attribute names, and Document Type Definitions (DTDs) and XML Schemas for validating XML documents. Sections 12.8–12.9 present additional XML technologies and key JavaScript capabilities for loading and manipulating XML programmatically—this material is optional but is recommended if you plan to use XML in your own applications. Finally, Section 12.10 introduces RSS—an XML format used to syndicate simple website content—and shows how to format RSS elements using JavaScript and other technologies presented in this chapter.

12.2 XML Basics

XML permits document authors to create *markup* (i.e., a text-based notation for describing data) for virtually any type of information. This enables document authors to create entirely new markup languages for describing any type of data, such as mathematical formulas, software-configuration instructions, chemical molecular structures, music, news, recipes and financial reports. XML describes data in a way that both human beings and computers can understand.

Figure 12.1 is a simple XML document that describes information for a baseball player. We focus on lines 5–9 to introduce basic XML syntax. You'll learnyou'll learn about the other elements of this document in Section 12.3.

XML documents contain text that represents content (i.e., data), such as John (line 6 of Fig. 12.1), and *elements* that specify the document's structure, such as firstName (line 6 of Fig. 12.1). XML documents delimit elements with *start tags* and *end tags*. A start tag consists of the element name in *angle brackets* (e.g., <player> and <firstName> in lines

```
1   <?xml version = "1.0"?>
2
3   <!-- Fig. 12.1: player.xml -->
4   <!-- Baseball player structured with XML -->
5   <player>
6      <firstName>John</firstName>
7      <lastName>Doe</lastName>
8      <battingAverage>0.375</battingAverage>
9   </player>
```

Fig. 12.1 | XML that describes a baseball player's information.

5 and 6, respectively). An end tag consists of the element name preceded by a *forward slash (/)* in angle brackets (e.g., `</firstName>` and `</player>` in lines 6 and 9, respectively). An element's start and end tags enclose text that represents a piece of data (e.g., the player's `firstName`—John—in line 6, which is enclosed by the `<firstName>` start tag and `</firstName>` end tag). Every XML document must have exactly one *root element* that contains all the other elements. In Fig. 12.1, the root element is `player` (lines 5–9).

XML-based markup languages—called XML *vocabularies*—provide a means for describing data in standardized, structured ways. Some XML vocabularies include XHTML (Extensible HyperText Markup Language), MathML (for mathematics), VoiceXML™ (for speech), CML (Chemical Markup Language—for chemistry), XBRL (Extensible Business Reporting Language—for financial data exchange) and others that we discuss in Section 12.7.

Massive amounts of data are currently stored on the Internet in many formats (e.g., databases, web pages, text files). Much of this data, especially that which is passed between systems, will soon take the form of XML. Organizations see XML as the future of data encoding. Information technology groups are planning ways to integrate XML into their systems. Industry groups are developing custom XML vocabularies for most major industries that will allow business applications to communicate in common languages. For example, many web services allow web-based applications to exchange data seamlessly through standard protocols based on XML.

The next generation of the web is being built on an XML foundation, enabling you to develop more sophisticated web-based applications. XML allows you to assign meaning to what would otherwise be random pieces of data. As a result, programs can "understand" the data they manipulate. For example, a web browser might view a street address in a simple web page as a string of characters without any real meaning. In an XML document, however, this data can be clearly identified (i.e., marked up) as an address. A program that uses the document can recognize this data as an address and provide links to a map of that location, driving directions from that location or other location-specific information. Likewise, an application can recognize names of people, dates, ISBN numbers and any other type of XML-encoded data. The application can then present users with other related information, providing a richer, more meaningful user experience.

Viewing and Modifying XML Documents
XML documents are highly portable. Viewing or modifying an XML document—which is a text file that usually ends with the *.xml* filename extension—does not require special software, although many software tools exist, and new ones are frequently released that

make it more convenient to develop XML-based applications. Any text editor that supports ASCII/Unicode characters can open XML documents for viewing and editing. Also, most web browsers can display XML documents in a formatted manner that shows the XML's structure. Section 12.3 demonstrates this in Internet Explorer and Firefox. An important characteristic of XML is that it is both human and machine readable.

Processing XML Documents

Processing an XML document requires software called an *XML parser* (or *XML processor*). A parser makes the document's data available to applications. While reading an XML document's contents, a parser checks that the document follows the syntax rules specified by the W3C's XML Recommendation (www.w3.org/XML). XML syntax requires a single root element, a start tag and end tag for each element, and properly nested tags (i.e., the end tag for a nested element must appear before the end tag of the enclosing element). Furthermore, XML is case sensitive, so the proper capitalization must be used in elements. A document that conforms to this syntax is a *well-formed XML document* and is syntactically correct. We present fundamental XML syntax in Section 12.3. If an XML parser can process an XML document successfully, that XML document is well-formed. Parsers can provide access to XML-encoded data in well-formed documents only.

Often, XML parsers are built into software or available for download over the Internet. Some popular parsers include *Microsoft XML Core Services (MSXML)*—which is included with Internet Explorer, the Apache Software Foundation's *Xerces* (xml.apache.org) and the open-source *Expat XML Parser* (expat.sourceforge.net).

Validating XML Documents

An XML document can reference a *Document Type Definition (DTD)* or a *schema* that defines the proper structure of the XML document. When an XML document references a DTD or a schema, some parsers (called *validating parsers*) can read the DTD/schema and check that the XML document follows the structure defined by the DTD/schema. If the XML document conforms to the DTD/schema (i.e., the document has the appropriate structure), the XML document is *valid*. For example, if in Fig. 12.1 we were referencing a DTD that specified that a player element must have firstName, lastName and battingAverage elements, then omitting the lastName element (line 7 in Fig. 12.1) would invalidate the XML document player.xml. However, the XML document would still be well-formed, because it follows proper XML syntax (i.e., it has one root element, each element has a start tag and an end tag, and the elements are nested properly). By definition, a valid XML document is well-formed. Parsers that cannot check for document conformity against DTDs/schemas are *nonvalidating parsers*—they determine only whether an XML document is well-formed, not whether it is valid.

We discuss validation, DTDs and schemas, as well as the key differences between these two types of structural specifications, in Sections 12.5–12.6. For now, note that schemas are XML documents themselves, whereas DTDs are not. As you'll learn in Section 12.6, this difference presents several advantages in using schemas over DTDs.

Software Engineering Observation 12.1

DTDs and schemas are essential for business-to-business (B2B) transactions and mission-critical systems. Validating XML documents ensures that disparate systems can manipulate data structured in standardized ways and prevents errors caused by missing or malformed data.

Formatting and Manipulating XML Documents
Most XML documents contain only data, not formatting instructions, so applications that process XML documents must decide how to manipulate or display the data. For example, a PDA (personal digital assistant) may render an XML document differently than a wireless phone or a desktop computer. You can use *Extensible Stylesheet Language (XSL)* to specify rendering instructions for different platforms. We discuss XSL in Section 12.8.

XML-processing programs can also search, sort and manipulate XML data using XSL. Some other XML-related technologies are XPath (XML Path Language—a language for accessing parts of an XML document), XSL-FO (XSL Formatting Objects—an XML vocabulary used to describe document formatting) and XSLT (XSL Transformations—a language for transforming XML documents into other documents). We present XSLT and XPath in Section 12.8.

12.3 Structuring Data

In this section and throughout this chapter, we create our own XML markup. XML allows you to describe data precisely in a well-structured format.

XML Markup for an Article
In Fig. 12.2, we present an XML document that marks up a simple article using XML. The line numbers shown are for reference only and are not part of the XML document.

This document begins with an *XML declaration* (line 1), which identifies the document as an XML document. The *version attribute* specifies the XML version to which the document conforms. The current XML standard is version 1.0. Though the W3C released a version 1.1 specification in February 2004, this newer version is not yet widely supported. The W3C may continue to release new versions as XML evolves to meet the requirements of different fields.

Portability Tip 12.1

Documents should include the XML declaration to identify the version of XML used. A document that lacks an XML declaration might be assumed to conform to the latest version of XML—when it does not, errors could result.

```
 1   <?xml version = "1.0"?>
 2
 3   <!-- Fig. 12.2: article.xml -->
 4   <!-- Article structured with XML -->
 5   <article>
 6      <title>Simple XML</title>
 7      <date>July 4, 2007</date>
 8      <author>
 9         <firstName>John</firstName>
10         <lastName>Doe</lastName>
11      </author>
12      <summary>XML is pretty easy.</summary>
13      <content>This chapter presents examples that use XML.</content>
14   </article>
```

Fig. 12.2 | XML used to mark up an article.

As in most markup languages, blank lines (line 2), white spaces and indentation help improve readability. Blank lines are normally ignored by XML parsers. XML comments (lines 3–4), which are delimited by `<!--` and `-->`, can be placed almost anywhere in an XML document and can span multiple lines. There must be exactly one end marker (`-->`) for each begin marker (`<!--`).

Common Programming Error 12.1

Placing any characters, including white space, before the XML declaration is an error.

Common Programming Error 12.2

In an XML document, each start tag must have a matching end tag; omitting either tag is an error. Soon, you'll learn how such errors are detected.

Common Programming Error 12.3

XML is case sensitive. Using different cases for the start tag and end tag names for the same element is a syntax error.

In Fig. 12.2, `article` (lines 5–14) is the root element. The lines that precede the root element (lines 1–4) are the XML *prolog*. In an XML prolog, the XML declaration must appear before the comments and any other markup.

The elements we use in the example do not come from any specific markup language. Instead, we chose the element names and markup structure that best describe our particular data. You can invent elements to mark up your data. For example, element `title` (line 6) contains text that describes the article's title (e.g., `Simple XML`). Similarly, `date` (line 7), `author` (lines 8–11), `firstName` (line 9), `lastName` (line 10), `summary` (line 12) and `content` (line 13) contain text that describes the date, author, the author's first name, the author's last name, a summary and the content of the document, respectively. XML element names can be of any length and may contain letters, digits, underscores, hyphens and periods. However, they must begin with either a letter or an underscore, and they should not begin with "xml" in any combination of uppercase and lowercase letters (e.g., `XML`, `Xml`, `xML`), as this is reserved for use in the XML standards.

Common Programming Error 12.4

Using a white-space character in an XML element name is an error.

Good Programming Practice 12.1

XML element names should be meaningful to humans and should not use abbreviations.

XML elements are *nested* to form hierarchies—with the root element at the top of the hierarchy. This allows document authors to create parent/child relationships between data. For example, elements `title`, `date`, `author`, `summary` and `content` are nested within `article`. Elements `firstName` and `lastName` are nested within `author`. We discuss the hierarchy of Fig. 12.2 later in this chapter (Fig. 12.25).

Common Programming Error 12.5

Nesting XML tags improperly is a syntax error. For example, `<x><y>hello</x></y>` is an error, because the `</y>` tag must precede the `</x>` tag.

Any element that contains other elements (e.g., article or author) is a *container element*. Container elements also are called *parent elements*. Elements nested inside a container element are *child elements* (or children) of that container element. If those child elements are at the same nesting level, they are *siblings* of one another.

Viewing an XML Document in Internet Explorer and Firefox

The XML document in Fig. 12.2 is simply a text file named article.xml. This document does not contain formatting information for the article. This is because XML is a technology for describing the structure of data. Formatting and displaying data from an XML document are application-specific issues. For example, when the user loads article.xml in Internet Explorer, MSXML (Microsoft XML Core Services) parses and displays the document's data. Firefox has a similar capability. Each browser has a built-in *style sheet* to format the data. Note that the resulting format of the data (Fig. 12.3) is similar to the format of the listing in Fig. 12.2. In Section 12.8, we show how to create style sheets to transform your XML data into various formats suitable for display.

Note the minus sign (–) and plus sign (+) in the screen shots of Fig. 12.3. Although these symbols are not part of the XML document, both browsers place them next to every container element. A minus sign indicates that the browser is displaying the container element's child elements. Clicking the minus sign next to an element collapses that element (i.e., causes the browser to hide the container element's children and replace the minus sign with a plus sign). Conversely, clicking the plus sign next to an element expands that element (i.e., causes the browser to display the container element's children and replace the plus sign with a minus sign). This behavior is similar to viewing the directory structure on your system in Windows Explorer or another similar directory viewer. In fact, a directory structure often is modeled as a series of tree structures, in which the *root* of a tree represents a disk drive (e.g., C:), and *nodes* in the tree represent directories. Parsers often store XML data as tree structures to facilitate efficient manipulation, as discussed in Section 12.9.

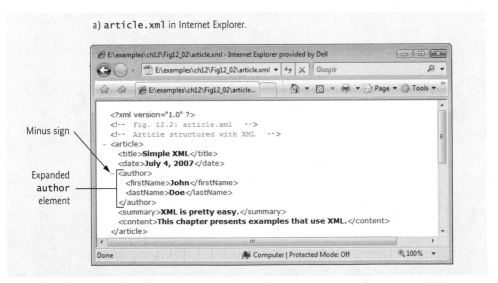

a) article.xml in Internet Explorer.

Fig. 12.3 | article.xml displayed by Internet Explorer 7 and Firefox 3. (Part 1 of 2.)

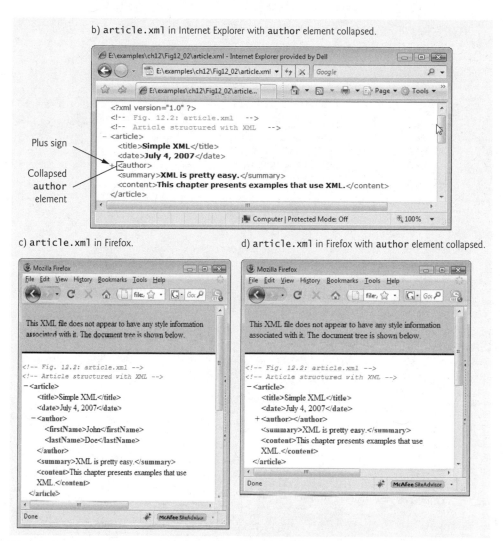

Fig. 12.3 | `article.xml` displayed by Internet Explorer 7 and Firefox 3. (Part 2 of 2.)

[*Note:* In Windows XP and Windows Vista, by default Internet Explorer displays all the XML elements in expanded view, and clicking the minus sign (Fig. 12.3(a)) does not do anything. To enable collapsing and expanding, right click the *Information Bar* that appears just below the **Address** field and select **Allow Blocked Content....** Then click **Yes** in the pop-up window that appears.]

XML Markup for a Business Letter

Now that you've seen a simple XML document, let's examine a more complex XML document that marks up a business letter (Fig. 12.4). Again, we begin the document with the XML declaration (line 1) that states the XML version to which the document conforms.

Line 5 specifies that this XML document references a DTD. Recall from Section 12.2 that DTDs define the structure of the data for an XML document. For example, a DTD

```
 1   <?xml version = "1.0"?>
 2
 3   <!-- Fig. 12.4: letter.xml -->
 4   <!-- Business letter marked up as XML -->
 5   <!DOCTYPE letter SYSTEM "letter.dtd">
 6
 7   <letter>
 8      <contact type = "sender">
 9         <name>Jane Doe</name>
10         <address1>Box 12345</address1>
11         <address2>15 Any Ave.</address2>
12         <city>Othertown</city>
13         <state>Otherstate</state>
14         <zip>67890</zip>
15         <phone>555-4321</phone>
16         <flag gender = "F" />
17      </contact>
18
19      <contact type = "receiver">
20         <name>John Doe</name>
21         <address1>123 Main St.</address1>
22         <address2></address2>
23         <city>Anytown</city>
24         <state>Anystate</state>
25         <zip>12345</zip>
26         <phone>555-1234</phone>
27         <flag gender = "M" />
28      </contact>
29
30      <salutation>Dear Sir:</salutation>
31
32      <paragraph>It is our privilege to inform you about our new database
33         managed with XML. This new system allows you to reduce the
34         load on your inventory list server by having the client machine
35         perform the work of sorting and filtering the data.
36      </paragraph>
37
38      <paragraph>Please visit our website for availability and pricing.
39      </paragraph>
40
41      <closing>Sincerely,</closing>
42      <signature>Ms. Jane Doe</signature>
43   </letter>
```

Fig. 12.4 | Business letter marked up as XML.

specifies the elements and parent/child relationships between elements permitted in an XML document.

Error-Prevention Tip 12.1

An XML document is not required to reference a DTD, but validating XML parsers can use a DTD to ensure that the document has the proper structure.

Portability Tip 12.2

Validating an XML document helps guarantee that independent developers will exchange data in a standardized form that conforms to the DTD.

The DOCTYPE reference (line 5) contains three items, the name of the root element that the DTD specifies (letter); the keyword **SYSTEM** (which denotes an *external DTD*—a DTD declared in a separate file, as opposed to a DTD declared locally in the same file); and the DTD's name and location (i.e., letter.dtd in the current directory; this could also be a fully qualified URL). DTD document filenames typically end with the *.dtd* extension. We discuss DTDs and letter.dtd in detail in Section 12.5.

Several tools (many of which are free) validate documents against DTDs (discussed in Section 12.5) and schemas (discussed in Section 12.6). A free XML validator can be found at www.xmlvalidation.com. This validator can validate XML documents against both DTDs and schemas. You can paste your XML code into the provided text area, or upload the XML document (Fig. 12.5(a)). If you wish to validate the document against a DTD, simply click the **validate** button after pasting in your code or uploading the document. The next screen will prompt you to paste in your DTD code or upload the DTD file (Fig. 12.5(b)). The output (Fig. 12.6) shows the results of validating the document using this online validator—in this case, no errors were found so the XML document is valid. Visit www.w3.org/XML/Schema for a list of additional validation tools.

Root element letter (lines 7–43 of Fig. 12.4) contains the child elements contact, contact, salutation, paragraph, paragraph, closing and signature. Data can be placed between an elements' tags or as *attributes*—name/value pairs that appear within

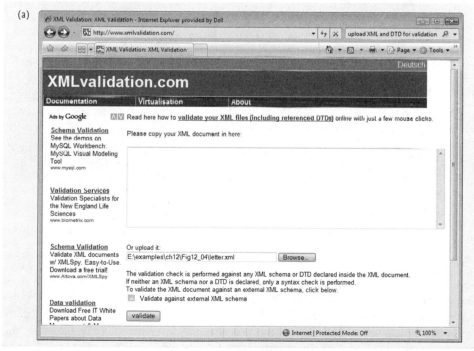

Fig. 12.5 | Validating an XML document with Microsoft's XML Validator. (Part 1 of 2.)

(b)

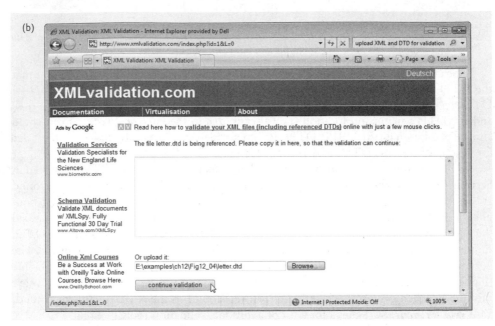

Fig. 12.5 | Validating an XML document with Microsoft's XML Validator. (Part 2 of 2.)

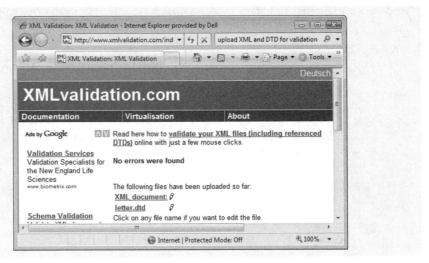

Fig. 12.6 | Validation result using Microsoft's XML Validator.

the angle brackets of an element's start tag. Elements can have any number of attributes (separated by spaces) in their start tags. The first contact element (lines 8–17) has an attribute named type with *attribute value* "sender", which indicates that this contact element identifies the letter's sender. The second contact element (lines 19–28) has attribute type with value "receiver", which indicates that this contact element identifies the letter's recipient. Like element names, attribute names are case sensitive, can be any length, may contain letters, digits, underscores, hyphens and periods, and must begin with either a letter or an underscore character. A `contact` element stores various items of information about a contact, such as the contact's name (represented by element `name`), address (represented by elements `address1`, `address2`, `city`, `state` and `zip`), phone number (represented by element `phone`) and gender (represented by attribute `gender` of element `flag`). Element `salutation` (line 30) marks up the letter's salutation. Lines 32–39 mark up the letter's body using two `paragraph` elements. Elements `closing` (line 41) and `signature` (line 42) mark up the closing sentence and the author's "signature," respectively.

Common Programming Error 12.6

Failure to enclose attribute values in double ("") or single (' ') quotes is a syntax error.

Line 16 introduces the *empty element* `flag`. An empty element is one that does not have any content. Instead, an empty element sometimes places data in attributes. Empty element `flag` has one attribute that indicates the gender of the contact (represented by the parent `contact` element). Document authors can close an empty element either by placing a slash immediately preceding the right angle bracket, as shown in line 16, or by explicitly writing an end tag, as in line 22.

> **<address2></address2>**

Note that the `address2` element in line 22 is empty because there is no second part to this contact's address. However, we must include this element to conform to the structural rules specified in the XML document's DTD—`letter.dtd` (which we present in Section 12.5). This DTD specifies that each `contact` element must have an `address2` child element (even if it is empty). In Section 12.5, you'll learn how DTDs indicate required and optional elements.

12.4 XML Namespaces

XML allows document authors to create custom elements. This extensibility can result in *naming collisions* among elements in an XML document that each have the same name. For example, we may use the element `book` to mark up data about a Deitel publication. A stamp collector may use the element `book` to mark up data about a book of stamps. Using both of these elements in the same document could create a naming collision, making it difficult to determine which kind of data each element contains.

An XML *namespace* is a collection of element and attribute names. XML namespaces provide a means for document authors to unambiguously refer to elements with the same name (i.e., prevent collisions). For example,

> **<subject>**Geometry**</subject>**

and

> **<subject>**Cardiology**</subject>**

use element `subject` to mark up data. In the first case, the subject is something one studies in school, whereas in the second case, the subject is a field of medicine. Namespaces can differentiate these two `subject` elements—for example:

> **<highschool:subject>**Geometry**</highschool:subject>**

and

<medicalschool:subject>Cardiology</medicalschool:subject>

Both highschool and medicalschool are *namespace prefixes*. A document author places a namespace prefix and colon (:) before an element name to specify the namespace to which that element belongs. Document authors can create their own namespace prefixes using virtually any name except the reserved namespace prefix xml. In the next subsections, we demonstrate how document authors ensure that namespaces are unique.

Common Programming Error 12.7

Attempting to create a namespace prefix named xml in any mixture of uppercase and lowercase letters is a syntax error—the xml namespace prefix is reserved for internal use by XML itself.

Differentiating Elements with Namespaces

Figure 12.7 demonstrates namespaces. In this document, namespaces differentiate two distinct elements—the file element related to a text file and the file document related to an image file.

```
 1  <?xml version = "1.0"?>
 2
 3  <!-- Fig. 12.7: namespace.xml -->
 4  <!-- Demonstrating namespaces -->
 5  <text:directory
 6     xmlns:text = "urn:deitel:textInfo"
 7     xmlns:image = "urn:deitel:imageInfo">
 8
 9     <text:file filename = "book.xml">
10        <text:description>A book list</text:description>
11     </text:file>
12
13     <image:file filename = "funny.jpg">
14        <image:description>A funny picture</image:description>
15        <image:size width = "200" height = "100" />
16     </image:file>
17  </text:directory>
```

Fig. 12.7 | XML namespaces demonstration.

Lines 6–7 use the XML-namespace reserved attribute ***xmlns*** to create two namespace prefixes—text and image. Each namespace prefix is bound to a series of characters called a *Uniform Resource Identifier (URI)* that uniquely identifies the namespace. Document authors create their own namespace prefixes and URIs. A URI is a way to identifying a resource, typically on the Internet. Two popular types of URI are *Uniform Resource Name (URN)* and *Uniform Resource Locator (URL)*.

To ensure that namespaces are unique, document authors must provide unique URIs. In this example, we use the text urn:deitel:textInfo and urn:deitel:imageInfo as URIs. These URIs employ the URN scheme frequently used to identify namespaces. Under this naming scheme, a URI begins with "urn:", followed by a unique series of additional names separated by colons.

Another common practice is to use URLs, which specify the location of a file or a resource on the Internet. For example, www.deitel.com is the URL that identifies the home page of the Deitel & Associates website. Using URLs guarantees that the namespaces are unique because the domain names (e.g., www.deitel.com) are guaranteed to be unique. For example, lines 5–7 could be rewritten as

```
<text:directory
    xmlns:text = "http://www.deitel.com/xmlns-text"
    xmlns:image = "http://www.deitel.com/xmlns-image">
```

where URLs related to the deitel.com domain name serve as URIs to identify the text and image namespaces. The parser does not visit these URLs, nor do these URLs need to refer to actual web pages. They each simply represent a unique series of characters used to differentiate URI names. In fact, any string can represent a namespace. For example, our image namespace URI could be hgjfkdlsa4556, in which case our prefix assignment would be

```
xmlns:image = "hgjfkdlsa4556"
```

Lines 9–11 use the text namespace prefix for elements file and description. Note that the end tags must also specify the namespace prefix text. Lines 13–16 apply namespace prefix image to the elements file, description and size. Note that attributes do not require namespace prefixes (although they can have them), because each attribute is already part of an element that specifies the namespace prefix. For example, attribute filename (line 9) is implicitly part of namespace text because its element (i.e., file) specifies the text namespace prefix.

Specifying a Default Namespace

To eliminate the need to place namespace prefixes in each element, document authors may specify a *default namespace* for an element and its children. Figure 12.8 demonstrates using a default namespace (urn:deitel:textInfo) for element directory.

Line 5 defines a default namespace using attribute xmlns with no prefex specified, but with a URI as its value. Once we define this default namespace, child elements belonging to the namespace need not be qualified by a namespace prefix. Thus, element file (lines 8–10) is in the default namespace urn:deitel:textInfo. Compare this to lines 9–10 of Fig. 12.7, where we had to prefix the file and description element names with the namespace prefix text.

```
1   <?xml version = "1.0"?>
2
3   <!-- Fig. 12.8: defaultnamespace.xml -->
4   <!-- Using default namespaces -->
5   <directory xmlns = "urn:deitel:textInfo"
6      xmlns:image = "urn:deitel:imageInfo">
7
8      <file filename = "book.xml">
9         <description>A book list</description>
10     </file>
11
12     <image:file filename = "funny.jpg">
13        <image:description>A funny picture</image:description>
14        <image:size width = "200" height = "100" />
15     </image:file>
16  </directory>
```

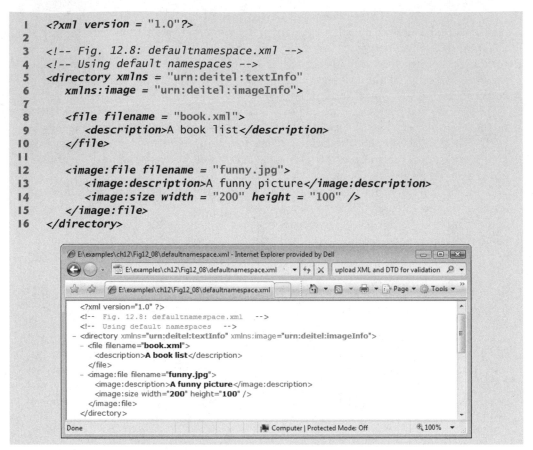

Fig. 12.8 | Default namespace demonstration.

The default namespace applies to the directory element and all elements that are not qualified with a namespace prefix. However, we can use a namespace prefix to specify a different namespace for a particular element. For example, the file element in lines 12–15 includes the image namespace prefix, indicating that this element is in the urn:deitel:imageInfo namespace, not the default namespace.

Namespaces in XML Vocabularies
XML-based languages, such as XML Schema (Section 12.6) and Extensible Stylesheet Language (XSL) (Section 12.8), often use namespaces to identify their elements. Each of these vocabularies defines special-purpose elements that are grouped in namespaces. These namespaces help prevent naming collisions between predefined elements and user-defined elements.

12.5 Document Type Definitions (DTDs)
Document Type Definitions (DTDs) are one of two main types of documents you can use to specify XML document structure. Section 12.6 presents W3C XML Schema documents, which provide an improved method of specifying XML document structure.

Software Engineering Observation 12.2

XML documents can have many different structures, and for this reason an application cannot be certain whether a particular document it receives is complete, ordered properly, and not missing data. DTDs and schemas (Section 12.6) solve this problem by providing an extensible way to describe XML document structure. Applications should use DTDs or schemas to confirm whether XML documents are valid.

Software Engineering Observation 12.3

*Many organizations and individuals are creating DTDs and schemas for a broad range of applications. These collections—called **repositories**—are available free for download from the web (e.g., www.xml.org, www.oasis-open.org).*

Creating a Document Type Definition

Figure 12.4 presented a simple business letter marked up with XML. Recall that line 5 of letter.xml references a DTD—letter.dtd (Fig. 12.9). This DTD specifies the business letter's element types and attributes, and their relationships to one another.

A DTD describes the structure of an XML document and enables an XML parser to verify whether an XML document is valid (i.e., whether its elements contain the proper attributes and appear in the proper sequence). DTDs allow users to check document structure and to exchange data in a standardized format. A DTD expresses the set of rules for document structure using an EBNF (Extended Backus-Naur Form) grammar. DTDs are not themselves XML documents. [*Note:* EBNF grammars are commonly used to define programming languages. To learn more about EBNF grammars, visit en.wikipedia.org/wiki/EBNF or www.garshol.priv.no/download/text/bnf.html.]

```
1   <!-- Fig. 12.9: letter.dtd        -->
2   <!-- DTD document for letter.xml -->
3
4   <!ELEMENT letter ( contact+, salutation, paragraph+,
5      closing, signature )>
6
7   <!ELEMENT contact ( name, address1, address2, city, state,
8      zip, phone, flag )>
9   <!ATTLIST contact type CDATA #IMPLIED>
10
11  <!ELEMENT name ( #PCDATA )>
12  <!ELEMENT address1 ( #PCDATA )>
13  <!ELEMENT address2 ( #PCDATA )>
14  <!ELEMENT city ( #PCDATA )>
15  <!ELEMENT state ( #PCDATA )>
16  <!ELEMENT zip ( #PCDATA )>
17  <!ELEMENT phone ( #PCDATA )>
18  <!ELEMENT flag EMPTY>
19  <!ATTLIST flag gender (M | F) "M">
20
21  <!ELEMENT salutation ( #PCDATA )>
22  <!ELEMENT closing ( #PCDATA )>
23  <!ELEMENT paragraph ( #PCDATA )>
24  <!ELEMENT signature ( #PCDATA )>
```

Fig. 12.9 | Document Type Definition (DTD) for a business letter.

Common Programming Error 12.8

For documents validated with DTDs, any document that uses elements, attributes or nesting relationships not explicitly defined by a DTD is an invalid document.

Defining Elements in a DTD

The *ELEMENT element type declaration* in lines 4–5 defines the rules for element letter. In this case, letter contains one or more contact elements, one salutation element, one or more paragraph elements, one closing element and one signature element, in that sequence. The *plus sign (+) occurrence indicator* specifies that the DTD requires one or more occurrences of an element. Other occurence indicators include the *asterisk (*)*, which indicates an optional element that can occur zero or more times, and the *question mark (?)*, which indicates an optional element that can occur at most once (i.e., zero or one occurrence). If an element does not have an occurrence indicator, the DTD requires exactly one occurrence.

The contact element type declaration (lines 7–8) specifies that a contact element contains child elements name, address1, address2, city, state, zip, phone and flag—in that order. The DTD requires exactly one occurrence of each of these elements.

Defining Attributes in a DTD

Line 9 uses the *ATTLIST attribute-list declaration* to define a type attribute for the contact element. Keyword *#IMPLIED* specifies that if the parser finds a contact element without a type attribute, the parser can choose an arbitrary value for the attribute or can ignore the attribute. Either way the document will still be valid (if the rest of the document is valid)—a missing type attribute will not invalidate the document. Other keywords that can be used in place of #IMPLIED in an ATTLIST declaration include *#REQUIRED* and *#FIXED*. #REQUIRED specifies that the attribute must be present in the element, and #FIXED specifies that the attribute (if present) must have the given fixed value. For example,

```
<!ATTLIST address zip CDATA #FIXED "01757">
```

indicates that attribute zip (if present in element address) must have the value 01757 for the document to be valid. If the attribute is not present, then the parser, by default, uses the fixed value that the ATTLIST declaration specifies.

Character Data vs. Parsed Character Data

Keyword *CDATA* (line 9) specifies that attribute type contains *character data* (i.e., a string). A parser will pass such data to an application without modification.

Software Engineering Observation 12.4

DTD syntax cannot describe an element's or attribute's data type. For example, a DTD cannot specify that a particular element or attribute can contain only integer data.

Keyword *#PCDATA* (line 11) specifies that an element (e.g., name) may contain *parsed character data* (i.e., data that is processed by an XML parser). Elements with parsed character data cannot contain markup characters, such as less than (<), greater than (>) or ampersand (&). The document author should replace any markup character in a #PCDATA element with the character's corresponding *character entity reference*. For example, the character entity reference < should be used in place of the less-than symbol (<), and the character entity reference > should be used in place of the greater-than symbol (>). A

document author who wishes to use a literal ampersand should use the entity reference
& instead—parsed character data can contain ampersands (&) only for inserting entities.

Common Programming Error 12.9

*Using markup characters (e.g., <, > and &) in parsed character data is an error. Use character
entity references (e.g., <, > and &) instead.*

Defining Empty Elements in a DTD

Line 18 defines an empty element named flag. Keyword *EMPTY* specifies that the element
does not contain any data between its start and end tags. Empty elements commonly describe data via attributes. For example, flag's data appears in its gender attribute (line 19).
Line 19 specifies that the gender attribute's value must be one of the enumerated values
(M or F) enclosed in parentheses and delimited by a vertical bar (|) meaning "or." Note that
line 19 also indicates that gender has a default value of M.

Well-Formed Documents vs. Valid Documents

In Section 12.3, we demonstrated how to use an online XML validator to validate an XML
document against its specified DTD. The validation revealed that the XML document
letter.xml (Fig. 12.4) is well-formed and valid—it conforms to letter.dtd (Fig. 12.9).
Recall that a well-formed document is syntactically correct (i.e., each start tag has a corresponding end tag, the document contains only one root element, etc.), and a valid document contains the proper elements with the proper attributes in the proper sequence. An
XML document cannot be valid unless it is well-formed.

When a document fails to conform to a DTD or a schema, the XML validator we
demonstrated in Section 12.3 displays an error message. For example, the DTD in
Fig. 12.9 indicates that a contact element must contain the child element name. A document that omits this child element is still well-formed, but is not valid. In such a scenario,
the XML validator displays an error message like the one in Fig. 12.10.

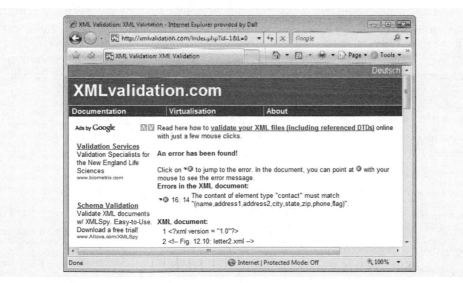

Fig. 12.10 | XML Validator displaying an error message.

12.6 W3C XML Schema Documents

In this section, we introduce schemas for specifying XML document structure and validating XML documents. Many developers in the XML community believe that DTDs are not flexible enough to meet today's programming needs. For example, DTDs lack a way of indicating what specific type of data (e.g., numeric, text) an element can contain, and DTDs are not themselves XML documents, forcing developers to learn multiple grammars and developers to create multiple types of parsers. These and other limitations have led to the development of schemas.

Unlike DTDs, schemas do not use EBNF grammar. Instead, schemas use XML syntax and are actually XML documents that programs can manipulate. Like DTDs, schemas are used by validating parsers to validate documents.

In this section, we focus on the W3C's *XML Schema* vocabulary (note the capital "S" in "Schema"). We use the term XML Schema in the rest of the chapter whenever we refer to W3C's XML Schema vocabulary. For the latest information on XML Schema, visit www.w3.org/XML/Schema. For tutorials on XML Schema concepts beyond what we present here, visit www.w3schools.com/schema/default.asp.

Recall that a DTD describes an XML document's structure, not the content of its elements. For example,

<quantity>5**</quantity>**

contains character data. If the document that contains element quantity references a DTD, an XML parser can validate the document to confirm that this element indeed does contain PCDATA content. However, the parser cannot validate that the content is numeric; DTDs do not provide this capability. So, unfortunately, the parser also considers

<quantity>hello**</quantity>**

to be valid. An application that uses the XML document containing this markup should test that the data in element quantity is numeric and take appropriate action if it is not.

XML Schema enables schema authors to specify that element quantity's data must be numeric or, even more specifically, an integer. A parser validating the XML document against this schema can determine that 5 conforms and hello does not. An XML document that conforms to a schema document is *schema valid*, and one that does not conform is *schema invalid*. Schemas are XML documents and therefore must themselves be valid.

Validating Against an XML Schema Document
Figure 12.11 shows a schema-valid XML document named book.xml, and Fig. 12.12 shows the pertinent XML Schema document (book.xsd) that defines the structure for book.xml. By convention, schemas use the *.xsd* extension. We used an online XSD schema validator provided at

www.xmlforasp.net/SchemaValidator.aspx

to ensure that the XML document in Fig. 12.11 conforms to the schema in Fig. 12.12. To validate the schema document itself (i.e., book.xsd) and produce the output shown in Fig. 12.12, we used an online XSV (XML Schema Validator) provided by the W3C at

www.w3.org/2001/03/webdata/xsv

These free tools enforce the W3C's specifications for XML Schemas and schema validation.

Figure 12.11 contains markup describing several Deitel books. The books element (line 5) has the namespace prefix deitel, indicating that the books element is a part of the http://www.deitel.com/booklist namespace.

```
 1   <?xml version = "1.0"?>
 2
 3   <!-- Fig. 12.11: book.xml -->
 4   <!-- Book list marked up as XML -->
 5   <deitel:books xmlns:deitel = "http://www.deitel.com/booklist">
 6      <book>
 7         <title>Visual Basic 2005 How to Program, 3/e</title>
 8      </book>
 9      <book>
10         <title>Visual C# 2005 How to Program, 2/e</title>
11      </book>
12      <book>
13         <title>Java How to Program, 7/e</title>
14      </book>
15      <book>
16         <title>C++ How to Program, 6/e</title>
17      </book>
18      <book>
19         <title>Internet and World Wide Web How to Program, 4/e</title>
20      </book>
21   </deitel:books>
```

Fig. 12.11 | Schema-valid XML document describing a list of books.

```
 1   <?xml version = "1.0"?>
 2
 3   <!-- Fig. 12.12: book.xsd          -->
 4   <!-- Simple W3C XML Schema document -->
 5   <schema xmlns = "http://www.w3.org/2001/XMLSchema"
 6      xmlns:deitel = "http://www.deitel.com/booklist"
 7      targetNamespace = "http://www.deitel.com/booklist">
 8
 9      <element name = "books" type = "deitel:BooksType"/>
10
11      <complexType name = "BooksType">
12         <sequence>
13            <element name = "book" type = "deitel:SingleBookType"
14               minOccurs = "1" maxOccurs = "unbounded"/>
15         </sequence>
16      </complexType>
17
18      <complexType name = "SingleBookType">
19         <sequence>
20            <element name = "title" type = "string"/>
21         </sequence>
22      </complexType>
23   </schema>
```

Fig. 12.12 | XML Schema document for book.xml. (Part 1 of 2.)

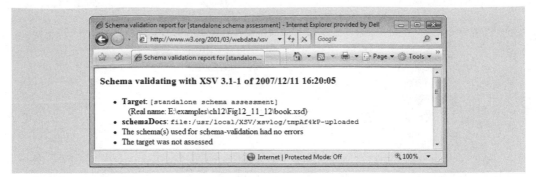

Fig. 12.12 | XML Schema document for book.xml. (Part 2 of 2.)

Creating an XML Schema Document

Figure 12.12 presents the XML Schema document that specifies the structure of book.xml (Fig. 12.11). This document defines an XML-based language (i.e., a vocabulary) for writing XML documents about collections of books. The schema defines the elements, attributes and parent/child relationships that such a document can (or must) include. The schema also specifies the type of data that these elements and attributes may contain.

Root element *schema* (Fig. 12.12, lines 5–23) contains elements that define the structure of an XML document such as book.xml. Line 5 specifies as the default namespace the standard W3C XML Schema namespace URI—*http://www.w3.org/2001/XMLSchema*. This namespace contains predefined elements (e.g., root-element schema) that comprise the XML Schema vocabulary—the language used to write an XML Schema document.

Portability Tip 12.3

W3C XML Schema authors specify URI http://www.w3.org/2001/XMLSchema when referring to the XML Schema namespace. This namespace contains predefined elements that comprise the XML Schema vocabulary. Specifying this URI ensures that validation tools correctly identify XML Schema elements and do not confuse them with those defined by document authors.

Line 6 binds the URI http://www.deitel.com/booklist to namespace prefix deitel. As we discuss momentarily, the schema uses this namespace to differentiate names created by us from names that are part of the XML Schema namespace. Line 7 also specifies http://www.deitel.com/booklist as the *targetNamespace* of the schema. This attribute identifies the namespace of the XML vocabulary that this schema defines. Note that the targetNamespace of book.xsd is the same as the namespace referenced in line 5 of book.xml (Fig. 12.11). This is what "connects" the XML document with the schema that defines its structure. When an XML schema validator examines book.xml and book.xsd, it will recognize that book.xml uses elements and attributes from the http://www.deitel.com/booklist namespace. The validator also will recognize that this namespace is the namespace defined in book.xsd (i.e., the schema's targetNamespace). Thus the validator knows where to look for the structural rules for the elements and attributes used in book.xml.

Defining an Element in XML Schema

In XML Schema, the *element* tag (line 9) defines an element to be included in an XML document that conforms to the schema. In other words, element specifies the actual *ele-*

ments that can be used to mark up data. Line 9 defines the `books` element, which we use as the root element in `book.xml` (Fig. 12.11). Attributes **name** and **type** specify the element's name and type, respectively. An element's type indicates the data that the element may contain. Possible types include XML Schema-defined types (e.g., `string`, `double`) and user-defined types (e.g., `BooksType`, which is defined in lines 11–16). Figure 12.13 lists several of XML Schema's many built-in types. For a complete list of built-in types, see Section 3 of the specification found at `www.w3.org/TR/xmlschema-2`.

XML Schema type	Description	Ranges or structures	Examples
string	A character string		"hello"
boolean	True or false	true, false	true
decimal	A decimal numeral	$i * (10^n)$, where i is an integer and n is an integer that is less than or equal to zero.	5, -12, -45.78
float	A floating-point number	$m * (2^e)$, where m is an integer whose absolute value is less than 2^{24} and e is an integer in the range -149 to 104. Plus three additional numbers: positive infinity, negative infinity and not-a-number (NaN).	0, 12, -109.375, NaN
double	A floating-point number	$m * (2^e)$, where m is an integer whose absolute value is less than 2^{53} and e is an integer in the range -1075 to 970. Plus three additional numbers: positive infinity, negative infinity and not-a-number (NaN).	0, 12, -109.375, NaN
long	A whole number	-9223372036854775808 to 9223372036854775807, inclusive.	1234567890, -1234567890
int	A whole number	-2147483648 to 2147483647, inclusive.	1234567890, -1234567890
short	A whole number	-32768 to 32767, inclusive.	12, -345
date	A date consisting of a year, month and day	yyyy-mm with an optional dd and an optional time zone, where yyyy is four digits long and mm and dd are two digits long.	2005-05-10
time	A time consisting of hours, minutes and seconds	hh:mm:ss with an optional time zone, where hh, mm and ss are two digits long.	16:30:25-05:00

Fig. 12.13 | Some XML Schema types.

In this example, books is defined as an element of type deitel:BooksType (line 9). BooksType is a user-defined type (lines 11–16) in the http://www.deitel.com/booklist namespace and therefore must have the namespace prefix deitel. It is not an existing XML Schema type.

Two categories of type exist in XML Schema—*simple types* and *complex types*. Simple and complex types differ only in that simple types cannot contain attributes or child elements and complex types can.

A user-defined type that contains attributes or child elements must be defined as a complex type. Lines 11–16 use element ***complexType*** to define BooksType as a complex type that has a child element named book. The sequence element (lines 12–15) allows you to specify the sequential order in which child elements must appear. The element (lines 13–14) nested within the complexType element indicates that a BooksType element (e.g., books) can contain child elements named book of type deitel:SingleBookType (defined in lines 18–22). Attribute ***minOccurs*** (line 14), with value 1, specifies that elements of type BooksType must contain a minimum of one book element. Attribute ***maxOccurs*** (line 14), with value ***unbounded***, specifies that elements of type BooksType may have any number of book child elements.

Lines 18–22 define the complex type SingleBookType. An element of this type contains a child element named title. Line 20 defines element title to be of simple type string. Recall that elements of a simple type cannot contain attributes or child elements. The schema end tag (</schema>, line 23) declares the end of the XML Schema document.

A Closer Look at Types in XML Schema

Every element in XML Schema has a type. Types include the built-in types provided by XML Schema (Fig. 12.13) or user-defined types (e.g., SingleBookType in Fig. 12.12).

Every simple type defines a ***restriction*** on an XML Schema-defined type or a restriction on a user-defined type. Restrictions limit the possible values that an element can hold.

Complex types are divided into two groups—those with ***simple content*** and those with ***complex content***. Both can contain attributes, but only complex content can contain child elements. Complex types with simple content must extend or restrict some other existing type. Complex types with complex content do not have this limitation. We demonstrate complex types with each kind of content in the next example.

The schema document in Fig. 12.14 creates both simple types and complex types. The XML document in Fig. 12.15 (laptop.xml) follows the structure defined in Fig. 12.14 to describe parts of a laptop computer. A document such as laptop.xml that conforms to a schema is known as an ***XML instance document***—the document is an instance (i.e., example) of the schema.

```
1   <?xml version = "1.0"?>
2   <!-- Fig. 12.14: computer.xsd -->
3   <!-- W3C XML Schema document    -->
4
5   <schema xmlns = "http://www.w3.org/2001/XMLSchema"
6      xmlns:computer = "http://www.deitel.com/computer"
7      targetNamespace = "http://www.deitel.com/computer">
```

Fig. 12.14 | XML Schema document defining simple and complex types. (Part 1 of 2.)

```
 8
 9        <simpleType name = "gigahertz">
10           <restriction base = "decimal">
11              <minInclusive value = "2.1"/>
12           </restriction>
13        </simpleType>
14
15        <complexType name = "CPU">
16           <simpleContent>
17              <extension base = "string">
18                 <attribute name = "model" type = "string"/>
19              </extension>
20           </simpleContent>
21        </complexType>
22
23        <complexType name = "portable">
24           <all>
25              <element name = "processor" type = "computer:CPU"/>
26              <element name = "monitor" type = "int"/>
27              <element name = "CPUSpeed" type = "computer:gigahertz"/>
28              <element name = "RAM" type = "int"/>
29           </all>
30           <attribute name = "manufacturer" type = "string"/>
31        </complexType>
32
33        <element name = "laptop" type = "computer:portable"/>
34     </schema>
```

Fig. 12.14 | XML Schema document defining simple and complex types. (Part 2 of 2.)

Line 5 declares the default namespace to be the standard XML Schema namespace—any elements without a prefix are assumed to be in the XML Schema namespace. Line 6 binds the namespace prefix computer to the namespace http://www.deitel.com/computer. Line 7 identifies this namespace as the targetNamespace—the namespace being defined by the current XML Schema document.

To design the XML elements for describing laptop computers, we first create a simple type in lines 9–13 using the *simpleType* element. We name this simpleType gigahertz because it will be used to describe the clock speed of the processor in gigahertz. Simple types are restrictions of a type typically called a *base type*. For this simpleType, line 10 declares the base type as decimal, and we restrict the value to be at least 2.1 by using the *minInclusive* element in line 11.

Next, we declare a complexType named CPU that has *simpleContent* (lines 16–20). Remember that a complex type with simple content can have attributes but not child elements. Also recall that complex types with simple content must extend or restrict some XML Schema type or user-defined type. The *extension* element with attribute *base* (line 17) sets the base type to string. In this complexType, we extend the base type string with an attribute. The *attribute* element (line 18) gives the complexType an attribute of type string named model. Thus an element of type CPU must contain string text (because the base type is string) and may contain a model attribute that is also of type string.

Last, we define type `portable`, which is a `complexType` with complex content (lines 23–31). Such types are allowed to have child elements and attributes. The element *all* (lines 24–29) encloses elements that must each be included once in the corresponding XML instance document. These elements can be included in any order. This complex type holds four elements—`processor`, `monitor`, `CPUSpeed` and `RAM`. They are given types `CPU`, `int`, `gigahertz` and `int`, respectively. When using types `CPU` and `gigahertz`, we must include the namespace prefix `computer`, because these user-defined types are part of the `computer` namespace (`http://www.deitel.com/computer`)—the namespace defined in the current document (line 7). Also, `portable` contains an attribute defined in line 30. The `attribute` element indicates that elements of type `portable` contain an attribute of type `string` named `manufacturer`.

Line 33 declares the actual element that uses the three types defined in the schema. The element is called `laptop` and is of type `portable`. We must use the namespace prefix `computer` in front of `portable`.

We have now created an element named `laptop` that contains child elements `processor`, `monitor`, `CPUSpeed` and `RAM`, and an attribute `manufacturer`. Figure 12.15 uses the `laptop` element defined in the `computer.xsd` schema. Once again, we used an online XSD schema validator (`www.xmlforasp.net/SchemaValidator.aspx`) to ensure that this XML instance document adheres to the schema's structural rules.

Line 5 declares namespace prefix `computer`. The `laptop` element requires this prefix because it is part of the `http://www.deitel.com/computer` namespace. Line 6 sets the laptop's `manufacturer` attribute, and lines 8–11 use the elements defined in the schema to describe the laptop's characteristics.

This section introduced W3C XML Schema documents for defining the structure of XML documents, and we validated XML instance documents against schemas using an online XSD schema validator. Section 12.7 discusses several XML vocabularies and demonstrates the MathML vocabulary. Section 12.10 demonstrates the RSS vocabulary.

```
 1   <?xml version = "1.0"?>
 2
 3   <!-- Fig. 12.15: laptop.xml            -->
 4   <!-- Laptop components marked up as XML -->
 5   <computer:laptop xmlns:computer = "http://www.deitel.com/computer"
 6      manufacturer = "IBM">
 7
 8      <processor model = "Centrino">Intel</processor>
 9      <monitor>17</monitor>
10      <CPUSpeed>2.4</CPUSpeed>
11      <RAM>256</RAM>
12   </computer:laptop>
```

Fig. 12.15 | XML document using the `laptop` element defined in `computer.xsd`.

12.7 XML Vocabularies

XML allows authors to create their own tags to describe data precisely. People and organizations in various fields of study have created many different kinds of XML for structuring data. Some of these markup languages are: *MathML (Mathematical Markup*

Language), Scalable Vector Graphics (SVG), Wireless Markup Language (WML), Extensible Business Reporting Language (XBRL), Extensible User Interface Language (XUL) and *Product Data Markup Language (PDML)*. Two other examples of XML vocabularies are W3C XML Schema and the Extensible Stylesheet Language (XSL), which we discuss in Section 12.8. The following subsections describe MathML and other custom markup languages.

12.7.1 MathML™

Until recently, computers typically required specialized software packages such as TeX and LaTeX for displaying complex mathematical expressions. This section introduces MathML, which the W3C developed for describing mathematical notations and expressions. One application that can parse, render and edit MathML is the W3C's *Amaya*™ browser/editor, which can be downloaded from

www.w3.org/Amaya/User/BinDist.html

This page contains download links for several platforms. Amaya documentation and installation notes also are available at the W3C website. Firefox also can render MathML, but it requires additional fonts. Instructions for downloading and installing these fonts are available at www.mozilla.org/projects/mathml/fonts/. You can download a plug-in (www.dessci.com/en/products/mathplayer/) to render MathML in Internet Explorer .

MathML markup describes mathematical expressions for display. MathML is divided into two types of markup—*content* markup and *presentation* markup. Content markup provides tags that embody mathematical concepts. Content MathML allows programmers to write mathematical notation specific to different areas of mathematics. For instance, the multiplication symbol has one meaning in set theory and another meaning in linear algebra. Content MathML distinguishes between different uses of the same symbol. Programmers can take content MathML markup, discern mathematical context and evaluate the marked-up mathematical operations. Presentation MathML is directed toward formatting and displaying mathematical notation. We focus on Presentation MathML in the MathML examples.

Simple Equation in MathML

Figure 12.16 uses MathML to mark up a simple expression. For this example, we show the expression rendered in Firefox.

By convention, MathML files end with the .mml filename extension. A MathML document's root node is the math element, and its default namespace is http://www.w3.org/1998/Math/MathML (line 7). The *mn element* (line 8) marks up a number. The *mo element* (line 9) marks up an operator (e.g., +). Using this markup, we define the expression 2 + 3 = 5, which any MathML capable browser can display.

```
1    <?xml version="1.0" encoding="iso-8859-1"?>
2    <!DOCTYPE math PUBLIC "-//W3C//DTD MathML 2.0//EN"
3        "http://www.w3.org/TR/MathML2/dtd/mathml2.dtd">
4
```

Fig. 12.16 | Expression marked up with MathML and displayed in Firefox. (Part 1 of 2.)

```
5   <!-- Fig. 12.16: mathml1.mml -->
6   <!-- MathML equation. -->
7   <math xmlns="http://www.w3.org/1998/Math/MathML">
8      <mn>2</mn>
9      <mo>+</mo>
10     <mn>3</mn>
11     <mo>=</mo>
12     <mn>5</mn>
13  </math>
```

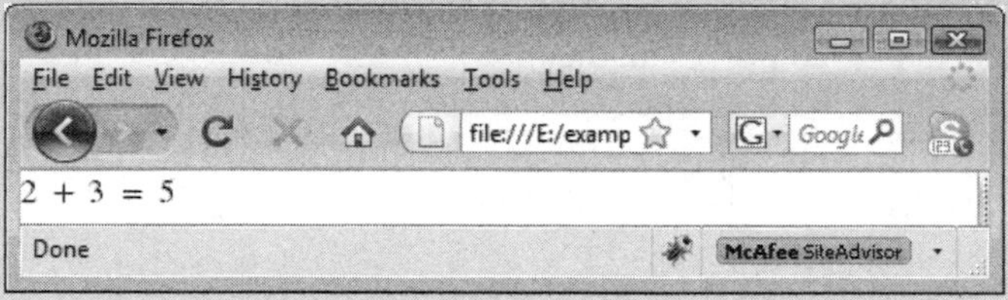

Fig. 12.16 | Expression marked up with MathML and displayed in Firefox. (Part 2 of 2.)

Algebraic Equation in MathML

Let's consider using MathML to mark up an algebraic equation containing exponents and arithmetic operators (Fig. 12.17). For this example, we again show the expression rendered in Firefox.

```
1   <?xml version="1.0" encoding="iso-8859-1"?>
2   <!DOCTYPE math PUBLIC "-//W3C//DTD MathML 2.0//EN"
3      "http://www.w3.org/TR/MathML2/dtd/mathml2.dtd">
4
5   <!-- Fig. 12.17: mathml2.html -->
6   <!-- MathML algebraic equation. -->
7   <math xmlns="http://www.w3.org/1998/Math/MathML">
8      <mn>3</mn>
9      <mo>&InvisibleTimes;</mo>
10     <msup>
11        <mi>x</mi>
12        <mn>2</mn>
13     </msup>
14     <mo>+</mo>
15     <mn>x</mn>
16     <mo>&minus;</mo>
17     <mfrac>
18        <mn>2</mn>
19        <mi>x</mi>
20     </mfrac>
21     <mo>=</mo>
22     <mn>0</mn>
23  </math>
```

Fig. 12.17 | Algebraic equation marked up with MathML and displayed in the Firefox browser. (Part 1 of 2.)

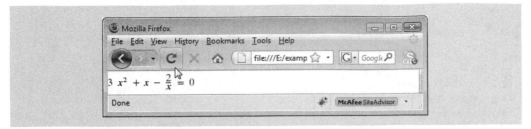

Fig. 12.17 | Algebraic equation marked up with MathML and displayed in the Firefox browser. (Part 2 of 2.)

Line 9 uses *entity reference ⁢* to indicate a multiplication operation without explicit *symbolic representation* (i.e., the multiplication symbol does not appear between the 3 and x). For exponentiation, lines 10–13 use the msup element, which represents a superscript. This *msup element* has two children—the expression to be superscripted (i.e., the base) and the superscript (i.e., the exponent). Correspondingly, the msub element represents a subscript. To display variables such as x, line 11 uses *identifier element mi*.

To display a fraction, lines 17–20 uses the *mfrac element*. Lines 18–19 specify the numerator and the denominator for the fraction. If either the numerator or the denominator contains more than one element, it must appear in an mrow element.

Calculus Expression in MathML

Figure 12.18 marks up a calculus expression that contains an integral symbol and a square-root symbol.

Lines 8–30 group the entire expression in an *mrow element*, which is used to group elements that are positioned horizontally in an expression. The entity reference *∫* (line 10) represents the integral symbol, while the *msubsup element* (lines 9–17) specifies the subscript and superscript a base expression (e.g., the integral symbol). Element mo marks up the integral operator. The msubsup element requires three child elements—an operator (e.g., the integral entity, line 10), the subscript expression (line 11) and the superscript expression (lines 12–16). Element mn (line 11) marks up the number (i.e., 0) that represents the subscript. Element mrow (lines 12–16) marks up the superscript expression (i.e., $1-y$).

Element *msqrt* (lines 18–27) represents a square-root expression. Line 28 introduces entity reference δ for representing a lowercase delta symbol. Delta is an operator, so line 28 places this entity in element mo. To see other operations and symbols in MathML, visit www.w3.org/Math.

```
1    <?xml version="1.0" encoding="iso-8859-1"?>
2    <!DOCTYPE math PUBLIC "-//W3C//DTD MathML 2.0//EN"
3       "http://www.w3.org/TR/MathML2/dtd/mathml2.dtd">
4
5    <!-- Fig. 12.18 mathml3.html -->
6    <!-- Calculus example using MathML -->
```

Fig. 12.18 | Calculus expression marked up with MathML and displayed in the Amaya browser. [Courtesy of World Wide Web Consortium (W3C).] (Part 1 of 2.)

```
 7   <math xmlns="http://www.w3.org/1998/Math/MathML">
 8       <mrow>
 9           <msubsup>
10               <mo>&int;</mo>
11               <mn>0</mn>
12               <mrow>
13                   <mn>1</mn>
14                   <mo>&minus;</mo>
15                   <mi>y</mi>
16               </mrow>
17           </msubsup>
18           <msqrt>
19               <mn>4</mn>
20               <mo>&InvisibleTimes;</mo>
21               <msup>
22                   <mi>x</mi>
23                   <mn>2</mn>
24               </msup>
25               <mo>+</mo>
26               <mi>y</mi>
27           </msqrt>
28           <mo>&delta;</mo>
29           <mi>x</mi>
30       </mrow>
31   </math>
```

Fig. 12.18 | Calculus expression marked up with MathML and displayed in the Amaya browser. [Courtesy of World Wide Web Consortium (W3C).] (Part 2 of 2.)

12.7.2 Other Markup Languages

Literally hundreds of markup languages derive from XML. Every day developers find new uses for XML. Figure 12.20 summarizes a few of these markup languages. The website

> www.service-architecture.com/xml/articles/index.html

provides a nice list of common XML vocabularies and descriptions.

12.8 Extensible Stylesheet Language and XSL Transformations

Extensible Stylesheet Language (XSL) documents specify how programs are to render XML document data. XSL is a group of three technologies—*XSL-FO (XSL Formatting Objects)*, *XPath (XML Path Language)* and *XSLT (XSL Transformations)*. XSL-FO is a vocabulary for specifying formatting, and XPath is a string-based language of expressions

Markup language	Description
Chemical Markup Language (CML)	Chemical Markup Language (CML) is an XML vocabulary for representing molecular and chemical information. Many previous methods for storing this type of information (e.g., special file types) inhibited document reuse. CML takes advantage of XML's portability to enable document authors to use and reuse molecular information without corrupting important data in the process.
VoiceXML™	The VoiceXML Forum founded by AT&T, IBM, Lucent and Motorola developed VoiceXML. It provides interactive voice communication between humans and computers through a telephone, PDA (personal digital assistant) or desktop computer. IBM's VoiceXML SDK can process VoiceXML documents. Visit www.voicexml.org for more information on VoiceXML.
Synchronous Multimedia Integration Language (SMIL™)	SMIL is an XML vocabulary for multimedia presentations. The W3C was the primary developer of SMIL, with contributions from some companies. Visit www.w3.org/AudioVideo for more on SMIL.
Research Information Exchange Markup Language (RIXML)	RIXML, developed by a consortium of brokerage firms, marks up investment data. Visit www.rixml.org for more information on RIXML.
Geography Markup Language (GML)	OpenGIS developed the Geography Markup Language to describe geographic information. Visit www.opengis.org for more information on GML.
Extensible User Interface Language (XUL)	The Mozilla Project created the Extensible User Interface Language for describing graphical user interfaces in a platform-independent way.

Fig. 12.19 | Various markup languages derived from XML.

used by XML and many of its related technologies for effectively and efficiently locating structures and data (such as specific elements and attributes) in XML documents.

The third portion of XSL—XSL Transformations (XSLT)—is a technology for transforming XML documents into other documents—i.e., transforming the structure of the XML document data to another structure. XSLT provides elements that define rules for transforming one XML document to produce a different XML document. This is useful when you want to use data in multiple applications or on multiple platforms, each of which may be designed to work with documents written in a particular vocabulary. For example, XSLT allows you to convert a simple XML document to an XHTML document that presents the XML document's data (or a subset of the data) formatted for display in a web browser.

Transforming an XML document using XSLT involves two tree structures—the *source tree* (i.e., the XML document to be transformed) and the *result tree* (i.e., the XML document to be created). XPath is used to locate parts of the source-tree document that match *templates* defined in an *XSL style sheet.* When a match occurs (i.e., a node matches a template), the matching template executes and adds its result to the result tree. When there are no more matches, XSLT has transformed the source tree into the result tree. The XSLT does not analyze every node of the source tree; it selectively navigates the source tree using XPath's select and match attributes. For XSLT to function, the source tree must be properly structured. Schemas, DTDs and validating parsers can validate document structure before using XPath and XSLTs.

A Simple XSL Example

Figure 12.20 lists an XML document that describes various sports. The output shows the result of the transformation (specified in the XSLT template of Fig. 12.21) rendered by Internet Explorer.

To perform transformations, an XSLT processor is required. Popular XSLT processors include Microsoft's MSXML and the Apache Software Foundation's *Xalan 2* (xml.apache.org). The XML document in Fig. 12.20 is transformed into an XHTML document by MSXML when the document is loaded in Internet Explorer. MSXML is both an XML parser and an XSLT processor. Firefox also includes an XSLT processor.

```
1   <?xml version = "1.0"?>
2   <?xml-stylesheet type = "text/xsl" href = "sports.xsl"?>
3
4   <!-- Fig. 12.20: sports.xml -->
5   <!-- Sports Database -->
6
7   <sports>
8      <game id = "783">
9         <name>Cricket</name>
10
11         <paragraph>
12            More popular among commonwealth nations.
13         </paragraph>
14      </game>
15
16      <game id = "239">
17         <name>Baseball</name>
18
19         <paragraph>
20            More popular in America.
21         </paragraph>
22      </game>
23
24      <game id = "418">
25         <name>Soccer (Futbol)</name>
26
27         <paragraph>
28            Most popular sport in the world.
29         </paragraph>
30      </game>
31   </sports>
```

Fig. 12.20 | XML document that describes various sports. (Part 1 of 2.)

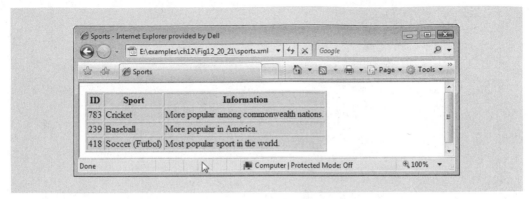

Fig. 12.20 | XML document that describes various sports. (Part 2 of 2.)

Line 2 (Fig. 12.20) is a *processing instruction (PI)* that references the XSL style sheet sports.xsl (Fig. 12.21). A processing instruction is embedded in an XML document and provides application-specific information to whichever XML processor the application uses. In this particular case, the processing instruction specifies the location of an XSLT document with which to transform the XML document. The *<?* and *?>* (line 2, Fig. 12.20) delimit a processing instruction, which consists of a *PI target* (e.g., xml-stylesheet) and a *PI value* (e.g., type = "text/xsl" href = "sports.xsl"). The PI value's type attribute specifies that sports.xsl is a text/xsl file (i.e., a text file containing XSL content). The href attribute specifies the name and location of the style sheet to apply—in this case, sports.xsl in the current directory.

Software Engineering Observation 12.5

XSL enables document authors to separate data presentation (specified in XSL documents) from data description (specified in XML documents).

Common Programming Error 12.10

You will sometimes see the XML processing instruction <?xml-stylesheet?> written as <?xml:stylesheet?> with a colon rather than a dash. The version with a colon results in an XML parsing error in Firefox.

Figure 12.21 shows the XSL document for transforming the structured data of the XML document of Fig. 12.20 into an XHTML document for presentation. By convention, XSL documents have the filename extension *.xsl*.

```
1   <?xml version = "1.0"?>
2   <!-- Fig. 12.21: sports.xsl -->
3   <!-- A simple XSLT transformation -->
4
5   <!-- reference XSL style sheet URI -->
6   <xsl-stylesheet version = "1.0"
7      xmlns:xsl = "http://www.w3.org/1999/XSL/Transform">
8
```

Fig. 12.21 | XSLT that creates elements and attributes in an XHTML document. (Part 1 of 2.)

```
 9    <xsl:output method = "html" omit-xml-declaration = "no"
10       doctype-system =
11          "http://www.w3c.org/TR/xhtml1/DTD/xhtml1-strict.dtd"
12       doctype-public = "-//W3C//DTD XHTML 1.0 Strict//EN"/>
13
14    <xsl:template match = "/"> <!-- match root element -->
15
16    <html xmlns = "http://www.w3.org/1999/xhtml">
17       <head>
18          <title>Sports</title>
19       </head>
20
21       <body>
22          <table border = "1" bgcolor = "wheat">
23             <thead>
24                <tr>
25                   <th>ID</th>
26                   <th>Sport</th>
27                   <th>Information</th>
28                </tr>
29             </thead>
30
31             <!-- insert each name and paragraph element value -->
32             <!-- into a table row. -->
33             <xsl:for-each select = "/sports/game">
34                <tr>
35                   <td><xsl:value-of select = "@id"/></td>
36                   <td><xsl:value-of select = "name"/></td>
37                   <td><xsl:value-of select = "paragraph"/></td>
38                </tr>
39             </xsl:for-each>
40          </table>
41       </body>
42    </html>
43
44    </xsl:template>
45 </xsl:stylesheet>
```

Fig. 12.21 | XSLT that creates elements and attributes in an XHTML document. (Part 2 of 2.)

Lines 6–7 begin the XSL style sheet with the *stylesheet* start tag. Attribute *version* specifies the XSLT version to which this document conforms. Line 7 binds namespace prefix *xsl* to the W3C's XSLT URI (i.e., http://www.w3.org/1999/XSL/Transform).

Lines 9–12 use element *xsl:output* to write an XHTML document type declaration (DOCTYPE) to the result tree (i.e., the XML document to be created). The DOCTYPE identifies XHTML as the type of the resulting document. Attribute method is assigned "html", which indicates that HTML is being output to the result tree. Attribute *omit-xml-dec-laration* specifies whether the transformation should write the XML declaration to the result tree. In this case, we do not want to omit the XML declaration, so we assign to this attribute the value "no". Attributes doctype-system and doctype-public write the DOC-TYPE DTD information to the result tree.

XSLT uses *templates* (i.e., *xsl:template* elements) to describe how to transform particular nodes from the source tree to the result tree. A template is applied to nodes that are specified in the required match attribute. Line 14 uses the *match* attribute to select the *document root* (i.e., the conceptual part of the document that contains the root element and everything below it) of the XML source document (i.e., sports.xml). The XPath character / (a forward slash) always selects the document root. Recall that XPath is a string-based language used to locate parts of an XML document easily. In XPath, a leading forward slash specifies that we are using *absolute addressing* (i.e., we are starting from the root and defining paths down the source tree). In the XML document of Fig. 12.20, the child nodes of the document root are the two processing instruction nodes (lines 1–2), the two comment nodes (lines 4–5) and the sports element node (lines 7–31). The template in Fig. 12.21, line 14, matches a node (i.e., the root node), so the contents of the template are now added to the result tree.

The MSXML processor writes the XHTML in lines 16–29 (Fig. 12.21) to the result tree exactly as it appears in the XSL document. Now the result tree consists of the DOCTYPE definition and the XHTML code from lines 16–29. Lines 33–39 use element *xsl:for-each* to iterate through the source XML document, searching for game elements. Attribute *select* is an XPath expression that specifies the nodes (called the *node set*) on which the xsl:for-each operates. Again, the first forward slash means that we are using absolute addressing. The forward slash between sports and game indicates that game is a child node of sports. Thus, the xsl:for-each finds game nodes that are children of the sports node. The XML document sports.xml contains only one sports node, which is also the document root node. After finding the elements that match the selection criteria, the xsl:for-each processes each element with the code in lines 34–38 (these lines produce one row in a table each time they execute) and places the result of lines 34–38 in the result tree.

Line 35 uses element *value-of* to retrieve attribute id's value and place it in a td element in the result tree. The XPath symbol @ specifies that id is an attribute node of the context node game. Lines 36–37 place the name and paragraph element values in td elements and insert them in the result tree. When an XPath expression has no beginning forward slash, the expression uses *relative addressing*. Omitting the beginning forward slash tells the xsl:value-of select statements to search for name and paragraph elements that are children of the context node, not the root node. Due to the last XPath expression selection, the current context node is game, which indeed has an id attribute, a name child element and a paragraph child element.

Using XSLT to Sort and Format Data

Figure 12.22 presents an XML document (sorting.xml) that marks up information about a book. Note that several elements of the markup describing the book appear out of order (e.g., the element describing Chapter 3 appears before the element describing Chapter 2). We arranged them this way purposely to demonstrate that the XSL style sheet referenced in line 2 (sorting.xsl) can sort the XML file's data for presentation purposes.

```
1   <?xml version = "1.0"?>
2   <?xml-stylesheet type = "text/xsl" href = "sorting.xsl"?>
3
```

Fig. 12.22 | XML document containing book information. (Part 1 of 2.)

```
4    <!-- Fig. 12.22: sorting.xml -->
5    <!-- XML document containing book information -->
6    <book isbn = "999-99999-9-X">
7       <title>Deitel&apos;s XML Primer</title>
8
9       <author>
10         <firstName>Jane</firstName>
11         <lastName>Blue</lastName>
12      </author>
13
14      <chapters>
15         <frontMatter>
16            <preface pages = "2" />
17            <contents pages = "5" />
18            <illustrations pages = "4" />
19         </frontMatter>
20
21         <chapter number = "3" pages = "44">Advanced XML</chapter>
22         <chapter number = "2" pages = "35">Intermediate XML</chapter>
23         <appendix number = "B" pages = "26">Parsers and Tools</appendix>
24         <appendix number = "A" pages = "7">Entities</appendix>
25         <chapter number = "1" pages = "28">XML Fundamentals</chapter>
26      </chapters>
27
28      <media type = "CD" />
29   </book>
```

Fig. 12.22 | XML document containing book information. (Part 2 of 2.)

Figure 12.23 presents an XSL document (sorting.xsl) for transforming sorting.xml (Fig. 12.22) to XHTML. Recall that an XSL document navigates a source tree and builds a result tree. In this example, the source tree is XML, and the output tree is XHTML. Line 14 of Fig. 12.23 matches the root element of the document in Fig. 12.22. Line 15 outputs an html start tag to the result tree. In line 16, the <xsl:apply-templates/> element specifies that the XSLT processor is to apply the xsl:templates defined in this XSL document to the current node's (i.e., the document root's) children. The content from the applied templates is output in the html element that ends at line 17.

```
1    <?xml version = "1.0"?>
2
3    <!-- Fig. 12.23: sorting.xsl -->
4    <!-- Transformation of book information into XHTML -->
5    <xsl:stylesheet version = "1.0"
6       xmlns:xsl = "http://www.w3.org/1999/XSL/Transform">
7
8       <!-- write XML declaration and DOCTYPE DTD information -->
9       <xsl:output method = "html" omit-xml-declaration = "no"
10         doctype-system = "http://www.w3.org/TR/xhtml11/DTD/xhtml11.dtd"
11         doctype-public = "-//W3C//DTD XHTML 1.1//EN"/>
12
```

Fig. 12.23 | XSL document that transforms sorting.xml into XHTML. (Part 1 of 3.)

```
13    <!-- match document root -->
14    <xsl:template match = "/">
15        <html xmlns = "http://www.w3.org/1999/xhtml">
16            <xsl:apply-templates/>
17        </html>
18    </xsl:template>
19
20    <!-- match book -->
21    <xsl:template match = "book">
22        <head>
23            <title>ISBN <xsl:value-of select = "@isbn"/> -
24                <xsl:value-of select = "title"/></title>
25        </head>
26
27        <body>
28            <h1 style = "color: blue"><xsl:value-of select = "title"/></h1>
29            <h2 style = "color: blue">by
30                <xsl:value-of select = "author/lastName"/>,
31                <xsl:value-of select = "author/firstName"/></h2>
32
33            <table style = "border-style: groove; background-color: wheat">
34
35                <xsl:for-each select = "chapters/frontMatter/*">
36                    <tr>
37                        <td style = "text-align: right">
38                            <xsl:value-of select = "name()"/>
39                        </td>
40
41                        <td>
42                            ( <xsl:value-of select = "@pages"/> pages )
43                        </td>
44                    </tr>
45                </xsl:for-each>
46
47                <xsl:for-each select = "chapters/chapter">
48                    <xsl:sort select = "@number" data-type = "number"
49                        order = "ascending"/>
50                    <tr>
51                        <td style = "text-align: right">
52                            Chapter <xsl:value-of select = "@number"/>
53                        </td>
54
55                        <td>
56                            <xsl:value-of select = "text()"/>
57                            ( <xsl:value-of select = "@pages"/> pages )
58                        </td>
59                    </tr>
60                </xsl:for-each>
61
62                <xsl:for-each select = "chapters/appendix">
63                    <xsl:sort select = "@number" data-type = "text"
64                        order = "ascending"/>
```

Fig. 12.23 | XSL document that transforms `sorting.xml` into XHTML. (Part 2 of 3.)

```
65                   <tr>
66                       <td style = "text-align: right">
67                           Appendix <xsl:value-of select = "@number"/>
68                       </td>
69
70                       <td>
71                           <xsl:value-of select = "text()"/>
72                           ( <xsl:value-of select = "@pages"/> pages )
73                       </td>
74                   </tr>
75               </xsl:for-each>
76           </table>
77
78           <br /><p style = "color: blue">Pages:
79               <xsl:variable name = "pagecount"
80                   select = "sum(chapters//*/@pages)"/>
81               <xsl:value-of select = "$pagecount"/>
82               <br />Media Type: <xsl:value-of select = "media/@type"/></p>
83           </body>
84       </xsl:template>
85   </xsl:stylesheet>
```

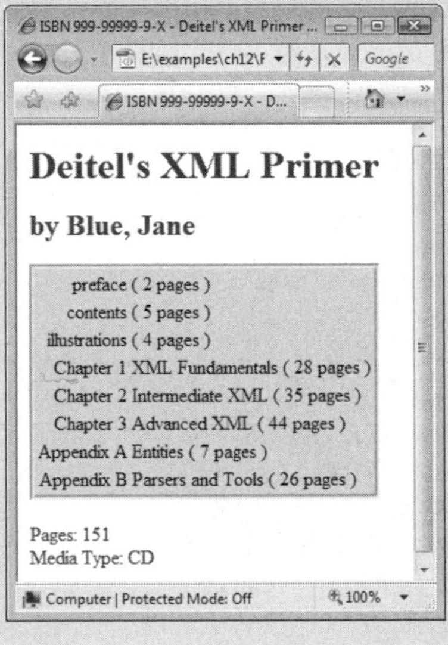

Fig. 12.23 │ XSL document that transforms `sorting.xml` into XHTML. (Part 3 of 3.)

Lines 21–84 specify a template that matches element book. The template indicates how to format the information contained in book elements of `sorting.xml` (Fig. 12.22) as XHTML.

Lines 23–24 create the title for the XHTML document. We use the book's ISBN (from attribute `isbn`) and the contents of element `title` to create the string that appears in the browser window's title bar (**ISBN 999-99999-9-X - Deitel's XML Primer**).

Line 28 creates a header element that contains the book's title. Lines 29–31 create a header element that contains the book's author. Because the context node (i.e., the current node being processed) is book, the XPath expression author/lastName selects the author's last name, and the expression author/firstName selects the author's first name.

Line 35 selects each element (indicated by an asterisk) that is a child of element frontMatter. Line 38 calls *node-set function **name*** to retrieve the current node's element name (e.g., preface). The current node is the context node specified in the xsl:for-each (line 35). Line 42 retrieves the value of the pages attribute of the current node.

Line 47 selects each chapter element. Lines 48–49 use element ***xsl:sort*** to sort chapters by number in ascending order. Attribute ***select*** selects the value of attribute number in context node chapter. Attribute ***data-type***, with value "number", specifies a numeric sort, and attribute ***order***, with value "ascending", specifies ascending order. Attribute data-type also accepts the value "text" (line 63), and attribute order also accepts the value "descending". Line 56 uses *node-set function **text*** to obtain the text between the chapter start and end tags (i.e., the name of the chapter). Line 57 retrieves the value of the pages attribute of the current node. Lines 62–75 perform similar tasks for each appendix.

Lines 79–80 use an ***XSL variable*** to store the value of the book's total page count and output the page count to the result tree. Attribute ***name*** specifies the variable's name (i.e., pagecount), and attribute select assigns a value to the variable. Function ***sum*** (line 80) totals the values for all page attribute values. The two slashes between chapters and * indicate a *recursive descent*—the MSXML processor will search for elements that contain an attribute named pages in all descendant nodes of chapters. The XPath expression

    //*

selects all the nodes in an XML document. Line 81 retrieves the value of the newly created XSL variable pagecount by placing a dollar sign in front of its name.

Summary of XSL Style-Sheet Elements

This section's examples used several predefined XSL elements to perform various operations. Figure 12.24 lists these elements and several other commonly used XSL elements. For more information on these elements and XSL in general, see www.w3.org/Style/XSL.

Element	Description
<xsl:apply-templates>	Applies the templates of the XSL document to the children of the current node.
<xsl:apply-templates match = "*expression*">	Applies the templates of the XSL document to the children of *expression*. The value of the attribute match (i.e., *expression*) must be an XPath expression that specifies elements.
<xsl:template>	Contains rules to apply when a specified node is matched.
<xsl:value-of select = "*expression*">	Selects the value of an XML element and adds it to the output tree of the transformation. The required select attribute contains an XPath expression.

Fig. 12.24 | XSL style-sheet elements. (Part 1 of 2.)

Element	Description
`<xsl:for-each select = "expression">`	Applies a template to every node selected by the XPath specified by the `select` attribute.
`<xsl:sort select = "expression">`	Used as a child element of an `<xsl:apply-templates>` or `<xsl:for-each>` element. Sorts the nodes selected by the `<xsl:apply-template>` or `<xsl:for-each>` element so that the nodes are processed in sorted order.
`<xsl:output>`	Has various attributes to define the format (e.g., XML, XHTML), version (e.g., 1.0, 2.0), document type and media type of the output document. This tag is a top-level element—it can be used only as a child element of an `xml:stylesheet`.
`<xsl:copy>`	Adds the current node to the output tree.

Fig. 12.24 | XSL style-sheet elements. (Part 2 of 2.)

This section introduced Extensible Stylesheet Language (XSL) and showed how to create XSL transformations to convert XML documents from one format to another. We showed how to transform XML documents to XHTML documents for display in a web browser. Recall that these transformations are performed by MSXML, Internet Explorer's built-in XML parser and XSLT processor. In most business applications, XML documents are transferred between business partners and are transformed to other XML vocabularies programmatically. Section 12.9 discusses the XML Document Object Model (DOM) and demonstrates how to manipulate the DOM of an XML document using JavaScript.

12.9 Document Object Model (DOM)

Although an XML document is a text file, retrieving data from the document using traditional sequential file processing techniques is neither practical nor efficient, especially for adding and removing elements dynamically.

Upon successfully parsing a document, some XML parsers store document data as tree structures in memory. Figure 12.25 illustrates the tree structure for the root element of the document `article.xml` (Fig. 12.2). This hierarchical tree structure is called a *Document Object Model* (*DOM*) *tree*, and an XML parser that creates this type of structure is known as a *DOM parser*. Each element name (e.g., `article`, `date`, `firstName`) is represented by a node. A node that contains other nodes (called *child nodes* or children) is called a *parent node* (e.g., `author`). A parent node can have many children, but a child node can have only one parent node. Nodes that are peers (e.g., `firstName` and `lastName`) are called *sibling nodes*. A node's *descendant nodes* include its children, its children's children and so on. A node's *ancestor nodes* include its parent, its parent's parent and so on. Many of the XML DOM capabilities you'll see in this section are similar or identical to those of the XHTML DOM you learned in Chapter 10.

The DOM tree has a single *root node*, which contains all the other nodes in the document. For example, the root node of the DOM tree that represents `article.xml` contains a node for the XML declaration (line 1), two nodes for the comments (lines 3–4) and a node for the XML document's root element `article` (line 5).

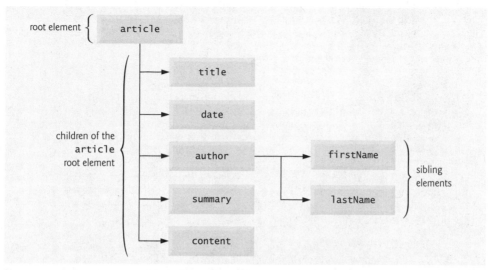

Fig. 12.25 | Tree structure for the document `article.xml` of Fig. 12.2.

To introduce document manipulation with the XML Document Object Model, we provide a scripting example (Fig. 12.26) that uses JavaScript and XML. This example loads the XML document `article.xml` (Fig. 12.2) and uses the XML DOM API to display the document's element names and values. The example also provides buttons that enable you to navigate the DOM structure. As you click each button, an appropriate part of the document is highlighted. All of this is done in a manner that enables the example to execute in both Internet Explorer 7 and Firefox 2 (and higher). Figure 12.26 lists the JavaScript code that manipulates this XML document and displays its content in an XHTML page.

Overview of the body Element
Lines 203–217 create the XHTML document's body. When the body loads, its onload event calls our JavaScript function `loadXMLDocument` to load and display the contents of `article.xml` in the div at line 216 (outputDiv). Lines 204–215 define a form consisting of five buttons. When each button is pressed, it invokes one of our JavaScript functions to navigate `article.xml`'s DOM structure.

```
1   <?xml version = "1.0" encoding = "utf-8"?>
2   <!DOCTYPE html PUBLIC "-//W3C//DTD XHTML 1.0 Strict//EN"
3      "http://www.w3.org/TR/xhtml1/DTD/xhtml1-strict.dtd">
4
5   <!-- Fig. 12.26: XMLDOMTraversal.html -->
6   <!-- Traversing an XML document using the XML DOM. -->
7   <html xmlns = "http://www.w3.org/1999/xhtml">
8   <head>
9      <title>Traversing an XML document using the XML DOM</title>
10     <style type = "text/css">
```

Fig. 12.26 | Traversing an XML document using the XML DOM. (Part 1 of 9.)

```
11          .highlighted { background-color: yellow }
12          #outputDiv { font: 10pt "Lucida Console", monospace; }
13      </style>
14      <script type="text/javascript">
15      <!--
16      var doc; // variable to reference the XML document
17      var outputHTML = ""; // stores text to output in outputDiv
18      var idCounter = 1; // used to create div IDs
19      var depth = -1; // tree depth is -1 to start
20      var current = null; // represents the current node for traversals
21      var previous = null; // represent prior node in traversals
22
23      // load XML document based on whether the browser is IE7 or Firefox
24      function loadXMLDocument( url )
25      {
26          if ( window.ActiveXObject ) // IE7
27          {
28              // create IE7-specific XML document object
29              doc = new ActiveXObject( "Msxml2.DOMDocument.6.0" );
30              doc.async = false; // specifies synchronous loading of XML doc
31              doc.load( url ); // load the XML document specified by url
32              buildHTML( doc.childNodes ); // display the nodes
33              displayDoc();
34          } // end if
35          else if ( document.implementation &&
36              document.implementation.createDocument ) // other browsers
37          {
38              // create XML document object
39              doc = document.implementation.createDocument( "", "", null );
40              doc.load( url ); // load the XML document specified by url
41              doc.onload = function() // function to execute when doc loads
42              {
43                  buildHTML( doc.childNodes ); // called by XML doc onload event
44                  displayDoc(); // display the HTML
45              } // end XML document's onload event handler
46          } // end else
47          else // not supported
48              alert( 'This script is not supported by your browser' );
49      } // end function loadXMLDocument
50
51      // traverse xmlDocument and build XHTML representation of its content
52      function buildHTML( childList )
53      {
54          ++depth; // increase tab depth
55
56          // display each node's content
57          for ( var i = 0; i < childList.length; i++ )
58          {
59              switch ( childList[ i ].nodeType )
60              {
61                  case 1: // Node.ELEMENT_NODE; value used for portability
62                      outputHTML += "<div id=\"id" + idCounter + "\">";
63                      spaceOutput( depth ); // insert spaces
```

Fig. 12.26 | Traversing an XML document using the XML DOM. (Part 2 of 9.)

```
64          outputHTML += childList[ i ].nodeName; // show node's name
65          ++idCounter; // increment the id counter
66
67          // if current node has children, call buildHTML recursively
68          if ( childList[ i ].childNodes.length != 0 )
69              buildHTML( childList[ i ].childNodes );
70
71          outputHTML += "</div>";
72          break;
73       case 3: // Node.TEXT_NODE; value used for portability
74       case 8: // Node.COMMENT_NODE; value used for portability
75          // if nodeValue is not 3 or 6 spaces (Firefox issue),
76          // include nodeValue in HTML
77          if ( childList[ i ].nodeValue.indexOf( "   " ) == -1 &&
78              childList[ i ].nodeValue.indexOf( "      " ) == -1 )
79          {
80              outputHTML += "<div id=\"id" + idCounter + "\">";
81              spaceOutput( depth ); // insert spaces
82              outputHTML += childList[ i ].nodeValue + "</div>";
83              ++idCounter; // increment the id counter
84          } // end if
85       } // end switch
86    } // end for
87
88    --depth; // decrease tab depth
89 } // end function buildHTML
90
91 // display the XML document and highlight the first child
92 function displayDoc()
93 {
94    document.getElementById( "outputDiv" ).innerHTML = outputHTML;
95    current = document.getElementById( 'id1' );
96    setCurrentNodeStyle( current.id, true );
97 } // end function displayDoc
98
99 // insert non-breaking spaces for indentation
100 function spaceOutput( number )
101 {
102    for ( var i = 0; i < number; i++ )
103    {
104       outputHTML += "   ";
105    } // end for
106 } // end function spaceOutput
107
108 // highlight first child of current node
109 function processFirstChild()
110 {
111    if ( current.childNodes.length == 1 && // only one child
112       current.firstChild.nodeType == 3 )  // and it's a text node
113    {
114       alert( "There is no child node" );
115    } // end if
```

Fig. 12.26 | Traversing an XML document using the XML DOM. (Part 3 of 9.)

```
116        else if ( current.childNodes.length > 1 )
117        {
118           previous = current; // save currently highlighted node
119
120           if ( current.firstChild.nodeType != 3 ) // if not text node
121              current = current.firstChild; // get new current node
122           else // if text node, use firstChild's nextSibling instead
123              current = current.firstChild.nextSibling; // get first sibling
124
125           setCurrentNodeStyle( previous.id, false ); // remove highlight
126           setCurrentNodeStyle( current.id, true ); // add highlight
127        } // end if
128        else
129           alert( "There is no child node" );
130     } // end function processFirstChild
131
132     // highlight next sibling of current node
133     function processNextSibling()
134     {
135        if ( current.id != "outputDiv" && current.nextSibling )
136        {
137           previous = current; // save currently highlighted node
138           current = current.nextSibling; // get new current node
139           setCurrentNodeStyle( previous.id, false ); // remove highlight
140           setCurrentNodeStyle( current.id, true ); // add highlight
141        } // end if
142        else
143           alert( "There is no next sibling" );
144     } // end function processNextSibling
145
146     // highlight previous sibling of current node if it is not a text node
147     function processPreviousSibling()
148     {
149        if ( current.id != "outputDiv" && current.previousSibling &&
150           current.previousSibling.nodeType != 3 )
151        {
152           previous = current; // save currently highlighted node
153           current = current.previousSibling; // get new current node
154           setCurrentNodeStyle( previous.id, false ); // remove highlight
155           setCurrentNodeStyle( current.id, true ); // add highlight
156        } // end if
157        else
158           alert( "There is no previous sibling" );
159     } // end function processPreviousSibling
160
161     // highlight last child of current node
162     function processLastChild()
163     {
164        if ( current.childNodes.length == 1 &&
165           current.lastChild.nodeType == 3 )
166        {
167           alert( "There is no child node" );
168        } // end if
```

Fig. 12.26 | Traversing an XML document using the XML DOM. (Part 4 of 9.)

```
169          else if ( current.childNodes.length != 0 )
170          {
171             previous = current; // save currently highlighted node
172             current = current.lastChild; // get new current node
173             setCurrentNodeStyle( previous.id, false ); // remove highlight
174             setCurrentNodeStyle( current.id, true ); // add highlight
175          } // end if
176          else
177             alert( "There is no child node" );
178       } // end function processLastChild
179
180       // highlight parent of current node
181       function processParentNode()
182       {
183          if ( current.parentNode.id != "body" )
184          {
185             previous = current; // save currently highlighted node
186             current = current.parentNode; // get new current node
187             setCurrentNodeStyle( previous.id, false ); // remove highlight
188             setCurrentNodeStyle( current.id, true ); // add highlight
189          } // end if
190          else
191             alert( "There is no parent node" );
192       } // end function processParentNode
193
194       // set style of node with specified id
195       function setCurrentNodeStyle( id, highlight )
196       {
197          document.getElementById( id ).className =
198             ( highlight ? "highlighted" : "" );
199       } // end function setCurrentNodeStyle
200       // -->
201    </script>
202 </head>
203 <body id = "body" onload = "loadXMLDocument( 'article.xml' );">
204    <form action = "" onsubmit = "return false;">
205       <input type = "submit" value = "firstChild"
206          onclick = "processFirstChild()"/>
207       <input type = "submit" value = "nextSibling"
208          onclick = "processNextSibling()"/>
209       <input type = "submit" value = "previousSibling"
210          onclick = "processPreviousSibling()"/>
211       <input type = "submit" value = "lastChild"
212          onclick = "processLastChild()"/>
213       <input type = "submit" value = "parentNode"
214          onclick = "processParentNode()"/>
215    </form><br/>
216    <div id = "outputDiv"></div>
217 </body>
218 </html>
```

Fig. 12.26 | Traversing an XML document using the XML DOM. (Part 5 of 9.)

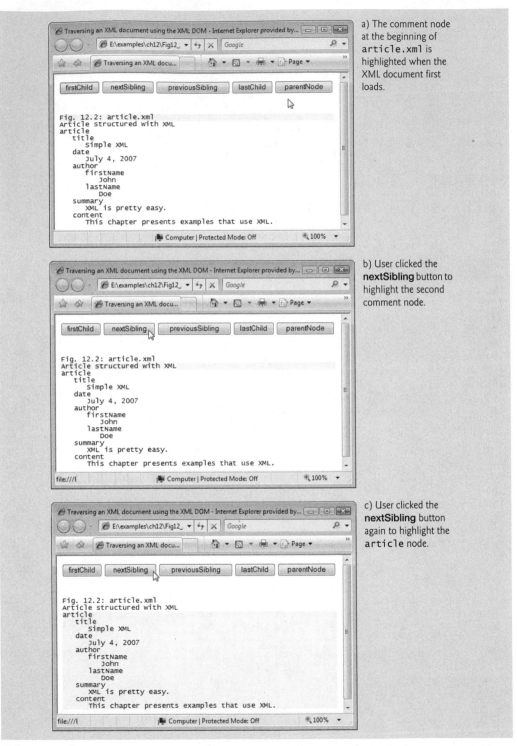

a) The comment node at the beginning of `article.xml` is highlighted when the XML document first loads.

b) User clicked the **nextSibling** button to highlight the second comment node.

c) User clicked the **nextSibling** button again to highlight the `article` node.

Fig. 12.26 | Traversing an XML document using the XML DOM. (Part 6 of 9.)

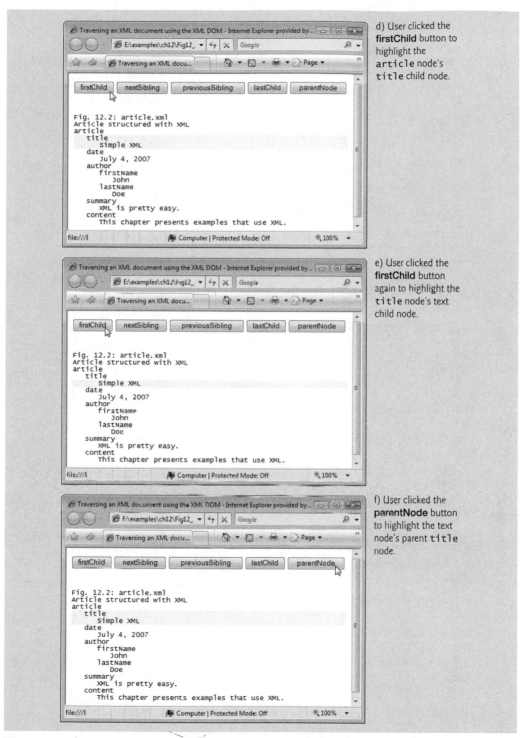

d) User clicked the **firstChild** button to highlight the `article` node's `title` child node.

e) User clicked the **firstChild** button again to highlight the `title` node's text child node.

f) User clicked the **parentNode** button to highlight the text node's parent `title` node.

Fig. 12.26 | Traversing an XML document using the XML DOM. (Part 7 of 9.)

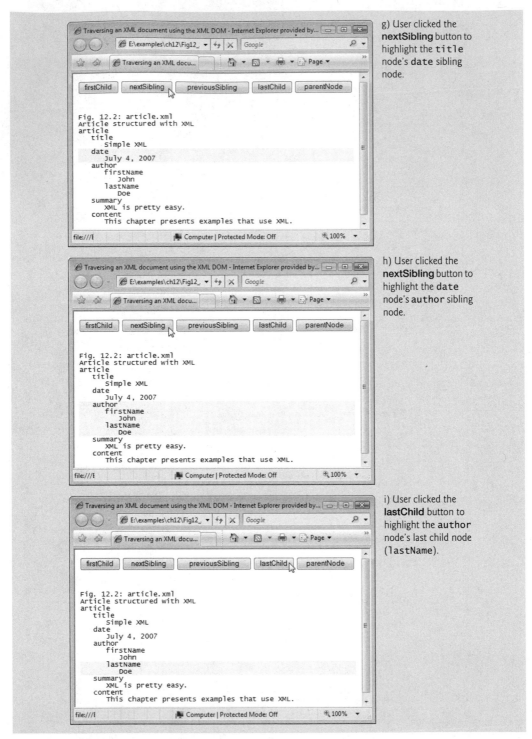

g) User clicked the **nextSibling** button to highlight the `title` node's `date` sibling node.

h) User clicked the **nextSibling** button to highlight the `date` node's `author` sibling node.

i) User clicked the **lastChild** button to highlight the `author` node's last child node (`lastName`).

Fig. 12.26 | Traversing an XML document using the XML DOM. (Part 8 of 9.)

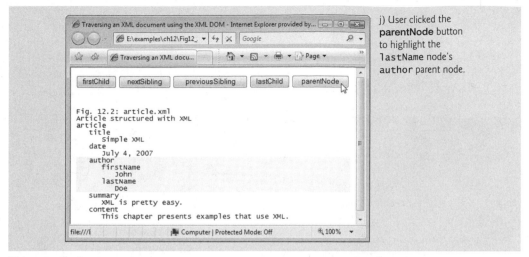

j) User clicked the
parentNode button
to highlight the
`lastName` node's
`author` parent node.

Fig. 12.26 | Traversing an XML document using the XML DOM. (Part 9 of 9.)

Global Script Variables

Lines 16–21 in the `script` element (lines 14–201) declare several variables used throughout the script. Variable `doc` references a DOM object representation of `article.xml`. Variable `outputHTML` stores the markup that will be placed in `outputDiv`. Variable `idCounter` is used to track the unique `id` attributes that we assign to each element in the `outputHTML` markup. These `id`s will be used to dynamically highlight parts of the document when the user clicks the buttons in the form. Variable `depth` determines the indentation level for the content in `article.xml`. We use this to structure the output using the nesting of the elements in `article.xml`. Variables `current` and `previous` track the current and previous nodes in `article.xml`'s DOM structure as the user navigates it.

Function loadXMLDocument

Function `loadXMLDocument` (lines 24–49) receives the URL of an XML document to load, then loads the document based on whether the browser is Internet Explorer 7 (26–34) or Firefox (lines 35–46)—the code for Firefox works in several other browsers as well. Line 26 determines whether `window.`***ActiveXObject*** exists. If so, this indicates that the browser is Internet Explorer. Line 29 creates a Microsoft `ActiveXObject` that loads Microsoft's *MSXML parser*, which provides capabilities for manipulating XML documents. Line 30 indicates that we'd like the XML document to be loaded synchronously, then line 31 uses the `ActiveXObject`'s *load method* to load `article.xml`. When this completes, we call our `buildHTML` method (defined in lines 52–89) to construct an XHTML representation of the XML document. The expression `doc.childNodes` is a list of the XML document's top-level nodes. Line 33 calls our `displayDoc` function (lines 92–97) to display the contents of `article.xml` in `outputDiv`.

If the browser is Firefox, then the document object's ***implementation*** property and the `implementation` property's ***createDocument*** method will exist (lines 35–36). In this case, line 39 uses the `createDocument` method to create an empty XML document object. If necessary, you can specify the XML document's namespace as the first argument and its root element as the second argument. We used empty strings for both in this example.

According to the site www.w3schools.com/xml/xml_parser.asp, the third argument is not implemented yet, so it should always be null. Line 40 calls its load method to load article.xml. Firefox loads the XML document asynchronously, so you must use the XML document's onload property to specify a function to call (an anonymous function in this example) when the document finishes loading. When this event occurs, lines 43–44 call buildHTML and displayDoc just as we did in lines 32–33.

Common Programming Error 12.11

Attempting to process the contents of a dynamically loaded XML document in Firefox before the document's onload event fires is a logic error. The document's contents are not available until the onload event fires.

Function *buildHTML*

Function buildHTML (lines 52–89) is a recursive function that receives a list of nodes as an argument. Line 54 increments the depth for indentation purposes. Lines 57–86 iterate through the nodes in the list. The switch statement (lines 59–85) uses the current node's **nodeType** *property* to determine whether the current node is an element (line 61), a text node (i.e., the text content of an element; line 73) or a comment node (line 74). If it is an element, then we begin a new div element in our XHTML (line 62) and give it a unique id. Then function spaceOutput (defined in lines 100–106) appends *nonbreaking spaces ( )*—i.e., spaces that the browser is not allowed to collapse or that can be used to keep words together—to indent the current element to the correct level. Line 64 appends the name of the current element using the node's **nodeName** *property*. If the current element has children, the length of the current node's childNodes list is nonzero and line 69 recursively calls buildHTML to append the current element's child nodes to the markup. When that recursive call completes, line 71 completes the div element that we started at line 62.

If the current element is a text node, lines 77–78 obtain the node's value with the **nodeValue** *property* and use the string method indexOf to determine whether the node's value starts with three or six spaces. Unfortunately, unlike MSMXL, Firefox's XML parser does not ignore the white space used for indentation in XML documents. Instead it creates text nodes containing just the space characters. The condition in lines 77–78 enables us to ignore these nodes in Firefox. If the node contains text, lines 80–82 append a new div to the markup and use the node's nodeValue property to insert that text in the div. Line 88 in buildHTML decrements the depth counter.

Portability Tip 12.4

Firefox's XML parser does not ignore white space used for indentation in XML documents. Instead, it creates text nodes containing the white-space characters.

Function *displayDoc*

In function displayDoc (lines 92–97), line 94 uses the DOM's getElementById method to obtain the outputDiv element and set its innerHTML property to the new markup generated by buildHTML. Then, line 95 sets variable current to refer to the div with id 'id1' in the new markup, and line 96 uses our setCurrentNodeStyle method (defined at lines 195–199) to highlight that div.

Functions *processFirstChild and processLastChild*

Function processFirstChild (lines 109–130) is invoked by the onclick event of the button at lines 205–206. If the current node has only one child and it's a text node (lines 111–112), line 114 displays an alert dialog indicating that there is no child node—we navigate only to nested XML elements in this example. If there are two or more children, line 118 stores the value of current in previous, and lines 120–123 set current to refer to its *firstChild* (if this child is not a text node) or its firstChild's *nextSibling* (if the firstChild is a text node)—again, this is to ensure that we navigate only to nodes that represent XML elements. Then lines 125–126 unhighlight the previous node and highlight the new current node. Function processLastChild (lines 162–178) works similarly, using the current node's *lastChild* property.

Functions *processNextSibling and processPreviousSibling*

Function processNextSibling (lines 133–144) first ensures that the current node is not the outputDiv and that nextSibling exists. If so, lines 137–140 adjust the previous and current nodes accordingly and update their highlighting. Function processPreviousSibling (lines 147–159) works similarly, ensuring first that the current node is not the outputDiv, that previousSibling exists and that previousSibling is not a text node.

Function *processParentNode*

Function processParentNode (lines 181–192) first checks whether the current node's *parentNode* is the XHTML page's body. If not, lines 185–188 adjust the previous and current nodes accordingly and update their highlighting.

Common DOM Properties

The tables in Figs. 12.27–12.32 describe many common DOM properties and methods. Some of the key DOM objects are *Node* (a node in the tree), *NodeList* (an ordered set of Nodes), *Document* (the document), *Element* (an element node), *Attr* (an attribute node) and *Text* (a text node). There are many more objects, properties and methods than we can possibly list here. Our XML Resource Center (www.deitel.com/XML/) includes links to various DOM reference websites.

Property/Method	Description
nodeType	An integer representing the node type.
nodeName	The name of the node.
nodeValue	A string or null depending on the node type.
parentNode	The parent node.
childNodes	A NodeList (Fig. 12.28) with all the children of the node.
firstChild	The first child in the Node's NodeList.
lastChild	The last child in the Node's NodeList.
previousSibling	The node preceding this node; null if there is no such node.
nextSibling	The node following this node; null if there is no such node.

Fig. 12.27 | Common Node properties and methods. (Part 1 of 2.)

Property/Method	Description
attributes	A collection of Attr objects (Fig. 12.31) containing the attributes for this node.
insertBefore	Inserts the node (passed as the first argument) before the existing node (passed as the second argument). If the new node is already in the tree, it is removed before insertion. The same behavior is true for other methods that add nodes.
replaceChild	Replaces the second argument node with the first argument node.
removeChild	Removes the child node passed to it.
appendChild	Appends the node it receives to the list of child nodes.

Fig. 12.27 | Common Node properties and methods. (Part 2 of 2.)

Property/Method	Description
item	Method that receives an index number and returns the element node at that index. Indices range from 0 to *length* − 1. You can also access the nodes in a NodeList via array indexing.
length	The total number of nodes in the list.

Fig. 12.28 | NodeList property and method.

Property/Method	Description
documentElement	The root node of the document.
createElement	Creates and returns an element node with the specified tag name.
createAttribute	Creates and returns an Attr node (Fig. 12.31) with the specified name and value.
createTextNode	Creates and returns a text node that contains the specified text.
getElementsByTagName	Returns a NodeList of all the nodes in the subtree with the name specified as the first argument, ordered as they would be encountered in a preorder traversal. An optional second argument specifies either the direct child nodes (0) or any descendant (1).

Fig. 12.29 | Document properties and methods.

Property/Method	Description
tagName	The name of the element.
getAttribute	Returns the value of the specified attribute.

Fig. 12.30 | Element property and methods. (Part 1 of 2.)

Property/Method	Description
setAttribute	Changes the value of the attribute passed as the first argument to the value passed as the second argument.
removeAttribute	Removes the specified attribute.
getAttributeNode	Returns the specified attribute node.
setAttributeNode	Adds a new attribute node with the specified name.

Fig. 12.30 | Element property and methods. (Part 2 of 2.)

Property	Description
value	The specified attribute's value.
name	The name of the attribute.

Fig. 12.31 | Attr properties.

Property	Description
data	The text contained in the node.
length	The number of characters contained in the node.

Fig. 12.32 | Text methods.

Locating Data in XML Documents with XPath

Although you can use XML DOM capabilities to navigate through and manipulate nodes, this is not the most efficient means of locating data in an XML document's DOM tree. A simpler way to locate nodes is to search for lists of nodes matching search criteria that are written as XPath expressions. Recall that XPath (XML Path Language) provides a syntax for locating specific nodes in XML documents effectively and efficiently. XPath is a string-based language of expressions used by XML and many of its related technologies (such as XSLT, discussed in Section 12.8).

Figure 12.33 enables the user to enter XPath expressions in an XHTML form. When the user clicks the **Get Matches** button, the script applies the XPath expression to the XML DOM and displays the matching nodes. Figure 12.34 shows the XML document sports.xml that we use in this example. [*Note:* The versions of sports.xml presented in Fig. 12.34 and Fig. 12.20 are nearly identical. In the current example, we do not want to apply an XSLT, so we omit the processing instruction found in line 2 of Fig. 12.20. We also removed extra blank lines to save space.]

The program of Fig. 12.33 loads the XML document sports.xml (Fig. 12.34) using the same techniques we presented in Fig. 12.26, so we focus on only the new features in this example. Internet Explorer 7 (MSXML) and Firefox handle XPath processing differently, so this example declares the variable browser (line 17) to store the browser that loaded the page. In function loadDocument (lines 20–40), lines 28 and 36 assign a string to variable browser indicating the appropriate browser.

```
1   <?xml version = "1.0" encoding = "utf-8"?>
2   <!DOCTYPE html PUBLIC "-//W3C//DTD XHTML 1.0 Strict//EN"
3      "http://www.w3.org/TR/xhtml1/DTD/xhtml1-strict.dtd">
4
5   <!-- Fig. 12.33: xpath.html -->
6   <!-- Using XPath to locate nodes in an XML document. -->
7   <html xmlns = "http://www.w3.org/1999/xhtml">
8   <head>
9      <title>Using XPath to Locate Nodes in an XML Document</title>
10     <style type = "text/css">
11        #outputDiv { font: 10pt "Lucida Console", monospace; }
12     </style>
13     <script type = "text/javascript">
14     <!--
15     var doc; // variable to reference the XML document
16     var outputHTML = ""; // stores text to output in outputDiv
17     var browser = ""; // used to determine which browser is being used
18
19     // load XML document based on whether the browser is IE7 or Firefox
20     function loadXMLDocument( url )
21     {
22        if ( window.ActiveXObject ) // IE7
23        {
24           // create IE7-specific XML document object
25           doc = new ActiveXObject( "Msxml2.DOMDocument.6.0" );
26           doc.async = false; // specifies synchronous loading of XML doc
27           doc.load( url ); // load the XML document specified by url
28           browser = "IE7"; // set browser
29        } // end if
30        else if ( document.implementation &&
31           document.implementation.createDocument ) // other browsers
32        {
33           // create XML document object
34           doc = document.implementation.createDocument( "", "", null );
35           doc.load( url ); // load the XML document specified by url
36           browser = "FF2"; // set browser
37        } // end else
38        else // not supported
39           alert( 'This script is not supported by your browser' );
40     } // end function loadXMLDocument
41
42     // display the XML document
43     function displayDoc()
44     {
45        document.getElementById( "outputDiv" ).innerHTML = outputHTML;
46     } // end function displayDoc
47
48     // obtain and apply XPath expression
49     function processXPathExpression()
50     {
```

Fig. 12.33 | Using XPath to locate nodes in an XML document. (Part 1 of 3.)

```
51          var xpathExpression = document.getElementById( "inputField" ).value;
52          outputHTML = "";
53
54          if ( browser == "IE7" )
55          {
56             var result = doc.selectNodes( xpathExpression );
57
58             for ( var i = 0; i < result.length; i++ )
59                outputHTML += "<div style='clear: both'>" +
60                   result.item( i ).text + "</div>";
61          } // end if
62          else // browser == "FF2"
63          {
64             var result = document.evaluate( xpathExpression, doc, null,
65                XPathResult.ANY_TYPE, null );
66             var current = result.iterateNext();
67
68             while ( current )
69             {
70                outputHTML += "<div style='clear: both'>" +
71                   current.textContent + "</div>";
72                current = result.iterateNext();
73             } // end while
74          } // end else
75
76          displayDoc();
77       } // end function processXPathExpression
78       // -->
79    </script>
80 </head>
81 <body id = "body" onload = "loadXMLDocument( 'sports.xml' );">
82    <form action = "" onsubmit = "return false;">
83       <input id = "inputField" type = "text" style = "width: 200px"/>
84       <input type = "submit" value = "Get Matches"
85          onclick = "processXPathExpression()"/>
86    </form><br/>
87    <div id = "outputDiv"></div>
88 </body>
89 </html>
```

(a)   (b)

Fig. 12.33 | Using XPath to locate nodes in an XML document. (Part 2 of 3.)

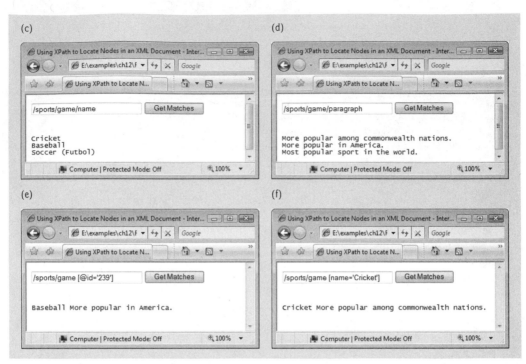

Fig. 12.33 | Using XPath to locate nodes in an XML document. (Part 3 of 3.)

```
 1   <?xml version = "1.0"?>
 2
 3   <!-- Fig. 12.34: sports.xml -->
 4   <!-- Sports Database       -->
 5   <sports>
 6      <game id = "783">
 7         <name>Cricket</name>
 8         <paragraph>
 9            More popular among commonwealth nations.
10         </paragraph>
11      </game>
12      <game id = "239">
13         <name>Baseball</name>
14         <paragraph>
15            More popular in America.
16         </paragraph>
17      </game>
18      <game id = "418">
19         <name>Soccer (Futbol)</name>
20         <paragraph>
21            Most popular sport in the world.
22         </paragraph>
23      </game>
24   </sports>
```

Fig. 12.34 | XML document that describes various sports.

When the body of this XHTML document loads, its onload event calls loadDocument (line 81) to load the sports.xml file. The user specifies the XPath expression in the input element at line 83. When the user clicks the **Get Matches** button (lines 84–85), its onclick event handler invokes our processXPathExpression function to locate any matches and display the results in outputDiv (line 87).

Function processXPathExpression (lines 49–77) first obtains the XPath expression (line 51). The document object's getElementById method returns the element with the id "inputField"; then we use its value property to get the XPath expression. Lines 54–61 apply the XPath expression in Internet Explorer 7, and lines 62–74 apply the XPath expression in Firefox. In IE7, the XML document object's *selectNodes method* receives an XPath expression as an argument and returns a collection of elements that match the expression. Lines 58–60 iterate through the results and mark up each one in a separate div element. After this loop completes, line 76 displays the generated markup in outputDiv.

For Firefox, lines 64–65 invoke the XML document object's *evaluate method*, which receives five arguments—the XPath expression, the document to apply the expression to, a namespace resolver, a result type and an XPathResult object into which to place the results. If the last argument is null, the function simply returns a new *XPathResult object* containing the matches. The namespace resolver argument can be null if you are not using XML namespace prefixes in the XPath processing. Lines 66–73 iterate through the XPathResult and mark up the results. Line 66 invokes the XPathResult's iterateNext method to position to the first result. If there is a result, the condition in line 68 will be true, and lines 70–71 create a div for that result. Line 72 then positions to the next result. After this loop completes, line 76 displays the generated markup in outputDiv.

Figure 12.35 summarizes the XPath expressions that we demonstrate in Fig. 12.33's sample outputs. For more information on using XPath in Firefox, visit the site developer.mozilla.org/en/docs/XPath. For more information on using XPath in Internet Explorer, visit msdn.microsoft.com/msdnmag/issues/0900/xml/.

Expression	Description
/sports	Matches all sports nodes that are child nodes of the document root node.
/sports/game	Matches all game nodes that are child nodes of sports, which is a child of the document root.
/sports/game/name	Matches all name nodes that are children of game. The game is a child of sports, which is a child of the document root.
/sports/game/paragraph	Matches all paragraphs that are children of game. The game is a child of sports, which is a child of the document root.
/sports/game [@id='239']	Matches the game node with the id number 239. The game is a child of sports, which is a child of the document root.
/sports/game [name='Cricket']	Matches all game nodes that contain a child element whose name is Cricket. The game is a child of sports, which is a child of the document root.

Fig. 12.35 | XPath expressions and descriptions.

12.10 RSS

RSS stands for *RDF (Resource Description Framework) Site Summary* and is also known as *Rich Site Summary* and *Really Simple Syndication*. RSS is an XML format used to syndicate website content, such as news articles, blog entries, product reviews, podcasts, vodcasts and more for inclusion on other websites. An RSS feed contains an *rss root element* with a `version` attribute and a *channel child element* with *item subelements*. Depending on the RSS version, the `channel` and `item` elements have certain required and optional child elements. The `item` elements provide the feed subscriber with a link to a web page or file, a title and description of the page or file. The most commonly used RSS feed versions are 0.91, 1.0, and 2.0, with RSS 2.0 being the most popular version. We discuss only RSS version 2.0 in this section.

RSS version 2.0, introduced in 2002, builds upon the RSS 0.9x versions. Version 2.0 does not contain length limitations or `item` element limitations of earlier versions, makes some formerly required elements optional, and adds new `channel` and `item` subelements. Removing length limitations on `item` descriptions allows RSS feeds to contain entire articles, blog entries and other web content. You can also have partial feeds that provide only a summary of the syndicated content. Partial feeds require the RSS subscriber to visit a website to view the complete content. RSS 2.0 allows `item` elements to contain an `enclosure` element providing the location of a media file that is related to the `item`. Such `enclosures` enable syndication of audio and video (such as podcasts and vodcasts) via RSS feeds.

By providing up-to-date, linkable content for anyone to use, RSS enables website developers to draw more traffic. It also allows users to get news and information from many sources easily and reduces content development time. RSS simplifies importing information from portals, weblogs and news sites. Any piece of information can be syndicated via RSS, not just news. After putting information in RSS format, an RSS program, such as a feed reader or aggregator, can check the feed for changes and react to them. For more details on RSS and for links to many RSS sites, visit our RSS Resource Center at www.deitel.com/RSS.

RSS 2.0 channel and item Elements

In RSS 2.0, the required child elements of `channel` are `description`, `link` and `title`, and the required child element of an `item` is either `title` or `description`. Figures 12.36–12.37 overview the child elements of `channels` and `items`, respectively.

Element	Description
title	The name of the channel or feed.
link	The URL to the website of the channel or feed the RSS is coming from.
description	A description of the channel or feed.
language	The language the channel is in, using W3C language values.
copyright	The copyright material of the channel or feed.
managingEditor	The e-mail address of the editor of the channel or feed.

Fig. 12.36 | channel elements and descriptions. (Part 1 of 2.)

Element	Description
webMaster	The e-mail address for the webmaster of the channel or feed.
pubDate	The date of the channel or feed release, using the RFC 822 Date and Time Specification—e.g., Sun, 14 Jan 2007 8:00:00 EST.
lastBuildDate	The last date the channel or feed was changed, using the RFC 822 Date and Time Specification.
category	The category (or several categories) of the channel or feed. This element has an optional attribute tag.
generator	Indicates the program that was used to generate the channel or feed.
docs	The URL of the documentation for the format used in the RSS file.
cloud	Specifies a SOAP web service that supports the rssCloud interface (cyber.law.harvard.edu/rss/soapMeetsRss.html#rsscloudInterface).
ttl	(Time To Live) A number of minutes for how long the channel or feed can be cached before refreshing from the source.
image	The GIF, JPEG or PNG image that can be displayed with the channel or feed. This element contains the required children title, link and url, and the optional children description, height and width.
rating	The PICS (Platform for Internet Content Selection) rating for the channel or feed.
textInput	Specifies a text input box to display with the channel or feed. This element contains the required children title, name, link and description.
skipHours	Tells aggregators which hours they can skip checking for new content.
skipDays	Tells aggregators which days they can skip checking for new content.

Fig. 12.36 | channel elements and descriptions. (Part 2 of 2.)

Element	Description
title	The title of the item.
link	The URL of the item.
description	The description of the item.
author	The e-mail address of the author of the item.
category	The category (or several categories) of the item. This element has an optional attribute tag.
comments	The URL of a page for comments related to the item.
enclosure	The location of a media object attached to the item. This element has the required attributes type, url and length.

Fig. 12.37 | item elements and descriptions. (Part 1 of 2.)

Element	Description
guid	(Globally Unique Identifier) A string that uniquely identifies the item.
pubDate	The date the item was published, using the RFC 822 Date and Time Specification—e.g., Sun, 14 Jan 2007 8:00:00 EST.
source	The RSS channel the item came from. This element has a required attribute url.

Fig. 12.37 | item elements and descriptions. (Part 2 of 2.)

Browsers and RSS Feeds

Many of the latest web browsers can now view RSS feeds, determine whether a website offers feeds, allow you to subscribe to feeds and create feed lists. An *RSS aggregator* keeps tracks of many RSS feeds and brings together information from the separate feeds. There are many RSS aggregators available, including Bloglines, BottomFeeder, FeedDemon, Microsoft Internet Explorer 7, Mozilla Firefox, My Yahoo, NewsGator and Opera 9.

To allow browsers and search engines to determine whether a web page contains an RSS feed, a link element can be added to the head of a page as follows:

```
<link rel = "alternate" type = "application/rss+xml" title = "RSS"
    href = "file">
```

Many sites provide RSS feed validators. Some examples of RSS feed validators are validator.w3.org/feed, feedvalidator.org, and www.validome.org/rss-atom/.

Creating a Feed Aggregator

The DOM and XSL can be used to create RSS aggregators. A simple RSS aggregator uses an XSL stylesheet to format RSS feeds as XHTML. Figure 12.38 loads two XML documents—an RSS feed (a small portion of which is shown in Fig. 12.39) and an XSL style sheet—then uses JavaScript to apply an XSL transformation to the RSS content and render it on the page. You'll notice as we discuss this program that there is little commonality between Internet Explorer 7 and Firefox with regard to programmatically applying XSL transformations. This is one of the reasons that JavaScript libraries have become popular in web development—they tend to hide such browser-specific issues from you. We discuss the Dojo toolkit—one of many popular JavaScript libraries—in Section 13.8. For more information on JavaScript libraries, see our JavaScript and Ajax Resource Centers (www.deitel.com/JavaScript/ and www.deitel.com/Ajax/, respectively).

```
1   <?xml version = "1.0" encoding = "utf-8"?>
2   <!DOCTYPE html PUBLIC "-//W3C//DTD XHTML 1.0 Strict//EN"
3       "http://www.w3.org/TR/xhtml1/DTD/xhtml1-strict.dtd">
4
5   <!-- Fig. 12.38: RssViewer.html -->
6   <!-- Simple RSS viewer. -->
7   <html xmlns = "http://www.w3.org/1999/xhtml">
8   <head>
```

Fig. 12.38 | Rendering an RSS feed in a web page using XSLT and JavaScript. (Part 1 of 4.)

```
 9      <title>Simple RSS Viewer</title>
10      <style type = "text/css">
11         #outputDiv { font: 12px Verdana, Geneva, Arial,
12                      Helvetica, sans-serif; }
13      </style>
14      <script type = "text/javascript">
15      <!--
16      var browser = ""; // used to determine which browser is being used
17
18      // is the browser Internet Explorer 7 or Firefox?
19      if ( window.ActiveXObject ) // IE7
20         browser = "IE7";
21      else if ( document.implementation &&
22         document.implementation.createDocument ) // FF2 and other browsers
23         browser = "FF2";
24
25      // load both the RSS feed and the XSL file to process it
26      function start()
27      {
28         if ( browser == "IE7" )
29         {
30            var xsl = loadXMLDocument( 'rss.xsl' ); // load XSL file
31            var rss = loadXMLDocument( 'deitel-20.xml' ); // load RSS feed
32            var result = applyTransform( rss, xsl ); // apply transform
33            displayTransformedRss( result ); // display feed info
34         } // end if
35         else if ( browser == "FF2" )
36         {
37            var xsl = loadXMLDocument( 'rss.xsl' ); // load XSL file
38            xsl.onload = function() // function to execute when xsl loads
39            {
40               var rss = loadXMLDocument( 'deitel-20.xml' ); // load RSS feed
41               rss.onload = function() // function to execute when rss loads
42               {
43                  var result = applyTransform( rss, xsl ); // apply transform
44                  displayTransformedRss( result ); // display feed info
45               } // end onload event handler for rss
46            } // end onload event handler for xsl
47         } // end else
48      } // end function start
49
50      // load XML document based on whether the browser is IE7 or Firefox
51      function loadXMLDocument( url )
52      {
53         var doc = ""; // variable to manage loading file
54
55         if ( browser == "IE7" ) // IE7
56         {
57            // create IE7-specific XML document object
58            doc = new ActiveXObject( "Msxml2.DOMDocument.6.0" );
59            doc.async = false; // specifies synchronous loading of XML doc
60            doc.load( url ); // load the XML document specified by url
61         } // end if
```

Fig. 12.38 | Rendering an RSS feed in a web page using XSLT and JavaScript. (Part 2 of 4.)

```
62          else if ( browser == "FF2" ) // other browsers
63          {
64             // create XML document object
65             doc = document.implementation.createDocument( "", "", null );
66             doc.load( url ); // load the XML document specified by url
67          } // end else
68          else // not supported
69             alert( 'This script is not supported by your browser' );
70
71          return doc; // return the loaded document
72       } // end function loadXMLDocument
73
74       // apply XSL transformation and show results
75       function applyTransform( rssDocument, xslDocument )
76       {
77          var result; // stores transformed RSS
78
79          // transform the RSS feed to XHTML
80          if ( browser == "IE7" )
81             result = rssDocument.transformNode( xslDocument );
82          else // browser == "FF2"
83          {
84             // create Firefox object to perform transformation
85             var xsltProcessor = new XSLTProcessor();
86
87             // specify XSL stylesheet to use in transformation
88             xsltProcessor.importStylesheet( xslDocument );
89
90             // apply the transformation
91             result =
92                xsltProcessor.transformToFragment( rssDocument, document );
93          } // end else
94
95          return result; // return the transformed RSS
96       } // end function applyTransform
97
98       // display the XML document and highlight the first child
99       function displayTransformedRss( resultXHTML )
100      {
101         if ( browser == "IE7" )
102            document.getElementById( "outputDiv" ).innerHTML = resultXHTML;
103         else // browser == "FF2"
104            document.getElementById( "outputDiv" ).appendChild(
105               resultXHTML );
106      } // end function displayTransformedRss
107      // -->
108      </script>
109   </head>
110   <body id = "body" onload = "start();">
111      <div id = "outputDiv"></div>
112   </body>
113   </html>
```

Fig. 12.38 | Rendering an RSS feed in a web page using XSLT and JavaScript. (Part 3 of 4.)

Fig. 12.38 | Rendering an RSS feed in a web page using XSLT and JavaScript. (Part 4 of 4.)

```
1   <?xml version="1.0" encoding="utf-8"?>
2
3   <!-- Fig. 12.39: deitel-20.xml -->
4   <!-- RSS 2.0 feed of Deitel Resource Centers -->
5   <rss version="2.0">
6      <channel>
7         <title>
8            Internet &#38; World Wide Web How to Program:
9            Deitel Resource Centers
10        </title>
11        <link>http://www.deitel.com/ResourceCenters.html</link>
12        <description>
13           Check out our growing network of Resource Centers that focus on
14           many of today's hottest programming, Web 2.0 and technology
15           topics. Start your search here for downloads, tutorials,
16           documentation, books, e-books, blogs, RSS feeds, journals,
17           articles, training, webcasts, podcasts, videos and more.
18        </description>
```

Fig. 12.39 | RSS 2.0 sample feed. (Part 1 of 2.)

```
19          <languague>en-us</languague>
20          <image>
21            <url>
22                http://www.deitel.com/Portals/0/deitel_transparent_smaller.png
23            </url>
24            <title>Deitel.com</title>
25            <link>http://www.deitel.com/</link>
26          </image>
27
28          <item>
29            <title>Adobe® Flex</title>
30            <link>http://www.deitel.com/Flex/</link>
31            <description>
32               <p>
33               Welcome to the Adobe® Flex™ Resource Center. Adobe Flex 2 is a
34               rich Internet application (RIA) framework that allows you to
35               create scalable, cross-platform, multimedia-rich applications
36               for delivery within the enterprise or across the Internet.
37               Start your search here for resources, downloads, tutorials,
38               documentation, books, e-books, articles, blogs and more that
39               will help you develop Flex applications.
40               </p>
41            </description>
42            <category>Programming</category>
43          </item>
44        </channel>
45    </rss>
```

Fig. 12.39 | RSS 2.0 sample feed. (Part 2 of 2.)

Determining the Browser Type and Loading the Documents

When this page first loads, lines 19–23 (Fig. 12.38) determine whether the browser is Internet Explorer 7 or Firefox and store the result in variable browser for use throughout the script. After the body of this XHTML document loads, its onload event calls function start (lines 26–48) to load RSS and XSL files as XML documents, and to transform the RSS. Since Internet Explorer 7 can download the files synchronously, lines 30–33 perform the loading, transformation and display steps sequentially. As mentioned previously, Firefox loads the files asynchronously. For this reason, line 37 starts loading the rss.xsl document (included with this example's code), and lines 38–46 register an onload event handler for that document. When the document finishes loading, line 40 begins loading the deitel-20.xml RSS document. Lines 41–45 register an onload event handler for this second document. When it finishes loading, lines 43–44 perform the transformation and display the results.

Transforming the RSS to XHTML

Function applyTransform (Fig. 12.38, lines 75–96) performs the browser-specific XSL transformations using the RSS document and XSL document it receives as arguments. Line 81 uses the MSXML object's built-in XSLT capabilities to apply the transformations. Method *transformNode* is invoked on the rssDocument object and receives the xslDocument object as an argument.

Firefox provides built-in XSLT processing in the form of the ***XSLTProcessor*** object (created at line 85). After creating this object, you use its ***importStylesheet*** method to specify the XSL stylesheet you'd like to apply (line 88). Finally, lines 91–92 apply the transformation by invoking the XSLTProcessor object's ***transformToFragment*** method, which returns a document fragment—i.e., a piece of a document. In our case, the rss.xsl document transforms the RSS into an XHTML table element that we'll append to the outputDiv element in our XHTML page. The arguments to transformToFragment are the document to transform and the document object to which the transformed fragment will belong. To learn more about XSLTProcessor, visit developer.mozilla.org/en/ docs/The_XSLT/JavaScript_Interface_in_Gecko.

In each browser's case, after the transformation, the resulting XHTML markup is assigned to variable result and returned from function applyTransform. Then function displayTransformedRss is called.

Displaying the XHTML Markup

Function displayTransformedRss (lines 99–106) displays the transformed RSS in the outputDiv element (line 111 in the body). In both Internet Explorer 7 and Firefox, we use the DOM method getElementById to obtain the outputDiv element. In Internet Explorer 7, the node's innerHTML property is used to add the table as a child of the outputDiv element (line 102). In Firefox, the node's appendChild method must be used to append the table (a document fragment) to the outputDiv element.

12.11 Web Resources

www.deitel.com/XML/

The Deitel XML Resource Center focuses on the vast amount of free XML content available online, plus some for-sale items. Start your search here for tools, downloads, tutorials, podcasts, wikis, documentation, conferences, FAQs, books, e-books, sample chapters, articles, newsgroups, forums, downloads from CNET's download.com, jobs and contract opportunities, and more that will help you develop XML applications.

13

Ajax-Enabled Rich Internet Applications

... the challenges are for the designers of these applications: to forget what we think we know about the limitations of the Web, and begin to imagine a wider, richer range of possibilities. It's going to be fun.
—Jesse James Garrett

Dojo is the standard library JavaScript never had.
—Alex Russell

To know how to suggest is the great art of teaching. To attain it we must be able to guess what will interest ...
—Henri-Fredreic Amiel

It is characteristic of the epistemological tradition to present us with partial scenarios and then to demand whole or categorical answers as it were.
—Avrum Stroll

O! call back yesterday, bid time return.
—William Shakespeare

OBJECTIVES

In this chapter you'll learn:

- What Ajax is and why it is important for building Rich Internet Applications.

- What asynchronous requests are and how they help give web applications the feel of desktop applications.

- What the XMLHttpRequest object is and how it's used to create and manage asynchronous requests to servers and to receive asynchronous responses from servers.

- Methods and properties of the XMLHttpRequest object.

- How to use XHTML, JavaScript, CSS, XML, JSON and the DOM in Ajax applications.

- How to use Ajax frameworks and toolkits, specifically Dojo, to conveniently create robust Ajax-enabled Rich Internet Applications.

- About resources for studying Ajax-related issues such as security, performance, debugging, the "back-button problem" and more.

13.1 Introduction

Despite the tremendous technological growth of the Internet over the past decade, the usability of web applications has lagged behind compared to that of desktop applications. Every significant interaction in a web application results in a waiting period while the application communicates over the Internet with a server. *Rich Internet Applications (RIAs)* are web applications that approximate the look, feel and usability of desktop applications. RIAs have two key attributes—performance and a rich GUI.

RIA performance comes from *Ajax (Asynchronous JavaScript and XML)*, which uses client-side scripting to make web applications more responsive. Ajax applications separate client-side user interaction and server communication, and run them in parallel, reducing the delays of server-side processing normally experienced by the user.

There are many ways to implement Ajax functionality. *"Raw" Ajax* uses JavaScript to send asynchronous requests to the server, then updates the page using the DOM (see Section 13.5). "Raw" Ajax is best suited for creating small Ajax components that asynchronously update a section of the page. However, when writing "raw" Ajax you need to deal directly with cross-browser portability issues, making it impractical for developing large-scale applications. These portability issues are hidden by *Ajax toolkits*, such as *Dojo* (Section 13.8), *Prototype, Script.aculo.us* and ASP.NET Ajax, which provide powerful ready-to-use controls and functions that enrich web applications, and simplify JavaScript coding by making it cross-browser compatible.

Traditional web applications use XHTML forms (Chapter 2) to build simple and thin GUIs compared to the rich GUIs of Windows, Macintosh and desktop systems in general. We achieve rich GUI in RIAs with Ajax toolkits and with RIA environments such as Adobe Flex, Microsoft Silverlight and JavaServer Faces. Such toolkits and environments provide powerful ready-to-use controls and functions that enrich web applications.

Previous chapters discussed XHTML, CSS, JavaScript, dynamic HTML, the DOM and XML. This chapter uses these technologies to build Ajax-enabled web applications. The client-side of Ajax applications is written in XHTML and CSS, and uses JavaScript to add functionality to the user interface. XML is used to structure the data passed between the server and the client. We'll also use JSON (JavaScript Object Notation) for this purpose. The Ajax component that manages interaction with the server is usually implemented with JavaScript's *XMLHttpRequest object*—commonly abbreviated as XHR. The server processing can be implemented using any server-side technology, such as PHP, ASP. NET, JavaServer Faces ot Ruby on Rails.

This chapter begins with several examples that build basic Ajax applications using JavaScript and the XMLHttpRequest object. We then build an Ajax application with a rich calendar GUI using the Dojo Ajax toolkit.

13.2 Traditional Web Applications vs. Ajax Applications

In this section, we consider the key differences between traditional web applications and Ajax-based web applications.

Traditional Web Applications

Figure 13.1 presents the typical interactions between the client and the server in a traditional web application, such as one that uses a user registration form. First, the user fills in the form's fields, then submits the form (Fig. 13.1, *Step 1*). The browser generates a request to the server, which receives the request and processes it (*Step 2*). The server generates and sends a response containing the exact page that the browser will render (*Step 3*), which causes the browser to load the new page (*Step 4*) and temporarily makes the browser window blank. Note that the client *waits* for the server to respond and *reloads the entire page* with the data from the response (*Step 4*). While such a ***synchronous request*** is being processed on the server, the user cannot interact with the client web page. Frequent long periods of waiting, due perhaps to Internet congestion, have led some users to refer to the World Wide Web as the "World Wide Wait." If the user interacts with and submits another form, the process begins again (*Steps 5–8*).

This model was originally designed for a web of hypertext documents—what some people call the "brochure web." As the web evolved into a full-scale applications platform, the model shown in Fig. 13.1 yielded "choppy" application performance. Every full-page refresh required users to re-establish their understanding of the full-page contents. Users began to demand a model that would yield the responsive feel of desktop applications.

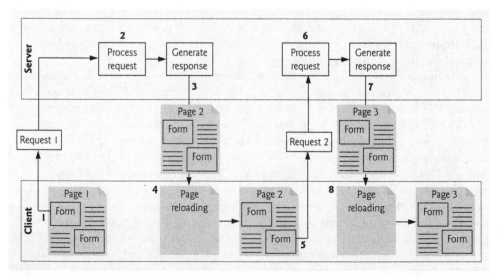

Fig. 13.1 | Classic web application reloading the page for every user interaction.

Ajax Web Applications

Ajax applications add a layer between the client and the server to manage communication between the two (Fig. 13.2). When the user interacts with the page, the client creates an XMLHttpRequest object to manage a request (*Step 1*). The XMLHttpRequest object sends the request to the server (*Step 2*) and awaits the response. The requests are *asynchronous*, so the user can continue interacting with the application on the client-side while the server processes the earlier request concurrently. Other user interactions could result in additional requests to the server (*Steps 3* and *4*). Once the server responds to the original request (*Step 5*), the XMLHttpRequest object that issued the request calls a client-side function to process the data returned by the server. This function—known as a *callback function*—uses *partial page updates* (*Step 6*) to display the data in the existing web page *without reloading the entire page*. At the same time, the server may be responding to the second request (*Step 7*) and the client-side may be starting to do another partial page update (*Step 8*). The callback function updates only a designated part of the page. Such partial page updates help make web applications more responsive, making them feel more like desktop applications. The web application does not load a new page while the user interacts with it.

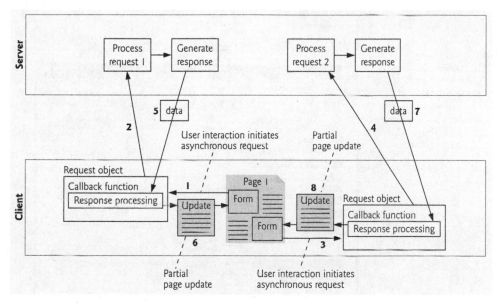

Fig. 13.2 | Ajax-enabled web application interacting with the server asynchronously.

13.3 Rich Internet Applications (RIAs) with Ajax

Ajax improves the user experience by making interactive web applications more responsive. Consider a registration form with a number of fields (e.g., first name, last name e-mail address, telephone number, etc.) and a **Register** (or **Submit**) button that sends the entered data to the server. Usually each field has rules that the user's entries have to follow (e.g., valid e-mail address, valid telephone number, etc.).

When the user clicks **Register**, a classic XHTML form sends the server all of the data to be validated (Fig. 13.3). While the server is validating the data, the user cannot interact

a) A sample registration form in which the user has not filled in the required fields, but attempts to submit the form anyway by clicking **Register**.

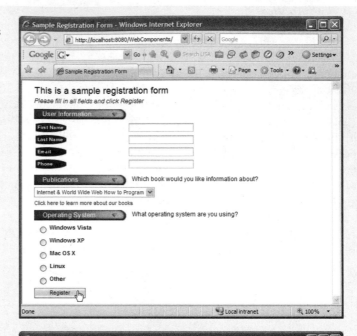

b) The server responds by indicating all the form fields with missing or invalid data. The user must correct the problems and resubmit the entire form repeatedly until all errors are corrected.

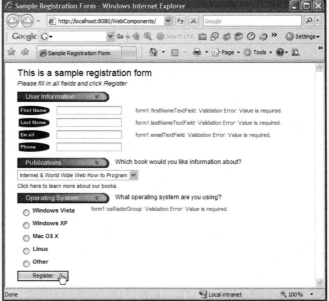

Fig. 13.3 | Classic XHTML form: User submits entire form to server, which validates the data entered (if any). Server responds indicating fields with invalid or missing data.

with the page. The server finds invalid data, generates a new page identifying the errors in the form and sends it back to the client—which renders the page in the browser. Once the user fixes the errors and clicks the **Register** button, the cycle repeats until no errors are found, then the data is stored on the server. The entire page reloads every time the user submits invalid data.

Ajax-enabled forms are more interactive. Rather than sending the entire form to be validated, entries are validated dynamically as the user enters data into the fields. For example, consider a website registration form that requires a unique e-mail address. When the user enters an e-mail address into the appropriate field, then moves to the next form field to continue entering data, an asynchronous request is sent to the server to validate the e-mail address. If the e-mail address is not unique, the server sends an error message that is displayed on the page informing the user of the problem (Fig. 13.4). By sending each entry asynchronously, the user can address each invalid entry quickly, versus making edits and resubmitting the entire form repeatedly until all entries are valid. Asynchronous requests could also be used to fill some fields based on previous fields (e.g., automatically filling in the "city" and "state" fields based on the zip code entered by the user).

Fig. 13.4 | Ajax-enabled form shows errors asynchronously when user moves to another field.

13.4 History of Ajax

The term Ajax was coined by Jesse James Garrett of Adaptive Path in February 2005, when he was presenting the previously unnamed technology to a client. The technologies of Ajax (XHTML, JavaScript, CSS, the DOM and XML) have all existed for many years.

Asynchronous page updates can be traced back to earlier browsers. In the 1990s, Netscape's LiveScript made it possible to include scripts in web pages (e.g., web forms) that could run on the client. LiveScript evolved into JavaScript. In 1998, Microsoft introduced the XMLHttpRequest object to create and manage asynchronous requests and responses. Popular applications like Flickr and Google's Gmail use the XMLHttpRequest object to update pages dynamically. For example, Flickr uses the technology for its text editing, tagging and organizational features; Gmail continuously checks the server for new e-mail; and Google Maps allows you to drag a map in any direction, downloading the new areas on the map without reloading the entire page.

The name Ajax immediately caught on and brought attention to its component technologies. Ajax has become one of the hottest web-development technologies, enabling webtop applications to challenge the dominance of established desktop applications.

13.5 "Raw" Ajax Example Using the XMLHttpRequest Object

In this section, we use the XMLHttpRequest object to create and manage asynchronous requests. The XMLHttpRequest object (which resides on the client) is the layer between the client and the server that manages asynchronous requests in Ajax applications. This object is supported on most browsers, though they may implement it differently—a common issue in JavaScript programming. To initiate an asynchronous request (shown in Fig. 13.5), you create an instance of the XMLHttpRequest object, then use its open method to set up the request and its send method to initiate the request. We summarize the XMLHttpRequest properties and methods in Figs. 13.6–13.7.

Figure 13.5 presents an Ajax application in which the user interacts with the page by moving the mouse over book-cover images. We use the onmouseover and onmouseout events (discussed in Chapter 11) to trigger events when the user moves the mouse over and out of an image, respectively. The onmouseover event calls function getContent with the URL of the document containing the book's description. The function makes this request asynchronously using an XMLHttpRequest object. When the XMLHttpRequest object receives the response, the book description is displayed below the book images. When the user moves the mouse out of the image, the onmouseout event calls function clearContent to clear the display box. These tasks are accomplished without reloading the page on the client. You can test-drive this example at test.deitel.com/examples/jsfp/ajax/fig13_05/SwitchContent.html.

```
1   <?xml version = "1.0" encoding = "utf-8"?>
2   <!DOCTYPE html PUBLIC "-//W3C//DTD XHTML 1.0 Strict//EN"
3      "http://www.w3.org/TR/xhtml1/DTD/xhtml1-strict.dtd">
4
5   <!-- Fig. 13.5: SwitchContent.html -->
6   <!-- Asynchronously display content without reloading the page. -->
7   <html xmlns = "http://www.w3.org/1999/xhtml">
8   <head>
9      <style type="text/css">
10        .box { border: 1px solid black;
11               padding: 10px }
12     </style>
13     <title>Switch Content Asynchronously</title>
14     <script type = "text/javascript" language = "JavaScript">
15        <!--
16        var asyncRequest; // variable to hold XMLHttpRequest object
```

Fig. 13.5 | Asynchronously display content without reloading the page. (Part 1 of 3.)

```
17
18          // set up and send the asynchronous request
19          function getContent( url )
20          {
21             // attempt to create the XMLHttpRequest and make the request
22             try
23             {
24                asyncRequest = new XMLHttpRequest(); // create request object
25
26                // register event handler
27                asyncRequest.onreadystatechange = stateChange;
28                asyncRequest.open( 'GET', url, true ); // prepare the request
29                asyncRequest.send( null ); // send the request
30             } // end try
31             catch ( exception )
32             {
33                alert( 'Request failed.' );
34             } // end catch
35          } // end function getContent
36
37          // displays the response data on the page
38          function stateChange()
39          {
40             if ( asyncRequest.readyState == 4 && asyncRequest.status == 200 )
41             {
42                document.getElementById( 'contentArea' ).innerHTML =
43                   asyncRequest.responseText; // places text in contentArea
44             } // end if
45          } // end function stateChange
46
47          // clear the content of the box
48          function clearContent()
49          {
50             document.getElementById( 'contentArea' ).innerHTML = '';
51          } // end function clearContent
52          // -->
53       </script>
54    </head>
55    <body>
56       <h1>Mouse over a book for more information.</h1>
57       <img src =
58          "http://test.deitel.com/examples/jsfp/ajax/thumbs/cpphtp6.jpg"
59          onmouseover = 'getContent( "cpphtp6.html" )'
60          onmouseout = 'clearContent()'/>
61       <img src =
62          "http://test.deitel.com/examples/jsfp/ajax/thumbs/iw3htp4.jpg"
63          onmouseover = 'getContent( "iw3htp4.html" )'
64          onmouseout = 'clearContent()'/>
65       <img src =
66          "http://test.deitel.com/examples/jsfp/ajax/thumbs/jhtp7.jpg"
67          onmouseover = 'getContent( "jhtp7.html" )'
68          onmouseout = 'clearContent()'/>
```

Fig. 13.5 | Asynchronously display content without reloading the page. (Part 2 of 3.)

```
69      <img src =
70         "http://test.deitel.com/examples/jsfp/ajax/thumbs/vbhtp3.jpg"
71         onmouseover = 'getContent( "vbhtp3.html" )'
72         onmouseout = 'clearContent()'/>
73      <img src =
74         "http://test.deitel.com/examples/jsfp/ajax/thumbs/vcsharphtp2.jpg"
75         onmouseover = 'getContent( "vcsharphtp2.html" )'
76         onmouseout = 'clearContent()'/>
77      <img src =
78         "http://test.deitel.com/examples/jsfp/ajax/thumbs/chtp5.jpg"
79         onmouseover = 'getContent( "chtp5.html" )'
80         onmouseout = 'clearContent()'/>
81      <div class = "box" id = "contentArea"> </div>
82   </body>
83   </html>
```

a) User hovers over C++ *How to Program* book cover image, causing an asynchronous request to the server to obtain the book's description. When the response is received, the application performs a partial page update to display the description.

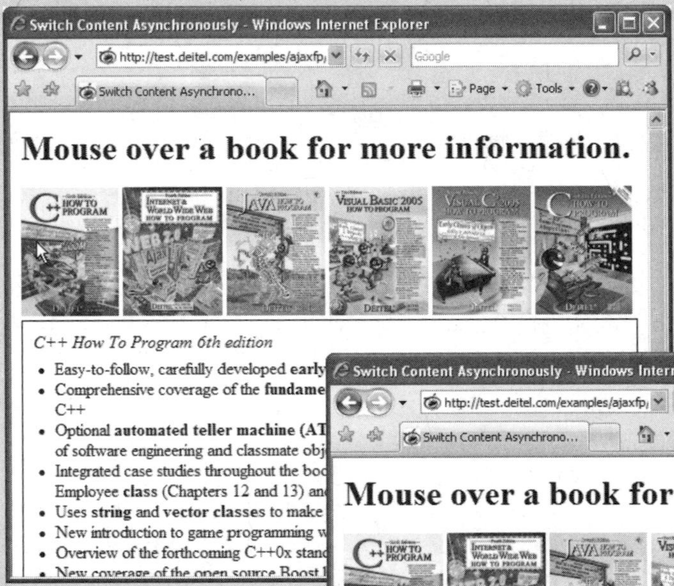

b) User hovers over *Java How to Program* book cover image, causing the process to repeat.

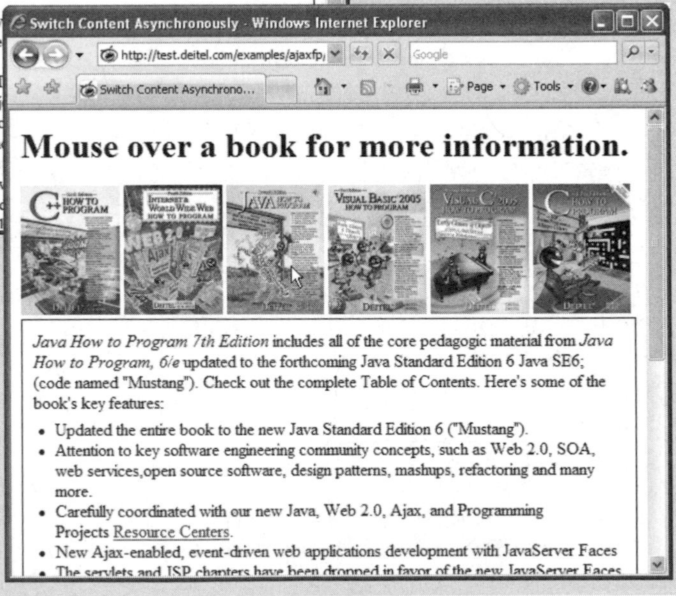

Fig. 13.5 | Asynchronously display content without reloading the page. (Part 3 of 3.)

Performance Tip 13.1

When an Ajax application requests a file from a server, such as an XHTML document or an image, the browser typically caches that file. Subsequent requests for the same file can load it from the browser's cache rather than making the round trip to the server again.

Software Engineering Observation 13.1

*For security purposes, the XMLHttpRequest object doesn't allow a web application to request resources from domain names other than the one that served the application. For this reason, the web application and its resources must reside on the same web server (this could be a web server on your local computer). This is commonly known as the **same origin policy (SOP)**. SOP aims to close a vulnerability called **cross-site scripting**, also known as **XSS**, which allows an attacker to compromise a website's security by injecting a malicious script onto the page from another domain. To learn more about XSS visit en.wikipedia.org/wiki/XSS. To get content from another domain securely, you can implement a server-side proxy—an application on the web application's web server—that can make requests to other servers on the web application's behalf.*

Asynchronous Requests

The function getContent (lines 19–35) sends the asynchronous request. Line 24 creates the XMLHttpRequest object, which manages the asynchronous request. We store the object in the global variable asyncRequest (declared at line 16) so that it can be accessed anywhere in the script.

Line 28 calls the XMLHttpRequest open method to prepare an asynchronous GET request. In this example, the url parameter specifies the address of an HTML document containing the description of a particular book. When the third argument is true, the request is asynchronous. The URL is passed to function getContent in response to the onmouseover event for each image. Line 29 sends the asynchronous request to the server by calling XMLHttpRequest send method. The argument null indicates that this request is not submitting data in the body of the request.

Exception Handling

Lines 22–34 introduce *exception handling*. An *exception* is an indication of a problem that occurs during a program's execution. The name "exception" implies that the problem occurs infrequently—if the "rule" is that a statement normally executes correctly, then the "exception to the rule" is that a problem occurs. Exception handling enables you to create applications that can resolve (or handle) exceptions—in some cases allowing a program to continue executing as if no problem had been encountered.

Lines 22–30 contain a ***try block***, which encloses the code that might cause an exception and the code that should not execute if an exception occurs (i.e., if an exception occurs in a statement of the try block, the remaining code in the try block is skipped). A try block consists of the keyword try followed by a block of code enclosed in curly braces ({}). If there is a problem sending the request—e.g., if a user tries to access the page using an older browser that does not support XMLHttpRequest—the try block terminates immediately and a ***catch block*** (also called a ***catch clause*** or ***exception handler***) catches (i.e., receives) and handles an exception. The catch block (lines 31–34) begins with the keyword catch and is followed by a parameter in parentheses (called the exception parameter) and a block of code enclosed in curly braces. The exception parameter's name (exception in this example) enables the catch block to interact with a caught exception object (for example, to obtain the name of the exception or an exception-specific error message via the exception object's `name` and `message` properties). In this case, we simply display our own error message `'Request Failed'` and terminate the `getContent` function. The request can fail because a user accesses the web page with an older browser or the content that is being requested is located on a different domain.

Callback Functions

The `stateChange` function (lines 38–45) is the callback function that is called when the client receives the response data. Line 27 registers function `stateChange` as the event handler for the `XMLHttpRequest` object's `onreadystatechange` event. Whenever the request makes progress, the `XMLHttpRequest` calls the `onreadystatechange` event handler. This progress is monitored by the `readyState` property, which has a value from 0 to 4. The value 0 indicates that the request is not initialized and the value 4 indicates that the request is complete—all the values for this property are summarized in Fig. 13.6. If the request completes successfully (line 40), lines 42–43 use the `XMLHttpRequest` object's `responseText` property to obtain the response data and place it in the `div` element named `contentArea` (defined at line 81). We use the DOM's `getElementById` method to get this `div` element, and use the element's `innerHTML` property to place the content in the `div`.

XMLHttpRequest Object Properties and Methods

Figures 13.6 and 13.7 summarize some of the `XMLHttpRequest` object's properties and methods, respectively. The properties are crucial to interacting with asynchronous requests. The methods initialize, configure and send asynchronous requests.

Property	Description
onreadystatechange	Stores the callback function—the event handler that gets called when the server responds.
readyState	Keeps track of the request's progress. It is usually used in the callback function to determine when the code that processes the response should be launched. The `readyState` value 0 signifies that the request is uninitialized; 1 signifies that the request is loading; 2 signifies that the request has been loaded; 3 signifies that data is actively being sent from the server; and 4 signifies that the request has been completed.
responseText	Text that is returned to the client by the server.
responseXML	If the server's response is in XML format, this property contains the XML document; otherwise, it is empty. It can be used like a document object in JavaScript, which makes it useful for receiving complex data (e.g. populating a table).
status	HTTP status code of the request. A `status` of 200 means that request was successful. A `status` of 404 means that the requested resource was not found. A `status` of 500 denotes that there was an error while the server was proccessing the request.

Fig. 13.6 | XMLHttpRequest object properties. (Part I of 2.)

Property	Description
statusText	Additional information on the request's status. It is often used to display the error to the user when the request fails.

Fig. 13.6 | XMLHttpRequest object properties. (Part 2 of 2.)

Method	Description
open	Initializes the request and has two mandatory parameters—method and URL. The method parameter specifies the purpose of the request—typically GET if the request is to take data from the server or POST if the request will contain a body in addition to the headers. The URL parameter specifies the address of the file on the server that will generate the response. A third optional boolean parameter specifies whether the request is asynchronous—it's set to true by default.
send	Sends the request to the sever. It has one optional parameter, data, which specifies the data to be POSTed to the server—it's set to null by default.
setRequestHeader	Alters the header of the request. The two parameters specify the header and its new value. It is often used to set the content-type field.
getResponseHeader	Returns the header data that precedes the response body. It takes one parameter, the name of the header to retrieve. This call is often used to determine the response's type, to parse the response correctly.
getAllResponseHeaders	Returns an array that contains all the headers that precede the response body.
abort	Cancels the current request.

Fig. 13.7 | XMLHttpRequest object methods.

13.6 Using XML and the DOM

When passing structured data between the server and the client, Ajax applications often use XML because it is easy to generate and parse. When the XMLHttpRequest object receives XML data, it parses and stores the data as an XML DOM object in the responseXML property. The example in Fig. 13.8 asynchronously requests from a server XML documents containing URLs of book-cover images, then displays the images in an HTML table. The code that configures the asynchronous request is the same as in Fig. 13.5. You can test-drive this application at test.deitel.com/examples/jsfp/ajax/fig13_08/ PullImagesOntoPage.html (the book-cover images will be easier to see on the screen).

When the XMLHttpRequest object receives the response, it invokes the callback function processResponse (lines 38–99). We use XMLHttpRequest object's responseXML property to access the XML returned by the server. Lines 41–42 check that the request was successful, and that the responseXML property is not empty. The XML file that we requested includes a baseURL node that contains the address of the image directory and a collection of cover nodes that contain image filenames. responseXML is a document object, so we can extract data from it using the XML DOM functions. Lines 47–52 use the DOM's method *getElementsByTagName* to extract all the image filenames from cover nodes and the URL of the directory from the baseURL node. Since the baseURL has no child nodes, we use item(0).firstChild.nodeValue to obtain the directory's address and store it in variable baseURL. The image filenames are stored in the covers array.

As in Fig. 13.5 we have a placeholder div element (line 126) to specify where the image table will be displayed on the page. Line 55 stores the div in variable output, so we can fill it with content later in the program.

Lines 58–93 generate an XHTML table dynamically, using the createElement, set-Attribute and appendChild DOM methods. Method createElement creates an XHTML element of the specified type. Method *setAttribute* adds or changes an attribute of an XHTML element. Method appendChild inserts one XHTML element into another. Lines 58 and 61 create the table and tbody elements, respectively. We restrict each row to no more than six images, which we track with variable rowCount variable. Each iteration of the for statement (lines 67–93) obtains the filename of the image to be inserted (lines 69–73), creates a table cell element where the image will be inserted (line 76) and creates an <img> element (line 77). Line 80 sets the image's src attribute to the image's URL, which we build by concatenating the filename to the base URL of the XHTML document. Lines 81–82 insert the <img> element into the cell and the cell into the table row. When the row has six cells, it is inserted into the table and a new row is created (lines 87–92). Once all the rows have been inserted into the table, the table is inserted into the placeholder element covers that is referenced by variable output (line 97). This element is located on the bottom of the web page.

Function clearTable (lines 102–105) is called to clear images when the user switches radio buttons. The text is cleared by setting the innerHTML property of the placeholder element to the empty string.

```
1    <?xml version = "1.0" encoding = "utf-8"?>
2    <!DOCTYPE html PUBLIC "-//W3C//DTD XHTML 1.0 Strict//EN"
3       "http://www.w3.org/TR/xhtml1/DTD/xhtml1-strict.dtd">
4
5    <!-- Fig. 13.8: PullImagesOntoPage.html -->
6    <!-- Image catalog that uses Ajax to request XML data asynchronously. -->
7    <html xmlns = "http://www.w3.org/1999/xhtml">
8    <head>
9    <title> Pulling Images onto the Page </title>
10   <style type = "text/css">
11      td { padding: 4px }
12      img { border: 1px solid black }
13   </style>
14   <script type = "text/javascript" language = "Javascript">
```

Fig. 13.8 | Image catalog that uses Ajax to request XML data asynchronously. (Part 1 of 4.)

```
15    var asyncRequest; // variable to hold XMLHttpRequest object
16
17    // set up and send the asynchronous request to the XML file
18    function getImages( url )
19    {
20        // attempt to create the XMLHttpRequest and make the request
21        try
22        {
23            asyncRequest = new XMLHttpRequest(); // create request object
24
25            // register event handler
26            asyncRequest.onreadystatechange = processResponse;
27            asyncRequest.open( 'GET', url, true ); // prepare the request
28            asyncRequest.send( null ); // send the request
29        } // end try
30        catch ( exception )
31        {
32            alert( 'Request Failed' );
33        } // end catch
34    } // end function getImages
35
36    // parses the XML response; dynamically creates a table using DOM and
37    // populates it with the response data; displays the table on the page
38    function processResponse()
39    {
40        // if request completed successfully and responseXML is non-null
41        if ( asyncRequest.readyState == 4 && asyncRequest.status == 200 &&
42            asyncRequest.responseXML )
43        {
44            clearTable(); // prepare to display a new set of images
45
46            // get the covers from the responseXML
47            var covers = asyncRequest.responseXML.getElementsByTagName(
48                "cover" )
49
50            // get base URL for the images
51            var baseUrl = asyncRequest.responseXML.getElementsByTagName(
52                "baseurl" ).item( 0 ).firstChild.nodeValue;
53
54            // get the placeholder div element named covers
55            var output = document.getElementById( "covers" );
56
57            // create a table to display the images
58            var imageTable = document.createElement( 'table' );
59
60            // create the table's body
61            var tableBody = document.createElement( 'tbody' );
62
63            var rowCount = 0; // tracks number of images in current row
64            var imageRow = document.createElement( "tr" ); // create row
65
```

Fig. 13.8 | Image catalog that uses Ajax to request XML data asynchronously. (Part 2 of 4.)

```
66              // place images in row
67              for ( var i = 0; i < covers.length; i++ )
68              {
69                  var cover = covers.item( i ); // get a cover from covers array
70
71                  // get the image filename
72                  var image = cover.getElementsByTagName( "image" ).
73                      item( 0 ).firstChild.nodeValue;
74
75                  // create table cell and img element to display the image
76                  var imageCell = document.createElement( "td" );
77                  var imageTag = document.createElement( "img" );
78
79                  // set img element's src attribute
80                  imageTag.setAttribute( "src", baseUrl + escape( image ) );
81                  imageCell.appendChild( imageTag ); // place img in cell
82                  imageRow.appendChild( imageCell ); // place cell in row
83                  rowCount++; // increment number of images in row
84
85                  // if there are 6 images in the row, append the row to
86                  // table and start a new row
87                  if ( rowCount == 6 && i + 1 < covers.length )
88                  {
89                      tableBody.appendChild( imageRow );
90                      imageRow = document.createElement( "tr" );
91                      rowCount = 0;
92                  } // end if statement
93              } // end for statement
94
95              tableBody.appendChild( imageRow ); // append row to table body
96              imageTable.appendChild( tableBody ); // append body to table
97              output.appendChild( imageTable ); // append table to covers div
98          } // end if
99      } // end function processResponse
100
101     // deletes the data in the table.
102     function clearTable()
103     {
104         document.getElementById( "covers" ).innerHTML = '';
105     }// end function clearTable
106     </script>
107 </head>
108 <body>
109     <input type = "radio" checked = "unchecked" name ="Books" value = "all"
110         onclick = 'getImages( "all.xml" )'/> All Books
111     <input type = "radio" checked = "unchecked"
112         name = "Books" value = "simply"
113         onclick = 'getImages( "simply.xml" )'/>  Simply Books
114     <input type = "radio" checked = "unchecked"
115         name = "Books" value = "howto"
116         onclick = 'getImages( "howto.xml" )'/> How to Program Books
117     <input type = "radio" checked = "unchecked"
118         name = "Books" value = "dotnet"
```

Fig. 13.8 | Image catalog that uses Ajax to request XML data asynchronously. (Part 3 of 4.)

```
119        onclick = 'getImages( "dotnet.xml" )'/> .NET Books
120    <input type = "radio" checked = "unchecked"
121        name = "Books" value = "javaccpp"
122        onclick = 'getImages( "javaccpp.xml" )'/> Java, C, C++ Books
123    <input type = "radio" checked = "checked" name = "Books" value = "none"
124        onclick = 'clearTable()'/> None
125    <br/>
126    <div id = "covers"></div>
127 </body>
128 </html>
```

a) User clicks the **All Books** radio button to display all the book covers. The application sends an asynchronous request to the server to obtain an XML document containing the list of book-cover filenames. When the response is received, the application performs a partial page update to display the set of book covers.

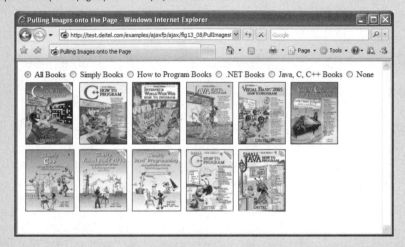

b) User clicks the **How to Program Books** radio button to select a subset of book covers to display. Application sends an asynchronous request to the server to obtain an XML document containing the appropriate subset of book-cover filenames. When the response is received, the application performs a partial page update to display the subset of book covers.

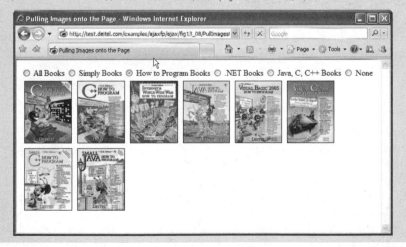

Fig. 13.8 | Image catalog that uses Ajax to request XML data asynchronously. (Part 4 of 4.)

13.7 Creating a Full-Scale Ajax-Enabled Application

Our next example demonstrates additional Ajax capabilities. The web application interacts with a web service to obtain data and to modify data in a server-side database. The web application and server communicate with a data format called JSON (JavaScript Object Notation). In addition, the application demonstrates server-side validation that occurs in parallel with the user interacting with the web application. You can test the application at `test.deitel.com/examples/jsfp/ajax/fig13_09_10/AddressBook.html`.

Using JSON

JSON (JavaScript Object Notation)—a simple way to represent JavaScript objects as strings—is an alternative way (to XML) for passing data between the client and the server. Each object in JSON is represented as a list of property names and values contained in curly braces, in the following format:

{ *"propertyName1"* : *value1*, *"propertyName2"* : *value2* }

Arrays are represented in JSON with square brackets in the following format:

[*value1*, *value2*, *value3*]

Each value can be a string, a number, a JSON representation of an object, `true`, `false` or `null`. You can convert JSON strings into JavaScript objects with JavaScript's `eval` function. To evaluate a JSON string properly, a left parenthesis should be placed at the beginning of the string and a right parenthesis at the end of the string before the string is passed to the `eval` function.

The `eval` function creates a potential security risk—it executes any embedded JavaScript code in its string argument, possibly allowing a harmful script to be injected into JSON. A more secure way to process JSON is to use a JSON parser. In our examples, we use the open source parser from `www.json.org/js.html`. When you download its Java-Script file, place it in the same folder as your application. Then, link the `json2.js` file into your XHTML file with the following statement in the `head` section:

```
<script type = "text/javascript" src = "json2.js">
```

You can now call function `JSON.parse`, which receives a JSON string and converts it to a JavaScript object.

JSON strings are easier to create and parse than XML, and require fewer bytes. For these reasons, JSON is commonly used to communicate in client/server interaction. For more information on JSON, visit our JSON Resource Center at `www.deitel.com/json`.

Rich Functionality

The previous examples in this chapter requested data from static files on the server. The example in Fig. 13.9 is an address-book application that communicates with a server-side application. The application uses server-side processing to give the page the functionality and usability of a desktop application. We use JSON to encode server-side responses and to create objects on the fly.

Initially the address book loads a list of entries, each containing a first and last name (Fig. 13.9(a)). Each time the user clicks a name, the address book uses Ajax functionality to load the person's address from the server and expand the entry *without reloading the page*

(Fig. 13.9(b))—and it does this *in parallel* with allowing the user to click other names. The application allows the user to search the address book by typing a last name. As the user enters each keystroke, the application asynchronously displays the list of names in which the last name starts with the characters the user has entered so far (Fig. 13.9(c), Fig. 13.9 (d) and Fig. 13.9(e))—a popular feature called *type ahead*.

The application also enables the user to add another entry to the address book by clicking the **addEntry** button (Fig. 13.9(f)). The application displays a form that enables live field validation. As the user fills out the form, the zip-code value is validated and used to generate the city and state (Fig. 13.9(g), Fig. 13.9(h) and Fig. 13.9(i)). The telephone number is validated for correct format (Fig. 13.9(j)). When the Submit button is clicked, the application checks for invalid data and stores the values in a database on the server (Fig. 13.9(k) and Fig. 13.9(l)). You can test-drive this application at test.deitel.com/examples/jsfp/ajax/fig13_09_10/AddressBook.html.

```
 1   <?xml version = "1.0" encoding = "utf-8"?>
 2   <!DOCTYPE html PUBLIC "-//W3C//DTD XHTML 1.0 Strict//EN"
 3      "http://www.w3.org/TR/xhtml1/DTD/xhtml1-strict.dtd">
 4
 5   <!-- Fig. 13.9 addressbook.html -->
 6   <!-- Ajax enabled address book application. -->
 7   <html xmlns = "http://www.w3.org/1999/xhtml">
 8   <head>
 9      <title>Address Book</title>
10      <link rel = "stylesheet" type = "text/css" href = "address.css" />
11      <script type = "text/javascript" src = "json2.js"></script>
12      <script type = "text/javascript">
13         <!--
14         // URL of the web service
15         var webServiceUrl = '/AddressBookWebService/Service.asmx';
16
17         var phoneValid = false; // indicates if the telephone is valid
18         var zipValid = false; //indicates if the zip code is valid
19
20         // get a list of names from the server and display them
21         function showAddressBook()
22         {
23            // hide the "addEntry" form and show the address book
24            document.getElementById( 'addEntry' ).style.display = 'none';
25            document.getElementById( 'addressBook' ).style.display = 'block';
26
27            var params = "[]"; // create an empty object
28            callWebService( 'getAllNames', params, parseData );
29         } // end function showAddressBook
30
31         // send the asynchronous request to the web service
32         function callWebService( method, paramString, callBack )
33         {
34            // build request URL string
35            var requestUrl = webServiceUrl + "/" + method;
36            var params = JSON.parse( paramString );
```

Fig. 13.9 | Ajax-enabled address-book application. (Part 1 of 10.)

```
37
38        // build the parameter string to add to the url
39        for ( var i = 0; i < params.length; i++ )
40        {
41            // checks whether it is the first parameter and builds
42            // the parameter string accordingly
43            if ( i == 0 )
44                requestUrl = requestUrl + "?" + params[ i ].param +
45                    "=" + params[ i ].value; // add first parameter to url
46            else
47                requestUrl = requestUrl + "&" + params[ i ].param +
48                    "=" + params[ i ].value; // add other parameters to url
49        } // end for
50
51        // attempt to send the asynchronous request
52        try
53        {
54            var asyncRequest = new XMLHttpRequest(); // create request
55
56            // set up callback function and store it
57            asyncRequest.onreadystatechange = function()
58            {
59                callBack( asyncRequest );
60            }; // end anonymous function
61
62            // send the asynchronous request
63            asyncRequest.open( 'GET', requestUrl, true );
64            asyncRequest.setRequestHeader("Accept",
65                "application/json; charset=utf-8" );
66            asyncRequest.send( "" ); // send request
67        } // end try
68        catch ( exception )
69        {
70            alert ( 'Request Failed' );
71        } // end catch
72    } // end function callWebService
73
74    // parse JSON data and display it on the page
75    function parseData( asyncRequest )
76    {
77        // if request has completed successfully process the response
78        if ( asyncRequest.readyState == 4 && asyncRequest.status == 200 )
79        {
80            // convert the JSON string to an Object
81            var data = JSON.parse( asyncRequest.responseText );
82            displayNames( data ); // display data on the page
83        } // end if
84    } // end function parseData
85
86    // use the DOM to display the retrieved address book entries
87    function displayNames( data )
88    {
```

Fig. 13.9 | Ajax-enabled address-book application. (Part 2 of 10.)

```
89          // get the placeholder element from the page
90          var listBox = document.getElementById( 'Names' );
91          listBox.innerHTML = ''; // clear the names on the page
92
93          // iterate over retrieved entries and display them on the page
94          for ( var i = 0; i < data.length; i++ )
95          {
96             // dynamically create a div element for each entry
97             // and a fieldset element to place it in
98             var entry = document.createElement( 'div' );
99             var field = document.createElement( 'fieldset' );
100            entry.onclick = handleOnClick; // set onclick event handler
101            entry.id = i; // set the id
102            entry.innerHTML = data[ i ].First + ' ' + data[ i ].Last;
103            field.appendChild( entry ); // insert entry into the field
104            listBox.appendChild( field ); // display the field
105         } // end for
106      } // end function displayAll
107
108      // event handler for entry's onclick event
109      function handleOnClick()
110      {
111         // call getAddress with the element's content as a parameter
112         getAddress( eval( 'this' ), eval( 'this.innerHTML' ) );
113      } // end function handleOnClick
114
115      // search the address book for input
116      // and display the results on the page
117      function search( input )
118      {
119         // get the placeholder element and delete its content
120         var listBox = document.getElementById( 'Names' );
121         listBox.innerHTML = ''; // clear the display box
122
123         // if no search string is specified all the names are displayed
124         if ( input == "" ) // if no search value specified
125         {
126            showAddressBook(); // Load the entire address book
127         } // end if
128         else
129         {
130            var params = '[{"param": "input", "value": "' + input + '"}]';
131            callWebService( "search",  params , parseData );
132         } // end else
133      } // end function search
134
135      // Get address data for a specific entry
136      function getAddress( entry, name )
137      {
138         // find the address in the JSON data using the element's id
139         // and display it on the page
140         var firstLast = name.split(" "); // convert string to array
```

Fig. 13.9 | Ajax-enabled address-book application. (Part 3 of 10.)

```
141        var requestUrl = webServiceUrl + "/getAddress?first="
142           + firstLast[ 0 ] + "&last=" + firstLast[ 1 ];
143
144        // attempt to send an asynchronous request
145        try
146        {
147           // create request object
148           var asyncRequest = new XMLHttpRequest();
149
150           // create a callback function with 2 parameters
151           asyncRequest.onreadystatechange = function()
152           {
153              displayAddress( entry, asyncRequest );
154           }; // end anonymous function
155
156           asyncRequest.open( 'GET', requestUrl, true );
157           asyncRequest.setRequestHeader("Accept",
158              "application/json; charset=utf-8"); // response datatype
159           asyncRequest.send( "" ); // send request
160        } // end try
161        catch ( exception )
162        {
163           alert ( 'Request Failed.' );
164        } // end catch
165     } // end function getAddress
166
167     // clear the entry's data.
168     function displayAddress( entry, asyncRequest )
169     {
170        // if request has completed successfully, process the response
171        if ( asyncRequest.readyState == 4 && asyncRequest.status == 200 )
172        {
173           // convert the JSON string to an object
174           var data = JSON.parse( asyncRequest.responseText );
175           var name = entry.innerHTML // save the name string
176           entry.innerHTML = name + '<br/>' + data.Street +
177              '<br/>' + data.City + ', ' + data.State
178              + ', ' + data.Zip + '<br/>' + data.Telephone;
179
180           // clicking on the entry removes the address
181           entry.onclick = function()
182           {
183              clearField( entry, name );
184           }; // end anonymous function
185
186        } // end if
187     } // end function displayAddress
188
189     // clear the entry's data
190     function clearField( entry, name )
191     {
192        entry.innerHTML = name; // set the entry to display only the name
```

Fig. 13.9 | Ajax-enabled address-book application. (Part 4 of 10.)

```
193        entry.onclick = function() // set onclick event
194        {
195           getAddress( entry, name ); // retrieve address and display it
196        }; // end function
197     } // end function clearField
198
199     // display the form that allows the user to enter more data
200     function addEntry()
201     {
202        document.getElementById( 'addressBook' ).style.display = 'none';
203        document.getElementById( 'addEntry' ).style.display = 'block';
204     } // end function addEntry
205
206     // send the zip code to be validated and to generate city and state
207     function validateZip( zip )
208     {
209        // build parameter array
210        var params = '[{"param": "zip", "value": "' + zip + '"}]';
211        callWebService ( "validateZip", params, showCityState );
212     } // end function validateZip
213
214     // get city and state that were generated using the zip code
215     // and display them on the page
216     function showCityState( asyncRequest )
217     {
218        // display message while request is being processed
219        document.getElementById( 'validateZip' ).
220           innerHTML = "Checking zip...";
221
222        // if request has completed successfully, process the response
223        if ( asyncRequest.readyState == 4 )
224        {
225           if ( asyncRequest.status == 200 )
226           {
227              // convert the JSON string to an object
228              var data = JSON.parse( asyncRequest.responseText );
229
230              // update zip code validity tracker and show city and state
231              if ( data.Validity == 'Valid' )
232              {
233                 zipValid = true; // update validity tracker
234
235                 // display city and state
236                 document.getElementById( 'validateZip' ).innerHTML = '';
237                 document.getElementById( 'city' ).innerHTML = data.City;
238                 document.getElementById( 'state' ).
239                    innerHTML = data.State;
240              } // end if
241              else
242              {
243                 zipValid = false; // update validity tracker
244                 document.getElementById( 'validateZip' ).
245                    innerHTML = data.ErrorText; // display the error
```

Fig. 13.9 | Ajax-enabled address-book application. (Part 5 of 10.)

```
246
247                      // clear city and state values if they exist
248                      document.getElementById( 'city' ).innerHTML = '';
249                      document.getElementById( 'state' ).innerHTML = '';
250               } // end else
251           } // end if
252           else if ( asyncRequest.status == 500 )
253           {
254               document.getElementById( 'validateZip' ).
255                   innerHTML = 'Zip validation service not avaliable';
256           } // end else if
257       } // end if
258   } // end function showCityState
259
260   // send the telephone number to the server to validate format
261   function validatePhone( phone )
262   {
263       var params = '[{ "param": "tel", "value": "' + phone + '"}]';
264       callWebService( "validateTel", params, showPhoneError );
265   } // end function validatePhone
266
267   // show whether the telephone number has correct format
268   function showPhoneError( asyncRequest )
269   {
270       // if request has completed successfully, process the response
271       if ( asyncRequest.readyState == 4 && asyncRequest.status == 200 )
272       {
273           // convert the JSON string to an object
274           var data = JSON.parse( asyncRequest.responseText );
275
276           if ( data.ErrorText != "Valid Telephone Format" )
277           {
278               phoneValid = false; // update validity tracker
279           } // end if
280           else
281           {
282               phoneValid = true; // update validity tracker
283           } // end else
284
285           document.getElementById( 'validatePhone' ).
286               innerHTML = data.ErrorText; // display the error
287       } // end if
288   } // end function showPhoneError
289
290   // enter the user's data into the database
291   function saveForm()
292   {
293       // retrieve the data from the form
294       var first = document.getElementById( 'first' ).value;
295       var last = document.getElementById( 'last' ).value;
296       var street = document.getElementById( 'street' ).value;
297       var city = document.getElementById( 'city' ).innerHTML;
```

Fig. 13.9 | Ajax-enabled address-book application. (Part 6 of 10.)

```
298            var state = document.getElementById( 'state' ).innerHTML;
299            var zip = document.getElementById( 'zip' ).value;
300            var phone = document.getElementById( 'phone' ).value;
301
302            // check if data is valid
303            if ( !zipValid || !phoneValid )
304            {
305               // display error message
306               document.getElementById( 'success' ).innerHTML =
307                  'Invalid data entered. Check form for more information';
308            } // end if
309            else if ( ( first == "" ) || ( last == "" ) )
310            {
311               // display error message
312               document.getElementById( 'success').innerHTML =
313                  'First Name and Last Name must have a value.';
314            } // end if
315            else
316            {
317               // hide the form and show the addressbook
318               document.getElementById( 'addEntry' )
319                  .style.display = 'none';
320               document.getElementById( 'addressBook' ).
321                  style.display = 'block';
322
323               // build the parameter to include in the web service URL
324               params = '[{"param": "first", "value": "' + first +
325                  '"}, { "param": "last", "value": "' + last +
326                  '"}, { "param": "street", "value": "'+ street +
327                  '"}, { "param": "city", "value": "' + city +
328                  '"}, { "param":  "state", "value:": "' + state +
329                  '"}, { "param": "zip", "value": "' + zip +
330                  '"}, { "param": "tel", "value": "' + phone + '"}]';
331
332               // call the web service to insert data into the database
333               callWebService( "addEntry", params, parseData );
334            } // end else
335         } // end function saveForm
336         //-->
337      </script>
338   </head>
339   <body onload = "showAddressBook()">
340      <div>
341         <input type = "button" value = "Address Book"
342            onclick = "showAddressBook()"/>
343         <input type = "button" value = "Add an Entry"
344            onclick = "addEntry()"/>
345      </div>
346      <div id = "addressBook" style = "display : block;">
347         Search By Last Name:
348         <input onkeyup = "search( this.value )"/>
349         <br/>
```

Fig. 13.9 | Ajax-enabled address-book application. (Part 7 of 10.)

```
350        <div id = "Names">
351        </div>
352     </div>
353     <div id = "addEntry" style = "display : none">
354        First Name: <input id = 'first'/>
355        <br/>
356        Last Name: <input id = 'last'/>
357        <br/>
358        <strong> Address: </strong>
359        <br/>
360        Street: <input id = 'street'/>
361        <br/>
362        City: <span id = "city" class = "validator"></span>
363        <br/>
364        State: <span id = "state" class = "validator"></span>
365        <br/>
366        Zip: <input id = 'zip' onblur = 'validateZip( this.value )'/>
367        <span id = "validateZip" class = "validator">
368        </span>
369        <br/>
370        Telephone:<input id = 'phone'
371           onblur = 'validatePhone( this.value )'/>
372        <span id = "validatePhone" class = "validator">
373        </span>
374        <br/>
375        <input type = "button" value = "Submit"
376           onclick = "saveForm()" />
377        <br/>
378        <div id = "success" class = "validator">
379        </div>
380     </div>
381 </body>
382 </html>
```

a) Page is loaded. All the entries are displayed.   b) User clicks on an entry. The entry expands, showing the address and the telephone.

Fig. 13.9 | Ajax-enabled address-book application. (Part 8 of 10.)

c) User types "B" in the search field. Application loads the entries whose last names start with "B".

d) User types "Bl" in the search field. Application loads the entries whose last names start with "Bl".

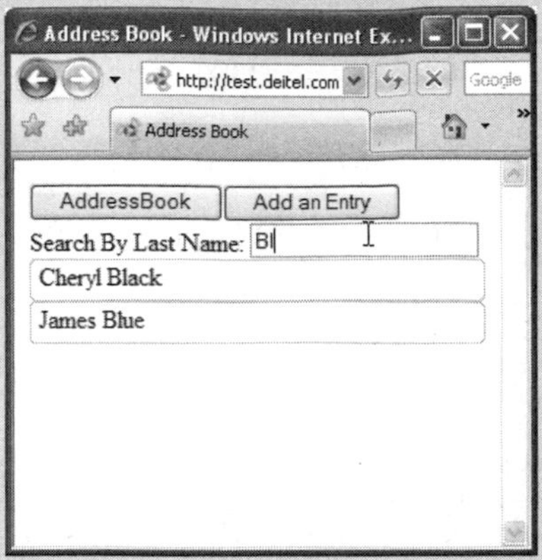

e) User types "Bla" in the search field. Application loads the entries whose last names start with "Bla".

f) User clicks **Add an Entry** button. The form allowing user to add an entry is displayed.

g) User types in a nonexistent zip code. An error is displayed.

h) User enters a valid zip code. While the server processes it, **Checking Zip...** is displayed on the page.

Fig. 13.9 | Ajax-enabled address-book application. (Part 9 of 10.)

i) The server finds the city and state associated with the zip code entered and displays them on the page.

j) The user enters a phone number and tries to submit the data. The application does not allow this, because the First Name and Last Name are empty.

k) The user enters the last name and the first name and clicks the Submit button.

l) The address book is redisplayed with the new name added in.

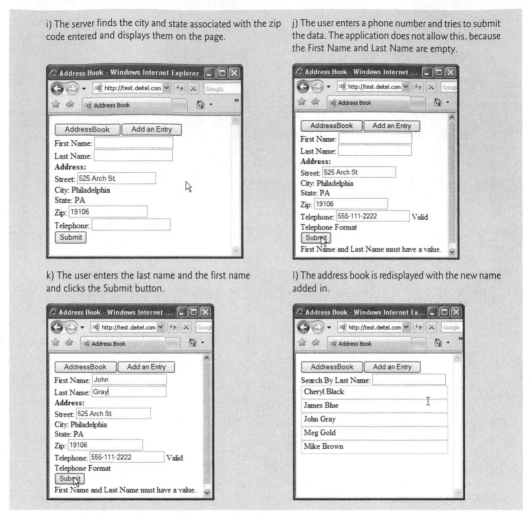

Fig. 13.9 | Ajax-enabled address-book application. (Part 10 of 10.)

Interacting with a Web Service on the Server

When the page loads, the onload event (line 339) calls the showAddressBook function to load the address book onto the page. Function showAddressBook (lines 21–29) shows the addressBook element and hides the addEntry element using the HTML DOM (lines 24–25). Then it calls function callWebService to make an asynchronous request to the server (line 28). Function callWebService requires an array of parameter objects to be sent to the server. In this case, the function we are invoking on the server requires no arguments, so line 27 creates an empty array to be passed to callWebService. Our program uses an ASP.NET web service that we created for this example to do the server-side processing. This web service is hosted at test.deitel.com. The web service contains a collection of methods that can be called from a web application. Our web service also invokes another web service from www.webservicex.net that validates a zip code and returns the corresponding city and state.

Software Engineering Observation 13.2

Keep in mind that when building systems that depend on web services, you are depending on the servers that host those services to be available, and you are introducing more potential points of failure into your system.

Function `callWebService` (lines 32–72) contains the code to call our web service, given a method name, an array of parameter bindings (i.e., the method's parameter names and argument values) and the name of a callback function. The web-service application and the method that is being called are specified in the request URL (line 35). When sending the request using the GET method, the parameters are concatenated URL starting with a ? symbol and followed by a list of *parameter=value* bindings, each separated by an &. Lines 39–49 iterate over the array of parameter bindings that was passed as an argument, and add them to the request URL. In this first call, we do not pass any parameters because the web method that returns all the entries requires none. However, future web method calls will send multiple parameter bindings to the web service. Lines 52–71 prepare and send the request, using similar functionality to the previous two examples. There are many types of user interaction in this application, each requiring a separate asynchronous request. For this reason, we pass the appropriate `asyncRequest` object as an argument to the function specified by the `callBack` parameter. However, event handlers cannot receive arguments, so lines 57–60 assign an anonymous function to `asyncRequest`'s onready-statechange property. When this anonymous function gets called, it calls function `callBack` and passes the `asyncRequest` object as an argument. Lines 64–65 set an `Accept` request header to receive JSON formatted data. Line 66 starts the asynchronous request.

Parsing JSON Data

Each of our web service's methods in this example returns a JSON representation of an object or array of objects. For example, when the web application requests the list of names in the address book, the list is returned as a JSON array, as shown in Fig. 13.10. Each object in Fig. 13.10 has the attributes `first` and `last`.

Line 11 links the `json2.js` script to the XHTML file so we can parse JSON data. When the `XMLHttpRequest` object receives the response, it calls function `parseData` (lines 75–84). Line 81 calls the `JSON.parse` function, which converts its JSON string argument into a JavaScript object. Then line 82 calls function `displayNames` (lines 87–106), which displays the first and last name of each address-book entry passed to it. Lines 90–91 use the DOM to store the placeholder `div` element `Names` in the variable `listbox`, and clear its content. Once parsed, the JSON string of address-book entries becomes an array, which this function traverses (lines 94–105).

```
1    [ { "first": "Cheryl", "last": "Black" },
2      { "first": "James", "last": "Blue" },
3      { "first": "Mike", "last": "Brown" },
4      { "first": "Meg", "last": "Gold" } ]
```

Fig. 13.10 | Address-book data formatted in JSON.

Creating XHTML Elements and Setting Event Handlers on the Fly

Line 99 uses an XHTML `fieldset` element to create a box in which the entry will be placed. Line 100 registers function `handleOnClick` as the `onclick` event handler for the div created in line 98. This enables the user to expand each address-book entry by clicking it. Function handleOnClick (lines 109–113) calls the getAddress function whenever the user clicks an entry. The parameters are generated dynamically and not evaluated until the getAddress function is called. This enables each function to receive arguments that are specific to the entry the user clicked. Line 102 displays the names on the page by accessing the first (first name) and last (last name) fields of each element of the data array.

Function getAddress (lines 136–166) is called when the user clicks an entry. This request must keep track of the entry where the address is to be displayed on the page. Lines 151–154 set the displayAddress function (lines 168–187) as the callback function, and pass it the entry element as a parameter. Once the request completes successfully, lines 174–178 parse the response and display the address. Lines 181–184 set the div's onclick event handler to function clearField (lines 190–197) to hide the address data when that div is clicked again. Lines 192–196 reset the entry's content and its onclick event handler to the values they had before the entry was expanded.

Implementing Type-Ahead

The input element declared in line 348 enables the user to search the address book by last name. As soon as the user starts typing in the input box, the onkeyup event handler calls the search function (lines 117–133), passing the input element's value as an argument. The search function performs an asynchronous request to locate entries with last names that start with its argument value. When the response is received, the application displays the matching list of names. Each time the user changes the text in the input box, function search is called again to make another asynchronous request.

Function search (lines 117–133) first clears the address-book entries from the page (lines 120–121). If the input argument is the empty string, line 126 displays the entire address book by calling function showAddressBook. Otherwise, lines 130–131 send a request to the server to search the data. Line 130 creates a JSON string to represent the parameter object that is passed to function callWebService. Line 131 converts the string to an object and invokes callWebService. When the server responds, callback function parseData is invoked, which calls displayNames to display the results on the page.

Implementing a Form with Asynchronous Validation

When the **Add an Entry** button (lines 343–344) is clicked, the addEntry function (lines 200–204) is called, which hides the addressBook element and shows the addEntry element that allows the user to add a person to the address book. The addEntry element (lines 353–380) contains a set of entry fields, some of which have event handlers that enable validation that occurs asynchronously as the user continues to interact with the page. When a user enters a zip code, the validateZip function (lines 207–212) is called. This function calls an external web service to validate the zip code. If it is valid, that external web service returns the corresponding city and state. Line 210 builds a parameter object containing validateZip's parameter name and argument value in JSON format. Line 211 calls the callWebService function with the appropriate method, the parameter object created in line 210 and showCityState (lines 216–258) as the callback function.

Zip-code validation can take a long time due to network delays. The showCityState function is called every time the request object's readyState property changes. Until the request completes, lines 219–220 display "Checking zip code..." on the page. After the request completes, line 228 converts the JSON response text to an object. The response object has four properties—`Validity`, `ErrorText`, `City` and `State`. If the request is valid, line 233 updates the `zipValid` variable that keeps track of zip-code validity (declared at line 18), and lines 237–239 show the city and state that the server generated using the zip code. Otherwise lines 243–245 update the `zipValid` variable and show the error code. Lines 248–249 clear the city and state elements. If our web service fails to connect to the zip-code validator web service, lines 252–256 display an appropriate error message.

Similarly, when the user enters the telephone number, the function `validatePhone` (lines 261–265) sends the phone number to the server. Once the server responds, the `showPhoneError` function (lines 268–288) updates the `validatePhone` variable (declared at line 17) and shows the message that the web service returned.

When the **Submit** button is clicked, function `saveForm` is called (lines 291–335). Lines 294–300 retrieve the data from the form. Lines 303–308 check if the zip code and telephone number are valid, and display the appropriate error message in the `Success` element on the bottom of the page. Before the data can be entered into a database on the server, both the first-name and last-name fields must have a value. Lines 309–314 check these fields. If they are empty, an appropriate error message is displayed. Once all the data entered is valid, lines 318–321 hide the entry form and show the address book. Lines 324–333 build the parameter object using JSON and send the data to the server using function `callWebService`. Once the server saves the data, it queries the database for an updated list of entries and returns them; then function `parseData` displays the entries on the page.

13.8 Dojo Toolkit

Developing web applications in general, and Ajax applications in particular, involves a certain amount of painstaking and tedious work. Cross-browser compatibility, DOM manipulation and event handling can get cumbersome, particularly as an application's size increases. Dojo is a free, open source JavaScript library that takes care of these issues. Dojo reduces asynchronous request handling to a single function call. Dojo also provides cross-browser DOM functions that simplify partial page updates. It covers many more areas of web development, from simple event handling to fully functional rich GUI controls.

To install Dojo, download the Dojo version 0.4.3 from `download.dojotoolkit.org/release-0.4.3/` to your hard drive. Extract the files from the archive file you downloaded to your web development directory or web server. Including the `dojo.js` script file in your web application will give you access to all the Dojo functions. To do this, place the following script in the head element of your XHTML document:

```
<script type = "text/javascript" src = "path/Dojo.js">
```

where *path* is the relative or complete path to the Dojo toolkit's files. The documentation for this version of Dojo is located at

```
dojotoolkit.org/book/dojo-book-0-4
```

[*Note:* More recent versions of Dojo are available from `dojotoolkit.org`; however, the example in this section will work only with version 0.4.3.]

Figure 13.11 is a calendar application that uses Dojo to create the user interface, communicate with the server asynchronously, handle events and manipulate the DOM. The calendar control (see the screen captures in Fig. 13.11) displays six weeks of dates. Various arrow buttons allow the user to traverse the calendar. When the user selects a date, an asynchronous request obtains that date's scheduled events. There is an **Edit** button next to each scheduled event. When it is clicked, the item is replaced by a text box with the item's content, a **Save** button and a **Cancel** button. When the user presses **Save**, an asynchronous request saves the new value to the server and displays it on the page. This feature, often referred to as *edit-in-place*, is common in Ajax applications. You can test-drive this application at test.deitel.com/examples/jsfp/ajax/fig13_11/calendar.html.

```
1   <?xml version = "1.0" encoding = "utf-8"?>
2   <!DOCTYPE html PUBLIC "-//W3C//DTD XHTML 1.0 Strict//EN"
3      "http://www.w3.org/TR/xhtml1/DTD/xhtml1-strict.dtd">
4
5   <!-- Fig. 13.11 Calendar.html -->
6   <!-- Calendar application built with dojo. -->
7   <html xmlns = "http://www.w3.org/1999/xhtml">
8   <head>
9      <script type = "text/javascript" src = "/dojo043/dojo.js"></script>
10     <script type = "text/javascript" src = "json2.js"></script>
11     <script type = "text/javascript">
12        <!--
13        // specify all the required dojo scripts
14        dojo.require( "dojo.event.*" ); // use scripts from event package
15        dojo.require( "dojo.widget.*" ); // use scripts from widget package
16        dojo.require( "dojo.dom.*" ); // use scripts from dom package
17        dojo.require( "dojo.io.*" ); // use scripts from the io package
18
19        // configure calendar event handler
20        function connectEventHandler()
21        {
22           var calendar = dojo.widget.byId( "calendar" ); // get calendar
23           calendar.setDate( "2007-07-04" );
24           dojo.event.connect(
25              calendar, "onValueChanged", "retrieveItems" );
26        } // end function connectEventHandler
27
28        // location of CalendarService web service
29        var webServiceUrl = "/CalendarService/CalendarService.asmx";
30
31        // obtain scheduled events for the specified date
32        function retrieveItems( eventDate )
33        {
34           // convert date object to string in yyyy-mm-dd format
35           var date = dojo.date.toRfc3339( eventDate ).substring( 0, 10 );
36
37           // build parameters and call web service
38           var params = '[{ "param":"eventDate", "value":"' +
39              date + "'}]";
40           callWebService( 'getItemsByDate', params, displayItems );
41        } // end function retrieveItems
42
43        // call a specific web service asynchronously to get server data
44        function callWebService( method, params, callback )
45        {
```

Fig. 13.11 | Calendar application built with Dojo. (Part 1 of 7.)

```
46          // url for the asynchronous request
47          var requestUrl = webServiceUrl + "/" + method;
48          var params = JSON.parse( paramString );
49
50          // build the parameter string to append to the url
51          for ( var i = 0; i < params.length; i++ )
52          {
53             // check if it is the first parameter and build
54             // the parameter string accordingly
55             if ( i == 0 )
56                requestUrl = requestUrl + "?" + params[ i ].param +
57                   "=" + params[ i ].value; // add first parameter to url
58             else
59                requestUrl = requestUrl + "&" + params[ i ].param +
60                   "=" + params[ i ].value; // add other parameters to url
61          } // end for
62
63          // call asynchronous request using dojo.io.bind
64          dojo.io.bind( { url: requestUrl, handler: callback,
65             accept: "application/json; charset=utf-8" } );
66       } // end function callWebService
67
68       // display the list of scheduled events on the page
69       function displayItems( type, data, event )
70       {
71          if ( type == 'error' ) // if the request has failed
72          {
73             alert( 'Could not retrieve the event' ); // display error
74          } // end if
75          else
76          {
77             var placeholder = dojo.byId( "itemList" ); // get placeholder
78             placeholder.innerHTML = ''; // clear placeholder
79             var items = JSON.parse( data ); // parse server data
80
81             // check whether there are events;
82             // if none then display message
83             if ( items == "" )
84             {
85                placeholder.innerHTML = 'No events for this date.';
86             }
87
88             for ( var i = 0; i < items.length; i++ )
89             {
90                // initialize item's container
91                var item = document.createElement( "div" );
92                item.id = items[ i ].id; // set DOM id to database id
93
94                // obtain and paste the item's description
95                var text = document.createElement( "div" );
96                text.innerHTML = items[i].description;
97                text.id = 'description' + item.id;
98                dojo.dom.insertAtIndex( text, item, 0 );
```

Fig. 13.11 | Calendar application built with Dojo. (Part 2 of 7.)

```
 99
100                    // create and insert the placeholder for the edit button
101                    var buttonPlaceHolder = document.createElement( "div" );
102                    dojo.dom.insertAtIndex( buttonPlaceHolder, item, 1 );
103
104                    // create the edit button and paste it into the container
105                    var editButton = dojo.widget.
106                       createWidget( "Button", {}, buttonPlaceHolder );
107                    editButton.setCaption( "Edit" );
108                    dojo.event.connect(
109                       editButton, 'buttonClick', handleEdit );
110
111                    // insert item container in the list of items container
112                    dojo.dom.insertAtIndex( item, placeholder, i );
113                 } // end for
114              } // end else
115           } // end function displayItems
116
117        // send the asynchronous request to get content for editing and
118        // run the edit-in-place UI
119        function handleEdit( event )
120        {
121           var id = event.currentTarget.parentNode.id; // retrieve id
122           var params = '[{ "param":"id", "value":"' + id +  '"}]';
123           callWebService( 'getItemById', params, displayForEdit );
124        } // end function handleEdit
125
126        // set up the interface for editing an item
127        function displayForEdit(type, data, event)
128        {
129           if ( type == 'error' ) // if the request has failed
130           {
131              alert( 'Could not retrieve the event' ); // display error
132           }
133           else
134           {
135              var item = JSON.parse( data ); // parse the item
136              var id = item.id; // set the id
137
138              // create div elements to insert content
139              var editElement = document.createElement( 'div' );
140              var buttonElement = document.createElement( 'div' );
141
142              // hide the unedited content
143              var oldItem = dojo.byId( id ); // get the original element
144              oldItem.id = 'old' + oldItem.id; // change element's id
145              oldItem.style.display = 'none'; // hide old element
146              editElement.id = id; // change the "edit" container's id
147
148              // create a textbox and insert it on the page
149              var editArea = document.createElement( 'textarea' );
150              editArea.id = 'edit' + id; // set textbox id
151              editArea.innerHTML = item.description; // insert description
```

Fig. 13.11 | Calendar application built with Dojo. (Part 3 of 7.)

```
152            dojo.dom.insertAtIndex( editArea, editElement, 0 );
153
154            // create button placeholders and insert on the page
155            // these will be transformed into dojo widgets
156            var saveElement = document.createElement( 'div' );
157            var cancelElement = document.createElement( 'div' );
158            dojo.dom.insertAtIndex( saveElement, buttonElement, 0 );
159            dojo.dom.insertAtIndex( cancelElement, buttonElement, 1 );
160            dojo.dom.insertAtIndex( buttonElement, editElement, 1 );
161
162            // create "save" and "cancel" buttons
163            var saveButton =
164               dojo.widget.createWidget( "Button", {}, saveElement );
165            var cancelButton =
166               dojo.widget.createWidget( "Button", {}, cancelElement );
167            saveButton.setCaption( "Save" ); // set saveButton label
168            cancelButton.setCaption( "Cancel" ); // set cancelButton text
169
170            // set up the event handlers for cancel and save buttons
171            dojo.event.connect( saveButton, 'buttonClick', handleSave );
172            dojo.event.connect(
173               cancelButton, 'buttonClick', handleCancel );
174
175            // paste the edit UI on the page
176            dojo.dom.insertAfter( editElement, oldItem );
177         } // end else
178      } // end function displayForEdit
179
180      // sends the changed content to the server to be saved
181      function handleSave( event )
182      {
183         // grab user entered data
184         var id = event.currentTarget.parentNode.parentNode.id;
185         var descr = dojo.byId( 'edit' + id ).value;
186
187         // build parameter string and call the web service
188         var params = '[{ "param":"id", "value":"' + id +
189            '"}, {"param": "descr", "value":"' + descr + '"}]';
190         callWebService( 'Save', params, displayEdited );
191      } // end function handleSave
192
193      // restores the original content of the item
194      function handleCancel( event )
195      {
196         var voidEdit = event.currentTarget.parentNode.parentNode;
197         var id = voidEdit.id; // retrieve the id of the item
198         dojo.dom.removeNode( voidEdit, true ); // remove the edit UI
199         var old = dojo.byId( 'old' + id ); // retrieve pre-edit version
200         old.style.display = 'block'; // show pre-edit version
201         old.id = id; // reset the id
202      } // end function handleCancel
203
```

Fig. 13.11 | Calendar application built with Dojo. (Part 4 of 7.)

```
204        // displays the updated event information after an edit is saved
205        function displayEdited( type, data, event )
206        {
207           if ( type == 'error' )
208           {
209              alert( 'Could not retrieve the event' );
210           }
211           else
212           {
213              editedItem = JSON.parse( data ); // get updated description
214              var id = editedItem.id; // obtain the id
215              var editElement = dojo.byId( id ); // get the edit UI
216              dojo.dom.removeNode( editElement, true ); // delete edit UI
217              var old = dojo.byId( 'old' + id ); // get item container
218
219              // get pre-edit element and update its description
220              var oldText = dojo.byId( 'description' + id );
221              oldText.innerHTML = editedItem.description;
222
223              old.id = id; // reset id
224              old.style.display = 'block'; // show the updated item
225           } // end else
226        } // end function displayEdited
227
228        // when the page is loaded, set up the calendar event handler
229        dojo.addOnLoad( connectEventHandler );
230        // -->
231     </script>
232     <title> Calendar built with dojo </title>
233  </head>
234  <body>
235     Calendar
236     <div dojoType = "datePicker" style = "float: left"
237        widgetID = "calendar"></div>
238     <div id = "itemList" style = "float: left"></div>
239  </body>
240  </html>
```

a) DatePicker Dojo widget
after the web page loads.

Fig. 13.11 | Calendar application built with Dojo. (Part 5 of 7.)

b) User selects a date and the application asynchronously requests a list of events for that date and displays the results with a partial page update.

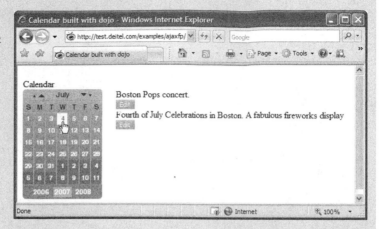

c) User clicks the **Edit** button to modify an event's description.

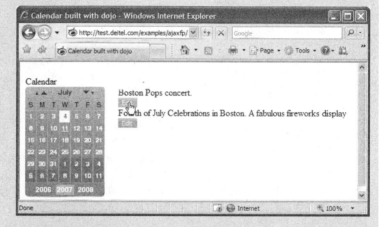

d) Application performs a partial page update, replacing the original description and the **Edit** button with a text box, **Save** button and **Cancel** button. User modifies the event description and clicks the **Save** button.

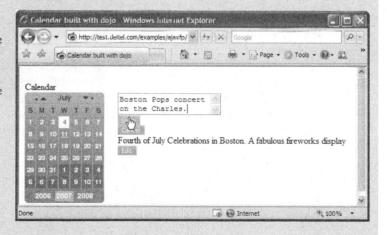

Fig. 13.11 | Calendar application built with Dojo. (Part 6 of 7.)

d) The **Save** button's event handler uses an asynchronous request to update the server and uses the server's response to perform a partial page update, replacing the editing GUI components with the updated description and an **Edit** button.

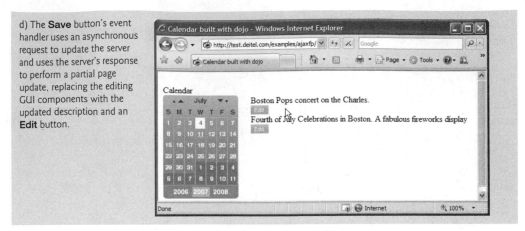

Fig. 13.11 | Calendar application built with Dojo. (Part 7 of 7.)

Loading Dojo Packages

Lines 9–17 load the Dojo framework. Line 9 links the dojo.js script file to the page, giving the script access to all the functions in the Dojo toolkit. Dojo is organized in packages of related functionality. Lines 14–17 use the dojo.require call, provided by the dojo.js script to include the packages we need. The dojo.io package functions communicate with the server, the dojo.event package simplifies event handling, the dojo.widget package provides rich GUI controls, and the dojo.dom package contains additional DOM functions that are portable across many different browsers.

The application cannot use any of this functionality until all the packages have been loaded. Line 229 uses the dojo.addOnLoad method to set up the event handling after the page loads. Once all the packages have been loaded, the connectEventHandler function (lines 20–26) is called.

Using an Existing Dojo Widget

A *Dojo widget* is any predefined user interface element that is part of the Dojo toolkit. The calendar control on the page is the DatePicker widget. To incorporate an existing Dojo widget onto a page, you must set the DojoType attribute of any HTML element to the type of widget that you want it to be (line 236). Dojo widgets also have their own widgetID property (line 237). Line 22 uses the dojo.widget.byId method, rather than the DOM's document.getElementById method, to obtain the calendar widget element. The dojo.events.connect method links functions together. Lines 24–25 use it to connect the calendar's onValueChanged event handler to the retrieveItems function. When the user picks a date, a special onValueChanged event that is part of the DatePicker widget calls retrieveItems, passing the selected date as an argument. The retrieveItems function (lines 32–41) builds the parameters for the request to the server, and calls the callWeb-Service function. Line 35 uses the dojo.date.toRfc3339 method to convert the date passed by the calendar control to *yyyy-mm-dd* format.

Asynchronous Requests in Dojo

The callWebService function (lines 44–66) sends the asynchronous request to the specified web-service method. Lines 47–61 build the request URL using the same code as

Fig. 13.9. Dojo reduces the asynchronous request to a single call to the dojo.io.bind method (lines 64–65), which works on all the popular browsers such as Firefox, Internet Explorer, Opera, Mozilla and Safari. The method takes an array of parameters, formatted as a JavaScript object. The url parameter specifies the destination of the request, the handler parameter specifies the callback function, and the mimetype parameter specifies the format of the response. The handler parameter can be replaced by the load and error parameters. The function passed as load handles successful requests and the function passed as error handles unsuccessful requests.

Response handling is done differently in Dojo. Rather than calling the callback function every time the request's readyState property changes, Dojo calls the function passed as the "handler" parameter when the request completes. In addition, in Dojo the script does not have access to the request object. All the response data is sent directly to the callback function The function sent as the handler argument must have three parameters—type, data and event.

In the first request, the function displayItems (lines 69–115) is set as the callback function. Lines 71–74 check if the request is successful, and display an error message if it isn't. Lines 77–78 obtain the place-holder element (itemList), where the items will be displayed, and clear its content. Line 79 converts the JSON response text to a JavaScript object, using the same code as the example in Fig. 13.9.

Partial Page Updates Using Dojo's Cross-Browser DOM Manipulation Capabilities
The Dojo toolkit (like most other Ajax libraries) provides functionality that enables you to manipulate the DOM in a cross-browser portable manner. Lines 83–86 check if the server-side returned any items, and display an appropriate message if it didn't. For each item object returned from the server, lines 91–92 create a div element and set its id to the item's id in the database. Lines 95–97 create a container element for the item's description. Line 98 uses Dojo's dojo.dom.insertAtIndex method to insert the description element as the first element in the item's element.

For each entry, the application creates an **Edit** button that enables the user to edit the event's content on the page. Lines 101–109 create a Dojo Button widget programmatically. Lines 101–102 create a buttonPlaceHolder div element for the button and paste it on the page. Lines 105–106 convert the buttonPlaceHolder element to a Dojo Button widget by calling the dojo.widget.createWidget function. This function takes three parameters—the type of widget to be created, a list of additional widget parameters and the element which is to be converted to a Dojo widget. Line 107 uses the button's setCaption method to set the text that appears on the button. Line 112 uses the insertAtIndex method to insert the items into the itemList placeholder, in the order in which they were returned from the server.

Adding Edit-In-Place Functionality
Dojo Button widgets use their own buttonClick event instead of the DOM onclick event to store the event handler. Lines 108–109 use the dojo.event.connect method to connect the buttonClick event of the Dojo Button widget and the handleEdit event handler (lines 119–124). When the user clicks the **Edit** button, the Event object gets passed to the event handler as an argument. The Event object's currentTarget property contains the element that initiated the event. Line 121 uses the currentTarget property to obtain the id of the item. This id is the same as the item's id in the server database. Line 123

calls the web service's `getItemById` method, using the `callWebService` function to obtain the item that needs to be edited.

Once the server responds, function `displayForEdit` (lines 127–178) replaces the item on the screen with the user interface for editing the item's content. The code for this is similar to the code in the `displayItems` function. Lines 129–132 make sure the request was successful and parse the data from the server. Lines 139–140 create the container elements into which we insert the new user-interface elements. Lines 143–146 hide the element that displays the item and change its `id`. Now the `id` of the user-interface element is the same as the `id` of the item that it's editing stored in the database. Lines 149–152 create the text-box element that will be used to edit the item's description, paste it into the text box, and paste the resulting text box on the page. Lines 156–173 use the same syntax that was used to create the **Edit** button widget to create **Save** and **Cancel** button widgets. Line 176 pastes the resulting element, containing the text box and two buttons, on the page.

When the user edits the content and clicks the **Cancel** button, the `handleCancel` function (lines 194–202) restores the item element to what it looked like before the button was clicked. Line 198 deletes the edit UI that was created earlier, using Dojo's `removeNode` function. Lines 200–201 show the item with the original element that was used to display the item, and change its `id` back to the item's `id` on the server database.

When the user clicks the **Save** button, the `handleSave` function (lines 181–191) sends the text entered by the user to the server. Line 185 obtains the text that the user entered in the text box. Lines 188–190 send to the server the `id` of the item that needs to be updated and the new description.

Once the server responds, `displayEdited` (lines 205–226) displays the new item on the page. Lines 214–217 contain the same code that was used in `handleCancel` to remove the user interface used to edit the item and redisplay the element that contains the item. Line 221 changes the item's description to its new value.

13.9 Web Resources

www.deitel.com/ajax

Our Ajax Resource Center contains links to some of the best Ajax resources on the web from which you can learn more about Ajax and its component technologies. Find categorized links to Ajax tutorials, tools, code, forums, books, libraries, frameworks, conferences, podcasts and more. See our comprehensive list of developer toolkits and libraries. Visit the most popular Ajax community websites and blogs. Explore many popular commercial and free open-source Ajax applications. Download code snippets and complete scripts that you can use on your own website. Also, be sure to visit our Resource Centers with information on Ajax's component technologies, including XHTML (www.deitel.com/xhtml/), CSS 2.1 (www.deitel.com/css21/), XML (www.deitel.com/XML/) and JavaScript (www.deitel.com/javascript/). For a complete Resource Center list, visit

www.deitel.com/ResourceCenters.html

XHTML Special Characters

The table of Fig. A.1 shows many commonly used XHTML special characters—called ***character entity references*** by the World Wide Web Consortium. For a complete list of character entity references, see the site www.w3.org/TR/REC-html40/sgml/entities.html.

Character	XHTML encoding	Character	XHTML encoding
non-breaking space		ê	&#234;
§	&#167;	ì	&#236;
©	&#169;	í	&#237;
®	&#174;	î	&#238;
¼	&#188;	ñ	&#241;
½	&#189;	ò	&#242;
¾	&#190;	ó	&#243;
à	&#224;	ô	&#244;
á	&#225;	õ	&#245;
â	&#226;	÷	&#247;
ã	&#227;	ù	&#249;
å	&#229;	ú	&#250;
ç	&#231;	û	&#251;
è	&#232;	•	&#8226;
é	&#233;	™	&#8482;

Fig. A.1 | XHTML special characters.

B

XHTML Colors

Colors may be specified by using a standard name (such as aqua) or a hexadecimal RGB value (such as #00FFFF for aqua). Of the six hexadecimal digits in an RGB value, the first two represent the amount of red in the color, the middle two represent the amount of green in the color and the last two represent the amount of blue in the color. For example, black is the absence of color and is defined by #000000, whereas white is the maximum amount of red, green and blue and is defined by #FFFFFF. Pure red is #FF0000, pure green (which the standard calls lime) is #00FF00 and pure blue is #00FFFF. Note that green in the standard is defined as #008000. Figure B.1 contains the XHTML standard color set. Figure B.2 contains the XHTML extended color set.

Color name	Value	Color name	Value
aqua	#00FFFF	navy	#000080
black	#000000	olive	#808000
blue	#0000FF	purple	#800080
fuchsia	#FF00FF	red	#FF0000
gray	#808080	silver	#C0C0C0
green	#008000	teal	#008080
lime	#00FF00	yellow	#FFFF00
maroon	#800000	white	#FFFFFF

Fig. B.1 | XHTML standard colors and hexadecimal RGB values.

Color name	Value	Color name	Value
aliceblue	#F0F8FF	dodgerblue	#1E90FF
antiquewhite	#FAEBD7	firebrick	#B22222
aquamarine	#7FFFD4	floralwhite	#FFFAF0
azure	#F0FFFF	forestgreen	#228B22
beige	#F5F5DC	gainsboro	#DCDCDC
bisque	#FFE4C4	ghostwhite	#F8F8FF
blanchedalmond	#FFEBCD	gold	#FFD700
blueviolet	#8A2BE2	goldenrod	#DAA520
brown	#A52A2A	greenyellow	#ADFF2F
burlywood	#DEB887	honeydew	#F0FFF0
cadetblue	#5F9EA0	hotpink	#FF69B4
chartreuse	#7FFF00	indianred	#CD5C5C
chocolate	#D2691E	indigo	#4B0082
coral	#FF7F50	ivory	#FFFFF0
cornflowerblue	#6495ED	khaki	#F0E68C
cornsilk	#FFF8DC	lavender	#E6E6FA
crimson	#DC143C	lavenderblush	#FFF0F5
cyan	#00FFFF	lawngreen	#7CFC00
darkblue	#00008B	lemonchiffon	#FFFACD
darkcyan	#008B8B	lightblue	#ADD8E6
darkgoldenrod	#B8860B	lightcoral	#F08080
darkgray	#A9A9A9	lightcyan	#E0FFFF
darkgreen	#006400	lightgoldenrodyellow	#FAFAD2
darkkhaki	#BDB76B	lightgreen	#90EE90
darkmagenta	#8B008B	lightgrey	#D3D3D3
darkolivegreen	#556B2F	lightpink	#FFB6C1
darkorange	#FF8C00	lightsalmon	#FFA07A
darkorchid	#9932CC	lightseagreen	#20B2AA
darkred	#8B0000	lightskyblue	#87CEFA
darksalmon	#E9967A	lightslategray	#778899
darkseagreen	#8FBC8F	lightsteelblue	#B0C4DE
darkslateblue	#483D8B	lightyellow	#FFFFE0
darkslategray	#2F4F4F	limegreen	#32CD32
darkturquoise	#00CED1	linen	#FAF0E6
darkviolet	#9400D3	magenta	#FF00FF
deeppink	#FF1493	mediumaquamarine	#66CDAA
deepskyblue	#00BFFF	mediumblue	#0000CD
dimgray	#696969	mediumorchid	#BA55D3

Fig. B.2 | XHTML extended colors and hexadecimal RGB values. (Part 1 of 2.)

Color name	Value	Color name	Value
mediumpurple	#9370DB	plum	#DDA0DD
mediumseagreen	#3CB371	powderblue	#B0E0E6
mediumslateblue	#7B68EE	rosybrown	#BC8F8F
mediumspringgreen	#00FA9A	royalblue	#4169E1
mediumturquoise	#48D1CC	saddlebrown	#8B4513
mediumvioletred	#C71585	salmon	#FA8072
midnightblue	#191970	sandybrown	#F4A460
mintcream	#F5FFFA	seagreen	#2E8B57
mistyrose	#FFE4E1	seashell	#FFF5EE
moccasin	#FFE4B5	sienna	#A0522D
navajowhite	#FFDEAD	skyblue	#87CEEB
oldlace	#FDF5E6	slateblue	#6A5ACD
olivedrab	#6B8E23	slategray	#708090
orange	#FFA500	snow	#FFFAFA
orangered	#FF4500	springgreen	#00FF7F
orchid	#DA70D6	steelblue	#4682B4
palegoldenrod	#EEE8AA	tan	#D2B48C
palegreen	#98FB98	thistle	#D8BFD8
paleturquoise	#AFEEEE	tomato	#FF6347
palevioletred	#DB7093	turquoise	#40E0D0
papayawhip	#FFEFD5	violet	#EE82EE
peachpuff	#FFDAB9	wheat	#F5DEB3
peru	#CD853F	whitesmoke	#F5F5F5
pink	#FFC0CB	yellowgreen	#9ACD32

Fig. B.2 | XHTML extended colors and hexadecimal RGB values. (Part 2 of 2.)

JavaScript Operator Precedence Chart

C.1 Operator Precedence Chart

This appendix contains the operator precedence chart for JavaScript/ECMAScript (Fig. C.1). The operators are shown in decreasing order of precedence from top to bottom.

Operator	Type	Associativity
. [] ()	member access array indexing function calls	left to right
++ -- - ~ ! delete new typeof void	increment decrement unary minus bitwise complement logical NOT deletes an array element or object property creates a new object returns the data type of its argument prevents an expression from returning a value	right to left
* / %	multiplication division modulus	left to right

Fig. C.1 | JavaScript/ECMAScript operator precedence and associativity. (Part 1 of 2.)

Operator	Type	Associativity
+ - +	addition subtraction string concatenation	left to right
<< >> >>>	left shift right shift with sign extension right shift with zero extension	left to right
< <= > >= instanceof	less than less than or equal greater than greater than or equal type comparison	left to right
== != === !==	equality inequality identity nonidentity	left to right
&	bitwise AND	left to right
^	bitwise XOR	left to right
|	bitwise OR	left to right
&&	logical AND	left to right
||	logical OR	left to right
?:	conditional	right to left
= += -= *= /= %= &= ^= |= <<= >>= >>>=	assignment addition assignment subtraction assignment multiplication assignment division assignment modulus assignment bitwise AND assignment bitwise exclusive OR assignment bitwise inclusive OR assignment bitwise left shift assignment bitwise right shift with sign extension assignment bitwise right shift with zero extension assignment	right to left

Fig. C.1 | JavaScript/ECMAScript operator precedence and associativity. (Part 2 of 2.)

Index

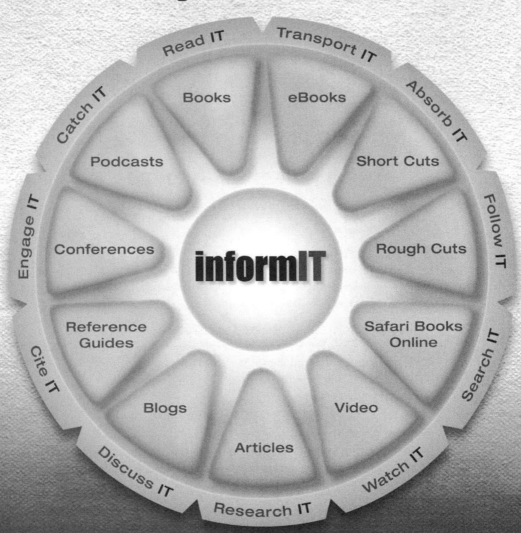

LearnIT at InformIT

Go Beyond the Book

11 WAYS TO LEARN IT at **www.informIT.com/learn**

The online portal of the information technology
publishing imprints of Pearson Education

FREE Online Edition

Your purchase of *JavaScript™ for Programmers* includes access to a free online edition for 45 days through the Safari Books Online subscription service. Nearly every Prentice Hall book is available online through Safari Books Online, along with more than 5,000 other technical books and videos from publishers such as Addison-Wesley Professional, Cisco Press, Exam Cram, IBM Press, O'Reilly, Que, and Sams.

SAFARI BOOKS ONLINE allows you to search for a specific answer, cut and paste code, download chapters, and stay current with emerging technologies.

Activate your FREE Online Edition at
www.informit.com/safarifree

> **STEP 1:** Enter the coupon code: VQAOJFH.

> **STEP 2:** New Safari users, complete the brief registration form.
> Safari subscribers, just log in.

If you have difficulty registering on Safari or accessing the online edition, please e-mail customer-service@safaribooksonline.com